Personal Liberty and Community Safety

Pretrial Release in the Criminal Court

THE PLENUM SERIES IN CRIME AND JUSTICE

Series Editors:
James Alan Fox, *Northeastern University, Boston, Massachusetts*
Joseph Weis, *University of Washington, Seattle, Washington*

CONTEMPORARY MASTERS IN CRIMINOLOGY
Edited by Joan McCord and John H. Laub

CRIMINAL INCAPACITATION
William Spelman

DELINQUENCY CAREERS IN TWO BIRTH COHORTS
Paul E. Tracy, Marvin E. Wolfgang, and Robert M. Figlio

PERSONAL LIBERTY AND COMMUNITY SAFETY
Pretrial Release in the Criminal Court
John S. Goldkamp, Michael R. Gottfredson, Peter R. Jones, and Doris Weiland

RACE AND THE JURY
Racial Disenfranchisement and the Search for Justice
Hiroshi Fukurai, Edgar W. Butler, and Richard Krooth

RAPE LAW REFORM
A Grassroots Revolution and Its Impact
Cassia Spohn and Julie Horney

A Continuation Order Plan is available for this series. A continuation order will bring delivery of each new volume immediately upon publication. Volumes are billed only upon actual shipment. For further information please contact the publisher.

Personal Liberty and Community Safety

Pretrial Release in the Criminal Court

John S. Goldkamp
Temple University
Philadelphia, Pennsylvania

Michael R. Gottfredson
University of Arizona
Tucson, Arizona

Peter R. Jones
Temple University
Philadelphia, Pennsylvania

and

Doris Weiland
Crime and Justice Research Institute
Philadelphia, Pennsylvania

Plenum Press • New York and London

Library of Congress Cataloging-in-Publication Data

Personal liberty and community safety : pretrial release in the criminal court / John S. Goldkamp ... [et al.].
p. cm. -- (Plenum series in crime and justice)
Includes bibliographical references and index.
ISBN 0-306-44879-3
1. Pre-trial release--Florida--Miami. 2. Bail--Florida--Miami. 3. Preventive detention--Florida--Miami. 4. Pre-trial release--Arizona--Phoenix. 5. Bail--Arizona--Phoenix. 6. Preventive detention--Arizona--Phoenix. I. Goldkamp, John S. II. Series.
KF9632.P48 1995
345.73'072--dc20
[347.30572] 95-15677
CIP

ISBN 0-306-44879-3

A Division of Plenum Publishing Corporation
233 Spring Street, New York, N. Y. 10013

10 9 8 7 6 5 4 3 2 1

Printed in the United States of America

To the memory of Otto G. Goldkamp
his love and support are dearly missed

Foreword

The past 30 years have seen many attempts to reform the process that determines pretrial release or detention of the criminal accused in our court systems. Driven by concerns about fairness and equal treatment, reform efforts sought to lessen the disparity between outcomes received by defendants who were able to purchase their freedom and those who remained in jail simply because of their inability to post the required bond. Not surprisingly, at least to those working in the criminal courts, the vast majority of detainees were from the lowest socioeconomic strata of society, causing reformers to claim that the use of money bail was effective only in insuring detention of the poor and had little demonstrated ability to assure defendants' appearance in court—then arguably the only recognized legitimate goal of bail.

Modeled after the Vera-prototype of the 1960s, some jurisdictions developed pretrial services programs to aid the courts in deciding which defendants could be released at little risk under nonfinancial terms. Eligibility criteria adopted by these programs were often based on "community ties," reflecting the concept that defendants who were employed and had stable residences and good reputations in the community would not flee from their court appointments and could be released without financial conditions. Ironically, while this approach appeared eminently reasonably to the middle-class reformers who proposed it, it had little relevance to the type of person most commonly processed by the criminal courts. These defendants often had no jobs, no good record of employment, no stable residence, no upstanding community members to vouch for their reliability, and little education. In short, just as they were unlikely to be able to post very low amounts of cash bail, they were also unlikely to receive high community-ties ratings to earn recommendations for release on personal recognizance (nonfinancial release).

The inhumane jail conditions that sparked the first reform efforts in New York City in the early 1960s were not notably improved by the jail crowding that grew to major crisis proportions in many American cities during the 1970s and 1980s. These conditions are still severe in the 1990s as various policies, particularly relating to drugs, have added pressure to confine defendants at the local level. Communities that previously have shown little interest in bail reform now are facing expensive campaigns to build new jails. Some jurisdictions—like Miami and Phoenix, subjects of this book—have experienced more than one generation of costly construction, quickly discovering the adage "once built, soon filled." The search for alternatives to incarceration at the local level soon focused on the pretrial population because defendants held pending adjudication often made up half or more of persons confined in the local jail. In pretrial release processing, efforts focused on nonfinancial release strategies. Numerous pretrial release agencies and methodologies were funded in hopes that expensive jail construction could be avoided in exchange for effective management and supervision of released defendants.

Again, most of these efforts uncritically centered on the community-ties yardstick, sometimes using specific release conditions to address what were seen as attributes of defendants linked to the likelihood of failing to appear in court. Increasingly, criteria for "excluding" defendants from release options were added based on the nature of charges, prior arrests, and other factors viewed as relating to risk. As some progress was made in the design of release options and the deployment of nonfinancial release approaches, the public safety agenda traditionally underlying bail practices became the focus of greater attention. Crime by defendants on pretrial release became a sensitive political issue as many states and the federal system adopted preventive detention laws aimed squarely at concerns for defendant "dangerousness." Efforts aimed at insuring the appearance of defendants in court through effective use of nonfinancial release options were overtaken and outpaced by single-minded emphasis on community safety. Despite much research showing that prediction of future crime was very difficult and that the criteria associated with the new preventive detention laws were poor predictors, the detention-for-danger movement gained momentum and increased—rather than limited—the use of local confinement.

Given these broad developments, it is no surprise that in many places local administrators began to reexamine their basic assumptions in operating pretrial release programs and systems. The concept of risk became increasingly important and the community-ties driven approach to rating defendants' eligibility to release options was seen by many not only to be inadequate but also increasingly irresponsible. Not only did such measures failure to reduce the discriminatory impact of bail practices, they did not serve as useful indicators of likely risk of flight or crime among defendants. Moreover, it was becoming increasingly evident that, without a central involvement by judges in review and improvement of pretrial release and detention decision practices, what court programs or agencies did about pretrial release would have little impact.

This is precisely the situation I confronted when, as a recently appointed head of the pretrial services program in Miami, researchers Goldkamp and Gottfredson arrived in town to discuss the possibility of using research to examine pretrial release and detention fundamentally and to develop a resource for assisting the judiciary in restructuring and managing its decisionmaking in this area. After adjusting to the nervousness with which I viewed such no-holds-barred research, I entered into what would be a productive working relationship for the Dade County courts and for me personally as the administrator responsible for pretrial release. Together, a judicial working group identified areas of release and detention decisionmaking to be addressed by the research and collaborated in the development of pretrial release guidelines to shape judicial decisionmaking, management of release options, and review of confined defendants in the Dade jail. The research was a resource for tailor-made local problem solving that helped pinpoint areas in need of correction and for development of an information approach that took into consideration the need to plan release alternatives to correspond to the risks and problems of Dade felony defendants. In this specific approach to problems of pretrial release, I was introduced to a research-supported method for dealing with other areas of criminal justice functioning which would later prove valuable.

As ground-breaking as the guidelines research process was, the implementation process faced serious difficulties as the research neared its final stages. Issues relating to judicial discretion in release decisionmaking and political realities pose major challenges to fundamental reform, as, after all this time, the history of bail reform has demonstrated. This experience is well detailed in the chapters of this book and has important lessons for all interested in court and justice system improvement. Was the guidelines approach a success? Readers will draw their own conclusions. As a local administrator in Miami, I saw both the promise of the method and its impact as a catalyst for moving decisionmakers away from traditionally held concepts regarding bail, release, and detention and toward more rational and better managed procedures. The guidelines research process served as a critical forum for the local judicial and justice community to come together to work on difficult problems as part of a problem-solving team. The guidelines process in Miami opened the door to the notion that policies and practices in the local justice system could be examined and revised based on a solid assist from this sort of policy-relevant research; more recently, I have seen the results and benefits of this research process applied to the development of Miami's treatment drug court for felony defendants and its domestic violence court innovations. However the pretrial release guidelines in Miami fare, the lessons of the useful role of research in policy development and improvement of practice have been learned.

TIMOTHY J. MURRAY, Director
Office of Substance Abuse Control for Metropolitan Dade County
Dade County, Florida

Preface

In 1968, Herbert Packer wrote that "the more we learn about the Is of the criminal process, the more we are instructed about its Ought and the greater the gulf between Is and Ought appears to become."[1] This captures well a fundamental lesson of our cumulative research experience investigating bail practices in several major urban jurisdictions over a period of a decade. Careful examination of the "Is" in the inquiry into court practices we describe underscores the great gap yet separating current practice from the basic ideals announced by bail reform in the early 1960s and earlier. Indeed, it has been more than 70 years since the powerful critique of bail practices in Cleveland by Felix Frankfurter and Roscoe Pound and 67 years since Arthur Beeley raised fundamental questions about the jailing of poor defendants in Chicago. Perhaps it was Caleb Foote who four decades ago most eloquently depicted and questioned the unbridled exercise of discretion by judges and magistrates at bail in his devastating and now classic study of bail practices in Philadelphia.

The most frequent target of critics of American bail practices was the role of cash bail in pretrial release determinations which produced a system that discriminated among defendants on the basis of their ability to raise cash. Today, despite many revisions of state and federal law in this area, cash bail is still the principal device employed by judges and commissioners to cause the detention of defendants who are awaiting trial. Judges and magistrates still use dollars to divide defendants into two classes of accused—the confined and the released. Added to concerns about inherent economic discrimination associated with cash-for-release practices is the fact that for those who wish to escape prosecution, the reliance on cash bail guarantees that, for a price, freedom can be purchased. Contrary to conventional wisdom, cash bail has never been shown to be a deterrent to offending by defendants during the period of pretrial release; in fact, some have argued that the use of cash bail encourages

1. Herbert L. Packer, *The Limits of the Criminal Sanction* (Stanford, CA: Stanford University Press, 1968), p. 150.

crime as defendants seek ways to pay the bondsman or others who may have provided the capital for release. The role of cash bail, as we show in the following pages, is at the heart of the detention process and provides the oxygen for unfettered judicial discretion. Our study found that across jurisdictions, bail set at amounts over $500 was sufficient to cause the detention of the majority of defendants. As judicial discretion has resisted attempts at reform fairly easily, survival of the role of cash bail has been an essential ingredient. Even the Federal Bail Reform Act of 1984, which sought to outlaw the use of cash bail for causing detention, has not accomplished this goal in federal practice.

The other side-effects of a cash-bail driven release process are still not yet a thing of the past. In 1922, Frankfurter and Pound wrote a devastating critique of the bondsman whom they described as "anomalous" to American justice and as an "extra-legal parasite." In 1967, the American Bar Association recommended in its *Standards Relating to Pretrial Release* that "compensated sureties" be abolished. Yet in many American counties in the 1990s, bondsmen are still in business and—seemingly impervious to recent recession—thriving, forming in some states a powerful political lobby that aims to thwart justice reform that would eliminate the potential for profit from pretrial release decisionmaking. How the dollar and pretrial freedom became fused is peculiarly an American story; how profiteering and discrimination in pretrial release determinations can be abrogated is a challenge that will likely not have been met in the twentieth century.

In earlier work, we have referred to the advent of explicit preventive detention laws as the "second generation of bail reform" following on efforts to increase nonfinancial release and to rely on community ties-based indicators of releasability innovated by the Vera Institute of Justice in the early 1960s. The second generation reform efforts attempted to move the exercise of detention decisionmaking from its *sub rosa* realms in which cash bail is used flexibly to cause the detention of nearly any defendant into the sunlight of a reviewable detention process. Many versions of new laws in the states and the federal jurisdiction have sought to recognize a community protection priority in the bail process and to institute controls not possible when the operational preoccupation with defendant danger is simply ignored. Legislation, caselaw, and practice have directly or indirectly embraced the public safety agenda in ways not imaginable in law only a couple of decades ago. Provisions for detaining outright defendants deemed "dangerous" are now no longer scarce. In law and practice, however, the role of cash bail has generally been preserved or has somehow survived. What has resulted is not more rational and reasonably controlled exercise of detention decisionmaking, but rather a system that both allows some outright detention of dangerous defendants with slight increased due process protections and confinement through manipulation of cash bail in the traditional fashion at the discretion of the judge, commissioner, or magistrate. The overall effect has been to increase the discretion of the judiciary to confine defendants pending adjudication of their cases. Moreover, the unfair and unsavory side-effects of the cash bail system have therefore not been removed.

These facts notwithstanding, it is not accurate to say that bail, pretrial release, and detention practice—the "Is" of Packer's characterization—have not changed or been improved over the century. But as study and reform have sharpened our understanding of the nature of the process that determines the liberty or confinement of the accused, so too have they documented how difficult it has been to bring about meaningful change. Close inspection of this important liberty decision in practice reveals that the wide exercise of discretion by the judiciary at this stage of processing has stubbornly resisted legislative, advocacy, and administrative attempts at reform. The problem at the heart of pretrial release decisionmaking remains the exercise of discretion by judges, magistrates, and commissioners. In comparison to the failure to address discretion problems constructively, the achievements of bail reform seem marginal.

Continuing crises of jail-crowding in localities have demonstrated, however, that the day of judicial license in confinement decisionmaking without regard for impact on the justice system or on local resources may soon be over. Even with federal assistance, local jurisdictions do not have the resources to construct sufficient additional jail capacity to keep up with poorly managed judicial decision processes and endless popular policies to increase the use of confinement. There are fiscal as well as rational limits to the privilege and responsibility attached to judicial discretion in justice processing. Discretion needs to be reasonably exercised and effectively managed, with clear goals, adequate information, and suitable alternatives.

This book describes our attempts to involve research in a process of examination and policy reform of pretrial release and detention practices in the criminal courts in Boston, Miami, and Phoenix. An important aim is to understand better the role of judicial discretion in problems related to pretrial release and detention. Our research documents the uneven nature of judicial decisionmaking: In Philadelphia we established earlier that disparity in pretrial release decisionmaking by judges easily rivaled that found in sentencing and parole. Unevenness was a theme in judicial decisions in this research as well. Some judges preferred financial release and produced disproportionately high rates of detention, while several favored nonfinancial means generating extremely infrequent uses of detention. One judge in Miami generated particularly high rates of failure-to-appear among defendants released by him, but average rearrest rates. Another judge produced extremely low rates of reoffending, but was not so good at failures-to-appear. Predictors of judges' bail and release decisions were not notably related to prediction of pretrial flight and crime, principal concerns of the pretrial release decision. In two instances, judicial decisionmaking was, in contrast, rigidly inflexible: In Miami, judges tended to follow the traditional bond schedule practically without exception in determining bond. In Maricopa County, Superior Court commissioners almost as inflexibly followed the recommendation of the pretrial services agency, although we could not explain empirically how that recommendation was arrived at. A theme across the jurisdictions and decisionmakers studied was that, to a notable extent, decisionmaking could not be explained and seemed partly random in nature and effect. The challenge of the special research approach we present in these pages was to engage research as a practical resource in a process of judicial reform and policy development—to address the problems that were identified, clarify the character of the "Is" in judicial decisionmaking, and take several steps closer to the "Ought" of pretrial release and detention—in a manner never before attempted. We believe that, on the whole, the experiment of partnership between researchers and judicial leadership has led to many positive lessons that may hold the key to constructive reform of policy and practice in this important area of American justice.

JOHN S. GOLDKAMP
MICHAEL R. GOTTFREDSON
PETER R. JONES
DORIS WEILAND

Acknowledgments

This book is based on a major research undertaking involving three cities, five court systems, and scores of officials and staff who contributed to all that has been learned. Without the interest and commitment of these persons, the work could not have been completed and little could have been learned in this difficult area. The empirical basis of our discussion of judicial decisionmaking, discretion, bail, pretrial release, and detention involved a massive data collection effort that was made possible only because of the hard work and cooperation of many people in Maricopa County, Arizona; Dade County, Florida; Boston, Massachusetts; and in our home base at Temple University in Philadelphia. Although the numbers of individuals to whom we are indebted for their assistance is daunting, we would like to mention some of their names so that we can express our deepest gratitude to them.

We are appreciative of the support and patience of our funding agency, the National Institute of Justice of the U. S. Department of Justice, which sponsored this research in phases between 1984 and 1990 (under grant number 84-IJ-CX-056). During our work with the Superior Court in Maricopa County, we had the privilege of working with two presiding judges, the Honorable B. Michael Dann and Robert C. Broomfield, and three criminal presiding judges, the Honorable John H. Seidel, the Honorable Cecil Patterson, and the Honorable Thomas O'Toole. Under Judge Dann's firm leadership, the research process reached its culmination; pretrial release guidelines were finalized, implemented, evaluated and adjusted to new realities of processing. Our efforts in Maricopa County were also greatly assisted by Gordon W. Allison and his court administration staff, particularly Pete Anderson, Lance Wilson, and Mark Weinberg; Terri Jackson and Tom Morrison of Pretrial Services (and the entire pretrial services staff); and Superior Court commissioners Nastro (now Judge Nastro), Lobue, Strohson, Keifer, and Jackson.

In Dade County, we are greatly indebted for the assistance of a large number of persons. At the top of our list, however, are two individuals, the Honorable Gerald T. Wetherington, then Chief Judge of the 11th

Judicial Circuit, and Timothy J. Murray, then Director of the Pretrial Services Agency of the Metropolitan Dade County Corrections and Rehabilitation Department. Judge Wetherington was challenging, fair, and demanding in his appraisal of the research undertaking and supportive of its end product because of his determination to address Dade County's long-standing jail overcrowding difficulties. We are grateful for Timothy Murray's leadership and endless efforts in support of the research in Dade County; we were and are impressed by his example of dedication to public service, his wit, intelligence, and perseverance in bringing about needed change and were the beneficiaries of his profound good sense. He has since continued to distinguish himself as Director of the Office of Substance Abuse Control in Dade County, assisting in innovating the nation's first treatment drug court and in leading policy discussion and development in this area across the United States, and more recently in his new position in the Office of Justice Programs in the United States Department of Justice as Deputy Director.

We feel very fortunate for the opportunity to have worked with and learned from the Honorable Gerald Kogan, then Administrative Judge for the Criminal Division in Circuit Court and currently Justice of the Florida Supreme Court; former County Court Judge and current Deputy Court Administrator Chuck Edelstein; Fred Crawford, Director of Metropolitan Dade County Corrections and Rehabilitation Department; Deputy Director Kevin Hickey; and Assistant Division Director for Administration Frank Brophy. We were greatly impressed by the cooperation and professionalism of the Metro-Dade Corrections staff at that time, both at the jail and in the central office. It is impossible to express fully our gratitude and appreciation for the hard work and professional spirit Dade County's Pretrial Services staff at all levels during the period of our research there. Among those to whom we owe thanks most directly are Wilhemina Tribble, Julio Morales, Maxine Harris, Julie Oglesby, Will Davis, Larry Turini, and Mary (Mericie) Lantes, to confine ourselves to just a few of the many. In addition, we would like to thank M. David McGriff, then Criminal Court Coordinator and now distinguished Executive Director of the Advocate Program, Inc., for assisting us in working with court data, in obtaining access to the agencies holding the data we needed, and in appraising our findings with a sharp critical perspective and good humor.

We selected the Boston Courts in large part because of the interest expressed by the Honorable Arthur Mason, then Chief Administrative Justice of the Trial Court of the Commonwealth of Massachusetts; Henry L. Barr, then Administrator of the Trial Court; and the then Chief Administrative Justice the Honorable Thomas R. Morse, Chief Administrative Justice of the Superior Court of the Commonwealth of Massachusetts.

These individuals argued that the need for improvement in bail practices and the use of pretrial detention in the Boston area was great and, because of the crowding crisis at the Charles St. Jail, urgent. They have our heartfelt thanks. In the Boston Municipal Court, we had the pleasure of working under the guidance of two Chief Administrative Justices, the Honorable Theodore Glynn and the Honorable Joseph F. Feeney. We thank John Tobin, then Chief Probation Officer, and his staff, especially Francis Burke and Thomas Lally, and Robert E. Block, Assistant Clerk of the Boston Municipal Court, for his cooperation and assistance. A rather unique feature in our Boston work was the interest and cooperation of the office of District Attorney Newman Flanagan and his staff, particularly Paul Leary and Tom McDonough. Another very positive part of our research experience in that city was the interest and cooperation of two successive Suffolk County sheriffs, Dennis J. Kearney and Robert Ruffo. Above all others, these two individuals seemed eager for positive results from our research, seeing in it a possible resource, as we had hoped it would be, for addressing jail overcrowding. Nancy Waggner of the jail staff was particularly helpful in facilitating our data collection at the jail and in serving as a resource for us as we tried to understand Boston's processes and problems in the bail area. We are also grateful for the assistance of then Commissioner of Probation for the Commonwealth of Massachusetts Donald Cochran, and of Joyce Murphy, Superintendent of the Massachusetts Correctional Institution at Framingham.

In the sites, many hands deserve our gratitude for their labors in data collection. Our thanks to Linda Williams, Maureen Madden, and the many students and coders who worked on our data collection in Maricopa County. We are grateful for the efforts of Jaime Mervis, Andrea Goldblum, and our many coders in Miami. Finally, in regard to our work in Boston, we thank Russ Immarigeon and Janet Weiner and the staffs they supervised during data collection in the Boston courts.

Coordination and supervision of data collection in three geographically remote research sites placed a major responsibility on the shoulders of the research team's supervisory staff. We are grateful for the assistance of Dr. Kimberly Kempf, the project coordinator during the first phase of the project, who has since moved on to a very promising academic career, leading research projects of her own. Thanks also are due to Lisa Martin, Donna Richardson, and LaSaundra Scott ("Radar"), who was our secretary par excellence.

Due to limitations of space, we have not mentioned all of the persons who assisted or encouraged us during this large research undertaking. For those whose names we have not listed, please accept our warmest thanks for a job well done. Finally, however, in the final stages, as the completed research moved from study to book, we were assisted by the considerable contributions of Kathleen Ward, executive assistant at the Crime and Justice Research Institute in Philadelphia, whose tireless efforts in proofing, editing, creating graphics, and many aspects of production of the manuscript were indispensable. She has our deepest gratitude.

Portions of some chapters are rewritten from materials published elsewhere. We are grateful to the publishers for allowing us to use these materials here. Specifically, we are grateful to the University of Chicago Press for use of "Prediction in Criminal Justice Policy Development" (pp. 103–150 in D.M. Gottfredson and M. Tonry, eds., *Prediction and Classification,* Crime and Justice, vol. 9, 1987) (© 1987 by The University of Chicago Press. All rights reserved); Administrative Office of the Courts for use of "Judicial Responsibility for Pretrial Release Discrimination and the Information Role of Pretrial Services" (*Federal Probation,* 57/1:28–35); and The Board of Trustees of the University of Illinois for the use of "Guidelines for Incarceration Decisions: A Partisan Review" (*University of Illinois Law Review,* 1984/2: 291).

Contents

I: THE NEED FOR REFORM

I

THE NEED FOR REFORM

1

Bail, Pretrial Release, and Detention: The Critical Need for Judicial Reform

> The system is lax with those with whom it should be stringent and stringent with those with whom it could safely be less severe.
>
> ARTHUR BEELEY, *The Bail System in Chicago*, 1927

Criticisms of bail practices in the United States have been prevalent during most of this century.[1] A vast literature has documented the problems inherent in bail systems and attempts to institute reform.[2] Despite two generations of "bail reform," the first focusing on "community ties" and personal recognizance release and the second on public safety and preventive detention, pretrial release decisionmaking by the courts remains a central problem for criminal justice. In recent years, jail populations have grown to unprecedented levels, and jail overcrowding is now the rule, rather than the exception, in jurisdictions across the country. The numbers of persons confined before trial has outstripped any increase in crime, moving in lockstep with public-safety-oriented bail laws during the 1970s and 1980s that permit greater use detention. As the pressures mount to discover better approaches to managing the criminal caseload and the use of confinement at all stages of the criminal process, concern for the rights of individual defendants has waned. Serious problems of overcrowding in the nation's jails and perceived threats to public safety resulting from poor pretrial release practices overshadow questions about the quality of justice available to individual defendants and the popular, if not technical, meaning of "presumption of innocence."

Periodically, the evening news headlines a sensational crime committed by a person who was "out" on bail in connection with earlier criminal charges. Often, however, the earlier charges involved drug possession or theft, or some other offense that would have provided little hint of the later violent crime. In a 12-month period in Philadelphia during 1992–1993, nearly 1 in 5 of the more than 400 persons arrested for homicide had "skipped out" when released in earlier criminal cases and were already wanted for bench warrants at the time of their homicide arrests. According to a national study of the 75 most populous jurisdictions, on average, less than 1 in 5 felony defendants released before trial are rearrested for new offenses during the pretrial period.[3] About 1 in 10 are rearrested for felonies; fewer are rearrested for crimes of violence. To the public, these rare and sometimes horrible instances seem preventable in hindsight (Why didn't the system lock these defendants up?), but they are nearly impossible to foresee, at least when relying mainly on judicial intuition.

Newspapers in American cities also constantly remind readers that modern court systems still make mistakes. At the bail stage, where the volume of cases is usually great and the time spent deciding pretrial release for individual defendants quite brief, the operational assumption is that defendants are probably guilty and that it is better to err in the direction of too much caution. The result is overreliance on cash bail and often pretrial detention. During the spring of 1991, for example, the following headlines were seen in the *Philadelphia Inquirer* in March and May: "2 Cleared of Murder Charges—after 22 Months in Jail" (March 14); "Innocent Man Jailed for 27 Days" (May 18); "A Case of Mistaken Identity: An Innocent Man Is Put in Jail" (May 20). During March 1994, the *Philadelphia Daily News* featured a front-page series on "Bad Busts . . . When the Police Make Mistakes" (March 15–16).

Although reforms of the last 30 years have changed bail practices in many ways, they have skirted the principal issue: the responsibility of the judiciary to manage pretrial release decisionmaking and to ensure its quality. Judges point to uncertainty in the law about the legitimate purposes of bail and question the appropriateness of judicial "activism." They have decried the abysmal state of information available in the court system for the bail decision about defendants and their cases. They have blamed jail overcrowding crises for limiting their pretrial release choices and lamented the miserable conditions of courthouses and the scarcity of resources that could be directed at necessary improvements. Yet, with rare exception, courts have not undertaken rigorous self-analysis concerning their exercise of judicial discretion in pretrial release. Rarely has judicial leadership developed effective policies to manage the exercise of discretion at bail or to make judicial decisionmakers accountable to those policies.

It is fair to target the role of the judicial decisionmaker in assessing the state of affairs of pretrial release and detention because, despite scarce resources, poor information, and jail overcrowding, the critical nature of the pretrial release decision requires that criminal courts perform the function optimally. Given the mounting challenges posed to criminal justice by jail overcrowding, court backlogs, and drug-related criminal cases, the luxury of improvisational and unregulated pretrial-release decisionmaking and the license of free discretion in bail can no longer be afforded.

Having argued that courts have, on the whole, failed to take responsibility for managing discretion at the bail stage, we fully recognize that, even under the best of circumstances, the problems of pretrial release decisionmaking are not easy to resolve. In fact, the decisionmaker on a day-to-day basis faces fundamental questions that have been at the heart of long-standing debates concerning the appropriate goals of the pretrial release decision, the means available to achieve those goals, the criteria that should govern the release or detention of defendants before trial, and the consequences of bail decisions to defendants, society, and the court process. They are not questions necessarily or easily addressed by legislative enactment, no matter how "reform-oriented," or by perfunctory reference to court rules relating to bail.

In this book, we discuss an initiative undertaken by courts in several jurisdictions in partnership with social science researchers to examine pretrial release decisionmaking and to develop policy about the use of pretrial discretion. Our aim is to weigh the promise of a judge-centered approach to pretrial release policy and to describe a research approach intended to facilitate constructive change. The questions we address about the central judicial role in pretrial release and detention are now also being addressed in other settings, such as in certain treatment drug courts and domestic violence courts, where the presiding judge plays a more hands-on and activist role.

The dilemmas that have been faced historically by pretrial release systems in the United States can be summarized briefly as involving (1) questions about the legitimate purposes of bail; (2) the decision alternatives available at the pretrial release decision; (3) the appropriateness and quality of information used for making pretrial release decisions; and (4) the consequences (i.e., the equity, efficiency, and effectiveness) of pretrial release decisionmaking for criminal justice systems nationwide.

The Purpose(s) of Bail and Pretrial Detention

Until recently, there has been significant controversy about the legitimate goals of the bail decision and the legitimate uses of pretrial detention.

Early research and commentary documented illegal, punitive uses of bail and detention by criminal court judges.[4] During the 1960s and 1970s, the constitutional debate focused most often on whether, in addition to ensuring the appearance of defendants at court, judges could decide bail in response to the threat of additional crime during pretrial release.[5] The outcome of this debate has shifted noticeably: Until the late 1960s the practice of using pretrial detention to protect the public from dangerous defendants was highly controversial, but, in the 1980s particularly, it emerged from its *sub rosa* status to near-universal acceptance.[6] The passage of the Federal Bail Reform Act of 1984[7] (commonly referred to as the federal preventive detention law) and its subsequent favorable review in 1987 by the U.S. Supreme Court in *U.S. v. Salerno*[8] are only some of the most recent indications that the constitutionally acceptable goals of bail include public safety.

In fact, much of the momentum for change as well as the resistance to change American bail procedures can be traced to concerns for public safety and preoccupation with the select and "dangerous few" believed to be disproportionately responsible for serious crime. Thus, preventive detention legislation has sought to identify the dangerous defendants and to make it easier to confine them prior to adjudication of charges. At the same time, judges stubbornly defend their discretionary powers—and the all-purpose currency of cash bail—which they believe allow them to deal with dangerous defendants in their own, often highly subjective ways.

Decision Alternatives: Beyond Financial Bail

Providing alternatives to money bail has been a persistent aim of bail reform, precisely because money bail is used to cause pretrial detention. The original platform of bail reform included an attempt to persuade judges that many defendants who lacked financial resources could be released on personal recognizance (ROR) directly (as opposed to financial bond) and could be trusted to return to court faithfully when required.[9] Although this option has been employed much more widely over the last three decades, it is fair to conclude that optimum use of release on personal recognizance (ROR) has not been effectuated in all major jurisdictions.

Bail reform efforts have sought to introduce the use of other alternatives to traditional financial bail as well, such as "conditional release," the release before trial of defendants on various nonfinancial conditions often resembling conditions of probation more commonly reserved for adjudicated offenders.[10] Another innovation during the 1960s was deposit or "10 percent" bail, which allowed the defendant to deposit a small percentage of the full bail amount (roughly equivalent to the bondsman's usual fee) with the court. This deposit (usually minus a "service charge") was to be returned upon successful attendance at the required proceedings.[11]

Certainly, attempts to implement personal recognizance, conditional release and deposit bail have not always met with success. Perhaps the ultimate proof is that the use of financial conditions still predominates in most courts and that large numbers of defendants are to this day held in jail for want of posting cash bail—even under the federal law which appeared to prohibit this procedure. Failures have been due to the preference among judges for financial bail, to the flexible exercise of discretion to detain or release defendants associated with bail, and to the interests of bondsmen, whose livelihood is seriously threatened by shifts in court practices away from strict reliance on cash bail.[12]

Born partly of the necessity to relieve jail crowding and partly as a natural outgrowth of advances in rapidly changing technology, "new" alternatives in the form of pretrial drug testing (to determine the risk that defendants might pose and their eligibility for monitoring or treatment programs) and electronic monitoring (via "ankle bracelets" or other remote monitoring devices) have been implemented, with mixed results.[13]

The Relevancy of Information for Bail Decisions

An important contribution of the movement to reform bail practices in the United States was an emphasis on improving and broadening the information that ought to be considered by judges in their pretrial release determinations. The Vera Institute's New York program in the 1960s sought to encourage greater use of ROR at the initial appearance stage by providing judges with information regarding defendants' community and family ties.[14] This campaign was really an attempt to reexamine the criteria that should guide bail judges, who generally relied nearly exclusively on the perceived seriousness of defendants' charges. Efforts to broaden the kinds of information judges had available to guide selection among the various newly emerging bail options were reflected, for example, in the Federal Bail Reform Act of 1966. This law suggested a large number of criteria for judicial consideration.[15] Although this landmark legislation inspired similar legislation in the states, the guiding criteria suggested in state laws have ranged from none, or very few, to indicating such a large number as to offer little real guidance.[16] Furthermore, when criteria are specified, judges are not given guidance as to the relative importance of the different options.

Questions about the value of specific kinds of information for pretrial release decisions are even more fundamental. Researchers have raised issues about the actual ("objective" or statistical) versus presumed (theoretical or intuitive) value of particular kinds of information (such as defendants' charges or prior histories) and the standards that ought to govern their selection.[17] In the late 1980s and 1990s, debate has again surfaced about the utility of defendant drug abuse information. Proponents argue that much, if not all, of crime is tied to drugs, and that therefore drug information is essential to determining the level of risk posed by defendants. Some jurisdictions have implemented programs of pretrial drug testing, partly based on the hypothesis that such tests would contribute important data to judicial decisionmaking.[18]

Research has also focused on the kinds of information most predictive of defendant flight (failure to appear in court, or FTA) and crime,[19] and on the information actually employed by judges or determinative of their pretrial release decisions.[20] The gaps between what is *thought* by judges to be predictive of defendant performance during pretrial release, what *is* predictive, and what is predictive of judges' *bail choices* are key problems to be addressed, if rational pretrial-release decisionmaking is to be widely achieved.

Equity, Effectiveness, and Efficiency in Pretrial Release Decisions

Issues raised by pretrial release practices come into sharpest focus when it is recalled that the pretrial release decision has one consequence: the release or detention prior to their trial of persons accused of crime. A perennial criticism of traditional bail practices holds that a system allocating release and detention among the criminally accused on the basis of their ability to afford financial bail is inequitable because it discriminates on the basis of economic status. In fact, many have long questioned the very existence of financial bail as a means of determining pretrial release.[21] Indeed, much of the impetus toward the development of preventive detention laws—particularly the 1970 enactment of the District of Columbia preventive detention law and the Federal Bail Reform Act of 1984—was motivated by the wish to eliminate reliance on financial bail.

The issue of *equitable treatment* of defendants at pretrial release is broader than overreliance on cash bail. It also involves the availability of equal justice for the two classes of accused (those detained and those released before trial), the appropriateness of the criteria defining those classes, and the comparability of the treatment of similarly situated defendants at bail.[22] At the core of these issues concerning equity, of course, are questions about the goals of pretrial release and detention and about the information on the basis of which they should be pursued.

The utilitarian nature of bail decisions raises the question of effectiveness. The concept of *effectiveness* is complex because it can be viewed as minimizing the number of dangerous defendants released before trial (unsafe release) and/or as minimizing the unnecessary detention of defendants whose inappropriate detention would serve to exacerbate the condition of already hopelessly overcrowded jails. It is ineffective to release defendants who flee and commit crimes during pretrial release.[23] The current reexamination of bail and pretrial release laws is motivated principally by such effectiveness concerns.

Another increasingly important issue in this area is the pragmatic concern about resource *efficiency*. Procedures that result in unnecessary detention can ultimately prove very costly. Not only do crowded jails increase operational costs, but they also invite expensive lawsuits, crowding litigation, and fines for failing to comply with court orders and consent decrees. Similarly, it is inefficient to release defendants who fail to attend court, thereby causing delays in court proceedings and the need for reapprehension. It is costly to release defendants who commit new crimes during the period of provisional liberty prior to adjudication, costly to victims of their crimes, and costly to law enforcement and other criminal justice agencies that will ultimately have to reprocess the same individuals.

Bail and Jail Overcrowding

Historically, American jails have been the source of controversy and continuing concern because of crowded facilities and substandard conditions.[24] In fact, the pioneering research and commentary of Caleb Foote (1954) and the efforts of Louis Schweitzer and the Vera Institute of Justice in implementing bail reform programs in the early 1960s were in large part responses to the conditions of jails and the plight of their inmates. Despite over three decades of "bail reform," American jails today remain crowded and often substandard. Frequently, at least half the jail population consists of defendants detained prior to adjudication. This chronic situation cannot be explained by the crime rate alone, as the following statistics demonstrate.

According to the U.S. Department of Justice,[25] the one-day count of jail inmates in the United States increased 181 percent between 1978 and 1992, from 158,394 inmates to 444,584 inmates. The average daily population of inmates in American jails grew 94 percent between 1983 and 1992 alone—from 227,541 to 441,889 inmates. In 1978, 65 percent of jails were over "rated capacity"; by 1992, 99 percent were reported by the same source to be over capacity, while about 27 percent were under court orders relating to crowding or conditions of confinement.[26]

The burgeoning jail populations are not explained by a similar growth in serious crime. According to the National Crime Survey, for example, the number of total victimizations in the United States *declined* 18 percent from 1978 to 1992, and the number of violent crimes increased 10 percent during that period.[27] According to the FBI, arrests overall increased about 40 percent from 1990 to 1991; arrests for drug abuse violations increased 126 percent through 1989 and then declined notably after that to a level in 1991 still 84 percent above that of 1980.[28] In short, it is reasonable to assume that part of the growth in institutional populations was generated by judicial and other decisionmaking processes regulating the use of confinement, including pretrial release and sentencing, and revocation decisions. It is also probable that part of the impact was explained by justice policies associated with the War against Drugs during the 1980s.

Pretrial Release Guidelines: The Promise of a Rational Decisionmaking Approach

The difficult problems characterizing the pretrial release and detention process in the United States can be best understood as problems of decisionmaking. In general, the problem is defining an explicit court policy to guide pretrial release decisionmaking. On the level of the individual judicial decisionmaker, the problem is to develop a guiding resource with clear goals and a variety of appropriate pretrial-release options based on relevant and parsimonious information. In this book, we describe research in five courts in three urban settings documenting the experiences of guidelines development efforts designed to respond to the challenges faced by judiciaries with decisionmaking responsibilities for pretrial release.

This research represents the second stage in the development of the decision guidelines approach to pretrial release. The first stage involved an experiment conducted in the Philadelphia Municipal Court[29] in which judges and social scientists worked together to construct decision guidelines[30] and to determine whether their use by the court could productively address the kinds of problems noted above.

The Philadelphia study tested the proposition that the issues stubbornly characterizing the practice of bail were, like problems associated with other criminal-justice decision stages (such as parole and sentencing), best attacked as "normal" problems of decisionmaking, as "natural" to the exercise of discretionary judgment.[31] Inequitable treatment of defendants, flight and crime during pretrial release, and jail overcrowding were viewed as "normal" problems in the sense that they were artifacts of highly subjective decisionmaking by large numbers of judges who made use of few options, who relied on very little reliable information, and who made their decisions under conditions of low visibility, securely within the realm of judicial discretion.

The court-based self-help guidelines in Philadelphia were created as an explicit representation of court policy regarding bail and pretrial release and as a tool to aid the judge as the front-line decisionmaker in making better pretrial release decisions. The principal aim of the experiment was to study the promise of the self-help guidelines method as a means of assisting the court as a whole in making and managing better pretrial release decisions. Thus, concerns about defendant flight or defendant crime could best be addressed, it was argued, through structuring the pretrial release decision, managing the use of information, and providing systematic feedback on (both defendant and judicial) performance. At the same time, on a policy level, the Philadelphia guidelines were designed to respond to criticisms of the bail practices that were argued by critics to be responsible for jail crowding. By reviewing "bail" policy thoroughly and analyzing the impact of bail decisions, the municipal court judiciary was able to demonstrate that it had an appropriate policy and that it was able to monitor the results of its practices. Using the policy framework of the court's decision guidelines and the empirical analysis which supported their development, the municipal court had a powerful tool that could both facilitate the examination of specific problem areas (in the light of court policy) and enable a more systematic approach to release decisionmaking. Given the improvisation of *ad hoc* (and potentially self-defeating) emergency release measures by courts supervising overcrowding litigation in Philadelphia during that period,[32] the strong hope was that the court-based decision-guidelines approach to pretrial release pioneered by the municipal court judiciary could offer a more rational alternative to analyzing population crises as they presented themselves.

A Guidelines Approach to Decisionmaking

The idea of applying decision guidelines to the area of pretrial release derives from efforts aimed at reforming the paroling and sentencing functions during the early 1970s.[33] These efforts introduced the idea of decisionmaker-based self-help or voluntary attempts to bring about major system improvements. The National Council on Crime and Delinquency and the (then) U.S. Board of Parole proposed to study parole decisionmaking and to examine its implication for policy and practice. Using a variety of social science approaches, the researchers sought to examine the criteria relied on by parole board members in making their decisions and to facilitate an evaluation by the board of the appropriateness and efficacy of those criteria. As a result of this collaborative effort, and based on extensive policy debate, guidelines were developed that adopted specific criteria to guide parole board members' decisions in the majority of cases.

The categories of offenders used in the guidelines were based on a ranking of offense severity and a "salient factor score" that classified defendants according to their probability of success on parole if released. These dimensions were constructed after careful study of the relative importance in past decisionmaking of specific criteria, including ranking exercises by board members and hearing examiners to scale offense severities as well as actuarial analyses of failure on parole in large samples of parolees.[34]

The U.S. Parole Commission (the U.S. Board of Parole renamed) adopted guidelines in a matrix format for voluntary use by parole decisionmakers. The hypothesis was that the decisionmakers would find the guidelines helpful in the vast majority of cases; discretion whether to grant parole would be structured according to specific criteria designed to reflect known policy goals. The guidelines also recognized that unusual cases would warrant exceptional decisions on the basis of criteria not built into the guidelines. Exceptional decisions would be accompanied by written reasons so that decisionmakers would be accountable and so that the guidelines could later be analyzed for possible revision. The U.S. Parole Commission adopted parole decision guidelines fully in 1973. Experience with the federal parole guidelines has encouraged similar innovations in parole and sentencing in many states.

The second important stage of voluntary guidelines development was to determine whether the same collaborative strategy could be used to structure sentencing discretion. Feasibility studies were conducted by researchers working with D. Gottfredson and L. Wilkins to examine sentencing decisions in courts in Denver and Vermont. Empirical modeling of decisions was employed on samples of sentencing decisions, and these models were used to construct versions of guidelines that judges might choose to employ if guidelines were implemented.[35] In a second phase, voluntary guidelines were developed or implemented by courts in Chicago, Phoenix, Newark, and Denver between 1976 and 1978.[36]

Since the initial parole and sentencing guidelines projects, parole guidelines have been adopted in a number of states (including Arizona,

Florida, Georgia, Maryland, Minnesota, New York, Oklahoma, Oregon, and Washington), and several states and many local jurisdictions have developed some form of voluntary sentencing guidelines. The Philadelphia Court of Common Pleas developed such guidelines (without fully implementing them) as an offshoot of the Denver project. Michigan, Massachusetts, and New Jersey have engaged in the development of voluntary guidelines independent of the early research projects.[37] Florida and Maryland undertook comparable guidelines-development processes.[38]

In the late 1970s, however, guidelines development branched in two directions. Many jurisdictions continued to operate or to develop voluntary guidelines, while several states elected to create presumptive sentencing-guidelines systems. They are "presumptive" in that the applicable guideline ranges are legally presumed to apply in every case; decisionmakers may impose some other sentence if they give their reasons for concluding that the presumption is overcome, and the sufficiency of those reasons is typically subject to review on appeal. In 1978 Minnesota created a sentencing commission and charged it to develop guidelines for felony sentencing. These guidelines were to be followed in any case unless "substantial and compelling" reasons justified a "departure" (i.e., imposition of some other sentence). Evaluation of the early years of Minnesota's experience with guidelines revealed high levels of compliance with the guidelines and a reduction in sentencing disparities among felony cases.[39] Washington State and Pennsylvania developed and implemented presumptive sentencing-guidelines systems. Half a dozen other states have established sentencing commissions, and at the federal level the Comprehensive Crime Control Act of 1984 established the U.S. Sentencing Commission, which developed federal sentencing guidelines initially taking effect late in 1987 and undergoing revisions since that time.

After completion of the early work with parole and sentencing, and prior to most of the efforts to develop legislative guidelines for sentencing in states and the federal jurisdiction, a research effort was initiated to determine the feasibility of the voluntary guidelines approach for bail decisions in Philadelphia. The first version of pretrial release ("bail") guidelines was produced as a result of the feasibility research and then was implemented in an experiment in the Philadelphia Municipal Court between 1981 and 1983. The Philadelphia "bail guidelines" were formally adopted by the municipal court judiciary as court policy in 1983.[40]

The attempt to bring the guidelines approach to bear on reform of pretrial release clearly falls in the tradition of the voluntary guidelines efforts, although it could be argued that analogues to the legislatively imposed presumptive sentencing guidelines can be seen in the Federal Bail Reform Act of 1984 and recent changes in federal law governing pretrial release in the District of Columbia. The parallels with parole and sentencing decisionmaking are not perfect, however.

The *bail decision*, as the pretrial release decision has traditionally been known, is in some ways less complex and in other ways more of a dilemma than the sentencing and parole decisions. It is arguably less complex because the aims of pretrial release determinations are strictly utilitarian—by which we mean that the means employed can be evaluated in terms of the ends to be achieved—and thus not clouded (in theory at least) by punitive concerns of "just desert" or retribution. Yet, the bail decision may be more frustrating than the other decisions. If punishment of the accused cannot be one of the goals of pretrial release decisionmaking, it should be easy to measure its effects and to improve its practice, though this is rarely done. Because bail centers on prediction by the judge of a defendant's likely future conduct so that misconduct can be avoided (a utilitarian aim), it should be easier to comment on the effectiveness of pretrial release practices than on the effectiveness of sentencing practices (when sentencing goals are thought to involve deterrence or incapacitation, for example). Judges' bail decisions and their outcomes, the use of release and detention, and defendants' behavior during pretrial release can be observed, measured, and evaluated in a relatively straight-forward fashion, generally unobscured by the comparatively ponderous philosophical questions that surround debates on sentencing reform.

The decision guidelines for bail developed in the Philadelphia study (like those to be described later in this book that were developed in Boston, Maricopa County, and Dade County) were designed to be a court-based, voluntarily employed decisionmaking tool to assist judges in their pretrial release tasks. In appearance, as will be illustrated in later chapters, they have followed a familiar grid format[41] positing "presumptive" bail decisions for designated categories of defendants. The rationale behind the use of the guidelines is that, if they have been designed properly, they ought to be "followed" by judges in a majority of the cases. In a minority of instances, special features of cases would lead to decisions outside the choices suggested by the guidelines—in a more restrictive or less restrictive direction. Decisions outside the ranges suggested by the guidelines would be accompanied by notation by the judges of the reasons why an exception or "departure" was necessary. Later examination of departures, judges' reasons for departures (as well as other data relating to the pretrial release decisions), the use of pretrial detention, and the performance of defendants within specific guidelines categories would be used to modify the guidelines if necessary, or at least to feed back to the court information about their effects.

A Note on Terminology: Bail, Pretrial Release, and Pretrial Detention

Because some readers may (already) be confused by some of the terminology we employ, it may be helpful to clarify our terms briefly before proceeding further into the discussion. Perhaps most often confused are the terms *bail, bond,* and *pretrial release.* Bail is confusing because it is often taken to connote any option designed to permit the release of a defendant before trial with appropriate assurances. There is a history of scholarly debate about the purposes of bail and whether they included a concern that a defendant would not be held to answer charges. *Bail* could be taken to mean any arrangement devised to provide that assurance, from an individual's word or the word of a third party, to providing property or, most commonly in America, cash. To many, bail *refers* only to the use of a financial assurance, the posting of bond. *Bail setting,* then, is taken to refer to the assignment by a judge or judicial officer of an amount of cash bond.

Although it is true that cash or financial bail is by far the most often employed bail option (hence the reason for the popular assumption that bail is only financial), *bail decisionmaking* really refers to a full range of possible actions a judge could take in ensuring that a defendant will appear in court or, if released, will not pose a risk of crime to the community. One of the basic criticisms of the bail process has been its traditional reliance on cash bail,[42] its doubtful utility in ensuring the presence of the defendant, and its inherent unfairness to economically disadvantaged defendants. From the perspective of decisionmaking, the problem with a predominantly cash bail "bail" process is that the custody status of the individual remains to be decided by his or her ability to raise cash, not by a judge's decision to grant or deny release. During the bail reform movement of the 1960s, many convincingly argued that the proper term for the first judicial decisionmaking stage is the *pretrial release decision,* because the point of the decision after all was either to hold or to release defendants. In fact, one of the arguments made to support preventive detention legislation (both for the District of Columbia in 1970 and for the federal jurisdiction in the Federal Bail Reform Act of 1984) was that the fudge factor provided by cash choices, the ability to detain persons *sub rosa,* ought to be abolished in favor of a clear-cut release or detention decision at the "bail" stage.

When we refer to *bail guidelines,* we use the term in its proper, broad sense to suggest the selection of arrangements that could provide the assurance that a court needs to believe that a defendant will attend trial and refrain from criminal activity if at liberty in the interim. We denote the use of financial bail options by referring to them as *financial bail, cash bail,* or *bond.* We are convinced that, for reasons of clarity and for purpose of forthrightness in conceptualizing the early judicial decision, the terms *pretrial release* and *pretrial release guidelines* are greatly to be preferred. After all, we are focusing on the decision by the judiciary that results in the release or detention of defendants before trial, its consequences, and how it might be improved.

How This Book Is Organized

This book is organized in five basic parts. In Part I, we introduce the issues and problems at the core of the judicial exercise of pretrial release decisionmaking in the United States, issues that stubbornly defy reform. We then describe the voluntary guidelines rationale for addressing these problems. In addition, we review the initial experiment to implement pretrial release guidelines in Philadelphia. This sets the stage for the main focus of the book, a study of the efforts to bring guidelines to bear on pretrial release problems in court systems in three large urban jurisdictions. In Part II, we describe the court systems in Dade County, Florida; Boston, Massachusetts; and Maricopa County, Arizona; these were the focus of the research. We discuss the descriptive research undertaken in the first phase of guidelines development at those sites. In Part III, we review the construction of the decision guidelines at each of the sites and the concerns that shaped their development. We also estimate the impact the guidelines were likely to have, if they were to be successfully implemented. In Part IV, we describe the implementation and initial effects of the guidelines at each of the sites. Part V integrates findings from the separate experiences and draws conclusions about the promise of the self-help guidelines strategy as a resource for the judicial reform of pretrial release. Finally, we briefly revisit Philadelphia 10 years after the completion of the original bail guidelines experiment, as well as the Dade County and Maricopa County sites six years after the second-stage research, to learn how the original bail guidelines have fared since.

Notes

1. See, for example, Frankfurter and Pound (1922); Beeley (1927); Moley (1933); Foote (1954); Ares, Rankin, and Sturz (1963); Freed and Wald (1964); American Bar Association

(1968); Angel et al. (1971); Thomas (1976); National Association of Pretrial Services Agencies (1978); Goldkamp (1979).

2. See, for example, Foote (1954); Goldfarb (1967); Wice (1973); Thomas (1976); Goldkamp (1979); Goldkamp and Gottfredson (1985); Feeley (1983).
3. Reaves (1992).
4. Frankfurter and Pound (1922); Beeley (1927); Foote (1954).
5. Foote (1954); Freed and Wald (1964); American Bar Association (1968); Ervin (1971); Goldkamp (1979).
6. When Congress debated and then passed the "preventive detention" law for the District of Columbia in 1970, no other laws recognized any other goal than ensuring a defendant's appearance in court at the pretrial stage. See D.C. Code Ann. secs. 23 1321 to 23 1332 (1981 & Supp. 1985); *Hearings before the Subcomm. on Constitutional Rights of Comm. on the Judiciary*, 91st Cong., 2nd Sess. (1970). Since that time approximately 35 states, the District of Columbia, and the federal law have provisions that can be interpreted as allowing a public safety orientation (see Goldkamp 1985).
7. Federal Bail Reform Act of 1984, Pub. L. 98 473, tit. II, ch. 1, 98 Stat. 1976 (1984).
8. Salerno 481 U.S. 739 (1987).
9. Freed and Wald (1964).
10. For an analysis of the kinds of conditions provided for in the laws of the United States, see Goldkamp (1985). The Federal Bail Reform Act of 1984 and its predecessor, the Federal Bail Reform Act of 1966 (Pub. L. No. 89 465, sec. 3(a), 80 Stat. 214; codified as 18 U.S.C. sec. 3146, 1966), offer good examples of nonfinancial release conditions.
11. Deposit bail was intended to make release more affordable to defendants, while still holding them responsible for the entire amount should they fail to appear in court. Unlike the use of bondsmen, who would keep the fees whether defendants appeared or not, the deposit with the court was seen as providing some incentive for the defendant to return (to reclaim his or her bail minus a small service charge). Although "10 percent" bail, pioneered in Illinois, was the most common, jurisdictions varied in the amount of the total bail that would be required, ranging up to as much as 50 percent (see Goldkamp 1985).
12. The role of the bondsman in pretrial criminal justice has long been criticized. See, for example, the discussions of bondsmen in Frankfurter and Pound (1922) and Beeley (1927). The bondsmen today remain a powerful political force in many places and continue to resist reform of bail practices that they view as encroaching on their ability to do business.
13. See Jones and Goldkamp (1993); Britt, Gottfredson, and Goldkamp (1992); Goldkamp and Jones (1992); Goldkamp, Gottfredson, and Weiland (1990).
14. Recommendations for broader use of information at the bail stage, particularly information describing defendants' "social" background were made as early as 1927 (Beeley) and 1954 (Foote).
15. For a discussion of the criteria suggested by state and federal law for judicial bail determinations, see Goldkamp (1985).
16. Goldkamp (1979, 1985).
17. Goldkamp (1987). See, for example, Morris and Miller (1985), who argue that, although it is desirable to employ predictive information at the pretrial release stage that is empirically justified, it is not required constitutionally. Information that is thought to be appropriate is all that is necessary.
18. This hypothesis has now been examined in some detail (Wish and Johnson 1986; Carver 1986, 1993; Toborg and Bellassai 1988; Belenko and Mara-Drita 1987; Smith, Wish, and

Jarjoura 1989; Goldkamp, Gottfredson and Weiland 1990; Britt et al. 1992; Goldkamp and Jones 1992; Vischer 1992; Jones and Goldkamp 1993).

19. Clarke, Freeman, and Koch (1976); Gottfredson (1974); Roth and Wice (1978); Goldkamp (1983); Goldkamp and Gottfredson (1985); Toborg et al. (1987); Goldkamp (1987); Yezer et al. (1987a, b); Belenko and Mara-Drita (1987); Smith et al. (1989); Goldkamp, Gottfredson, and Weiland (1990).
20. See Roth and Wice (1978); Goldkamp (1979); Goldkamp and Gottfredson (1985); Goldkamp (1987); Goldkamp and Gottfredson (1988).
21. See, for example, Frankfurter and Pound (1922); Beeley (1927); Foote (1954); ABA (1968).
22. Goldkamp and Gottfredson (1985); Goldkamp (1979).
23. Smith (1993). Recent data show that an average of one in four felony defendants released before trial in the 75 most populous counties nationally fail to appear in court as required.
24. See, for example, Frankfurter and Pound (1922:375–388); Beeley (1927); National Commission on Law Observance and Enforcement (1931*b*:56–57).
25. See Flanagan, Hindelang, and Gottfredson (1979, Table 6.18); McGuire and Pastore (1994, Table 6.17); Bureau of Justice Statistics (1992:4).
26. See Flanagan and McGuire (1992:6.25, 6.51); Beck et al. (1993); Welsh and Smith (1992).
27. By 1991, crimes of violence victimizations had increased nearly 10 percent, while theft victimizations declined a further 6 percent (Flanagan and McGuire 1992, Table 3.2; Bureau of Justice Statistics 1992:4; Bastion 1993, Table 1). The rates of victimization (per 1,000) decreased 5 percent from 1978 to 1992 (Maquire and Pastore 1994).
28. McGuire and Flanagan (1991, Table 4.5)
29. Goldkamp and Gottfredson (1985).
30. Gottfredson, Wilkins, and Hoffman (1978).
31. Gottfredson and Gottfredson (1988).
32. See Goldkamp (1983).
33. Gottfredson et al. (1978).
34. Gottfredson et al. (1978).
35. Wilkins et al. (1976).
36. See Kress (1980).
37. Blumstein et al. (1983:126–183).
38. Carrow et al. (1985)
39. Knapp (1984*a*)
40. Goldkamp and Gottfredson (1985); Goldkamp (1987).
41. Ibid.
42. See, e.g., Beeley (1927); Foote (1954).

2

The Development and Implementation of Voluntary Guidelines in Criminal Justice

As the use of guidelines has become more common—and the word itself overused—doubts have been expressed by some critics about guidelines' ability to deliver on their original promise. Two broad sets of issues have been raised. The first involves the appropriateness of empirically based methods in guidelines development, and the second concerns the correctness of the statistical procedures employed in the construction of guidelines.

The Role of Predictive Methods

Three related questions lie at the heart of the debate concerning the use of predictive methods in developing decision guidelines: (1) Is it possible to infer "policy" meaningfully from predictive analyses? (2) What uses should and can be made of empirically based policy inferences in developing guidelines? (3) Have the statistical analyses used in guideline projects been appropriately selected and adequately performed?

1. *Inferring policy from statistical description.* The initial research projects on parole, sentencing, and bail guidelines collected and analyzed data describing samples of recent decisions. This was seen as facilitating discussion among the responsible decisionmakers of apparent operating policy and as setting the stage for constructing guidelines for future use.[1] This step employed multivariate statistical methods to model the decisions under study on the basis of knowledge of the attributes of the cases (i.e., their demographic, legal, social, and criminal history characteristics) that would have been available to decisionmakers when making their

decisions. The thesis was that, by finding commonalities in the ways that decisionmakers handle cases, researchers could identify underlying policies.

This key postulate has been challenged by a number of critics. The principal objection questions whether such statistical methods can capture inherent policy.[2] The more general criticism questions whether meaningful inferences about policy may be drawn from aggregate statistics, which, critics contend, produce illusory and misleading results. What is obtained, it is said, is an "average" profile of decisionmaking, which may be merely a statistical construct that reflects the actual policy of no individual judge.[3]

Proponents of the guidelines approach mean something different when they use the term *implicit policy*. What they mean by use of that term is indeed a statistical aggregate. They reason that the "empirical analyses of past decision practices are useful to policy development if they uncover sentencing (or paroling or bailing) behavior of the decisionmakers in the aggregate. . . . The bases of the estimates will capture as main determinants what we mean by policy—themes that seem to guide most decisionmakers in most cases" (Gottfredson and Gottfredson 1980:300). Rough statistical indicators of policy correlates are all that is needed in the collaborative research process employed in guidelines development. The interpretation of the statistical results is not a task for researchers only. Models of decisions are examined and debated for sense by the decisionmakers, who can confirm or refute the relevance of statistical correlates to decision policy.[4]

2. *Confusing descriptive and prescriptive uses.* Some critics have objected to decision guidelines on the basis of a belief that the empirical modeling of past practices leads inexorably to institutionalization of the status quo.[5] Similarly, assuming that the empirical description of justice decisions and the construction of decision guidelines are the same thing, Fisher and Kadane (1983) write that "we are uncomfortable with the whole enterprise of empirically based sentencing guidelines . . . first, they are by their nature unthoughtfully conservative . . . [they] strike us as a species of computer-driven conservatism" (p. 192).[6]

The developers of guidelines certainly conceived that guidelines could be designed solely to reflect and to better organize past decision practices,[7] but they also distinguished descriptive and prescriptive roles for modeling by using empirical methods. In the descriptive phase, decisions are examined for patterns that suggest policies, the principal idea being that discussion of what "ought to be" may usefully be grounded in a knowledge of what "is." In the prescriptive phase, descriptions of past practice can serve as the basis for identifying decision patterns that should be changed and for projecting the impact of alternative new policies. Proponents argue that the design of alternative models of decision guidelines that could be employed to shape future decisions is a distinct undertaking that involves the debate of the desirability of what "is" compared with competing visions of what "could be."

The distinction between the descriptive and the prescriptive empirical tasks is fundamental. Decisionmaking studies in other domains demonstrate that descriptions of what decisionmakers do often do not correspond with what they should do or even with what they believe they do.[8]

3. *The "rationality-cannot-reform" critique.* A third major critique is that decision guidelines are not an effective means of bringing about change. These doubts range from narrow criticisms of the guidelines method to more general, philosophical disagreements with the "rational-man" assumptions that underlie the voluntary guidelines approach.[9]

A "rational" conception of the human decisionmaker underlies the guidelines approach.[10] That conception assumes that decisionmakers will voluntarily seek optimal solutions to difficult choices, are interested in improving their understanding of the goals of their decisions, and see themselves as benefiting from information related to achievement of those goals and to the consequences of their decisions.

Some critics have plainly questioned these assumptions.[11] In a summary of an evaluation of the Maryland and Florida sentencing guidelines, both of which were to have had an empirical base, Carrow (1984) concluded that the major weaknesses of the guidelines systems she examined were not traceable to their "judicial origins or empirical design, but their voluntary implementation" (p. 171).

Proponents cite the experience of the U.S. Parole Commission and the bail guidelines experiment in Philadelphia as evidence that meaningful and measurable change can be effectuated by the voluntary guidelines method. Perhaps some forms of "voluntariness" carry with them powerful influences toward compliance. For example, a guidelines innovation adopted by a court of its own accord may be motivated by external pressures. Judges may fear that, if they refuse to revise sentencing practices, the legislature will mandate changes with which they disagree. Similarly, jail-crowding crises and litigation may motivate judges to worry about pretrial release decisionmaking.

In practice, the use of "voluntary" guidelines may not be entirely voluntary. Decisionmakers may be influenced by collegial pressure or may have little choice but to comply if the policy becomes a formal or informal court rule. Even without legislative backing, guidelines may be "enforced" informally by strong court leadership; conversely, they may fall quickly into disuse in the absence of commitment from the top or may be overwhelmed by emergency release decrees resulting from crowding litigation. To date, nevertheless, there is evidence that voluntary guidelines can produce effective and meaningful change.[12]

Statistical Methods

Critics argue that serious methodological weaknesses have characterized voluntary guidelines research. A lengthy list of problems has been detailed: the descriptive models at the heart of the guidelines have been seriously flawed; the models' predictive power has been unimpressively weak; and the models devised have institutionalized the discriminatory effects of status variables such as sex, race, or economic status or have failed to attend to the anticipated effects of classifications resulting from their adoption.[13]

1. *Flawed models.* Quality modeling is crucial. If researchers do not model decisions well, the examination of policy and practice will be faulty, and the resulting guidelines may be based on erroneous premises. Vigorous critiques of the statistical sophistication of some of the earlier guidelines have been offered.[14]

Poorly specified models may stem from a number of problems. Sampling may insufficiently or inequitably represent the decisionmakers whose decisions are the foundation of the modeling exercise; extrapolations of policy from such a sample may be too narrowly based. Sampling may also inadequately include entire categories of cases that, although essential to any sentencing scheme, may appear only rarely. Murder, rape, and robbery cases are less common than are less serious cases. To learn how these kinds of cases are "typically" handled, it may be necessary to design a sample to "overinclude" them.

In addition, samples serving as the basis for guidelines development may be too small for meaningful analysis if the researchers wish to weigh the relative strength of variables related to decisions, to assess possible interaction effects, or to validate results.[15] Rich et al. (1982, p. 71), for example, suggest that, by relying on a sample of 200 cases, the researchers who were developing sentencing guidelines in Denver employed a sample much too small for in-depth multivariate modeling.

Another problem is that variables included in empirical models may not reflect operating concerns (because of poor data, poor conceptualizations, or spurious correlations), and others that do influence policy may be omitted (because of measurement difficulties, poor theorizing, or missing information). The models that are produced may best be explained merely by the availability of some information in archival data and the unavailability of other information.

A related difficulty involves poor conceptualization and measurement of variables.[16] The measurement of sentencing decisions, for example, has been examined as a quasi-interval-level variable[17] in which zero represented nonincarcerative sanctions, and values of 1 or higher stood for periods of time to be served in incarceration. Such a measure may impractically combine qualitatively different decisions (the in-out decision and the length-of-sentence decision) in one criterion, serving neither well. Subsequent guidelines efforts have generally modeled the two aspects of sentencing decisions separately.[18]

Bail decisionmaking poses a similar measurement problem because of its different decision options (release on personal recognizance, cash bail, conditional release, and outright detention). Some researchers have employed an all-purpose criterion with values ranging from $0.00 (for personal recognizance) to positive dollar values (sometimes reaching into the millions).[19] More recently, the dependent variable has been conceptualized as a bifurcated or trifurcated decision (e.g., "release on recognizance," yes or no?; then, if no, cash amount).[20] In bail guidelines, each aspect has been modeled separately because of the apparently different orientations of the decision components and the difference in the factors that appear to predict each.[21]

The measurement of independent variables, particularly offense severity, has also posed problems.[22] Statutory offense definitions vary from jurisdiction to jurisdiction, so it is difficult to employ a measure that both reflects the treatment of severity locally and can serve as the basis for comparisons across jurisdictions. When offense severity is scaled without reference to statutory gradings, the resulting classification may be quite different still, as in the case of the original federal parole guidelines[23] and of the bail guidelines developed in Philadelphia.[24] Similarly, measurements of criminal history suffer reliability and validity weaknesses (Is an individual's record accurate or even available? When available, does the conviction offense correspond well with the crime committed?).

Misapplication of statistical techniques has been described as a source of poor modeling in guidelines efforts.[25] Ordinary least-squares regression, for example, has been applied to predictions of dichotomous criterion variables that have been treated as interval-level indicators without concern for the consequences. Often the distributions of these variables have been highly skewed (aggravating prediction errors) and nonlinear relations between the independent measures and the criterion variables not properly explored. Critics have urged that researchers pay more attention to the assumptions underlying specific statistical techniques in their application to guidelines modeling. However, because of the validity, reliability, and measurement difficulties characteristic of archival criminal justice data, comparisons of the relative power of simple versus "sophisticated" techniques suggest very little difference.[26]

In short, to the extent that the development of decision guidelines has relied on empirical modeling, the quality of statistical modeling tasks has become an important concern having implications for the final policy product. The various pitfalls have been well documented and debated in the critical literature. That specific errors have been made in the past, of course, does not mean they will be made again in the future.

2. *The poor predictive power of decision models.* A second technical criticism questions the power of the predictive equations on the basis of which decision models are developed and suggests that basing future policy on models whose accuracy ranges from weak to modest is misguided. Blumstein et al. (1983), for example, note that "sentencing models seldom explain more than a third of the variance in sentences, often less, and consequently provide at best a blurred picture of past patterns" (p. 149). The accuracy of predictive models may be linked to many issues, including sampling, reliability, measurement, and baseline rates. Often the behaviors of interest occur relatively rarely, thus increasing the difficulty of prediction.

Another explanation of the generally modest predictive power of decision models is that the large amount of unexplained variance associated with the modeling of sentencing, parole, and bail decisions reflects unpatterned or arbitrary decision practices, that is, "unwarranted variation."

Accuracy is also of concern when prescriptive guidelines classify individuals according to risk, as was done in the federal parole guidelines and in the Philadelphia bail guidelines. To the degree that guidelines decisions are based on empirical estimates of risk, legal, ethical, and moral questions about the predictive validity of the models employed assume critical dimensions.[27] In descriptive phases, the limitations of predictive analyses have important implications. If one concludes that the models predict poorly because data are highly incomplete, then at least the courts or other officials may have been shown that they have a major information problem. If, however, poor predictive models result from decisions that are not characterized by measurable patterns, different implications arise. The first might be that guidelines provide structure for the exercise of discretion because inconsistency or randomness reveals a great need for such a tool. The second implication arises from difficulty in designing guidelines that are really only "descriptive." If the only detectable patterns in sentencing decisions explain no more than one-third of the variance, for example, then it is not possible to construct guidelines based on knowledge of only that one-third variance and to have those guidelines produce decisions comparable to the original decisions. Sentencing decisions resulting from such guidelines would differ markedly from the decisions on which guidelines were modeled; if charge seriousness and prior criminal history accounted for one-third of the variance in the decisions that were being modeled descriptively, they would account for nearly 100 percent of the variance in future guidelines-generated decisions. Use of such a "descriptive" formula in creating new sentencing guidelines, thus, would amount to a normative decision to alter current practices, to focus them more rigorously on what were found to be main themes in current practices.

The development of predictive devices to assist decisionmakers in developing decision tools that are overtly predictive raises additional questions. In the original Philadelphia bail experiment, once judges decided that prediction of flight and crime during pretrial release should be a guidelines function, the limitations of prediction were discussed. The judges decided that a validated predictive instrument would be valuable because predictive judgments were unavoidable in deciding bail and because the statistically derived instrument would be an improvement over *ad hoc* judicial decisionmaking. Use of a prediction device did not change the need to worry about "bad" predictions at bail; this continued to be an important policy concern. There was hope, however, that the extent of such errors would be lessened.

3. *Classification and suspect models.* Reliance on predictive models of reoffending presents a number of classification issues. First, whatever the inadequacies of prediction devices, if they are used offenders will be incarcerated as a result of predictive classifications. Second, failure to recognize and address (or "purge") the effects of ethically or legally inappropriate factors (such as race, sex, or economic status) in guidelines development may cause or aggravate distorted outcome patterns. Critics have noted that researchers who have tried to eliminate the influence of status-related variables on the guidelines have failed to attend to methodological difficulties and may have institutionalized the negative effects of those variables on the guidelines. For example, guidelines may institutionalize the disadvantages experienced by minority groups under current decision practices.[28] The significance of this issue depends on the frequency with which such status relations are encountered in descriptive modeling of decisions. It is a concern that ought to be carefully investigated, particularly when descriptive modeling will serve as the basis for guidelines construction.[29]

Criticism of the guidelines approach has focused on empirical methods, challenged the capacity of the strategy to produce meaningful change, and outlined technical issues likely to undermine the integrity of guidelines. The broad criticisms have questioned whether meaningful "implicit policies" can be identified by use of empirical research and statistical analyses, asserted that the approach is apt to institutionalize the status quo, and questioned whether empirically based guidelines are capable of altering decision patterns unless they are based on some form of enforcing legal authority.

The initial attempt to test the strength of the voluntary guidelines approach in the area of pretrial release in the Philadelphia bail-guidelines experiment is germane to these debates for at least four reasons: The bail research followed the original conceptualization of the guidelines strategy. It was the first application of the guidelines approach to bail. The bail guidelines were evaluated by means of a rigorous experimental design—the first such design in any guidelines application. Appropriate statistical models were employed in their development.

The initial Philadelphia research showed that meaningful researcher–decisionmaker collaboration can produce both an informed examination of court policy and a thoughtful revision of decision practices. The findings were important because they helped to identify issues to be addressed in subsequent guidelines research. They also suggested that voluntary guidelines can be implemented and used by courts in the area of pretrial release and that they can produce needed change. The Philadelphia findings raised the possibility that, perhaps more effectively than in the areas of paroling and sentencing, the voluntary guidelines approach could offer courts a solid tool for managing and reviewing their pretrial release policies in the future and could improve the quality of decisionmaking.

The Philadelphia experiment and the subsequent extension of the concept to other courts described in this book should prevent overly hasty rejection of the potential strength of the guidelines strategy. The critical literature does, however, make an important point: The various technical tasks must be performed well, or the overall product will be suspect. Thus the performance of a host of research tasks, ranging from sample design and data collection and measurement to modeling the decisions under study, will determine the ultimate worth of the guidelines that result. It will be the contention of this book that the critical literature runs the risk of condemning the guidelines approach too readily on the basis of narrow technical concerns and may have discouraged further developments and experimentation in this area. (The technical points raised may or may not be important, depending on the individual case and the overall picture.)

Although technical questions in any research enterprise are important, the focus of the debate concerning the ultimate value of guidelines raises much larger questions about rigor and successful implementation. To a great extent, the mixed results in evaluation of guidelines systems may be explained by varying degrees of attention to implementation issues.

Innovations may fail through researchers' inability to work through practical operational matters that may be crucial to decisionmakers' considering how useful a particular innovation might be to them. These problems may stem from the relative inexperience of the researchers in dealing with implementation questions, the often unrealistic expectations placed on research projects to attend to implementation issues when limited resources barely provide the time or funding to accomplish basic research tasks, and the inevitable resistance in the criminal justice agency to innovation and change.

Indeed the resistance among decisionmakers to an innovation varies directly with the lack of concern shown about practical questions of implementation. If implementation issues are ignored and resistance is great (as is usual when decisionmakers are not consulted on impending reforms affecting them directly), then nonvoluntary methods seem to be the only recourse for bringing about change. However, criminal justice officials are skilled both in ignoring voluntary innovations and in circumventing nonvoluntary reforms imposed from the outside. Evaluations of nonvoluntary guidelines systems will thus certainly show the slippage that critics associate with the self-help guidelines approaches, if they have not already.

The original self-help, voluntary approach to guidelines emphasized implementation: collaborative working relations between researchers and agency officials, the definition of the "problems" by the decisionmakers themselves, the examination of policy questions through problem solving and debate, and the use of research to provide feedback for policy analysis. Of course, if the resulting "guidelines" have never been implemented well or even at all, they will not produce changes in decision patterns. However, criticism of particular applications—characterized by poor implementation—does not mean the concept itself is inappropriate. As additional and varied applications of guidelines are undertaken in the United States, a rigorous exploration of implementation questions that looks at both failures and successes should take priority. We should separate issues relating to criticisms of particular applications from those related to criticism of the underlying self-help guidelines paradigm.

Notes

1. Wilkins et al. (1976); Gottfredson et al. (1978); Goldkamp, Gottfredson, and Mitchell-Herzfeld (1981); Wilkins (1981).
2. Rich et al. (1982); Blumstein et al. (1983).
3. See, e.g., Rich et al. (1982).
4. Discussions of the process by which descriptive findings were interpreted by decisionmakers for their meaning and relevance to understanding operating policy in the development of parole and bail guidelines are found in Gottfredson et al. (1978) and Goldkamp and Gottfredson (1985).
5. See, e.g., Knapp (1984*b*).
6. See also von Hirsch (1982:173); Sparks (1983:232–33).
7. See the discussion in Rich et al. (1982) or Wilkins et al. (1976). Concerning the bail guidelines in Philadelphia, see also Goldkamp and Gottfredson (1985).
8. Gottfredson and Gottfredson (1986).
9. For example, Rich et al. (1982) seek to discredit the concept of decision guidelines as a vehicle for policy reform by highlighting the weaknesses of a specific application.
10. Gottfredson et al. (1978).
11. Rich et al. (1982:206).
12. Goldkamp and Gottfredson (1985); Goldkamp (1987).
13. Galegher and Carroll (1983:368).
14. Rich et al. (1982); Blumstein et al. (1983); Sparks (1983).
15. Sparks (1983:211–212).
16. Blumstein et al. (1983:83–84); Sparks (1983:209, 226).
17. Wilkins et al. (1976).
18. See, e.g., Blumstein et al. (1983).
19. Landes (1974).
20. Roth and Wice (1978); Goldkamp (1979).
21. Goldkamp (1979); Goldkamp and Gottfredson (1985).
22. Blumstein et al. (1983:108–110); Sparks (1983:226–227).
23. Gottfredson et al. (1978).
24. Goldkamp et al. (1981).
25. Blumstein et al. (1983:80); Sparks (1983:218–219); Gottfredson and Gottfredson (1986:127).
26. Gottfredson and Gottfredson (1979).
27. Cohen (1983); von Hirsch and Gottfredson (1984). See also Underwood (1979); Morris and Miller (1985).
28. Petersilia and Turner (1987).
29. Goldkamp (1987).

3

Evidence about Guidelines

The research described in subsequent chapters was predicated on the experience of our earlier work in the Philadelphia Municipal Court.[1] Perhaps the most fundamental question underlying the Philadelphia research was whether it would be possible *to review and change the exercise of judicial discretion at the bail stage* through this voluntary approach. Could the highly discretionary pretrial release decision be made more visible and therefore more accountable to acknowledged policy aims and governing criteria? Could the equity of bail decisions be improved so that similarly situated defendants would be treated more "similarly"? Could bail decisions be made more effective?

Even some of the simpler questions posed major challenges to judicial tradition in this area. Could or would judges work in a collaborative relationship with social scientists to review and debate pretrial release policy and to examine its *discretionary* practice through empirical means? Could decision guidelines be developed to assist judges in their day-to-day decisionmaking duties and the court as a whole in effectuating its overall pretrial release policy? If guidelines were developed, would judges make use of them in the manner intended? Would they note their reasons whey they disagreed with the choices suggested by guidelines so that the guidelines could later be reexamined and modified, if necessary? If used, would the voluntary guidelines system bring about change in important areas of concern?

Philadelphia had much to offer as a site for such feasibility research. The municipal court judiciary was concerned about the fairness and effectiveness of bail. A pretrial services agency had struggled with pretrial release reforms for a decade. Most important, the local correctional institutions, known as the Philadelphia Prisons, had been grappling with overcrowding and decrepit conditions since the 1960s. When the research began in 1978, overcrowding litigation—still ongoing at the time of this writing—was approximately eight years old, and pretrial detainees, making up more than half of the city's 3,000 inmates, represented a continuing source of difficulty for the existing confinement capacity.

Our Philadelphia research was initiated when a small judicial steering and policy committee, consisting of 6 judges (of the 20 who were sitting at the time) and the director of the pretrial services agency, was appointed by the president judge of the court. The working agreement between the court and the research team included an understanding that the project could be discontinued by the court at any time and that there was no commitment by the court in advance to adopt decision guidelines.

The researchers' role was to collect data related to bail decisions and their consequences, to analyze data in response to the specific interests and concerns of the steering committee, and to facilitate discussion of policy issues. For example, it was clear at the outset that the judges were concerned about unwarranted disparities in bail decisions. They also seemed eager to learn of the effectiveness of their decisions. They complained that they rarely had an opportunity to learn whether defendants were released or jailed and, if released, whether they absconded or committed additional crimes—except as a result of negative media coverage of the rare defendant released on personal recognizance who was immediately rearrested for a brutal crime.

We designed a data collection approach that permitted a focus on the decisions of individual judges (anonymously represented) and on specific categories of criminal cases. Because a random sample of recent bail decisions would not have included a balanced cross section of all the 20 judges who then had bail responsibilities nor a balanced selection of criminal cases (because misdemeanor charges were nearly three times more common than felonies in the population), a quota sample that was stratified by judge (20 categories) and charge (6 rankings) was employed. For each judge, the sample included 40 cases for each of the 6 rankings, in other words, 240 cases for each judge. Data were collected for more than 200 items of information for each of 4,800 bail decisions occurring between 1977 and 1979.[2] The data collected included information relating to the current charges and to past criminal history, prior performance on pretrial release, social background, demographics, and subsequent performance on release.

The Descriptive Phase

Before modeling bail decisions, the researchers confirmed with the judges the reasonableness of the bifurcated conceptualization of bail adopted in earlier research.[3] Thus the first modeling task was to "explain" an initial decision to grant a defendant release on personal recognizance (ROR) (a yes-or-no choice), and the second, for defendants not receiving ROR, was to predict the judge's selection of an amount of cash bail.

Given the different levels of measurement associated with the two decisions to be modeled, different multivariate techniques were employed to predict them. For the modeling of the ROR decision, a number of logit models were fitted on the basis of an examination of underlying bivariate relations. The most parsimonious model predicted the granting of ROR based on knowledge of a defendant's current charge, prior arrests, prior felony convictions, prior failures to appear in court, pending charges, employment, and living arrangements. The current charge was by far the dominant independent variable in the prediction of ROR. The defendant's race was not found to be important, but gender was.[4]

Multiple regression was employed to predict cash bail decisions. First, however, the criterion measure (i.e., amount of cash) was examined carefully. The distribution of cash bails was highly skewed (half the cash bails were below $1,000, although the range extended from $50 to $625,000). Moreover, contrary to the assumptions of the regression technique, cash bail patterns did not comport with an interval-level measure. Unlike a true interval measure, which is characterized by equidistant values ranging from $1.00 to $625,000, cash bail was set in 9 or 10 common amounts (e.g., $500, $1,000, $5,000, and $10,000) with other values rarely occurring. Bails of $279, for example, were never seen. To standardize the criterion measure and to allow the assumptions of multiple regression to apply, a logarithmic transformation of the criterion was employed. The final regression included 10 predictor variables that explained 47 percent of the variance in the transformed bail measure.[5] These included victim injury, current charge, number of different charges, presence of charges involving crimes against the person, number of prior convictions for serious person crimes, number of pending charges, age of the defendant, and the identity of the judge determining bail.

Thus, like other empirically based guidelines approaches, the Philadelphia approach had formulated "best" models that described the factors that apparently characterized decisions made by the judges. The important question was how these correlates were linked to bail policy for the judges of the Philadelphia Municipal Court. "Implicit policy" became "explicit" through discussion and debate of the meaning of the findings with the judges.

Discussion began with debate about the proper goals of bail.[6] Some judges, for example, argued that failure to recognize bail's public safety function would be a sham. (The legality of public safety as a goal of bail under Pennsylvania law was, at that time, uncertain in that, rather oddly, it appeared to be authorized only for consideration of ROR.) Others insisted that, until case law authorized judges setting bail to take "dangerousness" into account, the only acceptable bail goal was the appearance of defendants in court.

The multivariate findings were summarized and presented to the committee with this debate as a backdrop. The findings suggested to the steering and policy committee what appeared to be two different policy orientations for judges when considering ROR and when determining cash bail. The ROR decision represented a screening at which persons charged with offenses viewed as either serious or not had probabilities of ROR that could not be modified by other factors. Persons charged with serious crimes were unlikely ever to receive ROR, and those charged with trivial offenses were very likely to receive it. For defendants with charges of moderate seriousness, secondary factors such as evidence of solid community ties played an important role. The ROR stage was seen by the judges as an opportunity to screen out the "good-risk" defendants so they could be immediately released, and to select from the "moderate-risks" those who could be trusted for outright pretrial release. This decision and the factors on which it was based were more concerned with the defendant's potential for absconding than was the subsequent cash-bail-amount decision.

The cash bail stage appeared reserved for defendants who posed a very high risk of flight or who appeared to present possible danger to victims, witnesses, or the community. There was a heavy emphasis on the seriousness of the current criminal charge (4 of the 10 predictors were related to current charge) for the cash bail decision, a fact that seemed to make sense in light of this policy interpretation, as did the relative importance of the defendant's prior record. In contrast with the ROR decision, in which community ties and the defendant's record of prior attendance at court seemed to play an important role, none of these appeared influential in the judge's choice of a cash bail amount. However, whether a defendant was already on pretrial release at the time of the current charge was a marked concern.

One interesting finding was the relation between a defendant's age and the selection of cash bail (the younger the defendant, the lower the bail, other factors being equal). This was interpreted by the steering committee judges as reflecting the practice (engaged in by judges on some occasions) of not automatically giving young defendants ROR even if charged with nonserious offenses. Instead they would intentionally set bail at a very low amount so that the defendant would be compelled to call home for assistance, thus alerting the parents to a child in trouble—something that ROR release might not have accomplished.

Our finding of pronounced disparity in the assignment of cash bail had a major impact on the judges. Disparity was inferred from two findings. First, even after the analysis of 200 items of information, a great deal of variance remained unexplained. Although this might have resulted in part from failure to measure important variables, it was reasonable also to assume that bail decisions varied unsystematically. Second, after controlling for the effects of all other important correlates of cash bail, the identity of the judge deciding bail made a significant difference: An additional 10 percent of the variance was explained simply by adding the identities of the judges. Some of the judges' initial doubts about the equity of bail decisions in Philadelphia thus seemed to be supported by the modeling of cash bail decisions. This finding was viewed as especially important because disparity in the use of cash bail translated into disparity in the use of pretrial detention, because of differences in the ability to afford bail.

The Normative Phase

The consequences of the bail decisions were investigated, including the allocation of pretrial detention and the occurrence of absconding and rearrest of defendants during their pretrial release on bail or ROR. A follow-up study of the 4,800 defendants showed the correlates of pretrial flight and crime.[7] We demonstrated widely different rates of failure during pretrial release among defendants released by the different judges, and we developed models predicting pretrial flight and crime. The judges were struck by the lack of correspondence between the factors found to influence judicial decisions and the predictors of defendants' performance during pretrial release: The correlation was not significant ($r = -.02$). Gottfredson and Gottfredson (1986, Table 1) have demonstrated the consistency of this effect across a wide variety of justice decision settings.

At this point, with the support of the steering committee, guidelines development shifted to an explicitly prescriptive phase in which both the goals of bail and the criteria that ought to guide the bail decision were examined. The research task became the development of alternative models of bail guidelines that represented different policy orientations.

The debate by the judges focused on three competing models. One, a "status quo" model, employed the ROR and cash bail stages of the bail decision and scored and classified defendants on the basis of formulas derived from the final descriptive models of the ROR and cash bail decisions. The presumptive bail decisions established for this version of bail guidelines were expressed in ranges of cash derived from a study of how bail had typically been set in the recent past for categories of defendants. (The "categories" were determined from a classification analysis, the goal of which was to locate a small number of classes of defendants treated differently in the awarding of ROR or cash bail). The would-be presumptive decision ranges were fixed by the use of the amounts between which the middle 50 percent of bails had been set in each category in the past.

A second, "actuarial" model was based on refinement of the predictions of absconding and pretrial crime developed during the descriptive guidelines phase. The refined actuarial model was validated on an independent sample of Philadelphia defendants.[8] This model would determine bail by classifying defendants according to their probability of engaging in misconduct during pretrial release. One of the difficulties associated with this model was that judges did not overtly decide to release or detain defendants but shaped that outcome through the device of cash bail; the judges were reluctant to use such a framework to distinguish openly between release and detention. Thus the actuarial guidelines would have relied on an array of ROR, conditional release, and cash options aligned with increasing probabilities of misconduct during release. Nevertheless, the actuarial model was designed to address the predictive aims of bail. If it had been adopted, the model would have marked a dramatic departure from the then-current bail decisions by aligning future decisions more directly with the empirical correlates of risk.[9]

A third, "hybrid" model combined elements from the status quo and the actuarial models. The matrix was defined by two axes, one based on a measure of charge severity derived from the descriptive analysis of bail decisions and the other on a 5-part risk classification of defendants taken from the actuarial model. The 5-part risk dimension and the 15-part charge-severity dimension produced a grid of 75 cells, with presumptive bail decisions established by examining what judges had done with these categories in the past and the absconding, pretrial crime, and detention rates associated with them.

The policy implications of each model were debated by the steering committee. Although the status quo model might achieve greater consistency, the judges understood that this approach might institutionalize inequitable features of traditional practices and would rely on factors that were not highly correlated with risk of flight and pretrial crime. The actuarial model had the advantage of framing bail decisions in terms of the strongest predictors of pretrial misconduct. The judges were not ready, however, to "trust the computer" entirely, and they were sensitive to the controversy likely to surround bail practices that were based openly on predictions of future danger at that time. The hybrid model seemed to offer statistical guidance from the actuarial research as well as some grounding in tradition, and it was this model that the judges elected for use in a subsequent guidelines experiment (see Figure 3.1).

BAIL GUIDELINES: JUDICIAL WORKSHEET

Date ______ *Log #* ______ *Name of defendant* ______ *Police photo #* ______ *Calculated by* ______

Guidelines Matrix

Probability of Failure: Low ← → High

Charge Severity: Low (1) ↓ High (15)

1	ROR	ROR	ROR	ROR	ROR
2	ROR	ROR	ROR	ROR	ROR
3	ROR	ROR	ROR	ROR	ROR-$500
4	ROR	ROR	ROR	ROR	ROR-$500
5	ROR	ROR	ROR	ROR	ROR-$1,000
6	ROR	ROR	ROR	ROR-$1,000	$300-$1,000
7	ROR	ROR	ROR	ROR-$1,000	$300-$1,000
8	ROR	ROR	ROR	ROR-$1,000	$500-$1,000
9	ROR	ROR	ROR	$500-$1,500	$500-$1,500
10	ROR	ROR	ROR-$1,500	$500-$1,500	$500-$2,000
11	ROR-$1,500	ROR-$1,500	ROR-$1,500	$500-$2,000	$500-$2,000
12	ROR-$1,500	ROR-$1,500	$500-$1,500	$800-$2,500	$800-$3,000
13	$800-$3,000	$800-$3,000	$1,000-$3,000	$1,000-$5,000	$1,500-$5,000
14	$1,000-$3,000	$1,000-$3,000	$1,000-$3,000	$1,000-$5,000	$1,500-$5,000
15	$2,000-$7,500	$2,000-$7,500	$2,000-$7,500	$2,500-$7,500	$3,000 - $10,000

Guidelines Decision ______ Judicial Decision: ☐ ROR ☐ Financial (amount) $______

☐ IF DECISION DEPARTS FROM THE GUIDELINES, REASON(S):

- ☐ High probability that prosecution will be withdrawn
- ☐ High probability of conviction
- ☐ Defendant's demeanor in court room
- ☐ Defendant's physical or mental health
- ☐ To cause guardian to be informed of defendant's arrest
- ☐ Low probability of conviction
- ☐ Sponsor present at hearing
- ☐ Defendant's history of court appearances
- ☐ Defendant poses specific threat to witness or victim
- ☐ Presence of warrants, detainers, or warrant cards
- ☐ Other (explain): ______

Decision by ______

FIGURE 3.1. Bail guidelines: Judicial worksheet.

Flawed Modeling and Poor Predictive Power

Empirical modeling played a central role in the development of alternative versions of bail guidelines in the Philadelphia research and in the format ultimately selected for implementation in the Philadelphia Municipal Court. Most of the issues outlined in the critical literature pertaining to the quality of modeling procedures were addressed. For example, the sample was carefully crafted to reflect a balanced array of cases and to include equal numbers and kinds of cases for each of the presiding judges. Similarly, measurement of dependent and independent variables was attended to in the conceptualization of the bail decision, in the transformation of cash bail into a more useful (logarithmic) version, and in the careful analysis of charge severity.

Attention was paid to the assumptions underlying the application of analytic methods: Logit analysis was applied to the analysis of the use of ROR and prediction of pretrial misconduct, and regression procedures were used in the analysis of cash bail. Each of the solutions was validated on a separate sample before it was employed in developing descriptive-type guidelines alternatives.

Questions concerning the power of the predictive analyses were also important in the feasibility research. Although the analyses of decisions produced results generally stronger (e.g., in terms of R^2) than those reported in the sentencing literature (and the solutions validated well), unexplained variance was still a problem. For example, the best explanation of variance in cash bails accounted for less than 50 percent of the variance. If the judges had elected to implement "descriptive" guidelines for bail, this limitation could have become important. If, for example, identified correlates of decisions accounted for one-half of the variance in the decisions that were modeled descriptively, they should account for nearly 100 percent of the variance in future guidelines-generated decisions. Use of such a "descriptive" formula would amount to a normative decision to alter current practices, that is, to focus them more rigorously on what were found to be main themes in then current practices.

The predictive analyses of defendant flight and crime during pretrial release raised perhaps an even more important issue relating to the power of predictive models. Decision research in criminal justice and elsewhere has repeatedly demonstrated that statistical methods will better predict future events than will clinical or subjective methods.[10] Producing a trouble-free and powerful risk device is, however, not simple.

The study of defendant misconduct during pretrial release is hampered by several well-documented problems. First, from one perspective, samples are "biased." Only defendants who achieve pretrial release can be studied; little is known about the risks posed by those who are detained. In Philadelphia, nearly 90 percent of all defendants entering the system in the sample were released before the completion of their cases; 10 percent were thus excluded.

Second, data may be poor. In Philadelphia, a great many data were available because of elaborate interviews before initial appearances conducted by pretrial services staff and because criminal histories were reasonably accurate. Yet the reliability of some of the items stemming from defendant self-reports, such as drug history, was questionable.

Third, the outcomes of concern (i.e., flight from court or crime) are relatively rare occurrences and thus, from a statistical point of view, are difficult to predict. In the Philadelphia sample, 12 percent of released defendants were recorded as willful failures to appear in court, and 16 percent were rearrested for new crimes within a 120-day follow-up period (less than half for serious crimes).

Fourth, because of the sample and data limitations, final predictive solutions are not powerful. They result in more inaccurate than accurate predictions. Importantly, these "limited" models are still modestly successful when compared with the uneven record of judges who make predictions.

Many of these problems are, of course, well known. The solution involves two approaches: the careful validation of results of predictive analyses before implementation and the recognition of the limitations of predictive devices. Although predictive devices can help decisionmakers frame their decisions, they will produce errors that must be addressed, if possible through careful reviews and other due-process measures. Only after discussing the strengths and weaknesses of actuarial information did the Philadelphia judges decide to incorporate a risk dimension in their bail guidelines.

Testing the Impact of Voluntary Reform

Perhaps the principal criticism of empirically derived guidelines has been the charge that voluntary guidelines cannot achieve positive or meaningful changes. In its second phase, the Philadelphia research sought to test this criticism directly through a controlled experiment.

Development, selection, and refinement of a version of bail guidelines acceptable to the committee of judges were one matter; implementation of guidelines using an experimental research design was quite another.

Guided by the president judge of the municipal court, the researchers developed a plan to implement the guidelines through a rigorous experimental format to learn whether hypothesized benefits would occur.

The obstacles to conducting social experiments in courts are formidable. The biggest complication is to devise a method for randomizing the "treatment" among incoming criminal defendants so that the experiences of comparably situated defendants can be contrasted and inferences drawn about the new procedures. One approach would have been for each judge to set bail, alternating between the new bail guidelines and the normal methods. However, the logistics of conducting and monitoring such a system would be forbidding and prone to mix-ups. It is unlikely that, in practice, judges would shift neatly between guidelines and "normal" decision modes. The result would be that judges would mix the two approaches in their minds and carry out neither one in practice.

The strategy adopted was to assign judges to an experimental guidelines group or to a control group that would handle bail in the normal way. The goal was to produce sufficiently large numbers of guidelines decisions and nonguidelines decisions that were comparable in all ways except for the mode of the decision. The decisions of 16 judges over a period of approximately nine months were studied: 8 judges were randomly selected to employ guidelines; another 8 were randomly chosen to serve as controls, setting bail in the normal fashion. The 8 judges who served as "guidelines" judges were not selected on the basis of their philosophical predispositions toward innovation whether in the name of court reform or in the interest of progressive research.

Data were collected prospectively during 1981 and 1982 with the use of a sample stratified by judge and charge measures until 960 bail decisions had been produced for each of the experimental and control groups. (This approach yielded 120 bail decisions per judge, including 20 in each of the six charge categories.) The logistics of the experiment were demanding, given the two versions of paperwork that had to be processed through the early stages of the system, the coordination and monitoring of several participants in the pretrial process, and the around-the-clock schedules of judges who decided bail.[11]

The experiment examined whether decisions under the new guidelines differed from "normal" decisions in a number of ways. It was hypothesized, for example, that guidelines decisions would conform to the guidelines in a substantial majority of instances and that, when judges departed from the guidelines, they would note their reasons. It was hypothesized, therefore, that the visibility, rationality, equity, and effectiveness of the experimental judges' bail decisions would be enhanced in comparison with those of the control judges.

Several findings led the researchers to conclude that voluntary guidelines have an impact on decision practices at the bail stage and that the approach has promise for bringing about policy reform in key areas of criminal justice decisionmaking.

Perhaps the simplest and most important question asked was whether randomly "drafted" judges would use the bail guidelines as intended or would ignore or otherwise circumvent them. To measure this, bail decisions were compared for the experimental and control judges. A convincing majority of the decisions made by the guidelines judges—76 percent of all cases—fell within the presumptive decision ranges.

By contrast, only 57 percent of the nonguidelines judges' decisions fell within the guidelines' ranges. The difference, which was both statistically significant and substantial, demonstrated that the experimental judges followed the guidelines voluntarily in a large majority of the cases and that this represented a marked change in decision practice in the court.

A second important question was whether judges would give reasons when making decisions departing from those suggested by the guidelines. The judges were not accustomed to providing written reasons for many of their decisions in the criminal process and least of all for bail decisions. Again, however, the findings were reasonably encouraging. In 65 percent of the decisions that departed from the guidelines, the experimental judges noted reasons for their actions. Two judges conspicuously failed to give reasons. One appeared not to have understood the importance of the request to include reasons and therefore did not make the effort consistently; the other simply did not wish to provide reasons.

Two of the reasons most often given for departing decisions—the severity of the criminal charges and the defendant's history of failures to appear in court—were factors that had already been taken into account in designing the guidelines. It seemed, therefore, that judges were confused or that they misunderstood the notion of making exceptions to the guidelines. However, discussions with the judges concerned revealed that they had understood the aims of the guidelines quite well. They argued that charges were occasionally so serious—so violent or heinous—that extra weight beyond that provided by the guidelines ought to be given to the severity of charges. It was pointed out that, in the risk scale, negative points were assigned for 1 or 2 or more prior failures to appear in court. One judge argued that extra weight ought to be given when a defendant had had 12 prior absences in the last several years. (Most defendants charged with prostitution in the study had lengthy records of flight, after recording as many as 20 or more missed appearances in one year.) As a result, the researchers concluded that the notation of reasons had worked reasonably and that efforts should be made to encourage all judges using guidelines to make the effort to note them.

Another important question asked was whether the use of guidelines made bail decisions more systematic, less disparate, and more equitable. This required agreement on a definition of "similarly situated" that must be tied to the goals of the bail decision and to the criteria deemed appropriate to accomplishing these goals. Two measures were adopted. First, the criteria defining the bail guidelines were used as the framework for comparing the similarity of decisions given similar classes of defendants. Charge seriousness was employed as another—if more questionable—framework for evaluating the equity of the experimental bail decisions. We concluded that the variability in bail decisions for given categories of defendants (whether defined by guidelines or by charge) was more than halved by the use of the guidelines.[12]

On consideration of the findings of the experiment, the judges of the Philadelphia Municipal Court moved to adopt the guidelines for use by the full court in the spring of 1983. At the conclusion of this book, we revisit the status of the "bail guidelines" in Philadelphia a decade later.

As a first experiment, the results of the Philadelphia study were encouraging regarding the promise of voluntary decision guidelines for pretrial release. However, a number of important questions remained unanswered, questions we seek to address in this book. Perhaps the biggest concerned the generalizability of our approach: Would the initiative work in other court settings different from Philadelphia? In some respects the structure and function of the municipal court in Philadelphia are like those of most limited-jurisdiction courts in urban America. In other ways they are quite different, responding to a unique sociopolitical climate. During the time of the study, the leadership of the municipal court was strong and progressive and interested in improving the practices of the court, despite significant obstacles to change. The court as a whole was relatively sophisticated concerning ongoing developments in criminal justice. The research team had engaged in previous work with the court and had developed positive working relationships with all key personnel. The court records were, for that time, relatively automated, and the collection of excellent follow-up information was possible. Indeed, the court system had developed a comprehensive pretrial services agency, the leadership of which was attracted to the guidelines concept. However, the underlying hypothesis of the research was that the decision guidelines concept could provide a useful tool for courts generally, and the Philadelphia study mainly demonstrated its feasibility at one site, under one set of circumstances. The door was opened by the Philadelphia experience to ask whether the same strategy could be applied to pretrial problems faced by other courts under different circumstances. The research described in this book sought to determine how well the decision guidelines idea for pretrial release could be transferred to other very different settings.

A More Complete Test of Pretrial Release Guidelines

The research we discuss in this book began in 1984,[13] six years after the preliminary research began in Philadelphia. Concern about bail practices had grown, not lessened, during this time. In 1978, approximately 23 states and the District of Columbia had laws reflecting a public safety or "danger" orientation[14] by 1984 11 more states and the federal jurisdiction had altered their laws to permit a public safety or "danger" focus at the bail/pretrial release stage. Although by 1984 the U.S. Supreme Court had still not definitively addressed questions about the constitutionality of "preventive detention" or bail practices oriented toward public safety concerns, case law had contributed important decisions adding to the signs that the "danger" orientation was acceptable.[15] At the same time that legislatures and the U.S. Congress were revising their bail laws to incorporate public safety aims, jail overcrowding—one of the principal motivations for the original Vera reforms in the early 1960s and for the bail research in Philadelphia—had worsened considerably. Jail populations nationally had increased approximately 48 percent during that period; the unconvicted population had increased about 50 percent.

The problems of overcrowding and public safety made more critical the need to resolve the question about the transferability to other urban settings of the voluntary decision guidelines to reform pretrial release. One of the rationales of the guidelines strategy was that they could assist decisionmakers in adapting their decisionmaking behavior to the consequences of their decisionmaking policy. These consequences can easily include constraints deriving from jail capacity as well as concerns about community safety. Because the guidelines make provision for systematic feedback concerning the results of decisions, they can, in theory, adapt to changing policy orientations or unforeseen developments. One purpose of the research discussed in this book, then, is not only to determine whether bail guidelines could, in application to other settings, deliver on that promise as a decisionmaking resource shown in the Philadelphia experiment, but also whether they are useful to handle contemporary emphases on public safety and jail overcrowding.

We did not try to persuade other jurisdictions to employ the Philadelphia guidelines. Rather, the question we tried to answer was how the guidelines process—the creation and use of court-based self-help guidelines—could be adapted to different pretrial release concerns and with what results. An additional advantage of studying applications of bail guidelines in additional jurisdictions was that evidence concerning the assumptions underlying guidelines in the pretrial arena could be accumulated and knowledge could be gained of the relative strengths and weaknesses of guidelines under a variety of circumstances not touched upon in their initial implementation.

The guidelines approach involves analysis and revision of both policy and practice in targeted problem areas, undertaken on behalf of the decisionmakers themselves. It thus stands as a major contrast to legislative strategies involving pretrial release, which often sidestep day-to-day practicalities in the hope that the announcement of a favored policy will mandate stubborn problems out of existence. (A good example of that approach is the questionable impact that preventive detention laws have had on pretrial crime.) Furthermore, prior guidelines research signals alarm about possible inadvertent side effects of such policies on jail populations. Yet laws in many states have been broadened with the intent of increasing the probability that the courts will detain larger numbers of defendants outright. Most of these new laws have not greatly concerned themselves with empirical examination of what the courts actually do, or with the complexity of the pretrial release task they face.

The agenda for change implicit in decision guidelines is more sweeping than such legislative measures. Guidelines aim for nothing less than to shape day-to-day decisionmaking by affecting the rules and traditions involved in case decisionmaking. Yet the method for problem solving is more conservative in its targeted, iterative approach and is anchored in a firm understanding both of past practices and of projections of its likely impact on future practices. The Philadelphia research provided the first suggestion that change could be effectuated in an evolutionary fashion, on a category-by-category basis with an ability to adjust to emerging realities. By considering major research undertakings in three urban court systems, this book assesses whether the lessons, if not the detail, of the Philadelphia experience could be applied to other jurisdictions with equally satisfactory results, and whether, therefore, the court-based decision-guidelines strategy does indeed offer the judiciary an important policy tool, given the challenges faced by court and correctional systems alike.

Notes

1. Goldkamp and Gottfredson (1985); Goldkamp (1987).
2. For a full description of the research design and data collection, see Goldkamp et al. (1981).

3. Goldkamp (1979).
4. For an in-depth discussion of the modeling of ROR and of cash bail, see especially the technical appendices of Goldkamp et al. (1981).
5. For a discussion of the advantages and interpretation of a regression employing a dependent variable transformed into its logarithm, see Goldkamp et al. (1981, App. E.).
6. The debate concerning the proper goals for bail has been long and vigorous. Prior to 1970, when Congress enacted preventive detention legislation for the District of Columbia, the dominant view was that bail could be used only to ensure the presence of a defendant in court, although public safety goals were hotly debated. The model bail-reform legislation, the Federal Bail Reform Act of 1966, specifically states that ensuring the defendant's presence at trial is the sole legitimate goal in noncapital cases. Since 1970, however, danger-related provisions have been added to the bail laws of 34 states and the District of Columbia. In 1984, as part of the Comprehensive Crime Control Act of 1984, Congress enacted preventive detention legislation for the federal jurisdiction (see Goldkamp 1979, 1985).
7. For an in-depth discussion of the modeling of the performance of defendants during pretrial release, see the technical appendixes of Goldkamp et al. (1981).
8. The final risk model included five categories of defendants ranked from low to high probability of failing to appear in court, being rearrested for additional crimes, or both. For a technical discussion of the development and validation of this model, see Goldkamp et al. (1981). For an application of this risk model to a jail population in the context of emergency release measures in Philadelphia, see Goldkamp (1983).
9. The logit model predicting flight, crime, or both during pretrial release relied on knowledge of the age of a defendant (defendants over 44 years of age were assigned a low probability of misconduct); whether defendants had a phone; prior record of absconding; the existence of pending charges (whether this charge occurred while the defendant was already on pretrial release); prior arrests; the kind (as opposed to the severity) of the current charge; and the interaction of age and prior absconding (a defendant over 44 who had a record of prior absconding was an especially high risk) and distinguished between kind of current charge and prior record of arrests (a person charged with a serious crime against the person was a lower-probability risk, but such a person who also had a lengthy record of prior arrests was a high risk). See Goldkamp et al. (1981, Chap. 6).
10. Morris and Miller (1985).
11. For a discussion of the experiment, see Goldkamp and Gottfredson (1985).
12. Goldkamp and Gottfredson (1985).
13. The National Institute of Justice funded a broad research program for pretrial release guidelines in 1984 (Grant No. 84-IJ-CX-0056).
14. Of course, this is less remarkable than the increase from 1970 to 1978: Only the District of Columbia had a danger-oriented law in 1970.
15. See, for example, *Murphy v. Hunt*, 455 U.S. 478 (1982); *Hunt v. Roth*, 648 F.2d 1148 (8th Cir. 1981); *Parker v. Roth*, 202 Neb. 850, 278 N.W. 2d 106, cert. denied, 444 U.S. 920 (1979); *U.S. v. Edwards*, 430 A.2d 1321 (D.C. App. 1981) (en banc), cert. denied, 455 U.S. 1022 (1982); *Schall v. Martin*, 104 S.Ct. 2403.

II

THE PRETRIAL SYSTEMS IN THREE URBAN COURTS

4

The Courts in Boston, Dade County, and Maricopa County

Selection of the Research Sites

To begin our research, it was necessary to select three sites that not only had the willingness to participate in the self-study process but that also exhibited features likely to prove challenging for the method and to provide useful examples for other court systems. Selection of the sites was guided by three general principles: (1) they had to vary from Philadelphia and one another in legal and organizational structure; (2) they had to have concerns about aspects of bail and pretrial detention practices they would like to address; and (3) they had to have overcrowded jails.

The point of the first criterion, to be different from Philadelphia and one another, was simply intended to construct tests of the guidelines approach in diverse settings. We sought to learn whether the methodology could be tailored to address profitably the localized concerns of different kinds of courts operating in different environments. In this regard, one important consideration in choosing sites was the nature of the bail and pretrial release laws governing bail practices in the various states. The Philadelphia courts, of course, operated according to the dictates of Pennsylvania law. Pennsylvania law exhibited some of the reform-inspired provisions deriving from passage of the landmark bail reform legislation, the Federal Bail Reform Act of 1966.[1] For example, it included a presumption favoring the release of defendants before trial on personal recognizance (ROR), and it listed a large number of criteria judges should consider in making the bail decision. Unlike the model bail-reform legislation, however, Pennsylvania law did not specify that defendants should be released under the least onerous conditions possible. Moreover, the law was vague on whether the defendant's propensity to commit additional crimes was a legitimate concern.[2] We thus sought sites that differed in significant respects in the presumptions concerning pretrial release and the legitimate goals of the pretrial release decision.

In Philadelphia, the research and the guidelines system relied on the existence of a well-established pretrial-services agency. That agency had the responsibility for assembling background, criminal history, and case information by interviewing defendants before their first judicial appearance (referred to as preliminary arraignment in Pennsylvania) and by computer criminal-history checks. In addition, prior to the advent of guidelines, the pretrial services staff made recommendations concerning the suitability of ROR or, at a subsequent stage, the release of defendants on conditions. Because bail guidelines were intended, among other things, to be an informational tool, procedures for collecting, verifying, and summarizing information would play an important role in the eventual adoption of guidelines in a given jurisdiction. In reviewing sites for participation in the study, it was considered advantageous to choose at least one site having no formal pretrial-services support system. We thought it important to address the question of whether the existence of such an agency is a requisite for meaningful guidelines construction.

We also thought it desirable to incorporate variability in the structures of the court systems in which we were going to try to develop guidelines. Again, at the time of the initial experiment, the Philadelphia Municipal Court consisted of about 22 judges who rotated into the bail assignment. That court operated around the clock, every day of the year, and was highly centralized. It was administered by a president judge, chosen by the other sitting judges, all of whom had been elected. We wanted to know how applicable the guidelines concept is to other kinds of structures. Many "bail courts" consist of commissioners, appointed for the task by the leadership of the courts but having little or no other judicial experience. Some systems rely on a very small number of decisionmakers who "take turns" in the bail courts in addition to performing other substantial duties. Still others involve only a few judges or other judicial officers who spend most of their time deciding bail. In some courts, the bail decision is very nearly adversarial, and both the state and the defense are allowed to offer opinions and evidence. In other courts, an observer would find little more than the defendant, the judge, and the law enforcement agency responsible for the arrest. Some systems rely heavily on bail or bond schedules, with any hearings amounting to "appeals" of the schedule; others offer no guidelines of any sort other than the relatively vague factors permissible in statute. There are strongly led court systems in which the presiding judge dictates policy that is generally followed by other judges, and there are court systems where it is pretty much every judge for himself or herself. Our task was to incorporate as much variability as possible into our sites to test the generalizability of the guidelines concept. Clearly, we could not, with resources for three sites, tap all of the potentially important variability. Nor did we have a design that would permit the unambiguous partitioning of failure of decision guidelines according to dimensions such as those discussed above. But our aim in the second phase of testing guidelines for pretrial release decisionmaking was more modest. If the pretrial release guidelines could be designed and implemented in diverse sites, then, at least, the "uniqueness of Philadelphia" argument would not hold. If there were to be failures, we hoped to have gathered sufficient information to deduce why.

Our site selection also took into account jail crowding. One possible contributor to crowded jails is pretrial release practices that are inefficient and chaotic, practices that hold categories of defendants needlessly and nonsystematically. In Philadelphia, the jail facilities had been plagued by extreme overcrowding for more than a decade and had been under litigation and court intervention since 1971. In developing their guidelines, by conscious choice, the Philadelphia Municipal Court judges did not specifically build in provisions to accommodate jail population levels. However, later, during debates in that city about the "source" of overcrowding, the municipal court was able to use the guidelines both as evidence that it had examined and improved its bail practices and as a lens through which to assess the status of the pretrial population and the appropriateness of certain population reduction strategies affecting bail. A theme in this second phase of our research was to determine whether guidelines could be designed with more specific reference to the jail problems facing the jurisdictions to be studied.

With these criteria in mind, many of the major courts in the United States were contacted, and a reduced pool of candidate courts were visited by the research staff. As a result of the site visits, strong interest was expressed on the part of five judiciaries. The three finally chosen, included courts in Boston, Phoenix, and Miami.

The Boston Courts

Local Concerns about Jail Crowding and "Defaulting" Defendants

Boston appeared to be an excellent site for such a study not only because of its urban character, but because at the time the study was to be initiated there was evidence of strong public and judicial concern about jail overcrowding and the flight of defendants before trial. The bail practices in the Boston Municipal Court and the Suffolk County Superior Court, for example, had come under criticism in a *Boston Globe* series published during September 1984 questioning the apparently high rate of felony defendants who were able to thwart prosecution of their cases merely by not attending court. In a number of instances, defendants were located by the investigative reporters living undisturbed at their normal home addresses. During the spring of 1985, the local press featured the story of the mother who followed a young man she suspected might be her daughter's attacker after overhearing him describe the crime on a bus. Although this incident was picked up by the national media with a focus on its "self-help" implications for criminal justice, it was later discovered that the suspect had been on pretrial release and probation (in juvenile matters).

In addition, the overcrowded conditions of the Charles Street Jail serving Suffolk County at the heart of Boston had been the source of great media and even judicial attention. The jail, built in 1851, had in recent years exceeded its capacity of 266 detainees by a large margin and continued to suffer from a deteriorating physical plant. As the research staff were considering site alternatives, the overcrowding at the Charles Street Jail had become increasingly the center of public debate and media attention. Furthermore, decade-old litigation[3] had reached a decisive point. The judge presiding over the case had named a special committee to supervise emergency actions ordered to address the crowding problem. Because the facility dealt solely with a pretrial population, there appeared to be a serious interest on the part of the judicial leadership to consider the impact of bail practices on the jail population.

The Legal Context: Massachusetts Law Governing Bail

The Massachusetts law governing bail at that time restricted the goals of bail at a defendant's first appearance to ensuring appearance in court and clearly emphasized a presumption favoring release of defendants on personal recognizance (without financial conditions). In fact, the law provided defendants with a right to have the decision reviewed at the next Suffolk County Superior Court session when they had not secured ROR. Protection of the community from dangerous defendants was recognized as a bail agenda in the statute, but it was limited to the narrow instance when a newly arrested defendant was found to be on pretrial release pending adjudication of an earlier criminal charge.[4]

Under the law at that time, the Massachusetts judge might deny release to such a defendant after a hearing and upon a determination that there was probable cause to believe that the defendant had committed a crime during pretrial release and that the defendant would "seriously endanger any person or the community." Because of this special combination of a broad emphasis on ensuring appearance and release of defendants under nonfinancial conditions and a very narrow role for public safety concerns, the Massachusetts law presented an interesting legal framework within which to conduct the guidelines decisionmaking research. Indeed, it may be claimed that the Massachusetts law governing the bail practices of the Boston Municipal Court was at one end of a continuum of bail statutes; it placed a very heavy emphasis on the interest of pretrial defendants to liberty under the least restrictive conditions and a relatively light emphasis on the interest of the state (the commonwealth) in community safety. Overall, the interest of the state in an orderly justice process appeared to be the principal aim of the pretrial release decision.

Court Structure and the Pretrial Process in Boston

In 1984, the courts in Massachusetts were part of a recently unified state system led by the Chief Justice of the Supreme Judicial Court of the Commonwealth of Massachusetts and administered by the Chief Administrative Justice of the Trial Courts. The trial courts there include the "felony" or major trial courts known as the superior court; the limited-jurisdiction courts, including the district courts and the Boston Municipal Court; and others. Theoretically, the court "departments" within the trial courts are not organized in a hierarchical fashion; all report to the Chief Administrative Justice of the Trial Courts. Despite the new organizational chart, however, there were vestiges of political traditions that were not quite so horizontal, including the somewhat autonomous leanings of the judiciary of the Boston Municipal Court, which did not view itself as simply another district court. In planning our Boston study, we agreed initially to a two-pronged approach, with a primary emphasis on bail practices in the Boston Municipal Court (serving Suffolk County or central Boston) and a secondary emphasis on the Suffolk County Superior Court (which has statewide jurisdiction as the major felony or trial court as well as special relevance to Boston prosecutions).

Figure 4.1 illustrates the flow of criminal cases entering the system in the central Boston area, over which the Boston Municipal Court has jurisdiction. Bail is decided on both immediately after arrest at the police station (not by a judge but by a bail commissioner who is a judicial designee[5]) as well as, shortly thereafter, at the defendant's first appearance in court ("arraignment") by a Boston Municipal Court judge. All criminal cases—whether the equivalent of felonies or misdemeanors[6]—must be arraigned promptly in Boston Municipal Court. Between the arrests (many of which take place the night before) and morning arraignments, all defendants are processed by the court probation staff so that, ideally, information relating to a defendant's prior record and, often, previous court appearances and absences may be presented to the arraignment judge. If a defendant has not gained release at this stage, he or she

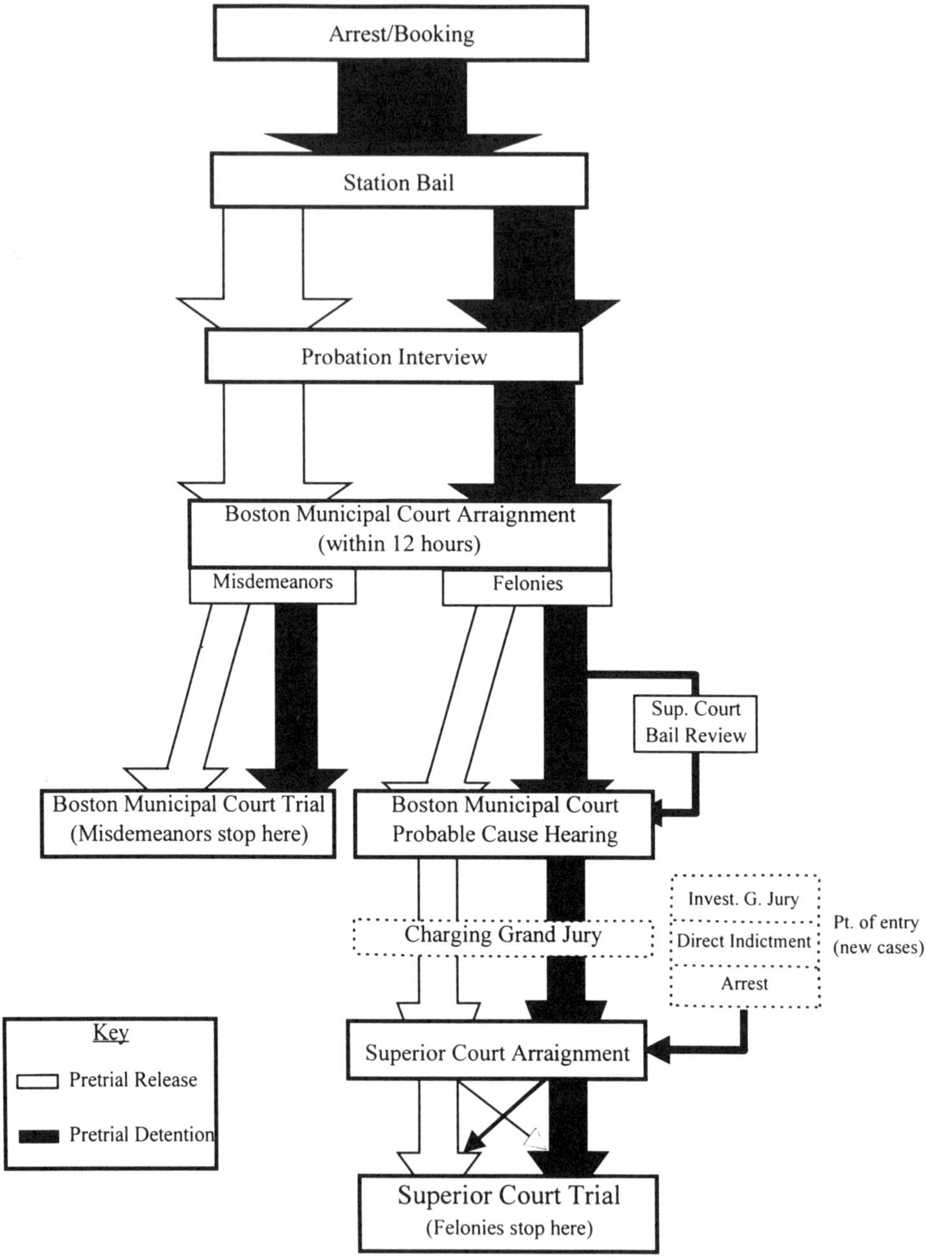

FIGURE 4.1. The processing of defendants in Boston, by pretrial custody status.

has the right to a review of bail by the Superior Court within 48 hours.

Serious felony cases (having penalties of five years or more) are next scheduled for "probable cause" (preliminary) hearings in municipal court to determine whether they will be bound over to superior court for trial. If bound over, cases are also reviewed by the grand jury, which must issue an indictment before a case can move to arraignment in the major trial court, the superior court. Bail, which may be reviewed at the probable cause stage, is redecided by a superior court judge at the superior court arraignment. Generally, cases in which the penalty will not include a sentence to the state prison system (i.e., misdemeanor and lesser felony cases) are scheduled for trial in municipal court. Although bail may be raised at a number of stages in the two-tiered court system, the key judicial stages of interest to this research were arraignment in municipal court, review of municipal court decisions in superior court, and arraignment in superior court.

The superior court is also a court of original jurisdiction for cases resulting from direct indictment by the investigating grand jury. Such felony cases have their first appearance at arraignment in superior court, at which charges are read and bail is decided.

In terms of structure, then, the Boston courts were in some respects similar to the Philadelphia system; the bail decision was made by several actors in the process, but fundamentally by lower-court judges whose bail setting was only one small part of their judicial activities. The court was "governed" by a chief administrative justice, who had general administrative responsibilities in addition to presiding over cases like the other judges.

Circuit and County Courts in Dade County

Public Safety and Jail Overcrowding in Dade County

Dade County has experienced one of the most rapid demographic changes of any American population center in the last decade and a half. Of the three research sites, it has the most diverse ethnic makeup. Not only has the area emerged as a nucleus of a large Hispanic population with roots in the Caribbean basin, but it has accepted several waves of refugee immigration from Cuba and Haiti that have taxed its resources. The rapid change has challenged law enforcement over the years in areas ranging from homicide to drug smuggling and has tested the ability of the criminal justice system to respond. The Dade County Jail, a predominantly pretrial institution, has been the focus of litigation in the federal district court since 1975[7] because of crowding-related problems. Although plans for new construction were on the books at the time of the guidelines research—and several generations of construction undertakings have transpired since—population pressures had increased in recent years and continued as of this writing to be a source of major concern to Dade County officials, including the judicial leadership.

The Legal Context: A Strong Public-Safety Orientation

In many ways, Florida stands in contrast to Massachusetts concerning the presumptions about bail. For several reasons, the then recently revised Florida law governing bail and pretrial release must certainly qualify as one of the most interesting of all laws in the states which had by then enacted new danger laws.[8] First, it was one of the few states explicitly stating the purpose of bail determinations in a bail statute:

> The purpose of a bail determination . . . is to ensure the appearance of the criminal defendant at subsequent proceedings and to protect the community against unreasonable danger from the criminal defendant.[9]

Second, detention based on public safety was expressly permitted. In redrafting the previous state law, the legislature announced its intention to detain upon arrest "persons committing serious criminal offenses, posing a threat to the safety of the community, or failing to appear for trial."[10] In fact, the Florida law departed from the laws of all other jurisdictions in announcing the primacy of public safety at the bail stage, instructing that "the primary consideration" in bail proceedings should "be the protection of the community from risk of physical harm of persons."[11]

This reform of Florida law accompanied a weakening of some of the emphases of reform statutes common since the bail reform movement of the 1960s. The principle of release under least restrictive conditions had been particularly diluted, notwithstanding legislative mention of "reducing the costs of incarceration by releasing . . . those persons not considered a danger . . . who meet certain criteria."[12] Drastically restricting the notion of presumed release on personal recognizance or release under least restrictive conditions, the Florida law only weakly suggested a preference for nonmonetary release "for any person" so fortunate as to be "granted pretrial release."[13] Because cash bond was retained under the Florida law, however, both the traditional *sub rosa* means of securing the detention of defendants and the more recent, formal preventive-detention procedures (requiring a hearing, etc.) existed side by side.

A final unique feature of the legal framework governing bail practices in Florida was the victims provision, which not only required that the state notify victims or witnesses when defendants gained pretrial release but also provided for "consultation" by the state's attorney with victims of felonies involving "physical or emotional injury or trauma" regarding pretrial release.[14]

Clearly, Florida met the (site selection) criterion that sought maximum variability in the state law about bail. When viewed in conjunction with Boston, Dade County might best be placed at the opposite end of the legal continuum, providing a test of the guidelines concept in an explicitly "danger"-oriented system.

Court Structure and the Pretrial Process in Dade County

The court system in Dade County was and still is structured hierarchically in two tiers. Judges are elected to each of the courts, and chief presiding judges are elected by vote of all presiding judges in each court. Although the county and circuit courts are separate organizations, they are closely tied by function and substantially influenced by the leadership of the chief administrative judge of the circuit court. Bail is largely the responsibility of the circuit (or major trial) court; however, county court judges preside over bond hearing (the initial bail decision in felony cases) for the circuit court during the week, and circuit court judges preside on a rotating basis on weekends. (Because of the large number of circuit court judges in the county, any given judge will decide bond relatively rarely.) All persons arrested in Dade County are booked at the central jail (Pretrial Detention Center) and, shortly after booking is completed, have the opportunity to post bond in an amount designated by the bond schedule—except for persons charged with nonbondable offenses.[15] If release is not secured at that point, felony defendants will have bond decided by a judge at the next bond hearing, which is scheduled twice daily and on weekends.

Defendants in misdemeanor cases who have not secured release immediately through the bond schedule will have the opportunity to have bail decided by a county court judge within a day at jail arraignments at which pleas are also accepted. Misdemeanor cases are scheduled for trial in county court, while felony cases are scheduled for arraignment and then trial in circuit court after a bond hearing in that court. Preliminary hearings in felony matters are not routinely held in Florida, but a so-called probable cause determination is made by judges at the bond hearing. Persons to whom bail has been denied (because the offenses are nonbondable) have a hearing within five days that reviews bail and probable cause.

Other than the booking-stage release available to all defendants via the bond schedule, the key bail stages in the Dade County courts are the misdemeanor arraignment and the bond hearing. Felony defendants are screened by a pretrial services program which is operated by the county corrections department (also responsible for the jail), usually prior to the bond hearing (see Figure 4.2). When guidelines research began, pretrial services program staff generally would make subjective recommendations to the bond hearing judge, either asking for custody of the defendant or not. If the court assigned a defendant to pretrial services for nonfinancial release, an "alternate bond" would be set at the same time. This alternate bond usually was the amount originally specified in the bond schedule on the basis of the ranking of the seriousness of the criminal charge.

Most defendants receiving referral to the pretrial services agency would then either be released immediately on personal recognizance, placed in a supervised release program, or allowed to post the alternate bond in the meantime. Because the corrections program actually has custody of these defendants, it does not generally release them until it is satisfied that it has sufficient background information. In some cases, it will subsequently decline to release defendants already given into its custody if later information suggests they are poor risks. Through administrative order of the circuit court, the pretrial services agency also has the power to release immediately persons charged with nonviolent felonies who have no record of prior convictions resulting in incarceration. A large number of defendants first booked on felony charges have their cases bound down (transferred) to county court to be handled as misdemeanor matters, in which case they begin processing at county court arraignment.

The structure of the Dade process introduced interesting dimensions to the test of the versatility of the guidelines concept in the area of pretrial release. The existence of a bond schedule offered an important consideration, as did the highly centralized character of the judicial process. Additionally, unlike in Boston, the role of the pretrial services agency was key in the selection of Dade County, although it had a distinctively different role to play in the process from that of the pretrial services agency in Philadelphia. The Dade County agency was also unusual because of its location in corrections, a contrast with Philadelphia's court-based agency.

Superior Court in Maricopa County

Public Safety, Jail Overcrowding, and Divided Jurisdiction in Maricopa County

At the beginning of the research in Maricopa County, jail overcrowding had been the subject of a federal suit since the late 1970s, a time when

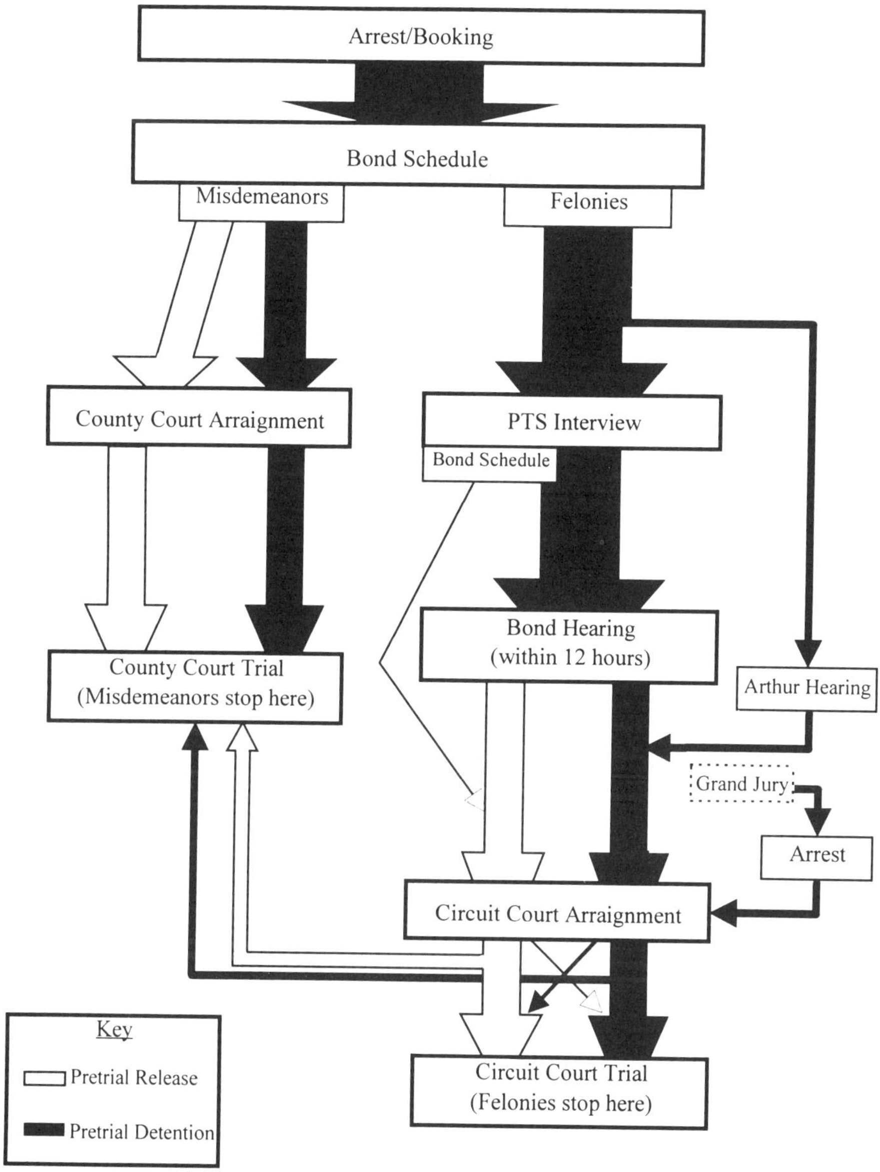

FIGURE 4.2. The processing of defendants in Dade County, by pretrial custody status.

the jail population had reached more than 1,550 in facilities with a capacity of 1,300.[16] The federal district court ordered a population limit and a plan to develop alternatives to incarceration, in addition to requiring other improvements. During the research, a new 3,000-bed jail facility was opened; it was immediately filled to capacity and began to experience crowding-related problems. Comprehensive action to address the pretrial and other aspects of the jail problem were made more difficult by the divided jurisdiction of the City of Phoenix (misdemeanor) and Maricopa County (state system) courts.

The Legal Context: A Recent Public-Safety Emphasis

Arizona statutes governing bail and pretrial release were revised in 1970, and the state constitution was amended in 1982, to permit the outright detention of defendants based on public safety concerns. Not only does the constitution now include the traditional limitation of a right to bail excluding persons charged with capital offenses, but persons charged with felonies who were on pretrial release in prior felony matters may be denied bail (and thereby release) categorically as well. The most recent amendment at the time of the research provided that defendants charged with felonies found to "pose a substantial danger to any other person or the community" may be detained if, after a detention hearing, no conditions of release can reasonably ensure the safety of the community.[17] Because felonies in Arizona include offenses for which the penalty may be one or more years of incarceration—a broader classification than in many states—the detention-for-danger provision may apply to a potentially large number of criminal cases. The Arizona law mentioned release on personal recognizance and on conditions but did not include a presumption for nonfinancial release or release under least restrictive conditions. The characteristics of the Arizona law thus seemed to place it somewhere between the laws of the other two sites on the conceptual continuum, although perhaps closer to Florida's example in its emphasis on defendant danger. The Arizona provision for a detention hearing for those the state seeks to detain outright because of dangerousness resembled Florida's "Arthur" procedures, and the lack of a strong presumption for least restrictive conditions sharply distinguished Arizona from Massachusetts.

Court Structure and the Pretrial Process in Maricopa County

Maricopa County includes the City of Phoenix, a number of surrounding population centers, and some rather remote rural areas. Jurisdiction for processing criminal cases was then and still is shared by the superior court, the Municipal Court of Phoenix, and local justice courts located in the outlying districts outside Phoenix. With few exceptions, the superior court, located in downtown Phoenix in a building then adjacent to the main jail, handled the initial appearances of all defendants charged with felonies and all arraignments for felony cases. (Some felony arrests in the most remote locations had initial appearances in justice courts.) The Phoenix Municipal Court was responsible for all misdemeanors falling within city limits, except for weekends, at which time they were processed by superior court.

Initial appearances for both misdemeanor and felony defendants in the county occurred in the basement of the jail attached to the superior court in adjoining rooms (see Figure 4.3). Five law-trained bail commissioners handled the bail tasks of both the superior and municipal courts through a cooperative agreement between the two courts. Preliminary hearings occur in the 18 justice-of-the-peace courts scattered through Maricopa County.

For about a decade, the superior court had administered a pretrial services program assigned the responsibility of interviewing felony defendants prior to initial appearance at the central Phoenix location and of presenting a recommendation with background information to the initial appearance commissioners. Misdemeanor cases were not served by a pretrial services program.

The central role played by the commissioners, with the administrative and policy oversight of the superior court, made the Maricopa court system of considerable interest in addressing the versatility of the guidelines approach to pretrial release. On the other hand, the presence of an existing pretrial services function, working under the direction of the court system, parallels the Philadelphia experience. Thus, Maricopa County appeared to provide an opportunity to examine the prospect for guidelines that was, as with Boston and Dade County, different enough from Philadelphia's example to lead us to believe that a meaningful test would be possible and fruitful.

Population, Crime, Criminal Court Caseload, and Jailing: A Comparison of the Research Sites

Quite obviously, the three court systems selected for the research were located in geographical areas—the Northeast, the Southeast, and the Southwest—that differed considerably in character. As population centers dealing with crime, they exhibited different histories as well.

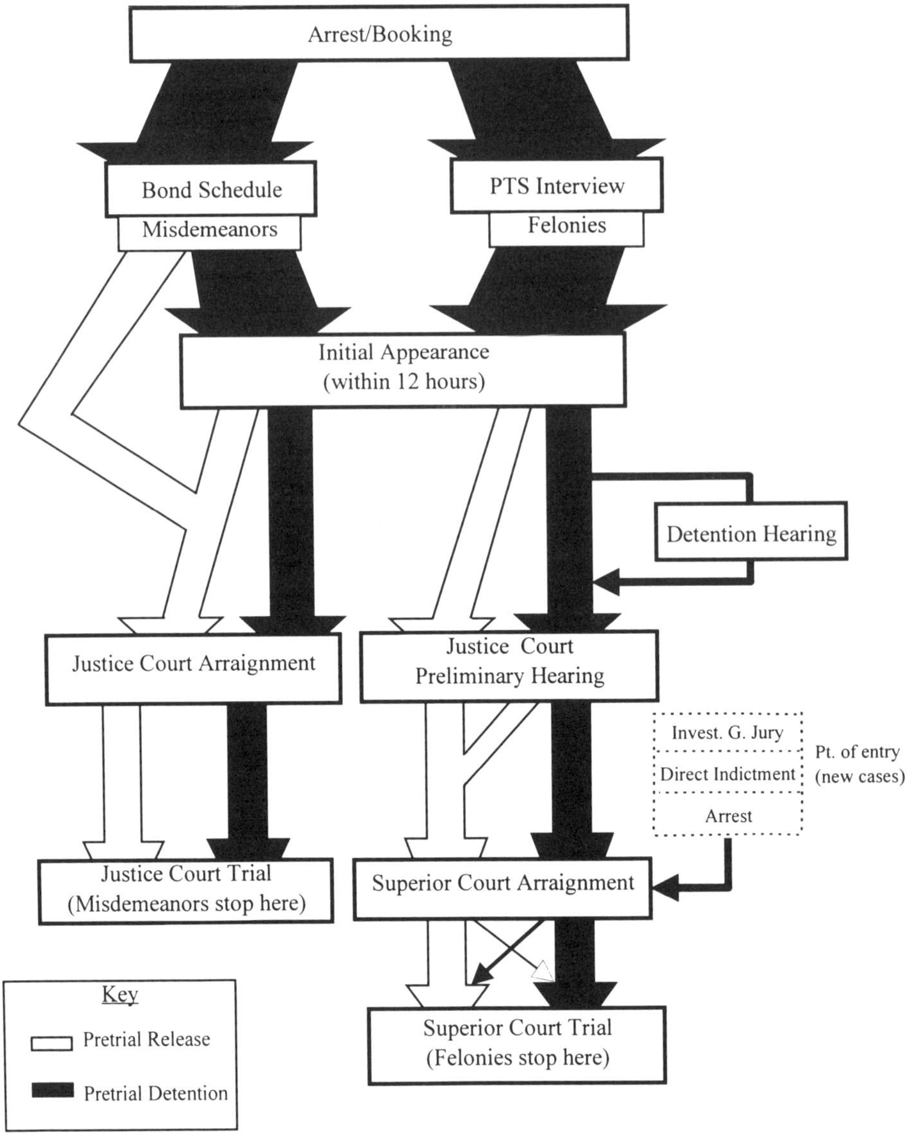

FIGURE 4.3. The processing of defendants in Maricopa County, by pretrial custody status.

Population Trends

The population trends in the three metropolitan areas in the years prior to our research were strikingly different. On one hand, the two southern cities, Miami (Dade County) and Phoenix (Maricopa County), showed remarkably similar patterns of growth; each had grown slowly but surely from under 1 million to just over 1.5 million inhabitants from the mid-1970s to the mid-1980s. On the other hand, for most of that period, the Boston metropolitan area, with just under 3 million people, had been experiencing a gradual and then a precipitous drop in population. This drop seemed to be reversing itself in 1983, just prior to the beginning of the research.

Offenses Known to the Police

Although the Uniform Crime Reports data describing crime reported to area police departments have well-known limitations, they still serve as useful rough indicators of the "crime problem" experienced by the justice systems at the sites studied. Figure 4.4 contrasts the number of total index offenses[18] per 100,000 inhabitants reported to the police in the three jurisdictions between 1975 and 1984. At the beginning of that period, Phoenix and Miami showed reported index offense rates markedly higher

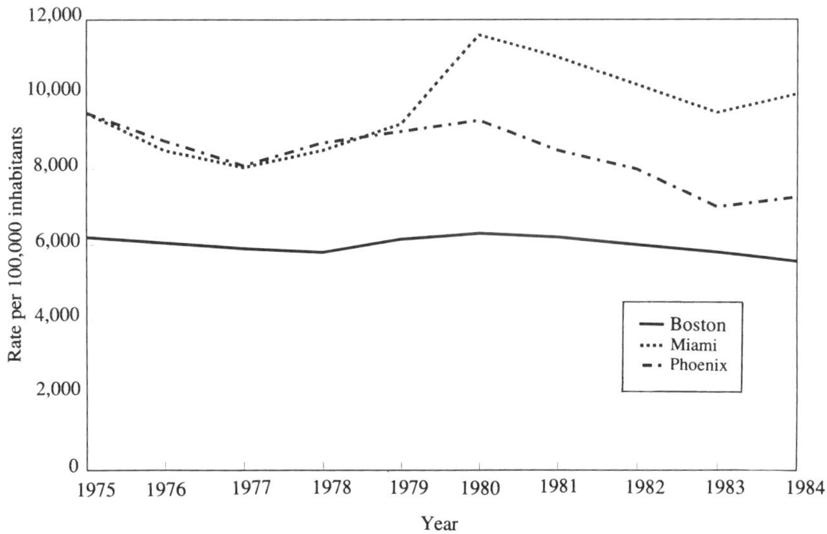

FIGURE 4.4. Total index offenses known to police per 100,000 inhabitants in Boston, Miami, and Phoenix (MSAs), 1975–1984. (*Source:* Adapted from Uniform Crime Reports, 1975–1984.)

than Boston's. However, while each of the jurisdictions revealed a slight decrease at first and then a slight increase, the similarities stopped in about 1978. Beginning in 1979, the crime rates in Miami increased abruptly. The rates in Phoenix began a notable decline, and in Boston, they showed a slight decline. By the end of the period, the Phoenix reported index crime rates were near the low level of the Boston rates, while the Miami rates were heading up again. Other differences are demonstrated when particular subcategories of crimes are considered in more detail. For example, when violent offenses reported to the police are compared (see Figure 4.5), the Miami area stands apart from the other two sites strikingly, both in its generally higher rates each year and in its generally upward thrust in violent offenses. Phoenix and Boston showed very similar patterns, ending up with rates only slightly higher than 10 years previously. When total property offenses are examined, the trends for the three sites do not differ strikingly, except that the Miami rates moved to the highest among the three sites by the decade's end to a point nearly one-third higher than Boston's.

Arrests

The characteristics of arrestees entering the systems at the three sites are important because arrest decisions by police establish the nature of

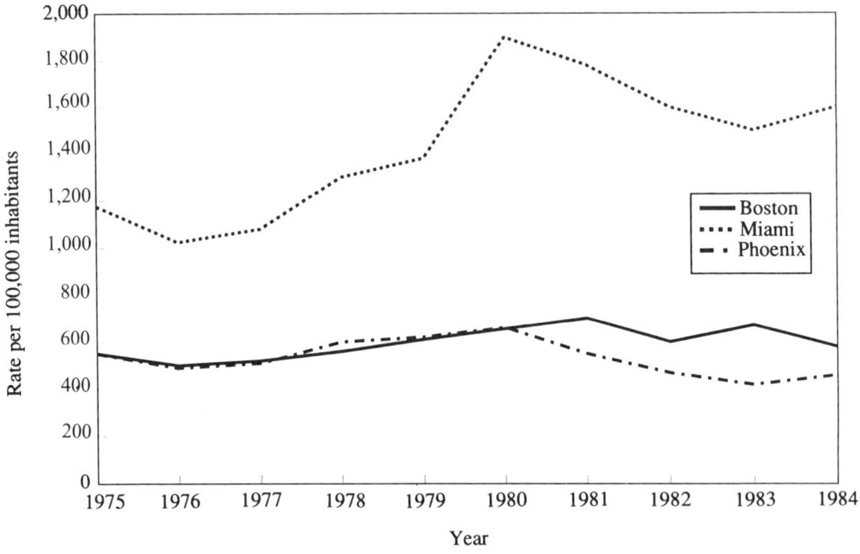

FIGURE 4.5. Total violent offenses known to police per 100,000 inhabitants in Boston, Miami, and Phoenix (MSAs), 1975–1984. (*Source:* Adapted from Uniform Crime Reports, 1975–1984.)

the caseload to be processed by the criminal courts and because of their possible influence on the local jail populations. Obtaining reliable and directly comparable arrest data is quite difficult, particularly in areas served by more than one police agency—as was the case at each of the sites. In fact, these data had to be requested from state agencies the size of whose reporting bases varied considerably. Arrests per 100,000 inhabitants for index offenses appear very similar in Miami and Phoenix through 1979, at about 11,000 arrests per 100,000 population. Rates for Miami then increased sharply to nearly 16,000, while those in Phoenix leveled off before declining to about 9,000 by 1984. The Miami rates had stabilized at about 14,000 per 100,000 by 1984.

Bail-Relevant Criminal Caseloads

Another way to contrast the sites is to compare the volume and nature of the bail-relevant caseloads that their respective court systems were dealing with. Figure 4.6 shows that during 1984, the year the study began, the Dade County courts processed an estimated 56,000 entering criminal cases, more than three times the volume entering each of the other two court systems.[19]

The caseloads differed also in the proportions of felonies and misdemeanors processed by the courts.[20] A majority of the cases processed by the Boston Municipal Court involved misdemeanor charges. In the Dade County courts, misdemeanor and felony cases entered in almost equal numbers during 1984. In the Maricopa County Superior Court, roughly 9 of 10 entering cases were felony matters during that time.

Because definitions of felony and misdemeanor crimes vary across the sites, Figure 4.6 further characterizes the kinds of criminal cases processed by the court systems by applying a modified version of the FBI's Uniform Crime Reports classification of offenses into index and nonindex offenses across jurisdictions.[21] Note that, according to this classification, a majority of the total cases entering each of the court systems annually involved nonindex charges. The second columns show the composition of the populations targeted as bail-relevant by the guidelines research: In the Boston Municipal Court, the relevant caseload in 1984 would have been composed of approximately 13 percent index cases and 87 percent nonindex cases. In Dade County, the courts ultimately requested a focus primarily on felony cases; thus the targeted population included offenses that were more serious, roughly 34 percent involving cases with index crimes. In Maricopa County, a felony focus was decided upon as well, and the targeted caseload in 1984 comprised about 35 percent index offense cases.

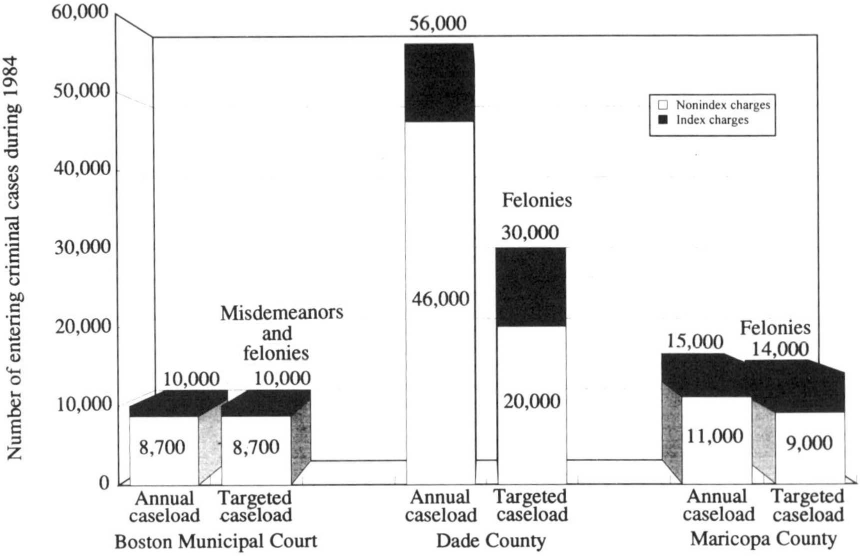

FIGURE 4.6. Estimated annual criminal caseload of entering ("new") cases in Boston Municipal Court, Dade County Circuit Court, and Maricopa County Superior Court during 1984, by seriousness of charges (modified index vs. nonindex).

Note: Charges were classified as nonindex versus index offenses using the FBI VCR method—except that larceny and motor vehicle theft were not included as index offenses. "Target caseload" refers to the part of the criminal caseload that the guidelines research would address.

The Local Jail Populations

Figure 4.7 depicts the estimated annual average daily populations[22] of unsentenced persons in the local jail facilities at each of the study sites during the years preceding and including the periods studied. The Dade and Maricopa County populations had been moving up rapidly, surpassing "crowded" levels around 1980 and heading toward their absolute ceilings (about 1,350 in Dade's detention center and about 1,500 in Maricopa's then new, 1985, facility). The population of the Suffolk County Jail (Boston's Charles Street Jail) had reached its maximum capacity of less than 300 inmates in the late 1970s; thus its flat curve gives a deceptive appearance of stability. (Its population had "stabilized" at overcrowded levels for most of the previous 10 years.)

Prior to the conclusion of our analyses of bail and pretrial-release decisionmaking data, we studied the jail populations at each location during the fall of 1985. Figure 4.8 summarizes the characteristics of the three populations and, in particular, persons awaiting trial.

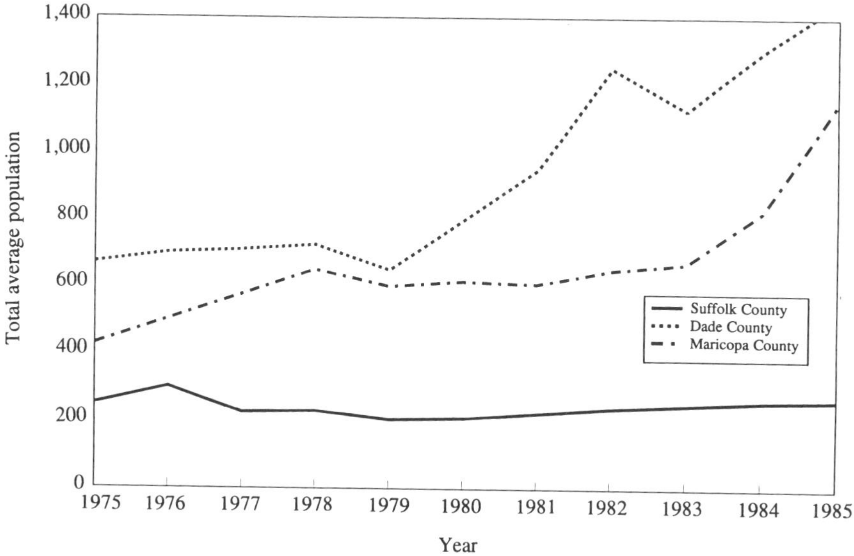

FIGURE 4.7. Estimated annual average daily pretrial population in the local jail, by research site, 1975–1985. (*Source:* Suffolk County Sheriff's Department, Metro-Dade Corrections and Rehabilitation Department, and Maricopa Sheriff's Department.)
Note: Population numbers for Dade County, 1975–1978, are estimates.

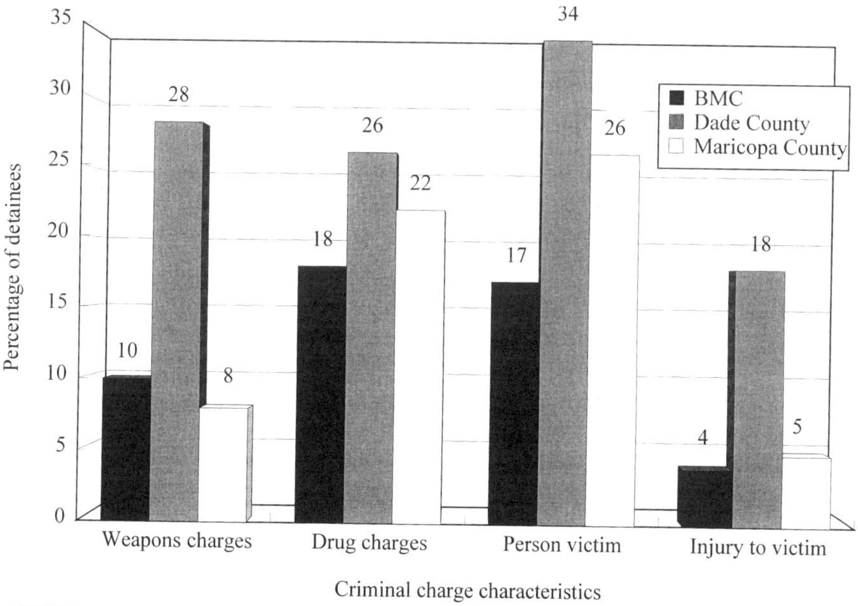

FIGURE 4.8. Criminal charges of defendants detained in local jails, by research site, on a single day in Fall 1985.

In Boston, nearly all jail inmates (about 96 percent) were inmates awaiting trial on the date of the jail profile (November 18, 1985). In Dade County, of the 2,900 persons confined in Dade facilities overall, roughly 58 percent were confined awaiting trial on the date of the study (September 19, 1985). In Maricopa County, the population of persons awaiting trial accounted for about 44 percent of all inmates in custody on the date of the study (September 21, 1985) (see Table 4.1). Of course, all persons held awaiting trial on particular charges were not confined exclusively for bail-related reasons: In Boston, 77 percent of detainees were held only because they could not post bail; in Dade County, 75 percent fell into that category; in Maricopa County, only 47 percent of the persons awaiting trial had no other reason associated with their confinement.

Figure 4.8 helps contrast the makeup of the local jail populations further by comparing the charges associated with their detained defendants. Detainees in the Dade County and Maricopa County jails showed

TABLE 4.1

Characteristics of Populations of Local Jail Facilities, by Site, by Custody Status, 1985

	Jail					
	Suffolk County[a]		Dade County[b]		Maricopa County[c]	
Population characteristics	Number	Percentage	Number	Percentage	Number	Percentage
Average annual total population for 1984[d]	320	—	2,800	—	1,840	—
Average annual population awaiting trial for 1984	310	—	1,349	—	937	—
Population on study date in 1985	323	—	2,900	—	2,484	—
Custody status of inmates						
Total	323	100.0	352	100.0	404	100.0
Awaiting trial	311	96.3	203	57.7	177	43.8
Other	12	3.7	149	42.3	227	56.2
Awaiting trial						
Total	311	100.0	203	100.0	177	100.0
Awaiting trial only	238	76.5	153	75.4	83	46.9
Awaiting trial and other	73	23.5	50	24.6	94	53.1

[a]Based on a 100 percent sample of persons in jail on November 18, 1985.
[b]Based on a 12 percent sample of persons in jail on September 19, 1985.
[c]Based on a 16 percent sample of persons in jail on September 21, 1985.
[d]These averages were based on head count data or other summary data provided by the jail officials at each site.

more than four times the proportion of defendants with cases involving weapons charges than defendants held in Boston on the study date. Dade County and Maricopa County defendants also held greater proportions of detainees having drug-related charges. In the Boston jail, proportionately more defendants were held on charges involving crimes against the person, and a slightly higher proportion of defendants had charges alleging harm to a victim than in the other jail facilities.

Clearly, the courts participating in the study exhibited criminal caseloads differing both in size and in the kinds of cases processed. They are in areas characterized by substantially different crime problems. This mix is precisely what we sought to mount a test of the guidelines approach under diverse conditions. The demonstration sites differed in governing pretrial release laws, court organization, region, crime problem, case mix, and demography. They shared general problems in their pretrial decisionmaking and concerns about jail overcrowding and community safety.

Notes

1. Pa. Rules. Crim. Pro. 4003 appeared to permit consideration of the danger defendants may pose to themselves or others in the judge's consideration of ROR, but not in the assignment of financial bail. While the prevailing interpretation of the law at the time was that the bail decision was to be based only on a concern about defendant flight, the judges of the Philadelphia Municipal Court decided as a matter of policy to include in the guidelines risk of rearrest as well as risk of flight.
2. See Goldkamp (1985) for discussion.
3. *Inmates of Suffolk County Jail v. Eisenstadt et al.*, 360 F. Supp. 676–693, 1973.
4. Ann. Laws Mass. C. 276:58.
5. The state office of the bail commissioner reports to the chief justice of the superior court.
6. Under common law in Massachusetts, crimes are not classified as felony or misdemeanor, but by whether they are eligible for state prison terms and the length of incarceration that may be imposed.
7. *Bridges v. Sandstrom*, F. Supp., U.S. District Court for So. Fla., No. 74 994, Jan. 2, 1975.
8. Fla. Stat. Ch. 903.046.
9. Fla. Stat. Ch. 907.041.
10. Id.
11. Id.
12. Id.
13. Id.
14. Fla. Stat. Ch. 960.30 (1984).
15. At the time of the research, the following offenses were nonbondable: murder, rape, robbery using a firearm or deadly weapon, sexual battery and other sex offenses, kidnapping, burglary with assault or armed, and possession of bombs or explosive devices.
16. *Hart v. Hill*, CIV 77 479 PHX EHC MS (1980). See Pryor and Murray (1981).
17. Ariz. Const. Art. II:22; Ariz. Stat. Art. 12:13 3961.

18. In its series *Crime in the United States* for the relevant years (see FBI, *Crime in the United States,* Washington, D.C.: U.S. Government Printing Office, 1975–1984), the Federal Bureau of Investigation lists the numbers of index crimes known to police per 100,000 inhabitants. Index offenses are murder, nonnegligent manslaughter, forcible rape, robbery, aggravated assault, burglary, larceny theft, motor vehicle theft, and arson.
19. We projected these estimates from the samples studied to arrive at an annualized criminal caseload in the criminal court systems. For example, in Maricopa County, the sample includes all relevant cases entering the system during June and July 1984, or during one-sixth of the year. Multiplied by 6, the sample provides a rough estimate for the courts' annual criminal caseload. In the Boston Municipal Court, the sample included all cases entering between April and October 1984, or during half a year. Of course, these estimates of annual bail-relevant criminal caseloads suffer important limitations. First, to the extent that the cases entering during the sample months differed from cases entering during other months, the annualized estimate is biased. (This would be more of a problem in Maricopa County and less of a problem in Boston, for example.) In addition, the estimate is of the annual bail-relevant criminal cases entering the respective court systems; excluded are the kinds of cases excluded from the samples (nonbondable criminal cases as well as cases involving only probation or parole revocation, only bench warrants, or warrants from other locations).
20. Note that the differing definitions of felony between Arizona, Florida, and Massachusetts make the comparisons uneven. In Arizona and Florida, offenses punishable by more than one year are classified as felonies. In Massachusetts, which does not formally classify offenses according to a felony or misdemeanor grading, offenses with incarcerative penalties of five years or more are considered felonies.
21. We dropped motor vehicle theft and larceny from the FBI's index offense list to provide a measure of more serious offenses. See Note 18, above.
22. These numbers are estimates because of the great difficulty in locating reliable data describing the jail populations in the jail systems over time. The Boston data, based on records of head counts taken over the years, appeared reasonably reliable (both for the total and the pretrial populations), particularly because the Charles Street Jail is largely a pretrial detention facility. The Dade pretrial population is based on averaging the daily head counts for unsentenced prisoners at the Women's Annex and the Dade County Detention Center, although we had to estimate the years before 1979 based on annual bookings. We discovered in examining the overall population of the Dade correctional facilities that the computerized list provided by the county overstated the population of the facilities between 16 and 25 percent when actual head-count lists were contrasted. Reliable daily head-count lists were available only from 1979 on. In Maricopa County, reasonably reliable population data were available from 1977 on. We should note as well the discrepancy between the jail's classification of sentenced versus unsentenced and our more precise definition of persons awaiting trial versus those not awaiting trial (persons awaiting trial as well as persons awaiting sentence, etc., are included among "unsentenced" inmates).

5

Design of the Research

Sampling Strategy and the Purposes of the Descriptive Phase

It is possible to construct guidelines to address pretrial release decisionmaking in a variety of ways.[1] Depending on the particular philosophy of guidelines construction that one adopts, there will be implications for the kinds of data to be collected (if, indeed, data are to be collected at all), the types of cases to be represented, and the decisionmakers to be included. It is essential, therefore, that we note assumptions that shaped the guidelines technique used in this study, as well as the data collection and empirical analyses undertaken in each of the jurisdictions.

First, we undertook to assist the site courts in *the development of voluntary guidelines.* The development of guidelines was itself a voluntary process in the sense that the courts agreed at first only to examine their pretrial-release practices through the use of descriptive research and to review the policy implications of what they found. There were no guarantees that the courts would choose to implement guidelines at the end of the collaborative research process. The participating courts merely agreed to work with the researchers in the development process and then to consider how some version of guidelines might or might not be designed to tackle important problem areas. It was understood that, at a point well along in the research process, each court would make a determination whether to make use of the resource developed or not. In other words, none of the courts committed themselves in advance to adopting a product sight unseen. Furthermore, the guidelines themselves were meant to be voluntary in their use, in the sense that they were to be developed as decisionmaker aids embodying court policy relating to pretrial release determinations and providing structure for the exercise of meaningful discretion.

Second, the guidelines research process was conceived of as involving *four distinct phases:*

- *Rigorous descriptive analysis of current (or recent past) practices,* which was meant to describe representative operating practices of the court as a whole.
- *Discussion with the court of the findings and their apparent implications for policy and the development of decision guidelines.*
- *Development and implementation of a finalized version of guidelines* (depending upon the court's decision to proceed).
- *Evaluation of initial use of the decision guidelines* and feedback to the court concerning their possible revision.

The General Research Plan

Data collection for the description of decisionmaking practices at the pretrial stage followed a similar plan in each of the courts, although the focus and the particular sampling strategy depended on a diagnosis of the criminal process and the areas that each of the judiciaries wished to emphasize. In general, we sought to collect data describing a large number of cases that had recently entered the criminal process at the bail and pretrial-release stage, to follow the cases through the system long enough to determine if they had secured release, and to observe whether they failed to appear in court or were rearrested while on release or, if they were not released before trial, to determine how long they were detained. We attempted to draw samples recent enough to reflect "current" court practices, but "old" enough to ensure that, by the end of data collection, most of the cases would have proceeded to final disposition.

The goal was to be able to examine factors influential in the judicial determination of bail, the determination of release, and the likelihood of flight or crime during pretrial release. Specific analyses in each of these areas were reported back to the courts as particular problem areas singled out for attention by them. In addition, the jail populations were analyzed so that inferences about the impact of pretrial release decisionmaking on the jail could be discussed. This general approach was adapted to the practicalities and interests of the courts at each of the sites. The strategies employed in each of the jurisdictions are briefly summarized here.

Maricopa County: Superior Court of Arizona

Discussion with the judicial leadership revealed that the principal thrust of the guidelines research in Maricopa County would focus on felony defendants. Thus, all "new" felony cases entering the process at initial appearance in superior court in Maricopa County during June and July 1984 were included in the sample of defendants studied for guidelines purposes. Although 3,667 defendants appeared before commissioners at initial appearance in superior court during that time, 1,435 were excluded because they were not relevant to the bail and pretrial-release questions being examined.[2] The remaining, total sample of entering felony cases included 2,232 defendants who had bail decided at initial appearance during June and July by five commissioners sitting at three sessions per day. Preliminary examination of the court records indicated that this procedure would result in sufficient numbers of serious cases (those which generally occur least frequently) to permit meaningful analyses and would also result in nearly proportionate representation of the five commissioners who were deciding bail in Maricopa.

A large amount of information was collected describing defendants and their cases from booking until their status eight months later. Cases were tracked for 90 days to learn whether pretrial release had occurred; if, by the time 90 days had elapsed, release had not occurred, the defendant was considered "detained" for the purposes of the research. If released at some point prior to 90 days after initial appearance, defendants were tracked on release to determine whether rearrests or failures to appear in court were recorded.

During the research, at a point about a year before the implementation of decision guidelines, a sample of the local jail population was also drawn (on September 21, 1985) to depict persons held in custody "on a given day." A 16 percent random sample of the 2,484 inmate population on that day yielded a sample of 405 persons for study.

Dade County: Circuit and County Courts

The committee of judges assembled to supervise the guidelines research in Dade County initially requested that both misdemeanor and felony cases be considered. Fortunately, all criminal cases were booked at the central jail before being channeled into the separate court systems (county court for misdemeanors and circuit court for felonies), so that a list of entering cases could be compiled for sampling purposes.

Because bond hearings for felony defendants (equivalent to initial appearance in Maricopa County) were to be an important focus, the scheduling of judges sitting at bond hearings had to be considered. It was found, for example, that one county court judge generally sat in circuit court to conduct bond hearings in felony cases during the week (9 to 4 o'clock), but that a variety of circuit court judges were rotated to sit at bond hearings on weekends. In order to include a sample of felony cases representing decisions of a sufficient number of judges, it was decided to sample weekends (Fridays, Saturdays, and Sundays). While this same county court judge would still be "overincluded" because he decided bond every Friday morning, many other judges decided bond on Friday afternoons and during the rest of the weekend. Analysis showed that these cases did not differ substantially from the kinds of cases processed during the week.

Populations of entering misdemeanor and felony defendants were defined with the help of the Research and Systems Division of the Dade County Court Administrative Office. Minus excluded cases (cases involving nonbondable offenses, fugitives, or escapees), 2,238 felony cases and 1,972 misdemeanor cases entered the system on weekends between June 1 and September 2, 1984. Since a sample of roughly 2,000 cases was desired and an emphasis on felony cases was considered important (because of bond hearing), a stratification with disproportionate sampling was employed. Roughly two-thirds of the weekend felony cases were randomly selected (n = 1,492), and one-fourth of the misdemeanor cases were randomly selected (n = 493), to produce a total sample of 1,985 cases. As with the Maricopa sample, a 90-day period was used to determine whether defendants gained release before trial; if they were released, we tracked their cases for 90 days to learn of any failures to appear in court or rearrests for new crimes.

On September 19, 1985, the collective population of the Metropolitan Dade Corrections and Rehabilitation Department jail facilities stood at 3,455. A random sample (n = 431) was drawn to describe that population on a "given day."

Boston: The Boston Municipal and Suffolk County Superior Courts

In discussing the appropriate focus of a guidelines development process in Boston courts, the trial court suggested that both the Boston Municipal Court (BMC—a central urban limited-jurisdiction court comparable to, but larger than, other district courts in the state) and the Suffolk County Superior Court (a state-level major trial court located in central Boston) might be worthwhile arenas for investigating and exploring bail issues. The municipal court was the court processing the largest volume of incoming criminal cases, though more misdemeanor than felony in number. However, the superior court received felony-level cases produced from direct indictments and cases bound over from the BMC and other district courts in the area, and it reviewed bail decisions of defendants detained after initial bail decisions at arraignment in the BMC or the other courts. The bail review function, mandated by statute,[3] seemed particularly important to study.

With primary emphasis given to the Boston Municipal Court, the two court systems were studied in the following manner. Cases entering the municipal court at arraignment were sampled by use of a list kept by Municipal Court Probation. To ensure that sufficient numbers of serious cases (which were relatively rare in the BMC caseload) were included in the study, cases entering between the beginning of April and the end of October 1984 (approximately 4,500 after subtracting exclusions[4]) were stratified on the basis of charge seriousness.[5] All of the serious cases (involving index offenses minus larceny and motor vehicle theft) during that period (n = 603) were included in the sample, and one-third of the roughly 4,000 less serious (nonindex) cases n = 1,376) were randomly taken, resulting in a total sample of 2,193 cases.

Several smaller samples were taken to investigate superior court case processing. First, to examine cases entering the judicial process directly at superior court arraignment, we randomly sampled one-third of the court's direct indictments for the year of 1984 to produce a sample of 356 cases. This excluded cases unavailable for coding because of sealed files.[6] Second, bail reviews were studied by including all available bail reviews (n = 564) during 1984 from any lower court in the area. To study "bind-over" cases entering superior court at the arraignment stage, we examined only the BMC cases that were bound over during the seven-month period in 1984 that had already been collected as part of the BMC sample (n = 164).

It was difficult to obtain systematic information describing subsequent criminal histories of defendants released before trial for the superior court and municipal court samples. Such information was not routinely available in a reliable form from the probation agencies, which generally held information relating to prior criminal records. Because criminal history was kept in manual card files by the Commissioner of Probation, separate sampling was required to obtain this important information. Given existing procedures, expense, time, and space, it was necessary to limit the request for record checks to two subsamples of defendants, one a 500-defendant random sample of the municipal court defendants, and the other the superior court's 356-defendant direct-indictment sample.

In addition, we studied all the cases (n = 324) held in the Charles Street (Suffolk County) Jail on November 18, 1985, in order to describe persons confined there on a "given" day.

The Collection of Defendant and Case Data in the Jurisdictions

Data collection was designed to permit us to address several analytic goals. First, it would be necessary to chart the progress of criminal cases as they passed through the early stages of the criminal process and beyond. This would be important so that key decisionmaking stages could be identified and their impact on later outcomes analyzed. Second, a central analytic goal was to examine a large sample of bail decisions made by a variety of judges or judicial officers so that inferences could be drawn about themes governing their transaction. Third, we wanted to examine the allocation of release and detention among entering defendants and attempt to discern patterns differentiating the two groups. Fourth, we wanted to follow the performance of defendants during pretrial release (at least for a 90-day period) and try to determine attributes of defendants or their cases that appeared related to misconduct (flight and crime). Finally, once decision guidelines were developed, it would be necessary to try to project the impact of their future implementation on like cases.

Accomplishment of these goals meant that several kinds of information were needed, including demographic, social-background, case-related, charge, and prior-criminal-history data. In practical terms, this meant that a number of agencies in each of the jurisdictions would have to be consulted. In Boston, for example, data collection required access to records located in eight agencies, including the Boston Municipal Court Clerk's Office, the Suffolk County Superior Court Clerk's Office, the Boston Municipal Court Probation Department, the Suffolk County Superior Court Probation Department, the Boston District Attorney's Office (two departments), the Office of the State Commissioner of Probation, the Office of the Suffolk County Sheriff, and the Massachusetts Correctional Institute at Framingham. No computerized files were available for court or case information or criminal history.

In Dade County, sources of data were located in records held by four principal agencies: The Research and Systems Division of the Administrative Office of Circuit Court, the Pretrial Services Division of Metropolitan Dade Corrections and Rehabilitation, and the offices of the Circuit Court Clerk and the County Court Clerk. The court assisted the research by providing computerized lists of entering criminal cases and allowing access to a computerized criminal history file.

In Maricopa County, the Court Administrator's Office of Superior Court, the Pretrial Services Division of Superior Court, and the Maricopa County Sheriff's Office offered access to the necessary files and provided computerized case and criminal-history information which greatly expedited data collection.

Although a great deal of information was collected describing large cohorts of cases entering the judicial processes, not all of the desired information was equally available in the three jurisdictions. Although this discovery is not in itself surprising, it foreshadowed information-related difficulties that would confront development of guidelines in one fashion or another later. Indeed, the presence or absence of particular data items is itself a significant finding of this research, documenting the considerable variability among these court systems in their "essential data base." The fact is that information deemed essential by one court for decisionmaking, another court would not even possess. Indeed, the information "base" on which some decisions rested would surprise the general public and criminal justice professionals alike.

Dade County, for example, did not routinely record certain kinds of demographic information that would have been helpful. Maricopa County did not always have certain charge-related and victim-related information available. Perhaps most dramatic was the large number of cases in Boston for which criminal history data (prior and subsequent to the case being studied) were not available at all.

The sites differed as well in the reliability of the data, even when available. For example, when defendants were interviewed by pretrial services in Dade and Maricopa counties concerning their drug abuse habits, the interviewers generally placed little faith in the responses obtained. In Boston, when criminal history information was available, it was not often complete; comparison of criminal history information from municipal court probation files, the jail files, and the probation commissioner's files showed inconsistencies.

Regardless of the quality or the quantity of the available information in the three sites, the data we collected represented the actual data that decisionmakers themselves had to rely on in setting bail. Whatever the deficiencies present in these data, they are the appropriate vehicle for beginning to model the decisions and review their consequences for the three sites.

The Criminal Caseload

Before discussing the findings from the guidelines research (in which we shall describe the processing of criminal cases and the character and consequences of the bail decisionmaking in each of the participating courts), we compare briefly the characteristics of the defendants and their cases entering the three systems at the time the guidelines research began.[7]

Demographic Characteristics

Slight differences among the courts were evident when the age and gender of the entering defendants are examined; more noticeable differences occurred when the race or ethnicity of defendants was considered. Dade County Circuit Court defendants, for example, were somewhat older (with a median age of 28 years) than defendants in the Boston Municipal Court and the Superior Court in Maricopa County (whose median ages were 25 and 26 years). Female defendants accounted for twice the proportion of defendants in the Boston Municipal Court (28 percent) of that in the circuit and superior courts (13 percent in each instance). White defendants accounted for only 22 percent of the caseload entering the circuit court in Dade County but were 42 percent of defendants in the Boston Municipal Court and 55 percent of the defendants entering the superior court in Maricopa County. Black defendants accounted for 45 percent of Boston defendants and 39 percent of Dade defendants, but only 15 percent of Maricopa defendants. The courts differed as well in the proportions of entering defendants who were Hispanic: in Dade County, 35 percent of entering defendants were Hispanic; in Maricopa County 26 percent were; but only 6 percent of Boston Municipal Court defendants were Hispanic.

Criminal Charges

Given the different jurisdictions of the participating courts, entering defendants in the three court systems could be distinguished on the basis of their criminal charges. As we noted above, the Boston Municipal Court accepted misdemeanor and felony cases for initial proceedings, though serious charges were comparatively rare. Both the circuit court in Dade County and the superior court in Maricopa County were primarily felony courts. However, beyond the gross differences in the seriousness of criminal charges associated with entering cases, a number of other charge-related characteristics set the courts apart from one another (see Figure 5.1).

First, using the modified index versus nonindex classification borrowed from the FBI as a gross measure of charge seriousness,[8] Figure 5.1 shows again the similarity in the charges of defendants entering the Maricopa and Dade courts (with 35 and 33 percent index charges, respectively) during that period, as well as the generally less serious nature of the offenses adjudicated by the Boston Municipal Court (only 13 percent of BMC defendants were charged with index-level offenses). The similarity of even the Dade County and Maricopa County court caseloads seemed to hide some important differences, however. Of the three courts, circuit court defendants were proportionately most often charged with weapons offenses (nearly three times the proportion of the other two courts), with drug offenses (a slightly greater proportion than the other courts), with crimes involving person victims (somewhat more than Maricopa defendants but twice the proportion of BMC defendants), and with crimes

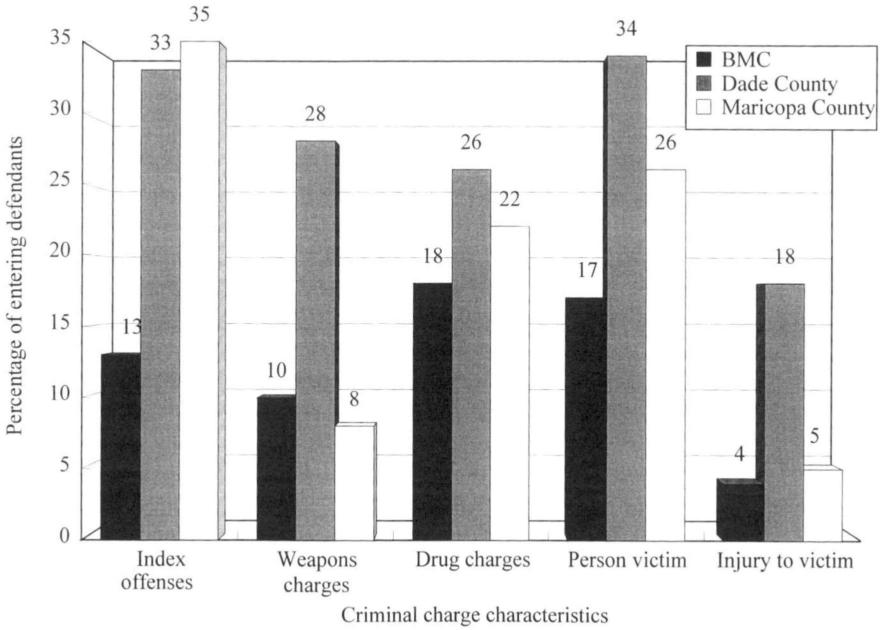

FIGURE 5.1. Comparison of criminal charges of defendants entering the criminal process in the Boston Municipal Court (BMC), Dade County Circuit Court, and Maricopa County Superior Court, 1984.

involving injury to victims (more than three times the proportion of the other courts).

Criminal History

Nearly half the Dade County and Maricopa County defendants had had arrests within the last three years.[9] Fewer BMC defendants showed recent arrests (37 percent compared with 51 and 49 percent of the other defendants, respectively). Each of the groups of defendants, however, showed just under one-fifth having prior arrests for serious crimes against the person. A slightly greater proportion of Dade defendants (31 percent) had prior arrests for drug-related offenses than Maricopa defendants (27 percent). Boston defendants had notably fewer prior arrests for drug offenses.

Dade defendants showed a higher proportion (56 percent) with previous convictions than both Maricopa (47 percent) and Boston (36 percent) defendants. Convictions for serious crimes against the person were rare among all defendants: 10 percent of Maricopa defendants, 5 percent of

Dade defendants, and 9 percent of Boston defendants had such histories. Maricopa defendants showed the highest rate of prior felony convictions (30 percent), when compared with the rates of Dade (20 percent) and Boston (14 percent) defendants. Maricopa defendants led the way in prior drug convictions (22 percent) over Dade (15 percent) and Boston (11 percent) defendants.

Clearly, there were some substantial differences among the caseload samples drawn for each of the sites in the characteristics of the defendants they included. In general, the Maricopa and Dade samples involved defendants with cases that were more serious than the cases in the Boston sample. There were greater proportions of minority group members in Maricopa and Dade than in Boston, and the prior records of the defendants in the Boston sample were less extensive. These differences, many of which certainly could influence pretrial release determinations and the consequences of release, make simple comparisons of the sites' caseloads difficult. In fact, when we do make comparisons later in this book, caution is observed so that these inherent differences can be taken into account.

Notes

1. Goldkamp and Gottfredson (1985); Gottfredson and Gottfredson (1984).
2. Exclusions included persons held on misdemeanor charges, persons appearing because of bench warrants or fugitive warrants only, and persons absent without leave from local or state correctional facilities. The rationale behind such exclusions was that more would be learned about typical pretrial-release decisionmaking by concentrating on criminal cases entering the system without mixing them with categories of special defendants whose cases could generally be handled quite differently.
3. See Mass. Gen. Laws Ann. vol. 45 sec. 58 (1987 Supp.).
4. Exclusions included cases listed for arraignment but not involving bail determinations, such as those dismissed or otherwise disposed at arraignment.
5. We employed a modified version of the FBI's Uniform Crime Reports nonindex versus index classification, dropping larceny and motor vehicle theft from the "index" category.
6. Thirty cases were either missing from the records or sealed and unavailable in this category.
7. See Goldkamp and Gottfredson (1988) for detailed description of the attributes of defendants and their criminal cases entering the criminal process in the remaining two courts studied, the Suffolk County Superior Court in Boston and the Dade County Court. After preliminary descriptive research focusing on both the Boston Municipal Court and the Suffolk County Superior Court, both courts agreed that the greatest impact could be produced by focusing on the Boston Municipal Court. In Dade County, a similar development occurred. At the outset, the judicial working committee—comprising circuit and count court judges—asked that the research focus on both misdemeanor and felony case processing. Near the conclusion of the descriptive phase of the research, the committee asked that the focus shift exclusively to felony cases—thus the emphasis on circuit court.

8. As we noted above, we have dropped larceny and motor vehicle theft from the FBI "index" category, but we otherwise have left the classification intact.
9. It may be useful to recall that the rigor of prior criminal history information may not be comparable in each jurisdiction. While each of the systems had its weaknesses and acknowledged shortcomings in its criminal history information (particularly its geographical limitations), the Boston information may have been most problematic. Thus, it is difficult to know whether differences in criminal history rates among the defendant groups are due to actual differences or differences in the thoroughness of the criminal history information available.

6

The Consequences of Bail Decisions in the Three Courts

In Some Ways Each Court Is Unique

In Chapter 4, we described the structure of the courts participating in the research and the paths taken by cases entering the criminal process. The first task of the research process in preparation for guidelines development involves a sort of "diagnosis," or mapping of the special features of pretrial release decisionmaking in the context of criminal processing. In this chapter, we employ a variety of special indicia that permit us to characterize pretrial release decisionmaking and place it in the context of processing.

Certainly, there were clear and important differences among the courts in the way things were done, in the way tasks were valued, and, even, in what things were called. One of the goals of the guidelines research was to recognize and address this uniqueness. For example, booking procedures were decentralized in Boston, carried out in each police precinct. Defendants were either temporarily held or released at the several police locations that fell within the jurisdiction of the Boston Municipal Court (BMC). However, all defendants had to report to the BMC for "arraignment" at the next scheduled session. Thus, "intake" was not "centralized" until the first judicial stage at which defendants were interviewed by BMC probation officers who conduct a record check, and then attend arraignment (which is held twice a day, weekdays). If they did not secure release as a result of the judge's bail decision at that stage, defendants were transferred to the Suffolk County Jail to await further proceedings.

In Maricopa County, booking procedures were heavily—if not totally—centralized. Most bookings occurred at the central jail location in Phoenix, at the same location where bail commissioners conducted initial appearances. Because of the very large distances between central Phoenix and the outlying towns in Maricopa County, some bookings occurred at police locations on the periphery of the county. Hence, most defendants were booked in the same building in which their initial appearance were to be held (three times a day, seven days a week) and were not released from custody until appearing before a superior court commissioner. If release was not secured, they were returned to the jail for further processing.

In Dade County, persons arrested for felony offenses were booked at the Dade County Pretrial Detention Center, which is located across the street from the criminal courts, where the bond hearing would occur. Interestingly, once the police finished with booking procedures, felony arrestees could gain immediate release by paying bond specified by a bond schedule, by making use of a bondsman, or by raising the required amount in other ways. If defendants did not gain release from jail at the booking stage, they were presented at the next bond hearing to a county court judge sitting in circuit court during weekdays or a circuit court judge if the arrest occurred on a weekend. (Bond hearings occurred twice daily, seven days a week). Defendants who did not gain release as a result of the bond hearing were returned to the jail to await further proceedings.

In Boston, a municipal court judge determined "bail" at "arraignment"; *bond* had a specific meaning designating special alternative financial arrangements equivalent to a particular bail amount. "Bondsmen" were very rarely in evidence. No "pretrial services" existed in Boston, although BMC Probation improvised several pretrial-services-like functions. In Dade County, "bail" was referred to as *bond,* which may be set according to the bond schedule or at the "bond hearing"; "bondsmen" may or may not be employed by the defendant to secure release. The "pretrial services" program in Dade County was a division of the corrections department with locations at the jail and the court. In Maricopa County, the superior court commissioner decided "pretrial release" at "initial appearance." This could involve nonfinancial release with particular "conditions of release" attached or "secured bond" (financial bail) with or without similar conditions. "Bondsmen" could be used as well in Maricopa County. The "pretrial services" program in Maricopa County was a division of court administration.

In Some Ways All Courts Are Similar

These structural, procedural, and local "cultural" differences notwithstanding, each system shares similarities with the others in the performance of bail and pretrial-release tasks. To put it simply, at some point, defendants are booked, presented to the judiciary, and may be released or detained pending adjudication—although not necessarily in that order. This similarity in the "things courts do" and the common focus on the deprivation of liberty permit some conceptual focus by allowing us to follow a similar strategy in each of the principal court systems. In each, the leadership of the courts assembled a working committee of judges and other related officials to participate in and to guide the guidelines research. The goal of these working committees ("Judicial Steering and Policy Committees") was to provide direction for the empirical investigation and "diagnosis" of the bail and pretrial-release decisionmaking apparatus, to surface policy issues of importance, and to shape, critique, and refine decision guidelines, when and if they emerged.

Thus, in Maricopa County, the presiding judge of the superior court convened a group to be chaired by the criminal presiding judge and to include a justice of the peace, court commissioners (who had bail responsibilities), a court administrator, and officials representing the pretrial services staff. In Dade County, a similar procedure was followed by the presiding judge. The criminal presiding judge chaired a working group of circuit and county court judges, the director of the pretrial services program, and the court's chief research officer. In Boston, the chief administrative justices of the Suffolk County Superior Court and the Boston Municipal Court convened separate committees to guide the guidelines research.

In its first phase, the goal of the process was to be descriptive and "diagnostic," educative as to the nature of bail practices and their impact, and to help surface key issues. In each of the research sites, data were collected describing a large number of defendants for whom bail decisions were made. Examination of their cases as they progressed into the criminal process and analysis of the decisions made about them as well as of their later outcomes provided the basis for a review of bail practices for a self-diagnosis and for discussion of particular features that the courts might wish to improve upon.

A brief description of the transaction of bail, pretrial release, and detention at each of the sites is presented in this chapter. The next chapters will focus in more depth on the special character of the findings at each site and on more in-depth analysis of bail decisionmaking and its effects.

Bail Decisions and Pretrial Release

Release at Booking and the Earliest Judicial Stage

Persons arrested on felony charges in Maricopa County did not have a means of gaining release at the booking stage. In Boston, in nearly half

(48 percent) of all cases during the period studied, arrested persons who were to be arraigned subsequently in municipal court gained release at the station house after booking. Dade County felony arrestees were able to post bond required by the bond schedule at the booking stage in about 20 percent of all cases.

In Boston and Maricopa County, all of the entering defendants had to appear before a judge (or judicial officer) at the first judicial stage (arraignment and initial appearance, respectively). In Dade County, only felony defendants who had not posted the bond amount noted on the bond schedule attended bond hearing in circuit court. In addition to the bond schedule releases (the 20 percent of entering cases noted above), an additional 1 percent of the studied defendants gained release before bond hearing because they were eligible for direct, administrative release by the pretrial services program.[1] In short, 79 percent of Dade felony defendants attended bond hearing to have bond determined by a judge.

In each of the jurisdictions, judges or commissioners employed financial bail (or bond), nonfinancial bail (personal recognizance release, or OR) and denied bond,[2] at the first judicial stage. Figure 6.1 depicts the use of these bail options among the three courts. Boston defendants were assigned nonfinancial release (ROR) in 69 percent of the cases, Dade defendants were given ROR 67 percent of the time, and Maricopa defendants were granted nonfinancial release in only 40 percent of the cases. Financial bail or bond was assigned most frequently in superior court (58 percent of the time) and notably less frequently in the other courts (30 percent of the time in circuit court and 29 percent of the time in the BMC). Denials of bail occurred in each court in 2 or 3 percent of the cases.

Even though bail or bond was used in similar proportions of cases in two of the courts, at least the financial option was used quite differently by each judiciary. Reflecting no doubt the large number of misdemeanor cases, the average (median) financial bail in the BMC, for example, was \$100. The median bond was \$3,750 in Dade County Circuit Court, however, but \$2,000 in Maricopa County Superior Court. This last difference is probably explained by the fact that, since financial bond is used so rarely in Dade County, it is relatively high when it is assigned. In Maricopa County, the superior court commissioners employ secured bond in a majority of cases but in lower amounts.

At arraignment in Boston Municipal Court, the judges assigned nonfinancial release 72 percent of the time, compared to 69 percent of the time in Dade County Circuit Court and only 41 percent of the time in Maricopa County Superior Court. Bail was rarely set in amounts over \$500 in Boston (3 percent of the cases). In Dade County, 6 percent of felony defendants were assigned bonds over \$10,000; such bonds were set 8 percent of the time in Maricopa County. Including ROR as \$0 bail, the median bail for

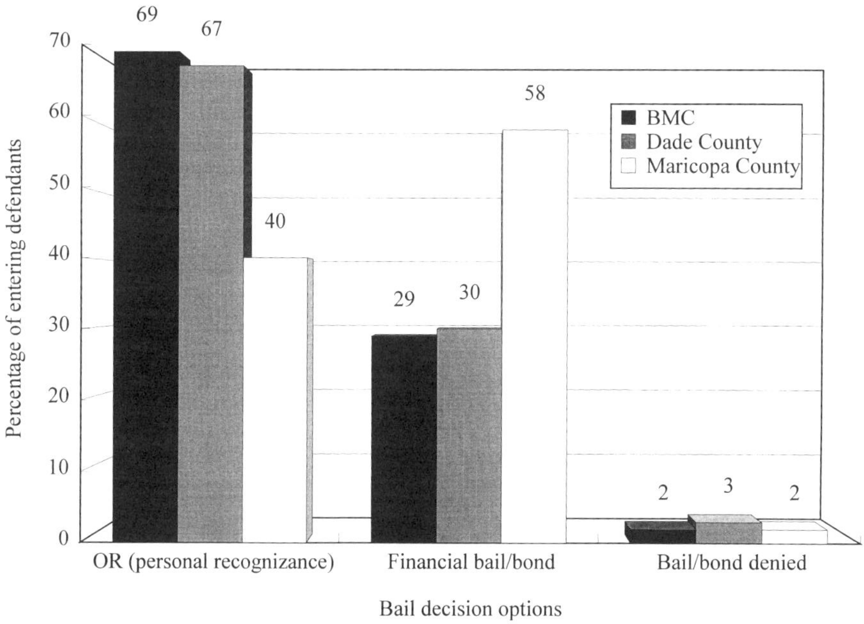

FIGURE 6.1. Use of bail decision options at first judicial stage in Boston Municipal Court, Dade County Circuit Court, and Maricopa County Superior Court, 1984.
Note: In Dade County, 20 percent of entering felony defendants secured release at booking prior to bond hearing (the first judicial stage).

Boston Municipal Court defendants was $0; for Dade defendants, it was $11; and for Maricopa defendants, it was $685.

Pretrial Release and Detention

The "bail" decision, how it is made, and its effects are at the heart of the guidelines research. However, one might choose to set aside the "niceties" of decisionmaking and ask, rather, what the results of the process were in terms of the release and detention of defendants and the performance of defendants who secured release. This is because, in most jurisdictions in the United States, the "bail" decision and the "release" or "detention" decision are not necessarily the same thing. Although judges in Boston, Dade, and Maricopa, may decide the release of defendants directly when selecting the personal recognizance (OR) option, they are not deciding detention directly when employing a financial option. Some defendants can afford release when bail is set at certain levels, and some cannot. Thus, while a judge may be hedging in the direction of making release unaffordable or affordable in particular cases, the release or detention outcome may be determined rather on the basis of a defendant's financial resources at the time of arrest.

Two useful ways of measuring pretrial detention and release among defendants entering the criminal process are (1) to determine release status shortly after the initial bail decisions, for example, within 24 hours of booking, or (2) to determine whether a defendant was ever released before the adjudication of his or her case.[3] Again, given the large number of misdemeanor cases entering the Boston court system and the frequent use of ROR and of low bails, it's not surprising that 78 percent of defendants gained release within 24 hours. Of the Dade felony defendants, 60 percent did, but only 45 percent of the felony defendants in superior court in Maricopa County gained release within 24 hours. Of BMC defendants, 94 percent were released within 90 days or prior to the adjudication of their cases; 80 percent in Dade ultimately secured pretrial release; and 55 percent of Maricopa defendants were released before trial.

Figure 6.2 compares the timing of release of defendants before trial in the three court systems. In each of the jurisdictions, the bulk of the releases that occurred had been effectuated within the first 24 hours or so. The initial "burst" of release in Maricopa was changed only very slightly and gradually, so that between 1 day and 90 days only an additional 10 percent of defendants gained pretrial release. In Boston and Dade County, that proportion of defendants was added to those released between Day 1 and Day 7. In Boston, a release rate of nearly 90 percent was reached initially and could be little improved upon through the remainder of the 90-day period of observation. In Dade County, still another 10 percent were released between the one-week and four-week mark, although the maximum release of 80 percent of felony defendants appears to have been reached by then and changed little after that.

Even in Boston, where at least a small number of defendants spend time in jail before trial, detention is brought about through the vehicle of cash bail. In fact, just the fact that the judge resorts to a financial bail increases the chances that the defendant will probably spend some time in detention. Of defendants for whom a cash bail was set, 58 percent were released within one day in Boston, 11 percent in Dade County, and 10 percent in Phoenix. Of Boston's financial defendants, 86 percent gained release within 90 days; only 51 percent of Dade County's financial bond defendants and 25 percent of Maricopa defendants gained release within that period. Interestingly, the average (median) bail paid by financial defendants securing release in the 1984 study varied across jurisdictions as well: The median posted bail in Boston was $100; in Dade, it was $4,000; and in Maricopa, it was $1,600.

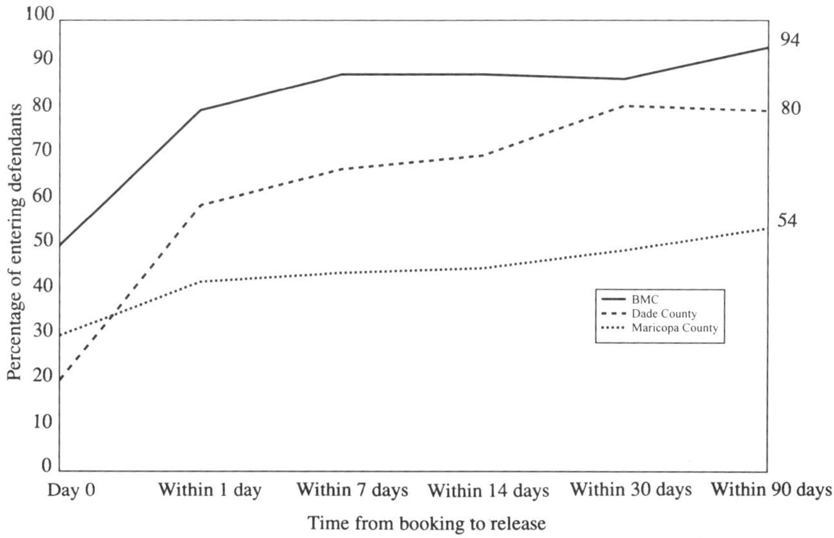

FIGURE 6.2. Days until release in Boston Municipal Court, Dade County Circuit Court, and Maricopa County Superior Court: Cumulative percentage of defendants released during 90 days following booking.

In Maricopa County, even bails under $500 appear to have caused the detention of a majority of defendants. In Boston and Dade, it required bails of over $500 to hold a majority of defendants, at least for some period. In Dade County, bonds of over $1,000 served to hold 9 out of 10 defendants in detention.

Detention as a Dynamic Measure: The Context of Case Processing

Although these two measures of the use of pretrial detention among entering criminal defendants are helpful in comparing the pretrial processing of cases in the three court systems, each measure has limitations. A more accurate picture of the detention resulting from bail decisionmaking may be important when considered in the context of the processing of cases within each of the courts.

For example, the measure of release throughout the pretrial period (through 90 days or until adjudication, whichever comes sooner) may be very misleading, depending upon the extent to which a jurisdiction disposes of cases prior to 90 days. The rate of adjudication (within 90 days) among the courts differed notably. The quickest pace was found in superior court in Maricopa County, where 89 percent of entering felony cases were adjudicated within 90 days of booking; 66 percent of the circuit court cases in Dade and 54 percent of Boston Municipal Court cases were completed within that period. Alternatively stated, after 90 days, only 11 percent of the caseload remained in the adjudicatory process in Maricopa County; 33 percent remained in Dade County; and 46 percent remained unresolved in Boston Municipal Court.

In each jurisdiction, a larger proportion of the cases of detained defendants than of released defendants was adjudicated within 90 days (see Figure 6.3). The difference in adjudication rates between detained and released defendants was greatest in Boston (53 percent of released vs. 76 percent of detained), was noticeable in Dade County (64 percent vs. 78 percent), and was slight in Maricopa County (87 percent vs. 93 percent). Several interpretations can be made of this finding. First, one might assume that this is evidence of "expedited" handling of the cases of detained defendants, a principle espoused in a number of recent laws.[4] Or second, one might conclude that detention brings about the conclusion of many cases, either as a pressure on the defendant to plead or as an incentive to agree to time served in exchange for release. In any event, these findings suggest that the magnitude of detention may be overestimated when measured in the manner we have chosen: Many cases are detained through their pretrial periods, but often these periods fall short of 90 days.

We also examined the frequency with which cases were completely "dropped" (dismissed by the judge, dropped by the prosecutor, or otherwise discharged) prior to 90 days. Dropped or dismissed cases further point to detention periods shorter than 90 days as well as detention that may have been inappropriate. (To the extent that the system has detained people whose cases are later dropped from the process, the use of detention in the first place may be questioned, at least using hindsight.[5])

We found a low dropout rate in the Boston Municipal Court (occurring in only 13 percent of the cases), but rather high rates in Dade County (47 percent) and Maricopa County (54 percent). That is, roughly half of entering felony defendants in Dade County and Maricopa County dropped out within 90 days of booking. The rates of dropout varied little by custody status in the jurisdictions. Nevertheless, one may conclude that a large number of detained defendants in two jurisdictions ultimately had their charges dropped or their cases dismissed.[6]

From the findings relating to the early adjudication of defendants' cases in each of the jurisdictions, we can draw the inference that many defendants who are detained "throughout their pretrial periods" are spending less than 90 days in confinement. The average (median) number of days spent in confinement by those detained in the three jurisdictions differed considerably: In Boston and Dade County, the median stays were relatively brief (13 and 20 days, respectively); in Maricopa County, the

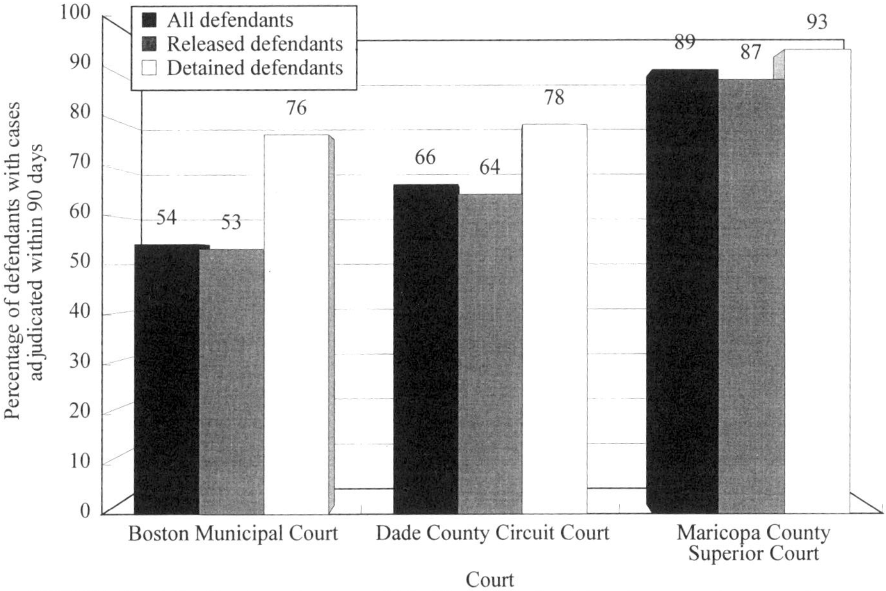

FIGURE 6.3. Adjudication of cases within 90 days of booking, by court, by custody status, 1984.

median stay of superior court detainees was 90 days. We may conclude that detention among Boston Municipal Court and Dade County detainees was shorter term, but that detention in Maricopa County was longer term, averaging roughly four times longer.[7]

Still a simpler measure of the pervasiveness of detention among entering criminal defendants at the three sites is to compare the jail days associated with their processing. Defendants entering the system through the municipal court in Boston and the circuit court in Dade County averaged 4.4 and 11.2 days in jail per defendant. Yet, in Maricopa County, the average was 42.7 days in jail per defendant. It was perhaps predictable that the Boston defendants would average the smallest amount of time in jail, considering the predominantly misdemeanor nature of their criminal charges. Particularly striking, however, was the large difference between the average jail times of Dade and Maricopa defendants, given the roughly comparable makeup of their criminal caseloads.

The Performance of Defendants during Pretrial Release: Flight and Rearrest

Despite the considerable variation in detention practices among the three jurisdictions (ranging from detention of 6 percent of entering defendants in Boston to 20 percent in Dade County and 45 percent in Maricopa County), a majority of defendants did gain release prior to adjudication of their cases. Figure 6.4 contrasts the performance of released defendants in municipal, circuit, and superior courts. During the period studied, Boston defendants who gained release failed to appear (FTA) in court 2.5 times as often as Maricopa defendants (who failed to appear 8 percent of the time) and twice as often as Dade defendants (who missed court 10 percent of the time).[8] Boston defendants also recorded slightly higher rearrest rates than the other two court systems; 13 percent were rearrested in Boston compared to 11 percent in Maricopa and 7 percent in Dade. Not more than 2 percent of released defendants were rearrested for "serious" crimes against the person at any of the sites.[9] When flight and crime measures are combined to form a general measure of misconduct during pretrial release, Dade defendants appeared to perform best overall: Only 15 percent failed to appear and/or were rearrested; Maricopa defendants "failed" 17 percent of the time; and Boston Municipal Court defendants performed most poorly, failing at roughly twice the rate of the other two jurisdictions (at 33 percent).

In the aggregate, these descriptive characteristics of our three sites establish the two themes noted at the outset of this chapter. The early

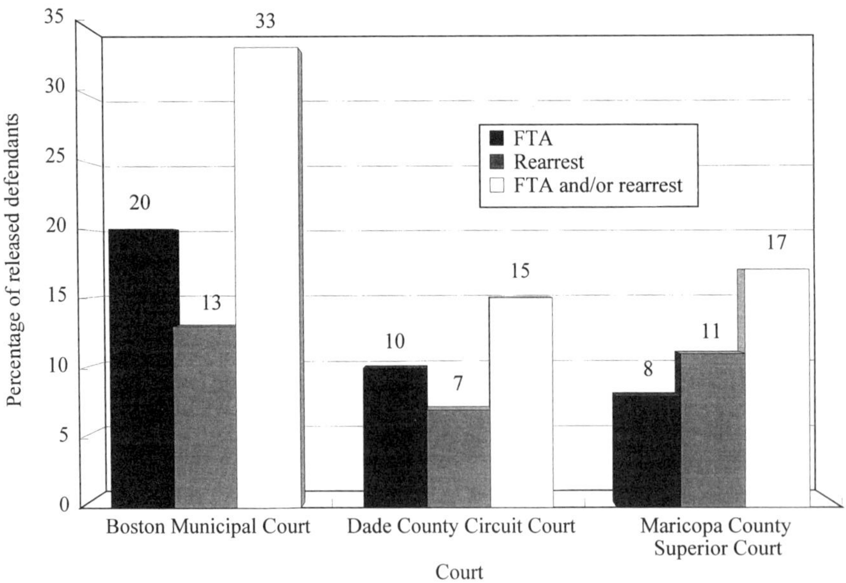

FIGURE 6.4. Defendant misconduct during pretrial release (failures to appear, rearrests, either or both), by court, 1984.

stages of the judicial process, from arrest to pleading, have commonalities regardless of jurisdiction. The bail decision under study has significant deprivation-of-liberty implications regardless of the court system. It also has implications for community safety and the integrity of the court system itself, although at substantially different levels depending on jurisdiction. The demonstration site courts also differed considerably in some ways relevant to the issue of guidelines: in time, in cases, in preferred release mechanisms, in detention levels, and so forth. The similarities suggest that guidelines may be appropriate; the differences present a challenge to their utility and acceptability. These differences must be kept firmly in mind as we now turn to a detailed study of the decisionmaking in the three courts.

Notes

1. By administrative order, the circuit court authorizes defendants charged with nonviolent offenses and having no prior convictions for violent offenses to be released directly by pretrial services.
2. The samples excluded categories of defendants for whom bond and thereby release could be routinely denied by statute. The denials of bail referred to in this instance were not provided for by statute; rather they reflected some informal denial policy, for example, concerning probation detainers or bench warrants followed within the courts.
3. The rationale behind use of the first measure is that it reflects the impact of the bail decision, while the second measure adds the effects of the system's other opportunities for release and review not directly tied to the initial bail decision. The second measure, release or detention within 90 days or prior to adjudication, whichever is sooner, is sometimes difficult to interpret. A defendant detained for 90 days (as long as his or her case has not been completed) will be considered detained under this measure, just as a defendant who was confined for two weeks and then had her or his case adjudicated.
4. See Goldkamp (1985, Figure 9, and accompanying text).
5. See Dan Freed's "imbalance ratio" (Feeley, 1979).
6. In Maricopa County, a large share of the early "dropouts" may be accounted for by the prosecutorial practice of "scratching" cases within the first 48 to 72 hours, often to be refiled by the prosecutor at a later date. The scratching or dropping of charges at this time results from the fact that the prosecutor does not routinely review criminal charges until several days after a defendant has been arrested. Cases are scratched when it appears that there is not enough evidence to support the prosecution of charges at that time. In Dade County, a similar phenomenon, but extending to 14 days, occurs because there is no routine indictment or preliminary hearing process to screen charges; rather, the prosecutor produces the information that serves as the basis of formal processing. As a result, a large number of cases are dropped at approximately the 14-day limit and/or a sizable number are transferred to county court for processing as misdemeanor cases.
7. We should note that the median days in confinement has an artificial ceiling of 90 days because of the approach taken in the research. We followed the progress of defendants' cases only up to 90 days to determine whether pretrial release was secured. If the defendant had not been released by that time and still had not had his or her case

adjudicated, no further effort was made to check for release before trial because of limitations of time and resources. Of course, many defendants may have been detained for longer periods—thus the odd-appearing finding that the median length of detention in Maricopa County among detainees was 90 days.

8. A "failure to appear" (FTA) was recorded in the study when a bench warrant (or *alias capiases* in Dade County) was issued for missing a required court appearance. Actual rates of failure to appear might have been higher if "unintentional" failures were included. For example, in Boston, 28 percent of released defendants missed a court appearance, although warrants were issued only for 20 percent. In each study, once it was determined that defendants had gained release, they were followed for 90 days or until their charges had been adjudicated, if earlier, to see if FTAs or arrests on new charges had occurred.
9. Serious rearrests include rearrests for the following kinds of offenses: murder, voluntary manslaughter, involuntary deviate sexual intercourse, forcible rape, statutory rape, robbery, kidnapping, aggravated assault, assault by a prisoner, arson with personal injury, and battery. Of course, the terminology describing criminal offenses varies from jurisdiction to jurisdiction; thus, by "serious offenses," we mean these offenses or their closest equivalents.

7

The Nature of Bail Decisionmaking in Maricopa County

Conceptual Issues about the Decision

We have already described some features of the defendants and their cases entering the three court systems. In Chapter 6, we briefly contrasted the decisions made about each cohort of defendants and their detention or release outcomes. We found differences among the sites in the characteristics of defendants entering the court systems and in the kinds of offenses with which they had been charged. In reviewing the bail decisions made regarding the entering defendants and the subsequent use of pretrial release and detention, we again noted key differences—even between Dade and Maricopa counties, the jurisdictions with the most similar felony caseloads. For example, although the Boston Municipal Court generated the highest rate of release among its heavily misdemeanant caseload, it also produced by far the highest rates of defendant misconduct during pretrial release. Circuit court in Dade County managed to release 80 percent of its felony defendants before trial and yet still succeeded in producing, of the three sites, the lowest flight and crime rates among defendants on pretrial release. Finally, the Superior Court in Maricopa County released dramatically fewer defendants than its companion courts, about half the proportion of defendants released by the Dade court. However, the frequent resort to pretrial detention in that jurisdiction did not produce misconduct rates that were even as good as those found in Dade County.

Beginning with this chapter, our objective is to focus more directly on the pretrial release decisionmaking generating these phenomena in each of the courts individually. To accomplish this, we begin with an attempt to define what we mean by the bail or pretrial-release decision, so that we have a common conceptual framework for analysis. Then, on the basis of large samples, we report on the results of statistical analyses designed to "predict" or "explain" pretrial release decisions made by judges and commissioners in each of the court systems. We then turn to detailed consideration of the consequences of pretrial release decisionmaking, the use of pretrial detention and release, and the performance of defendants gaining pretrial release. In this chapter, we examine decisionmaking in superior court in Maricopa County; in the next two chapters, we turn to practices in circuit court in Dade County and municipal court in Boston.

In analyzing bail decisions in each of the courts, we collected data that judges (and commissioners in Maricopa County) would have had available at the time of the bail task. (Of course, we made use of subsequent information to chart the later outcomes of the cases in which decisions had been made.) The purpose of these analyses was to discover patterns or regularities in decisionmaking associated with particular attributes of defendants or their cases. The assumption is that if patterns can be found in the types of variables used by these decisionmakers, then these patterns might represent important policy themes that implicitly guide the judges or commissioners in the setting of bail. The presence or absence of such patterns would provide the basis for a review of practice and discussion of policy among court officials, particularly when combined with the findings characterizing pretrial practices and case processing in each of the courts.

As a first step in the descriptive phase of guidelines development in each court, it was necessary to decide upon a useful way of conceptualizing the bail or pretrial-release decision. In the introduction to this book, we explained how the terms *bail, bond,* and *pretrial release* are often confused. The semantic confusion we described had its local variations in the parlance of the site courts. (For example, in Maricopa County, what was referred to as *bail* had a narrow, technical meaning, tied to use of property as assurance, and *secured bond* or *bailbond* was employed to refer to general financial conditions—which were known as *bail* in Boston and Philadelphia.) Because the technical "labels" were tied to how the decision function was conceptualized by judges, their meanings had to be addressed and incorporated from the outset.[1] Although perhaps an academic undertaking in its own right, the choice of a working model of the bail task for the purposes of guidelines development was accomplished through analysis and discussion with the judges at each of the separate sites. Although, on its face, the bail decision might not appear overly complex, theoretically at least it could be conceived of in different ways.

First, there was debate even within courts and among decisionmakers over the appropriate goals of the bail decision. In each of the states where the research was conducted, a provision authorizing consideration of the potential danger posed by a defendant could be found in the state law; the authorization was for broad consideration in Arizona and Florida but was strictly limited in Massachusetts law. In all three states, a main theme of the bail task was to ensure the attendance of defendants in court. Individual judges and court systems as a whole, therefore, varied according to the degree they considered either or both of these goals.

Beyond questions of appropriate goals, a working model of the bail task may be viewed in different ways. For example, is the bail decision a pretrial-release or detention decision or a (mostly financial) bond decision, of which release or detection is often the inadvertent result? Is the bail decision a simple single-choice decision? Or is it a decision consisting of contingent step-wise considerations?

As Figure 7.1 illustrates, several theoretical conceptualizations of the bail decision are possible and were considered by the judicial working groups in each location. Figure 7.1 displays, for example, four of the principal alternatives:

1. *Bail as a simple choice of a financial amount.* Under this alternative, the judge's task is relatively straightforward, involving only the choice of a financial amount ranging from ROR ($0) to any financial amount imaginable.

2. *Bail as a two-step choice.* Under this model, the judge performs a two-stage conceptual task. The initial "screening" stage involves a decision on whether a defendant is a nonfinancial or a financial candidate. At the second stage, if the defendant is a nonfinancial candidate, the judge may next decide whether or not any conditions ought to be attached to release, such as supervision or drug treatment. If the defendant is considered an appropriate financial candidate, the second stage consists of selecting a particular amount of financial bond.

3. *Bail as deciding release under the least restrictive conditions.* Another conceptualization derives from the laws of many states, the District of Columbia, and the federal jurisdiction and establishes a presumption that defendants should be released under the least restrictive conditions that ensure their appearance and minimize their threat to the community. Thus, a first task would be to decide whether or not a defendant can be released outright, on a mere promise to appear. If this would not satisfy the judge's perception of the risk posed by the defendant, he or she would then consider and/or reject options involving increasing restrictions on

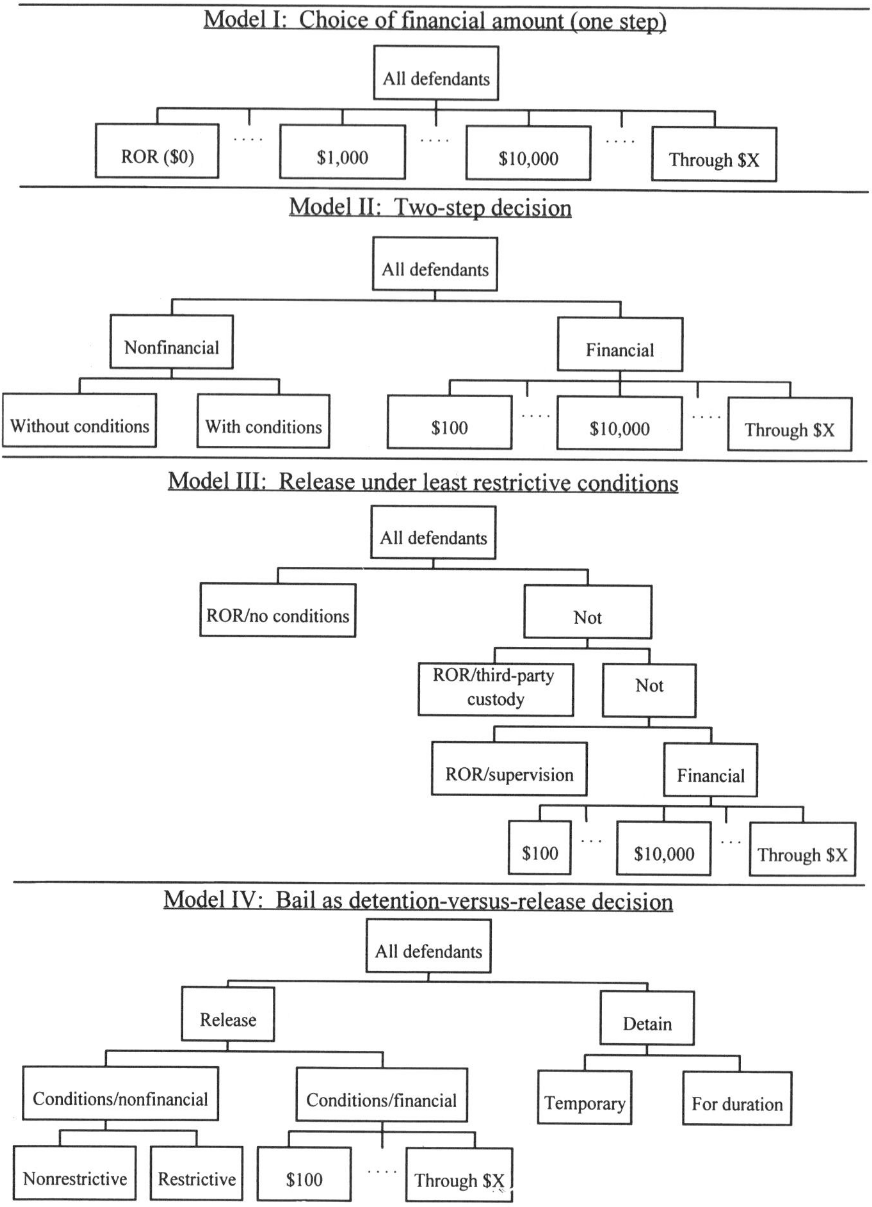

FIGURE 7.1. Alternative conceptualizations of bail/release decisions.

the defendant's liberty, such as third-party custody or supervision by a pretrial services program or a probation department. Resort to financial bond would be considered a comparatively drastic (and restrictive) decision choice. In some states, the judge can consider outright detention of the defendant after having rejected release under lesser options.[2]

4. *Bail as a detention versus release decision*. Finally, judges may make an outright detention-versus-release decision in each case. If the choice follows the theoretical model of the bail task outlined in the revised law governing pretrial release in the District of Columbia and in the recent federal legislation, the judge determines whether a defendant should be released or detained quite directly, in a first step. In a second step, the judge selects conditions of release, if any are to apply, or decides whether to detain the defendant temporarily (as when probation or parole violations or medical exams are involved) or for the full pretrial period. It can be argued, of course, that bail setting in traditional practice has followed this version, although in a *sub rosa* fashion. That is, judges have manipulated financial bail to set it either within or outside the reach of a defendant's ability to post it to cause his or her release or confinement.

These models of how the bail decision may be reached were discussed with the judicial working committees at each site until, in conjunction with analyses of the decisionmaking data, one version was chosen to serve as the vehicle for discussion and further analyses. Once a model could be agreed upon, analysis focused on explanation of the decisions made by the judges and commissioners.

Agreeing on a Working Model for Maricopa County

To begin examination of bail decisionmaking in superior court, we analyzed data describing 2,200 Maricopa County felony cases entering the system between the beginning of June and the end of July 1984. To find a working model of the bail task in Maricopa County—referred to there as the *pretrial release decision*—data were organized as if to comport with the four models depicted in Figure 7.1. Multivariate analyses were conducted to determine whether knowledge of defendant or case characteristics could explain variability in the various decisions or decision stages.[3]

The model subdividing the bail decision into consideration of the least restrictive release options in a sequential fashion (Model III) received little empirical support.[4] The model portraying the decision as a direct choice between release and detention (Model IV) was not regarded by the working committee as an intuitively justified representation of the way decisions were made, although it appeared to receive strong empirical support.[5] (Although this model may not have been viewed as accurately evoking the commissioners' conceptualization of the bail task, the release-versus-detention outcome may represent the effect of the commissioners' decisions quite well, and it is discussed in the next section.)

In a technical sense, both Model I and a modified version of Model II received strong empirical support, since defendant attributes or case characteristics were able to "explain" roughly 90 percent of the variance in decision choices. Analysis of Model II, the two-step version of the pretrial release decision, showed strong results in the first stage, where nonfinancial (ROR) versus financial (secured-bond) options were considered. In the second step, when the choice was to decide whether to assign conditions of release among nonfinancial defendants, the solution was decidedly weak. When the choice was an amount of secured bond, regression was moderately successful.

Because it appeared that little systematic differentiation among defendants was detectable in the second-stage, nonfinancial–condition decision, we concluded that the conditions or no-conditions subdecision would not play a role in a working model of the pretrial release task. The judicial committee concurred in this view; they argued that the first model (Model I) was perhaps too simplistic a framework and that they felt comfortable on an intuitive level with the modified version of Model II.

Factors Explaining Bail Choices in Maricopa County

Not surprisingly, it was found that variables explaining the bail decision in Maricopa County under Model I—as the simple choice of cash amounts (from ROR or $0 to any dollar amount)—were generally the same as those explaining the bail decision as a two-stage operation. The components of the two-step model, however, seemed to be influenced by different emphases and thus reflected qualitatively different decision concerns (see Table 7.1).

Defendants were more likely to be considered suitable candidates for nonfinancial than financial options when they had no outstanding warrants, were longer-term residents of Maricopa County, had no prior arrests, were not viewed by the police as posing risks of flight, had earned wages during the previous year, had not been charged with offenses involving use of a weapon, had no prior felony conviction, did not live alone, and, finally, were recommended for nonfinancial release by the pretrial services program. Thus, the "ROR decision" appeared influenced by "community ties" as well as some charge and prior-history variables. The selection of amounts of secured bond for defendants viewed as finan-

TABLE 7.1

Factors Influential in Commissioners' Decisions at Initial Appearance for Entering Felony Defendants (from Regression Analysis) Using Model I (Choice of Bail Amounts) and Model II (Two-Step Decision), Maricopa County[a] Superior Court, June–July, 1984

Model of pretrial release decision	Influential factors (explanatory variables)	r^2	Significance
Model 1			
Simple choice of financial amounts ($0 through any amount) ($n$ = 2,179)	Outstanding warrants		
	Police: risk of flight		
	Length of residence		
	Recent prior arrests		
	Robbery charges		
	Any sexual assault victims		
	Reported wages		
	Weapons used		
	Prior convictions/felonies		
	Lives alone	.34	<.00
	Nonfinancial recommendation[b]	.86	<.00
Model 2			
Two-step decision			
1. Choice of nonfinancial or financial options (n = 2,188)	Outstanding warrants		
	Length of residence		
	Recent prior arrests		
	Police: risk of flight		
	Reported wages		
	Weapons used		
	Prior convictions/felonies		
	Lives alone	.29	<.00
	Nonfinancial recommendation[b]	.90	<.00
2a. If nonfinancial: conditions versus no conditions of release (n = 892)	Drug-related offense		
	Defendant under 21		
	Present address in Maricopa		
	Number of victims		
	Length of residence	.07	<.00
	Nonfinancial recommendation[b]	.07	<.00
2b. If financial: selection of amount (n = 1,296)	Severity of most severe booking charge		
	Any sexual assault victims		
	Robbery charges		
	Police: risk of flight		
	Number of charges		
	Alcohol- or drug-related charge		
	Weaons used	.40	<.00
	Employment status	.40	<.00
	Nonfinancial recommendation[b]		

[a]Logit analyses were conducted to analyze Model II, Steps 1 and 2a. Under Model II, Step 1, the following factors fit the data well: outstanding warrants, length of residence, recent prior arrests, police noting risk of flight, and pretrial services recommendation for nonfinancial release (goodness of fit chi-sq. 83.69; degrees of freedom 127, P value .999). Without pretrial service recommendation, the logit model is not significant.

[b]The contribution of this variable to the explanation of variance when entered last may be estimated by subtracting the r^2 without the variable from the total r^2.

cial candidates, however, appeared more heavily oriented to considerations of the seriousness of the charges. These findings of different emphases in the ROR and financial choices correspond to findings in previous research that have been interpreted as reflecting a greater public safety or danger orientation among decisionmakers when financial bail is employed.

In several respects, these findings are of special note. In reviewing and interpreting them, the superior court commissioners appeared comfortable with the suggestion that these attributes of defendants and their cases played a primary role in their bail determinations. There was some surprise, however, as well as a little disbelief, in the finding that the police notation on the arrest report that the defendant was believed to pose a risk of flight was taken seriously by them. Although some admitted that they viewed the police information seriously, other commissioners stated that police officers generally viewed defendants as poor risks and almost always made that notation, and that this practice would cause them to view the notation with some skepticism.

Two findings, taken together, however, were of more important consequence for the guidelines research. The first was that, by statistical standards, and considering previous research, the power of the regression solutions—the ability to explain nearly 90 percent of the variance in decision choices made by the commissioners in superior court by using knowledge of eight or nine kinds of information about a defendant or his or her case—was extraordinary. (Usually, such analyses report explaining no more than 40 to 50 percent of the variance.) Ordinarily, such a successful analysis would permit the conclusion that we have rather certainly identified the factors that judges or commissioners rely on in making their decisions. Discussion in the working committee could now consider the policy implications of this result.

A second striking finding was the relative importance—indeed, dominance—of one piece of information: the recommendation of the pretrial services interviewer to the commissioner for either nonfinancial or financial bond. Of the 86 percent of variance explained in the analysis of the bail decision as a simple choice of financial amounts (Model I), knowledge of the pretrial services recommendation contributed 52 percent when entered last (i.e., when the effects of other relevant factors were controlled for). Of the 91 percent of variance explained in the analysis of the choice between nonfinancial and financial options, 61 percent was contributed by the pretrial services recommendation after controlling for other relationships. Stated another way, without knowledge of the pretrial services recommendation for ROR or secured bond in defendants' cases, we would have been able to report rather modest and tentative findings.

The Importance of the Pretrial Services Recommendation in the Commissioners' Pretrial Release Decisions

Without knowing much else, if we could know the staff's recommendation concerning nonfinancial or financial bond, we would make few mistakes in guessing what the commissioners subsequently decided. An examination of the data revealed that the commissioners' nonfinancial pretrial-release decisions, for example, agreed with the recommendations made by pretrial services in more than 96 percent of all cases. Moreover, given the recommendation of a secured-bond option, the odds were rather small that the defendant would secure release either within the next 24 hours or within 90 days. The secured-bond recommendation translated into a high probability that a defendant would be detained, other things being equal. Because of the apparent influence of the recommendations on initial-appearance decisionmaking, discussion in the superior court judicial working committee focused on looking for an explanation.

In trying to understand why the pretrial services recommendation appeared so influential, we considered several explanations:

1. The commissioners valued the recommendation highly because it represented an objective evaluation of defendants according to explicit screening criteria agreed upon by the commissioners. From an empirical perspective, this explanation would assume that known kinds of information (such as prior flight and prior record) would play a predictable part in an analysis of recommendations. If, for example, defendants with no local ties and with prior records of flight and long prior criminal histories of arrest were routinely "scored" in such a way by pretrial services that they were consistently not recommended for nonfinancial release, then defendant flight, local ties, and arrests would emerge as "predictors" of recommendations for ROR. This would in turn explain why the pretrial services recommendation had emerged as such a powerful predictor of commissioners' decisions.

2. An alternative hypothesis suggests that the recommendation was valued highly by commissioners in part because of the high regard they had for the independent (subjective) judgment of the pretrial services staff who interviewed defendants and reviewed background information before making up the recommendations. This explanation recognizes that the judgment—and therefore recommendations—of different interviewers could vary from staff member to staff member. Thus, for example, interviewers working on the night shifts might have been more conservative about their recommendations simply because it was more difficult for them to verify the information they were receiving. Or recommendations

could vary with the predilections and antipathies of individual interviewers as they reacted to criminal cases they confronted. A statistical analysis in this case would find that known criteria would be unlikely consistently to "explain" pretrial services recommendations, as the different interviewers reacted differently to information. Rather, recommendations would depend most often on the "recommender."

3. A third explanation also assumes that the pretrial services recommending process is subjective. This hypothesis does not explain the high rate of agreement between recommendations and commissioner decisions on the basis of high regard for the independent judgment of the pretrial services staff but sees the phenomenon as being the result of an accommodation of staff to decisionmaker. More specifically, perhaps pretrial services interviewers, having worked closely with the six commissioners over long periods, had learned to anticipate the ways in which their subjective recommendations would be received. For example, Staffer X might know that Commissioner Y would never entertain granting ROR in a case involving drunken driving. Over time, Staffer X has learned instead to recommend secured bond in those cases. Commissioner Y receives the recommendation he expects and, as a result, almost always agrees with it.

To determine which explanation was most likely, we examined the recommendations of the pretrial services staff much as we had examined the commissioners' decisions. We attempted to learn if we could predict recommendations (i.e., whether there was a recommendation for nonfinancial versus financial bond) using all the various items of information we had available. Unfortunately, not having anticipated this finding, we had not recorded the identity of each of the interviewers making recommendations.

What we found was that we were able to "explain" recommendation decisions rather modestly based on knowledge of the following kinds of defendant or case attributes:[6]

- Arrests within the last three years
- Length of residence in Maricopa County
- Outstanding warrants
- Prior felony convictions
- Living arrangements (alone or with others)
- Wages last year
- Robbery-related charges
- Prior misdemeanor convictions

To the extent that patterns governing the recommendations could be detected, it appeared that pretrial services interviewers were relying on apparently relevant kinds of information regarding the kinds of charges involved, the defendant's prior history, local ties, and income. When pretrial services staff were asked about the results, they agreed that, while no explicit screening criteria were employed to screen defendants systematically, interviewers were instructed to take these kinds of criteria into account in making their subjective recommendations. In fact, these are factors similar to those listed in the Arizona statutes and considered by judges and pretrial services programs in other parts of the country.

Thus recommendations were found to follow some, although weak, themes and could not be described as wholly random. However, it is also notable that—in terms of multiple-regression results—two-thirds of the variance went unexplained. This finding suggests either that recommendations were to a large extent athematic (random) or that we had failed to consider important information that could have increased our ability to account for the variability in recommendations. Given the large number of descriptors of defendants and their cases that were examined, this latter explanation is unlikely with a single exception. We did not record the identity of individual staff "recommenders," and it is possible that this information would have added substantially to our ability to predict recommendations. Had this been so, we would have been left with the conclusion that the recommendations depended substantially on the recommenders. This analysis does call into question the soundness of our initial hypothesis concerning the relationship between recommendations and commissioners' decisions: Explicit, consistently applied criteria were not found to govern objective recommendation policy.

From another angle, we could have asked whether, after controlling for the effects of the explaining variables listed above, analysis of commissioners' decisions indicated that the recommendation itself contributed powerfully to explaining outcomes in initial-appearance decisions. Here we were asking what effect the "unexplainable" part of the pretrial services recommendation had on the commissioners' decisions. When this analysis was carried out, we still found that, independent of other concerns, the pretrial services recommendation was the single dominant influence (see Table 7.1). Further analysis showed that, after controlling for these eight factors in analysis of commissioners' decisions, the powerful influence of the pretrial services recommendation remained (Table 7.1, Model 2, Step 1).

We conclude that the influence of the pretrial services recommendation was to a certain extent unique, not explained by available information, and relied on by commissioners at least partly as a recommendation (judgment) *per se*. While we have empirical evidence that emphasizes the highly subjective nature of the recommending function, we are not able to shed light on the second or third explanations above. That is, we cannot say whether commissioners were relying strongly on the largely unguided judgment of the pretrial services interviewers or whether the agreement between the two was the result of a flexible accommodation to commissioners' preferences by pretrial services recommenders.

This finding has important implications. Beyond their summary of information collected through the interview of defendants, the judgment of the pretrial services staff who prepared the recommendations for initial appearance played an important role in the commissioners' decisions. The recommendation heavily influenced the decision to place defendants in a nonfinancial versus financial (secured) bond category. However, it appeared to have little influence on the particular amount of secured bond chosen by the commissioners. Thus, where there was no recommendation to guide them, commissioners exercised more discretion and, as we see in the next section, produced decisions that varied considerably among them.

The Role of Charge Seriousness in Pretrial Release Decisions

The lack of influence of the seriousness of the charged offense on pretrial release determinations was unexpected. Although judicial reliance on the seriousness of the defendants' charges has been criticized in legal commentary concerning bail practices in the United States over the last 25 years, most previous research has nevertheless shown this factor to be the most powerful influence in initial-appearance decisions.[7] Charge seriousness did not appear to play the expected dominant role in Maricopa County release determinations that it has appeared to play in other jurisdictions. In the analysis of the pretrial services recommendation, the only charge-related factor to play even a marginal role was whether or not robbery charges were involved in the defendant's case. This may indicate a concern about seriousness on the part of the interviewers, or it may indicate a concern about a certain kind of charge. Overall, the general seriousness of the defendant's charges did not appear to be a dominant factor.

In our analysis of Model I, more charge-related measures appeared to figure into commissioners' decisions: the presence of robbery charges, of crimes with a victim of sexual violence, and of weapons charges. Although these factors point to the presence of charges for serious offenses, they reflect not general seriousness, but "kind-of-offense" concerns.

In Model II, in which the commissioners conceptually first sorted defendants into nonfinancial versus secured-bond categories, only the presence of weapons charges appeared to enter into the first decision step. However, in the second decision step, in which commissioners selected an amount of secured bond, nothing but charge severity (as measured by the statutory grading of offenses) played an influential role. After the statutory-ranking-of-charge measure (clearly an overall severity measure), most of the other factors importantly related to the selection of bond amounts seemed to reflect the presence or absence of various serious charges (see Table 7.1).

The surprising finding is that, unlike in other jurisdictions studied, the seriousness of the current charges was not the sole or dominant factor that commissioners relied on. Instead, they appeared to rely on the pretrial services recommendation, which we have seen was not dominated by the seriousness of the charged offense.[8]

Different Treatment of Similar Defendants Based on the Commissioner Presiding at Initial Appearance

Earlier research in Philadelphia suggested that, after taking into consideration other relevant factors, bail decisions varied significantly by judge. Particularly in the use of financial options, a defendant's bond depended on which official was presiding at initial appearance. In Maricopa, where initial-appearance responsibilities were handled by 5 commissioners (as opposed to 20 judges, as in Philadelphia), we also found a role for decisionmaker variation after controlling for other factors.

In the Model I framework, which conceptualizes the commissioner's choice as selection of a dollar amount, knowledge of the presiding commissioner contributed significantly (in a statistical sense) but not importantly to prediction of the initial-appearance decisions. In the two-step format (Model II), the presiding commissioner variable was not significant in the first-step decision (dividing defendants into financial versus nonfinancial groupings) but was significant in the second step, involving the selection of cash amounts. After other factors were held constant, knowledge of which commissioner was presiding increased our ability to account for variability in cash amount decisions by approximately 25 percent.

Apparently, commissioners tended to be consistent when they had recommendations to follow in choosing between ROR and secured bond, but they tended to act much less consistently in similar cases when, unguided, the task was to select amounts of secured bond. Because it is through secured bond that detention is achieved, this finding of decisionmaker disparity had important implications for the allocation of pretrial detention.

Pretrial Detention or Release Resulting from Initial Appearance

The commissioners did not entirely agree with the model of decisionmaking that assumed that the pretrial decision was, at least implicitly, a detention versus release decision. For the sake of argument, however, and because of the important impact of the pretrial release decision, we considered the initial-appearance decision tantamount to a choice of release versus confinement for felony defendants. This is perfectly reasonable because, in fact, a large share of pretrial release was determined directly when a commissioner assigned a nonfinancial release.

The data show that roughly 40 percent of felony defendants were released on nonfinancial conditions at initial appearance, that 47 percent overall gained release within 48 hours, and that 55 percent overall gained release prior to adjudication of their cases. Thus, a large majority (89 percent) of initial releases were a result of OR release at initial appearance, and almost three-quarters (73 percent) of all releases (early or later) were OR releases. It appears that because so few secured-bond defendants were released, the commissioner's resort to secured bond was tantamount to a detention decision. As we discussed earlier, irrespective of the dollar amount selected, only 14 percent of defendants secured release through secured bond within 48 hours. When a commissioner set secured bond in a case at $500 or higher, approximately 9 out of 10 defendants were detained for longer than 48 hours. Merely choosing a bond at that level was the functional equivalent of deciding that the defendant would be held.

Given the importance of the detention outcome of the initial-appearance decision (for the defendant, for the court, and for the jail), we examined the factors most influential in effectively dividing defendants into two classes of accused: the confined and the released.

In examining the allocation of release and detention among superior court defendants, multivariate analysis highlighted a number of charge and defendant variables as important:

- Whether the charges involved a Class 3 felony.
- The existence of outstanding warrants or detainers.

- Whether the defendant had a record of recent arrests (within the last three years).
- Whether the defendant reported earnings for the last year.
- Whether the defendant had a telephone.
- Whether the pretrial services staff recommended nonfinancial release.

Other factors being "held constant," defendants with outstanding warrants or detainers and/or having recent arrests had greater prospects of detention; having Class 3 felony charges, a verified local address, and a telephone lowered the defendant's chances of detention. These findings parallel those reported for the analysis of the bail decision: Community ties, criminal charge, and prior history measures played a role in differentiating the detained and released defendants. However, the pretrial services recommendation to the commissioner (for nonfinancial versus financial bond) once again predominated. In regression terms, it accounted for roughly twice the variance in custody outcomes of all the other items of information taken together.[9] If a defendant was recommended for secured bond instead of nonfinancial release by pretrial services, it was very likely that detention would result.[10]

The Performance of Defendants during Pretrial Release in Maricopa County

The Judicial Steering and Policy Committee in superior court was interested in examining the consequences of the pretrial release decisions occurring at initial appearance. The research followed Maricopa defendants for a period of 90 days from release to determine the extent of failures to appear in court (FTAs) and rearrests for crimes committed during the pretrial period. Earlier we noted that, of all felony defendants securing release prior to adjudication in Maricopa County, 8 percent failed to appear in court for a required proceeding, and 11 percent were rearrested for crimes occurring during the pretrial period. A major goal was to discover factors predictive of defendant misconduct during pretrial release.

At least four problems make statistical prediction of either version of pretrial misconduct difficult in Maricopa County (and elsewhere). First, statistically, it is difficult to predict rare occurrences—and certainly "failures" occurring in less than 1 in 10 cases of released defendants are rare.[11] Second, it is difficult to examine the phenomena of interest when only about half of all defendants secure pretrial release. The large detention proportion in Maricopa exacerbates this problem, and our study can analyze only a limited or selective sample of defendants. Many of those detained may have been good risks, but their detention means we cannot generalize about the risk characteristics of Maricopa defendants overall.[12] Third, since the system selectively detained higher-risk defendants (as opposed to randomly holding defendants regardless of their risk attributes), the bias problem is accentuated. Presumably, the task is to predict which defendants among the lower-risk releases would perform like higher-risk defendants, most of whom were likely to be detained. Finally, there is the very practical problem of information. The success of statistical prediction is tied to the availability and accuracy of descriptors of defendants' backgrounds, histories, and cases that may be related to outcomes during pretrial release. Jurisdictions vary in the degree and variety of information available.

Predictors of Pretrial Flight

Given the limitations caused by the high rate of detention and the low rate of flight among those who gained release, statistical efforts are unlikely to produce strong results. Nevertheless, in the analysis of FTAs, we discovered a model which fit the data well and helped to distinguish between defendants with lower and higher (flight) risk.[13] They included the following:

- *Police saw defendant as flight risk.* The police arrest report indicated that the arresting officer believed the defendant posed a risk of flight. This item increased the likelihood that defendants would flee.
- *Living alone* increased the defendant's risk of flight.
- *Charges involving a person victim.* When defendants were charged with crimes against the person, other factors held constant, they were less likely to fail to appear in court.
- *Defendant having telephone* lessened the prospects of subsequent flight from court.
- *Prior record of FTAs.* A prior history of failing to appear in court added to the chances that a defendant would do so again during pretrial release, other factors taken into account.

Predictors of Pretrial Crime

The limitations described above hampered discovery of predictors of the rearrest of defendants during pretrial release. Three factors related to rearrest during pretrial release at the bivariate level—prior FTAs, having more than one suspect involved in the alleged offense, and/or earning wages during the last year—produced a marginally acceptable prediction.[14]

Predictors of Misconduct Generally (Flight and/or Crime)

Because the decisionmakers might also have liked to consider defendant performance during pretrial release more generally as either flight or crime, we attempted to identify factors that could predict defendant failure during the pretrial release period. Multivariate analysis seeking to predict misconduct, as generally defined, identified the following attributes as important:[15]

- *Police viewed defendant as flight risk.* The arresting officer's notation of the defendant as a potential flight risk was related to greater chances of subsequent failure.
- *Charges involving crimes against the person* lessened the chances of subsequent misconduct.
- *Living alone* made the defendant a poorer risk than otherwise, once other relevant factors had been controlled for.
- *Robbery charges.* When robbery charges were included among the defendant's current charges, the odds for failure increased, after other factors were taken into account.
- *Prior history of FTAs* increased the chances of failure.
- *Police cited risk and defendant had prior FTAs (interaction).* When both factors were present, they increased the prospects that a defendant would engage in misconduct.
- *Police cited risk and defendant lived alone (interaction).* When both factors were present, they added to the probability of defendant failure.

Summary of Decisionmaking in Maricopa County

In this chapter, we have examined ways of looking at the superior court commissioners' decision task at initial appearance, we have attempted to discover the factors most influential in producing those decisions, and we have considered some of the critical outcomes of the decisions, such as release versus detention, and flight and pretrial crime.

Several findings seem especially important:

1. The pretrial-release decision could be conceptualized either as a two-step (nonfinancial versus financial; amount of financial bond) deci-

sion or as a choice of simple amounts of bond. It did not appear to operate as a choice of least restrictive alternatives, as legal theory might suggest.

2. The pretrial services recommendation played a powerful role in influencing the commissioners' choices.

3. The pretrial services recommendation could not be adequately "explained" statistically by available characteristics of defendants or their cases; rather, it appeared to some extent to be based on the subjective judgment of the recommenders. The recommendation was found not only to affect greatly choices between nonfinancial and secured-bond options, but to play an important part in determining whether a defendant gained release. The recommendation was not found to influence commissioners' choices when, having decided that secured bond was appropriate, they selected particular amounts of secured bond.

4. When commissioners resorted to use of secured bond, the result was that the vast majority of defendants were detained, at least temporarily. When secured bond exceeded $500—which it usually did—detention (for longer than 48 hours) resulted in approximately 90 percent of the cases.

5. In the selection of particular amounts of secured bond, when all other factors were held constant, the commissioner presiding at initial appearance had an important influence on the kinds of decisions defendants received.

6. An unusually large proportion of defendants were held before trial in Maricopa County (whether measured as detained for 24 hours or longer or as detention throughout the pretrial period).

7. Associated with the high rate of detention among Maricopa felony defendants were low rates of failure to appear and rearrest for crimes occurring during pretrial release. However, as we shall see in our discussion of Dade County, comparison with other jurisdictions suggested that similarly low rates could be achieved without such a frequent resort to pretrial detention. (See the discussion of the effectiveness of pretrial release practices in Chapter 10.)

8. We studied defendants who did achieve pretrial release for a follow-up period of 90 days to learn the nature and extent of pretrial flight and crime. Because of the low rates of failure among just over half of defendants who secured release, development of predictive factors associated with pretrial misconduct was constrained. Reasonably good predictions of flight (FTA) and failure during pretrial release were derived, but attempts to predict rearrest for crimes during pretrial release was not as successful.

Notes

1. Semantics became important much later, too, when, in Dade County, the chief judge decided that bail guidelines could not be called *bail guidelines* but should be called something that sounded more like what judges were used to. His choice was that they be named *uniform bond standards*.
2. For a detailed discussion of the principle of release under least restrictive conditions and analysis of state and federal laws, see Goldkamp (1985).
3. Statistical analyses of bail decisions or components of the decisions employed the following general procedures: The first task was to reduce the number of relationships under consideration for multivariate analyses between up to 60 independent variables and the various dependent measures. Correlations were first examined, as well as interrelationships among independent variables. As a rule of thumb, relationships showing a gamma of less than .2 were discarded.

   Subsequently, independent variables were grouped into one of several categories: demographic, charge-related, prior criminal history, and system-related. Multiple regression was then employed as a rough screening device to identify independent variables showing the greatest contributions to explaining the variance in the criterion. With the use of a best-subsets routine and controls (by altering the order of entry in regression), each category of independent variable was reduced to its strongest measures.

   If the dependent measure was interval-level (for example, we treated bail amount as an interval-level measure, although we employed the logarithm of the bail amount in analysis), we concluded the multivariate analysis with regression. If the dependent variable was dichotomous—and most were—we stopped regression analysis once we had roughly 10 or fewer candidate-independent variables remaining. At this stage, marginally related variables were temporarily kept in the analysis. For the dichotomous measures, we attempted to model decisions using logit procedures until we found a parsimonious model that best fit the data (including consideration of interactions). One advantage of using regression for screening analyses was that we were able to contrast the strength of solutions across jurisdictions using R^2.
4. As Figure 7.1 shows, this model subdivided the pretrial release decision into four decision components sequenced, according to restrictiveness, from least to most restrictive. In the first component, the commissioner decided whether to assign outright ROR without restrictive conditions (although standard conditions to appear and refrain from crime applied) or not. Without knowledge of the pretrial services recommendation for ROR instead of secured bond, nine independent variables explained about 19 percent of the variance (R^2 = .19); knowing the recommendation explained about 45 percent. The next step involved the choice, among those not receiving outright ROR, of whether to assign third-party release or not: Regression analysis was able to explain 10 percent of the variance with six independent variables (R^2 = .10) and 49 percent with knowledge of the recommendation. The next decision component decided, among persons not receiving outright ROR and not assigned third-party release, whether supervision by pretrial services would be assigned or not; here the R^2 was .08 based on five independent variables, but .70 when knowledge of the recommendation was added. In the last step, the choices had been narrowed to cash bond (secured bond), and the only decision was to select a given amount; this analysis is the same as discussed in the text above.
5. Knowledge of nine variables was able to explain 70 percent of the variance in release versus detention of Maricopa defendants.

6. Regression, used to reduce the data in preparation for logit analysis, produced an R^2 of .27 using eight independent variables. The final logit model including these variables produced a goodness-of-fit chi-squared of 128.24; $DF = 124$; and a P value of 0.38.
7. Severity of charge has not been found to relate to prediction of flight or crime during pretrial release, although kind of charged offense has.
8. Of course, one explanation for this rather unusual behavior may be that we do not measure the seriousness of the offenses charged very well if we employ the statutory classification of offenses as our rule. To examine this possibility, we decided to ignore the statutory grading and create instead a measure that might reflect the commissioners' views of offense severity. This alternate measure ranks all offenses (in our study) according to how often commissioners assigned nonfinancial release to defendants so charged, arguing that in the most serious cases nonfinancial release would be given very rarely, and that in the least serious cases it would be given quite frequently. When measured in this manner, we found that seriousness appeared to be even less influential than previously. For example, when we entered the statutory grading of offense last in a regression of commissioners' financial bond choices, the R^2 increased from .32 to .40. When the second, nonstatutory version of charge severity was entered last, the R^2 increased to only .37.
9. Logit analysis produced a model of the release–detention decision that fit the data substantially better when the pretrial services recommendation was included. (Without the recommendation, a successful model could not be generated.)
10. In regression analysis, the variables explained 40 percent of the variance. Entered last, the pretrial services recommendation increased the R^2 to .70. When logit analysis modeled detention versus release based on the first five variables listed in the text, a successful fit could not be achieved. Only with the addition of the recommendation was a model developed (goodness-of-fit chi-squared = 382.62; $DF = 448$; P value = 0.99; $n = 2{,}207$).
11. For a good discussion of statistical prediction of future events in criminal justice, see Gottfredson and Gottfredson (1986). Note that, in actuality, we are talking about *postdiction*, that is, trying to identify correlates of the phenomenon once it has already occurred as if we were predicting flight and crime from the vantage point of the bail–pretrial-release decision.
12. For discussions of the possible effects of selection bias on prediction of defendant misconduct during pretrial release, see Gottfredson (1976); Goldkamp (1979, 1984); Rhodes (1985); Smith et al. (1989); Goldkamp, Gottfredson, and Weilland (1990). Note that we have taken the position that, although released defendants may represent a biased subsample of all defendants, they are an appropriate and unbiased sample of defendants released in a jurisdiction. If the question is "Given the release practices in a jurisdiction, what are the predictors of misconduct?"—which in this research it is—then the best sample for studying the risk of misconduct during pretrial release is a sample of released defendants.
13. The logit model fit failure-to-appear modesty with the use of these five variables (goodness-of-fit chi-squared = 33.39; $DF = 27$; P value = 0.19).
14. Goodness-of-fit chi-squared = 1.5; $DF = 4$; P value = 0.83; $n = 1{,}211$.
15. Goodness-of-fit chi-squared = 13.73; $DF = 17$; P value = 0.69; $n = 1{,}211$.

8

The Nature of Bail Decisionmaking in Dade County

Initially, the Judicial Steering Committee in Dade County directed the research staff to examine bail and pretrial release practices for both misdemeanor and felony defendants. After discussion of the preliminary results at the first few meetings, the committee requested that we focus our attention on cases being processed as potentially bondable felonies.[1] The path taken by felony cases was quite different from the one followed by misdemeanors. Dade County felony arrestees were booked at the central pretrial-detention facility to await a bond hearing. The bond hearing, presided over by a county court judge during the week and a circuit court judge on weekends, could be held very shortly after arrest or as much as 12 hours later, depending on the timing of the arrest and the next scheduled court session. Theoretically, all bondable defendants were interviewed by pretrial services staff before the bond hearing; however, felony defendants had the opportunity to pay their bond as specified by a bond schedule, or to have the money posted by a friend, a relative, or a bondsman.

Early in our study of the bond–release process in Dade County, we discovered that pretrial release was determined at two early stages, rather than at one as in Maricopa County. First, nearly one-fifth of all defendants gained pretrial release by posting bond via the bond schedule at the jail before the bond hearing. Second, the remaining defendants appeared before a judge—after a pretrial services interview—for a bond hearing.

Release by Bond Schedule

Approximately 80 percent of felony defendants gained pretrial release within 90 days of booking in Dade County during the study period. However, nearly 20 percent secured release in less than 1 day by posting bond immediately after booking, by using the bond schedule. Thus, roughly one in five felony defendants gaining release did so promptly as a result of the bond schedule.

Like traditional bond schedules used earlier in the twentieth century, the Dade County bond schedule ranked offenses according to their seriousness[2] and assigned an amount of bond that must be posted to permit a defendant's early release. Certainly, members of the judicial working committee were aware of the controversy surrounding the use of bond schedules.[3] Critics have argued that schedules discriminate against poor defendants by setting a fixed price on release according to the charged offense rather than taking into account individual factors that may demonstrate the potential risk a defendant poses. In other words, what on the surface appears equitable—setting bonds for similar offenses at fixed levels—merely means that defendants who can raise bail can obtain release while those who cannot, do not. Bond schedules produce release or detention largely on the basis of a defendant's financial assets (or lack thereof) rather than on the basis of criteria related to his or her propensity toward flight or crime. Related to this criticism is the controversy surrounding the role of bondsmen, who, because of this structural role for financing in release determinations, enter the process for profit.

These criticisms prompted a detailed investigation of the role played by the bond schedule. If fully 20 percent of all entering defendants were paying for their release before appearing before a judge and before being reviewed by pretrial services, two important questions had to be asked:

1. How did defendants gaining release by paying the bond required by the schedule differ from those who appeared at the bond hearing and had bond set and release determined through judicial channels?
2. How did these defendants "perform" during pretrial release, compared to the other defendants who underwent a more thorough and thoughtful review prior to a bond decision or pretrial release?

These questions are important because, if we found, for example, that only a defendant's (on-hand) assets determined booking-stage release, we might question both the fairness and the effectiveness of the bond schedule. Fairness would be an issue because only those with financial resources were achieving release; effectiveness would be an issue because the availability of financial resources may not be a good determinant of a defendant's dependability.[4] (Consider the case of an alleged drug trafficker, for example, with plenty of assets but little intention of returning to court.) If defendants released at the booking stage differed little in the character of their cases or their likelihood of pretrial misconduct from those released later, we could focus on the optimal timing of release—early or late. The first question can be dealt with here; the second question is dealt with in a subsequent section which considers the performance of released Dade defendants.

The Determinants of Release at the Booking Stage

The ranking of offenses incorporated into the bond schedule appears to begin by categorizing defendants according to their statutory grading (Felonies 3, 2, or 1) and then subdivides those broad categories into subcategories judged to be worthy of lower or higher amounts of bond. The factors that differentiate among subcategories of bond appear to include various indices of the seriousness of the offense charged, such as whether the crime involved robbery or drug charges, whether force was used, and whether a weapon was used. When the bond schedule was used for obtaining release, the defendant had to post the amounts required for each of the charges—not just the most serious. The number of charges, by implication, was a factor in the schedule's ranking of the seriousness of the charges and in the prospects of a defendant's release by posting bond at booking. Under this system, it was possible for a defendant charged with several charges of lesser seriousness to have a higher bond to post than a defendant charged with one more serious charge.

We performed multivariate analysis of the factors associated with whether defendants secured release as a result of the bond schedule. Gaining release at the booking stage was related to the seriousness of charges as expected, since defendants charged with offenses ranked as more serious by the schedule (thus having higher bonds) would be less likely to obtain booking-stage release. Other factors, however, were much more important in the explanation of who gained release and who did not: a defendant's financial resources, living arrangements, recent prior arrests, and having a telephone were very influential. Those with resources, those not living with close family or friends, and those having a telephone were clearly more successful.[5]

Differences between Defendants Released at the Booking Stage and Defendants Released Later

The Dade County bail system did not release all defendants before trial. Some (20 percent) were released immediately as the result of the bond schedule mechanism, and some (another 60 percent) gained release later after going through the bond-hearing and early judicial-processing stages. Using multivariate analysis, we attempted to distinguish between the earlier and later releases. Given the information we had at our disposal, strong, clear differences were not found.

Because attributes differentiating defendants gaining release at the booking stage and defendants gaining release sometime later were not identified, we conclude that they did not appear to differ thematically from one another to a marked degree. Overall, therefore, of the defendants whom the system was going to release, whether a defendant gained release early or later occurred in large part randomly.

Decisionmaking at the Bond Hearing

For the remaining 80 percent of entering felony cases we studied during 1984, pretrial release or detention of defendants was determined by a judge's bond decision at the bond hearing in circuit court.[6] To simplify our analysis of an estimated 1,772 cases reaching this major decision stage, we once again discussed conceptualization of the judge's decision task with the Judicial Steering and Policy Committee that had been assembled by the presiding judge of circuit court and chaired by the criminal presiding judge. Like the Maricopa County judges and commissioners, the Dade County judges found it helpful to view the decision task as a two-part decision: the first part involving a choice between nonfinancial release and cash bond; the second involving selection of a form of nonfinancial release or, for financial defendants, a bond amount.

The Judges' Choice between Nonfinancial and Financial Bond

Although we attempted to determine how judges differentiated between candidates for nonfinancial release (of any form) and financial bond, statistical analyses were unable to detect strong systematic themes. To some extent, being charged with drug trafficking and other drug-related offenses, being charged with robbery, or being charged with first-degree felonies and having prior arrests for serious property offenses were associated with a higher probability of financial bond. Having a telephone decreased the odds of receiving financial bond.

There are several possible explanations for this rather surprising finding. First, perhaps we had not recorded important information concerning the defendant or his or her case during data collection and, as a result, were not able to detect its influence. Our major suspicion, however, is not that key information was missing from the various agency files and court records we examined, but that the pretrial services oral, in-court recommendation may have played a very important role. Because the oral recommendation was not documented, we were not able to record it with other data or to consider it in our analyses. If we assume that there was a great concordance between pretrial services recommendations and judges' bond-hearing decisions, we should have been better able to explain the judges' choice between financial and nonfinancial options statistically—if only that information had been available.

Thus, because pretrial services recommendations were not noted (i.e., did not leave a "paper trail"), we were unable to assess their importance in fact, particularly after the effects of other factors had been taken into account. Although this explanation is certainly possible, it would nevertheless be surprising if the pretrial services recommendations did not also rely on some criteria we had recorded and measured. Therefore, it remains unusual that these factors did not explain the judges' choices better and raises the possibility that judges as a group apply criteria inconsistently in their assignment of financial versus nonfinancial bond at the bond-hearing stage.[7] We also attempted to learn whether, when we held other factors constant, the judge presiding at the bond hearing made a difference in the likelihood that defendants would receive nonfinancial versus financial release. In fact, the presiding judge did make a statistically significant but practically inconsequential difference.

Choosing between Pretrial Services and Other Nonfinancial Options

Approximately 69 percent of felony defendants reaching the bond-hearing stage were assigned nonfinancial release of some sort. Roughly 70 percent of the defendants with nonfinancial decisions were assigned to pretrial services for supervision or routine notification. Judges had a number of nonfinancial pretrial-release options to consider, and therefore we sought to determine the kinds of attributes of defendants or their cases that may have played important roles in the judges' choices. At the time of the study, there were, in addition to ordinary pretrial services supervision, drug and alcohol referrals, a domestic abuse program, and a Hispanic support and supervisory program available for nonfinancial defendants and not associated with the pretrial services program.[8] Our analyses identified several themes differentiating modestly among defendants to be assigned to pretrial services and defendants to be assigned the other nonfinancial alternatives by judges at the bond hearing. Being Hispanic, having drug- or alcohol-related problems, and being charged with certain offenses increased the probability slightly that defendants would be assigned to the alternative programs.[9]

The Dominance of the Bond Schedule

Just less than one-third (31 percent) of felony defendants were assigned cash bond at the bond-hearing stage in circuit court. Although we noted above that we were not successful in establishing how these defendants differed from those given nonfinancial release, we next attempted to determine how judges chose among bond amounts in cases in which some form of nonfinancial release had been ruled out. We began by asking how important the bond schedule was in influencing the judges' choice of bond amount at the bond hearing. Our finding was that, in financial release cases, the amount suggested by the bond schedule was virtually the only governing factor. One additional factor was of marginal importance: If the defendant was charged with drug trafficking, cash bond was likely to be higher.

As a result of our analysis and discussion of the results with the Judicial Steering and Policy Committee in Dade County, we soon found that the conceptualization of the bail task we had employed (Model II in Chapter 7, Figure 7.1) did not apply well, principally because the bond schedule was such a powerful influence on bond-hearing decisionmaking. Before the bond hearing, 20 percent of entering felony defendants gained release on cash bond by using the bond schedule. The bond-hearing decision appeared largely to be a decision either to stick with the bond dictated by the bond schedule (this was the case with about 45 percent of defendants reaching the hearing) or to make an exception based on a rationale supported by the pretrial services recommendation or other organization and grant a nonfinancial release. This finding was so powerful that there was no detectable effect based on the presiding judge, once these factors had been taken into consideration, because there was nothing (no variability in decisions) left to explain statistically. (In other jurisdictions, we found a great diversity in cash bond decisions among judges, after other factors had been taken into account.)

The centrality of the bond schedule in judicial decisions at the bond hearing was also reflected in another unusual practice, referred to as *alternate bond.* Alternate bond was an amount of bond dictated by the bond schedule that was set as a "backup" when a nonfinancial release option was selected. The apparent rationale was that, if anything went wrong during the defendant's supervision by pretrial services, the defendant automatically had a financial bond requirement in effect. In some respects, then, alternate bond resembled what is referred to as *unsecured bond* in other jurisdictions. Unsecured bond is used in those locations to permit the release of defendants without requiring the posting of any financial security, but implying that, should the defendant violate any of the conditions of release, he or she would owe the specified amount of unsecured bond to the court (much as would a defaulting defendant who had had a cash bond set). This practice had another effect, however: It permitted defendants assigned to pretrial services for supervision during the pretrial period to "buy out" of that supervision. In essence, the defendant had the choice of either agreeing to the terms of supervision or to post the cash bond and avoid supervision.

The practice of alternate bond was unusual but can probably be explained as one reason judges felt more comfortable in employing nonfinancial release more frequently during the days when pretrial services were first being developed in Dade County. In a sense, the judge was able to shift the responsibility for nonfinancial release to the pretrial services agency, using alternate bond to say what the bond would have been, if he or she had not been persuaded to take a chance on pretrial services. This interpretation is further supported by the fact that the pretrial services program was run as part of the corrections department. Judges could assign nonfinancial release and feel that the defendant's behavior was now the responsibility of corrections, not of the court.

Release or Detention before Trial at the Booking and Bond-Hearing Stages

For the defendant, the courts, and the jail, perhaps the most important result of the booking stage or bond hearing was whether the defendant gained release or awaited proceedings in jail. Figure 8.1 depicts the stages at which Dade County felony defendants gained release from custody during the study period.

Release within Forty-Eight Hours of Booking

We examined the factors associated with release within 48 hours to determine the impact the bond schedule and the bond hearing had on the pretrial release or detention of defendants overall. Approximately two-thirds of defendants (66 percent) had secured release through one means or another by that time. We reasoned that, although approximately one-fifth of defendants were still able to secure release at a later date, defendants released early in the process as products of early decisions[10] may be said to have represented the system's "intentional" release decisions.

Multivariate analysis identified several defendant and case based factors as significant—if modest—predictors of the release or detention of defendants before trial as measured within 48 hours.[11] First, factors

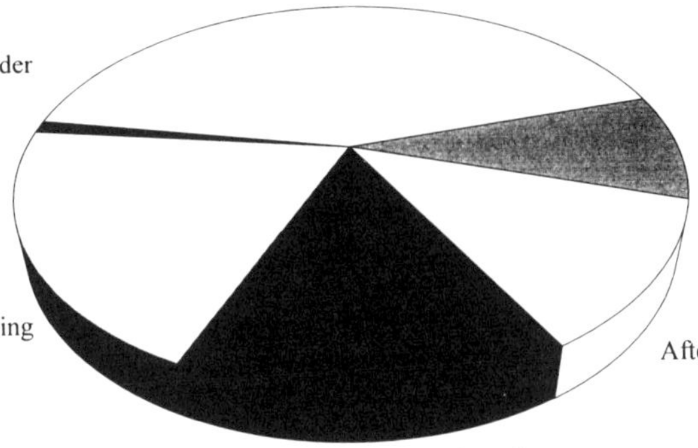

FIGURE 8.1. Pretrial release of felony defendants entering the criminal process in Dade County Circuit Court, by decision stages, Summer 1984.

related to the seriousness of a defendant's charges increased the likelihood that the defendant would not be released within two days. These included the seriousness ranking from the bond schedule and the presence of burglary and robbery charges. The assignment of a public defender reduced the likelihood of release within that period of time.[12] Records of recent arrests and prior convictions for property crimes and for misdemeanors were related to lower chances of release within 48 hours. A small but significant effect on a defendant's prospects for release was found when the identity of the judge sitting at the bond hearing was considered. (That is, the chances of release varied with the judge presiding.) On the whole, however, the analysis was not successful in identifying criteria that were strongly related to the prospects of release or detention at this stage. One interpretation of this finding may be that whether a defendant was released or detained at this stage was partly random.

Financial versus Nonfinancial Release

Among released defendants, we found important differences between those gaining release by posting cash and those released through nonfinancial means. Defendants assigned a public defender, charged with drug-related offenses, and who were employed had greater probabilities of release through cash bond. Having a verified local address and not living with a close family member increased the odds of financial release, when other factors were controlled for. Having prior failures to appear (FTAs) and being charged with a crime against a person or a crime involving stolen property increased the chances that the defendant would be released on financial bond. Being black and having bond decided by Judge "41" also increased the odds that release would be financial, other factors being held constant.[13]

These findings raise questions about the disadvantage regarding the chances of receiving nonfinancial release for persons who were black, persons who had public defenders, and persons who had bail decided by a particular judge. When the assignment of public counsel is taken as a surrogate measure of financial status (persons without arrests had public defenders assigned), it appears that black defendants without resources who gained release were more likely to post financial bond. Finally, the fact that the presence of one judge (Judge 41) in a case increased the odds of financial release raises serious questions about the even-handedness of that judge. The fact that this judge was frequently assigned bond-hearing duties increased our concern.

The Performance of Dade Felony Defendants during Pretrial Release

In Chapter 6, we reported that, of the Dade County felony defendants gaining release before trial, approximately 11 percent failed to appear in court and 6 percent were rearrested for crimes committed during the preadjudicatory period. Of course, the steering committee discussed whether these rates of defendant misconduct should be viewed as favorable or unfavorable statistics (we will treat this question about the "effectiveness of pretrial release" in Chapter 10) and asked us to develop a scheme for the prediction of flight and crime by defendants during pretrial release.

Prediction of Defendant Flight

Because of the unavailability of some defendant-related and other kinds of potentially relevant data in Dade County[14] and the relatively low rates of defendant misconduct, the multivariate analysis of failure to appear among defendants discovered only several weak predictors that helped distinguish among defendants with low and high (flight) risk, after we took the effects of other factors into account. Our best model of flight included the following factors:

- *Prior failures to appear* (based on bench warrants and/or *alias capiases*). The greater the number of prior failures to appear, the higher the likelihood of flight.

- *Judge deciding bond.* After other factors were controlled for, the judge who decided bond slightly but significantly affected the probability of defendant flight.[15]
- *Felony 2.* Charges designated by statute as Felony 2 added to the probability that a defendant would fail to appear in court.
- *Having a telephone.* Defendants having telephones showed a lower risk of flight, after other factors were controlled for.

Note that, although charge-related factors were related to the probability of flight (i.e., whether they were Felony 2, largely theft-related), the *general* seriousness of charges was not a statistically significant predictor. In addition, the identity of the judge deciding bail made a difference in the probability that defendants would flee. (Defendants released by Judge 36—a different judge from the one disproportionately employing financial release—showed higher rates of failure-to-appear.)

Prediction of Pretrial Crime

Prediction of rearrest for crimes committed by defendants during pretrial release was somewhat more successful. Two criminal-history measures figured most importantly in the model developed:

1. *Arrests within the last three years.* The greater the number of recent arrests, the higher the probability of rearrest during pretrial release, other factors being held constant.
2. *Prior felony convictions.* The presence of a felony record was related to increased odds of rearrest during release.

The general seriousness of the criminal charges (measured either by statutory grading or by the bond schedule ranking) was not related to rearrest. Although these two factors alone generated a satisfactory statistical model of rearrest, a better model was constructed when knowledge of the bond judge's identity and of whether the defendant had gained release before or after the bond-hearing stage was taken into account (both factors decreasing the prospects of rearrest). (Early release and *not* having bail decided by still a different judge, Judge 17, reduced the prospects for rearrests during pretrial release.)

Summary of Decisionmaking in Dade County

Summarized briefly, the multivariate analyses describing the release of felony defendants entering the criminal process in Dade County during the summer of 1984 produced the following principal findings:

1. Pretrial release or detention of defendants occurred as the result of two principal stages in Dade County: the booking stage (at which defendants could post the bond specified by the schedule) and the bond hearing (at which defendants could be released under nonfinancial conditions or have financial bond set). The bond schedule specified the bond to be paid by the defendant at booking according to a ranking of offenses. (In the event that defendants were charged with multiple offenses, each charge was ranked and assigned a bond amount.) Although to some extent persons charged with seriously ranked offenses showed poorer chances of posting bond at the booking stage than persons charged with offenses ranked less seriously, the principal determinants of release at the booking stage were factors indicative of a defendant's financial assets or ability to afford bond and were not related to his or her probability of flight or pretrial crime.

2. Persons securing release before the bond hearing via the bond schedule at the booking stage differed very little from persons securing release at later stages.

3. At the bond hearing, analysis organized the judges' choices into two stages for study: In the first, the judge decided between the appropriateness of financial and nonfinancial options; in the second, the judge decided which nonfinancial options (pretrial services versus others) and financial amounts were appropriate. In the first stage, roughly 69 percent of felony defendants were given nonfinancial options, and 31 percent had secured bond set at the bond hearing. Multivariate analysis was not able to explain very well how judges distinguished between nonfinancial and financial bond decisions, although weak themes were detected. When other factors were controlled for, the seriousness of the charges (from the bond schedule ranking) did not adequately explain the prospects of financial versus nonfinancial bond choices by the judges.

We drew two conclusions:

a. Probably, the in-court oral recommendation of staff of the pretrial services and other programs had great influence on the judges' choices at the bond hearing (since this was oral and not documented, this remains conjecture).

b. The choice between financial and nonfinancial options by judges at bond hearing was to some extent inconsistent and unpredictable. We can infer this despite the absence of pretrial services recommendations since these recommendations should have been based on criteria we did measure. Thus variables explaining the recommendation should emerge as factors in our analyses of judicial decisions. They did so only in a very weak sense.

4. Of the defendants receiving nonfinancial decisions at the bond hearing, approximately 70 percent were assigned to pretrial services. In

analyzing the judges' choices between pretrial services and other nonfinancial options, some patterns were found: Defendants living in the Dade area, defendants living with close family or friends, defendants having codefendants in their cases, and black defendants had greater chances of assignment to pretrial services. Hispanic defendants, defendants having prior felony convictions, and defendants charged with alcohol- or drug-related offenses had smaller likelihoods of nonfinancial release through pretrial services.

5. Approximately 31 percent of defendants reaching the bond hearing had (financial) bond set. Analysis of factors relied on by judges in selecting particular bond amounts revealed one major finding: The bond schedule ranking was the dominant factor in the selection of bond amounts. Whether or not the defendant's charges involved drug trafficking was also marginally influential in determining bond amount. The fact that the bond schedule served as the vehicle for the release of 20 percent of defendants after booking and functioned as a virtual judge's guide for the bonds of financial defendants at the bond hearing (another 24 percent of all defendants), as well as for the "alternate bonds" of the remaining defendants, suggests we reconsider the conceptual model of the bail task in Dade County. Rather than the "two-step" task we initially agreed to analyze (consisting of the choice between nonfinancial and financial options, and then of choosing nonfinancial conditions or the amount of financial bond), a more appropriate model proposes the bond schedule as the presumptive guide. Judges appeared to be asking the question of pretrial services, for example, "Why should I not assign the bond specified by the bond schedule in this case?"

6. Roughly two-thirds of felony defendants obtained release within 48 hours (81 percent were released within 90 days). Analysis at the post-bond-hearing stage (or within 48 hours of booking) showed some weak roles for several criteria determining release versus detention: Release *did* depend on the general seriousness of charges and the presence of burglary or robbery charges. Having a history of prior arrests and prior convictions for property crimes, as well as having been assigned a public defender, was associated with lowered chances for release within that period. We believe that, in this context, it is more appropriate to regard the appointment of the public defender as a reflection of a defendant's financial status, rather than a factor somehow lowering the defendant's prospects for release.

7. In general, the differentiation between detained and released defendants was not explained by multivariate analysis. We conclude that this inconsistent use of pretrial detention was the product of three phenomena: (a) the partly random effect of the bond schedule at the booking stage

on the release of defendants; (b) the partly random effect of the judge's choice between financial and nonfinancial options at the bond hearing; and (c) the partly random effect of the bond schedule on release when applied to the judge's selection of bond amounts at the bond hearing.

8. Of all felony defendants gaining release before adjudication, 25 percent gained release by means of the bond schedule at booking, 60 percent by nonfinancial bond, and 15 percent through financial bond after the bond hearing. The vast majority of defendants having cash bond set at the bond hearing were detained, at least for the short term; 85 percent were not released within 48 hours.

As described earlier, the level of bond set did not correspond directly with the odds of pretrial detention in Dade County. Rather, bond set in any amount over $500 detained a majority longer than two days. Bonds of over $1,000 detained defendants in at least 9 of 10 cases for two days or more; higher bonds were, in effect, "overkill." Thus, in a vast majority of cases receiving financial bond at the bond-hearing stage, the judge's resort to financial bond was tantamount to a detention decision, at least for the short term.

9. Bond-hearing defendants for whom bond was set had an increasing probability of release over time—from 15 percent within 2 days of booking to 52 percent within 90 days. The odds that bond defendants would secure release within 90 days were virtually unrelated to the amount of bond that had been set at the bond hearing. For example, 44 percent of defendants with bond set between $1,001 and $3,000 by the bond-hearing judge secured release within 90 days; 65 percent of defendants with bonds over $10,000 did. *Thus, particularly over the long run, bond amounts were not reliable yardsticks for determining detention.*

10. Multivariate analyses sought to identify factors predictive of failure to appear by and rearrest of defendants during pretrial release. Several factors, modest in their power, were identified. (Predictive analyses, their strengths and limitations, are discussed in more depth in Chapter 10.) *The general seriousness of criminal charges was not a predictor of (was not systematically related to) flight or crime by defendants who gained pretrial release.*

11. The means of release made a marginal difference in the prediction of rearrest: Pretrial services and surety release showed slightly lower probabilities of rearrest than other means of release, after the effects of other factors had been taken into account. In the prediction of failure to appear and the prediction of misconduct generally (either failure to appear or rearrest), means of release did not appear to make a meaningful difference.

12. Bond decisions and their outcomes (detention vs. release; FTA and rearrest) were affected somewhat by the identity of the judge presiding at

the bond hearing, after the effects of other factors were taken into account. In the analysis of FTA, if Judge 36 presided, the chances for flight were greater (he assessed prospective risks posed by defendants quite poorly). In the analysis of rearrests, *ceteris paribus,* the decisions of Judge 17, in contrast, were associated with lower probabilities of crime. (He apparently assessed prospective risks better than others.)

13. The seriousness of charges—for example, as ranked by the bond schedule—was very influential in multivariate analysis of bond and release decisions but was not statistically related to prediction of flight or pretrial crime.

14. Defendants released earlier by means of booking-stage bond-schedule release performed better than defendants released later. This raised the question of why later releases could not occur earlier, especially given the apparent randomness of their differentiation.

Notes

1. The following offenses listed under the Florida penal code were not bondable at the first judicial stage: attempt or solicitation for capital felony with a firearm (775.087); possession of bomb or explosive device (790.161); burglary or breaking and entering, armed (810.020); burglary with assault (810.020); forcible rape (794.021); kidnapping for ransom (805.020); kidnapping (787.01); murder in the first and second degree (782.040); rape (794.010); robbery using firearm or deadly weapon (812.130); sexual battery by threats (794.011); sexual battery on minor by adult (794.011); sexual battery on minor by minor (794.011); and sex offenses (794.021).
2. This is done periodically by a committee of judges and is based mostly on the way offenses are graded under the criminal code, with some exceptions principally relating to local ordinances.
3. For good examples of critical discussions in this area, see Beeley (1927); Foote (1954); ABA (1968).
4. Later in this chapter, we present our predictive analyses of pretrial flight and crime among Dade felony defendants who gained release. No factors that could be construed as relating to a defendant's assets or economic status emerged as predictors of misconduct during pretrial release.
5. Because a good measure of a defendant's immediate assets was not available in our data, we reasoned that the judge's determination that a defendant should be afforded a public defender could be used as a stand-in measure. If a judge at a bond hearing determined that a defendant did not have the ability to pay for his or her own counsel, we reasoned that this could serve as a measure of the defendant's resources. It turned out to be the most important factor in explaining who gained release at the booking stage. The logit model including this variable fits the data fairly well (goodness-of-fit chi-squared = 181.84; $DF = 252$; P value = 1.0). The parallel regression analysis produced an R^2 of 0.45 (n = 2,276).
6. Actually, the correct estimate is 79 percent; approximately 1 percent of defendants were permitted release by pretrial services under an administrative order of the court prior to the bond-hearing stage.

7. Or to be fair, we could also infer that judges may be very consistently following the recommendations of pretrial services staff, but that the recommendations of the staff are not explained by reliance on consistent, measurable criteria. Without data, we cannot say. We can only report the overall result, which was that the differentiation between use of nonfinancial and financial options at the bond decision cannot be well explained by the factors that were available to us in our research.
8. In the period between the background study of bail–pretrial-release practices and the development and implementation of guidelines, a number of these programs became organizationally affiliated with the pretrial services program.
9. These findings correspond logically to the fact that there were release programs available for Hispanic defendants, drug or alcohol abuse defendants, and domestic violence defendants.
10. For the purposes of this analysis, we considered the policy of permitting release through the bond schedule at booking a "decision."
11. A logit model could not be developed that fit the data sufficiently. The parallel regression analysis produced an R^2 of 0.12 with six variables.
12. We said earlier that this variable may also be understood as a "stand-in" indicator of a defendant's lack of financial assets. Thus the alternative interpretation is that, after the effects of charge-related factors are controlled for, lack of financial resources served to increase the probability of detention.
13. Without adding whether or not a public defender was assigned or whether or not Judge 41 presided at the bond hearing, a good logit model could not be constructed. With these, the model had a goodness-of-fit chi-squared of 258.20 ($DF = 242$; P value $= 0.23$; $n = 1{,}856$). The regression analysis using 11 variables produced an R^2 of 0.41 (with public defender and judge included).
14. See the discussion of some of the obstacles to successful statistical prediction described in the context of Maricopa County in Chapter 7.
15. The predictive analysis of failure to appear was conducted by the same method as analyses described earlier in this report. Bivariate analyses of a very large number of demographic, charge-related, prior-history, and system variables were conducted to identify relationships meeting a minimal statistical standard. Multiple regression was used next to help screen out independent variables having little explanatory power when controls were exercised. When a reasonably small number of candidate variables had been located in this manner, logit analysis was conducted to develop a model that fit the data well. In this analysis, a minimally adequate regression analysis was produced. The logit model based on the four variables noted in the text produced a goodness-of-fit chi-squared of 13.38 ($DF = 11$; P value $= 0.27$; $n = 1{,}840$).

9

The Nature of Bail Decisionmaking in Boston Municipal Court

The Limitations of Information

Our work in Boston, which began by working with two separate judicial steering and policy committees (one in the Suffolk County Superior Court and one in the Boston Municipal Court), shifted its focus to concentrate centrally on bail–pretrial-release decisionmaking in the Boston Municipal Court (BMC) as the work progressed into more advanced stages.[1] The working committee of BMC judges was often expanded into open meetings to include all judges of the court, schedules permitting. From the beginning, the discussions of research results and observation of bail practices in the Boston Municipal Court were marked by candor and skepticism. In the committee's direction to the research staff concerning which problems to investigate and in the judges' interpretations of the findings presented, consensus was not often achieved within the group. In agreeing on the importance of the guidelines research, many judges expressed the view that, although they recognized many problems in the bail system in their court, there was little else the judges themselves could do to improve matters.

In the view of some judges, the Boston Municipal Court was already releasing almost all of its criminal defendants because of the pressures resulting from the overcrowding of the local detention facility, the Charles Street Jail. These judges noted (and our research later confirmed) that several other courts in the Boston area—including the Suffolk County Superior Court—were more responsible for contributing to the population of the Charles Street Jail than was the municipal court. Other judges expressed frustration with the poor quality of the information they often received at the initial bail stage (at BMC arraignment), yet argued that improvements were impossible because of severe resource constraints. Indeed, some judges also expressed the fear that efforts to collect better information—such as would be involved in a guidelines program—would also cause the proceedings to bog down, contributing to additional system delay.

Along with the periodic meetings to discuss findings generated by the research, written questionnaires were submitted to all judges and interviews conducted with most of them. The interviews suggested that many judges were critical of important aspects of the system but were not hopeful that meaningful action could be undertaken successfully. In the questionnaires, judges ranked the availability of information as a key problem in performing bail-decisionmaking tasks. In fact, the items of information ranked by judges to be most essential at the bail determination were the same as those ranked the most often unavailable or unreliable. This theme of inadequate information was to become a fact of life with which the research staff would become closely familiar, and the one that most heavily influenced the outcome of the guidelines research in Boston.

In our discussion of data collection (see Chapter 5), we reported that, to assemble information that was as complete as possible pertaining to the cases of the defendants we studied, we examined the files and records of eight agencies.[2] Obviously, our ability to study bail decisions, release and detention, and their consequences depended on the availability and quality of information. Certain kinds of important information were unavailable in the Boston court system as compared with the Arizona and Florida courts involved in the study.[3] Two prime examples were criminal history information and arrest report information describing the alleged crime causing the defendant's arrest. (Interestingly, the assistant district attorney had this at arraignment, but the judge did not.)

We call attention to this issue—the availability and quality of information in the Boston court system—not only to explain the constraints imposed upon statistical analysis, but to underscore what may be an important, if obvious, finding. The research was constrained by uneven information pertaining to defendants and their cases even though research staff had the benefit of many months of searching and the cooperation of each of the agencies. Judges making real decisions at arraignment faced even greater constraints in obtaining sound information systematically just a few short hours after the defendant's arrest.

Against this background, our examination of bail decisions in approximately 2,000 cases (weighted $n = 4{,}500$ cases) entering the Boston Municipal Court between April and October 1984 centered on the following stages: (1) release at the booking stage prior to the defendants appearance in court; (2) bail decisionmaking in municipal court, including the influence of the assistant district attorney's recommendation; (3) release or custody after 24 hours; and (4) failure to appear in court and rearrest among released defendants.

The Determinants of Release or Custody after Police Booking

Just under half of the municipal court defendants had secured release at the police station just after arrest and prior to appearing in court as a result of having bail set or ROR assigned by a commissioner.[4] Multivariate analysis was employed to discover the factors most influential in determining whether a defendant would be released through the bail commissioner after booking or would remain in custody until arraignment in municipal court the next day.

We were unable to explain clearly the different prearraignment custody outcomes (release or detention), even considering all the information we had available.[5] Having analyzed the data available to the commissioners and yet being unable to "predict" their decisions, we are left to conclude that defendants were freed or held in custody until court on a nearly random basis. Although one might argue that this finding is not particularly important because of the relatively minor hardship imposed by the short period of police station custody before court—between 12 and 15 hours—it is a puzzling finding because of its apparent influence at later stages.

The Prosecutor's Recommendation Concerning Bail at Arraignment

In circuit court in Dade County and in superior court in Maricopa County, the judge's (or commissioner's) bail decision at initial appearance had the benefit of a recommendation from pretrial services staff who had interviewed the defendant and reviewed his or her background. In the Boston Municipal Court, the probation department improvised a similar role by orally presenting the available prior-record and court-attendance information to the judge at arraignment, except that a recommendation relating to the bail decision was not routinely made.

In observing the arraignment proceedings in the BMC, the research staff was struck by the active role played by the prosecutor in bail proceedings. In Dade County, the district attorney's staff played a role in the bond hearing, but not usually an influential one. In Maricopa County, a representative of the district attorney's office was not present for the initial bail determination. In the BMC, the prosecutor played a central role, which included reading to the judge information about the charges from the police arrest report (which, surprisingly, the judge did not have) and occasionally making a recommendation for higher bail.

The unusually influential role of the prosecutor required investigation, particularly the extent to which judges were influenced by the prosecutor's recommendation. Unfortunately, the decision to make a particular recommendation was often made on the spot and was not recorded. In discussion with the district attorney's staff, we learned that, in important cases, written notes—however informal—would probably have been placed in the case file. In fact, such hand-written recommendations were noted in 11 percent of the cases.

With little alternative, we reasoned that the influence of the prosecutor's recommendation would be tested by comparing cases with and without a written note. Although our interest in the assistant district attorney's recommendation was to learn of its influence on judicial decisions, we first needed to understand how the recommendation was derived, or what factors seemed to guide it. The available information did not explain the recommendation well. We conclude that the inability to explain statistically the presence of an assistant district attorney's recommendation may have stemmed from difficulty in obtaining an accurate written summary of the recommendation and the reasons behind it. We were informed by the district attorney's staff that this might often have had more to do with prosecutorial strategy than bail risk.) It may have also stemmed from the subjective nature of the assistant district attorney's recommendation, and from the differences likely to occur given the different approaches individual assistant district attorneys may have taken.

Arraignment: The Choice between Financial and Nonfinancial Bail

With the concurrence of the participating judges at our BMC meetings, we followed the conceptual models of the bail task we had employed in Arizona and Florida earlier and first looked at the judges' decision at arraignment in the BMC as involving two stages: the screening of defendants into nonfinancial (ROR) versus financial options; and selection of particular amounts of cash for cash candidates and conditions of release for nonfinancial candidates. In the first decision component, about 70 percent of all defendants had personal recognizance (ROR) set by BMC judges at arraignment, with the remaining 30 percent relegated to some amount of financial bail. Our meetings and discussions with the BMC judges, however, led us to approach our analyses somewhat differently in Boston from in the other jurisdictions. When we asked how bail decisions were made, we were frequently referred to the Massachusetts statute that outlines the criteria judges should take into consideration. The implication was that the judges decided bail by relying on the instructions provided by law.

To test this hypothesis, we first attempted to translate the 17 criteria listed in the law[6] into the attributes of the defendants and their cases measured in our data. For example, we assessed the "nature and circumstances of the offense" by considering any and all information we had available describing the alleged offense, its seriousness, injury to victims, use of force, presence and use of weapons and so on. In fact, we employed 20 items of information descriptive of a defendant's charges to measure the importance of this criterion in the law.

There were some criteria, such as the defendant's "reputation" and whether a defendant was "on release pending sentencing or appeal," that we were unable to measure. Other criteria we were unable to measure well or systematically for all defendants, such as the use of an alias or a fraudulent identification or a present drug dependency. Such information was simply not available or was available only in a small number of cases. In all, we selected 40 items of information to represent the 17 criteria suggested by the statue in our analysis of the judges' choice between nonfinancial and financial options. We found that knowledge of all of these factors failed to explain very well the variability in judges' choices between nonfinancial bail (ROR) and financial bail.[7] We concluded that knowledge of the criteria listed in the Massachusetts statute—roughly but generously measured—offered a rather poor prediction of how judges chose between nonfinancial and financial options.

Arraignment: The Selection of Cash Amounts in Financial Cases

Of the roughly 28 percent of defendants having financial bail set, more than half had bail set at $100 or less. Bail over $1,000 was exceedingly rare, occurring in 5 percent of all entering criminal cases. As low as the bail amounts in the BMC appeared to be, the use of cash bail by BMC judges was important because it was the vehicle by which detention of some defendants was obtained—whether temporarily or, in a small number of cases, throughout the pretrial period. When bail was set at $500 or less at arraignment, a majority (60 percent) of the cases secured immediate release. When bail was set over $500, a majority were not released within one day.

When examining the use of financial bail by the BMC judges at arraignment, we again sought to learn whether statutory or other criteria appeared to play influential roles in the judicial choice of specific bail amounts in cases in which financial bail was to be assigned. We were somewhat more successful in identifying criteria guiding this aspect of the judges' task. Several defendant and case attributes provided a modest explanation of the variability in selection of cash amounts.[8] The possible penalty associated with charges and several measures of the nature of the criminal charges appeared to account for the most influence among the factors representing the statutory criteria. In fact, the following charge-related measures were important: the overall seriousness of the most serious booking charge (based on possible sentence); a record of prior arrests for serious personal crimes; whether the charges involved serious crimes against the person; whether the charges involved sales of drugs (illegal distribution); whether the charges involved an index offense; and whether the defendant had a record of substance abuse. When other factors were controlled for the race and gender of defendants did not appear to influence judges' choices. We also found that two other factors made a significant though slight difference in the choice of cash bail amounts for BMC defendants, even after we took the effect of other factors into account: the presence of the assistant district attorney's recommendation and the identity of the particular judge presiding.

Although we were better able to "explain" the selection of cash amounts than the larger choice between nonfinancial and financial options, an important finding is that a large amount of the variability in judicial decisions could still not be explained by statutory or other factors. We concluded that, to a large extent, this was because decisions were not characterized by measurable patterns or themes and were inconsistent.

Release within 48 Hours of Booking

As we have noted previously, the major reason for examining bail decisions at the first judicial appearance is their practical result; the release or detention of defendants before trial. We reported that approximately 94 percent of all entering BMC defendants would gain release within 90 days or before the adjudication of their cases. This certainly represents a high rate of release among criminal defendants, but not unusually high when it is recalled that the BMC caseload substantially involved misdemeanor cases. While we may conclude that BMC defendants were seldom detained for long periods, a sizable proportion of defendants were jailed at least briefly. As discussed earlier, the majority of defendants having bail set at $500 or more by the municipal court judges were detained for some period longer than 24 hours; 9 out of 10 defendants with bails higher than $5,000 were held for some period.

We have already discussed the period spent in custody between arrest and arraignment of more than half of the entering defendants. Interestingly, 97 percent of defendants who had been released prior to arraignment were continued on release as a result of the judge's bail decision at arraignment, though 3 percent were taken into custody at that point. Of those held after booking until arraignment, 65 percent were released after bail, and 35 percent remained confined.

We examined detention of defendants after 48 hours, reasoning that the judges' decisions at arraignment would have had the most direct impact on the defendants' custody status by this point. Roughly 85 percent of defendants had gained release by that time; 15 percent remained confined. When we considered all the items of information describing defendants and their cases in multivariate analysis, we could not adequately explain release versus detention of defendants (as judged by finding a significant logit model).

Predicting the Performance of Defendants during Release

Like the judges in Miami and Phoenix, the Boston Municipal Court judges expressed an interest in learning of predictors of defendants failure to appear ("default") or crime during pretrial release. Thus the research staff attempted the same kinds of predictive analyses described above in the context of the Maricopa County and Dade County research. The judges were particularly interested in learning whether statistical analyses (not regarded equally by all participating judges, to be sure) would point to defendant attributes that they did not routinely consider or give sufficient weight to in their bail determinations.

Presentation of the predictive results to the BMC judges was introduced with a discussion of the limitations and uses of statistical prediction. For example, while at least some skepticism was voiced by the BMC judges concerning the value of statistical prediction, the research staff reported recent research showing the greater accuracy of statistical methods over subjective methods in predictive decisionmaking and explained the findings showing that statistical tools used in conjunction with the subjective judgment of decisionmakers can improve prediction over the level that would have been achieved by decisionmaker judgment alone. As the obstacles to good statistical prediction in criminal justice applications were reviewed with the working committee (see the discussion of prediction in Maricopa County in Chapter 7), it was clear that two problems would be particularly difficult in Boston: the quantity and quality of information available describing defendants, their histories, and their cases; and the availability of rearrest information in specific.

The measurement of defendant attendance in court (FTAs, or "defaults" in Boston) and rearrests for crimes occurring during the pretrial period each presented special problems. First, the study of defaults was facilitated by the fact that the clerk's office kept reliable records of defaults and the warrants that were issued as a result. Information concerning the rearrest of released defendants, however, was quite difficult to obtain because of the manual system of storing and retrieving criminal history in Massachusetts.[9] In fact, we were able to acquire such information only with the special cooperation of the commissioner of probation, who, still, could allow us to check the records of only a subsample of our BMC defendants. Because of the amount of labor required by the commissioner's staff to retrieve the arrest histories of 2,000 defendants during their particular pretrial release periods, we were able to gather follow-up information regarding arrest on only 414 of approximately 2,000 releases.[10] On the other hand, the prospect of sample bias was not going to present quite the problem encountered in Maricopa County, where only 55 percent of defendants gained release before trial. In the BMC, 94 percent gained release within the 90-day period and thus were at risk.

Prediction of Defendant Flight

As in the other jurisdictions studied, we followed the Boston defendants securing release after BMC arraignment for a period of 90 days or until their cases were adjudicated, whichever came first, to learn whether they absconded or were rearrested during the pretrial period. Default (failure-to-appear) information was available for our entire sample (approximately 29 percent of BMC defendants defaulted).

The purpose of multivariate analysis was to identify factors predictive of flight when taking into account the effects of other factors. Three independent variables and two interactions contributed to a model that fit the data adequately:[11]

- *Telephone.* After taking the effects of the other variables into account, having a telephone reduced the likelihood a defendant would fail to appear in court.
- *Employment status.* Being unemployed appeared to increase the prospects of defaulting.
- *History of prior defaults* increased the prospects for flight, other factors being held constant.
- *Telephone and prior defaults (interaction).* After the effects of other factors were taken into account, not having a phone *and* having prior defaults added to the chances that defendants would default.
- *Unemployed and recent prior failures to appear.* After the effects of other variables, being unemployed *and* having a prior history of defaults contributed to a higher probability of flight during pretrial release.

Prediction of Rearrest among BMC Releases

Our follow-up defendants for purposes of learning of rearrests for crimes alleged to have been committed during pretrial release was limited to the 414 case subsample of defendants who had to be specially checked through the records held by the commissioner of probation. As a result of the limited sample size, predictive analysis was more difficult. The variables included in one of the best models predicting rearrest included the following factors:[12]

- *Outstanding bench warrants* increased the prospects of rearrests for crimes committed during pretrial release.
- *Female victim of crime.* Charges involving a female crime victim added to the likelihood of rearrest.
- *Indication of history of substance abuse* increased the likelihood of rearrest.
- *Prior misdemeanor convictions* added to the likelihood of rearrest.
- *Outstanding warrants and female crime victim.* These two conditions together add to the likelihood of rearrest, after the effects of other factors had been taken into account.
- *Substance abuse and female crime victim.* The presence of these two factors interacted to add to the prospects of defendant rearrest.

Prediction of Defendant Misconduct Generally (Either Default or Rearrest)

Using the same 414 case subsample, we attempted to develop a model predictive of either rearrest or defaulting among defendants during pretrial release. Neither regression nor logit analysis produced a model that fit the data reasonably well.

Summary of Decisionmaking in the Boston Municipal Court

1. A first and fundamental finding in our study of bail in the Boston Municipal Court was discovered in trying to assemble data descriptive of defendants moving into the system: Important information describing defendants, their backgrounds, histories, and cases, was often not available—at least in reliable form—in time for judges' decisions at arraignment in the BMC. Information-related difficulties (which translated into data-related difficulties for the research staff) were obvious, both in terms of the needs of the bail–pretrial-release task at the arraignment stage and in comparison to other court systems.

In its efforts over many months to reconstruct information concerning the BMC cases in the study from the records of the cooperating agencies, the research team encountered serious problems relating to the availability and quality of important information. A key problem, for example, involved the availability and reliability of prior criminal-history information, though other kinds of information needs were also not consistently and rigorously met. Compared with those in other jurisdictions studied, Boston judges appeared sometimes to have to make bail decisions in the absence of critical information.

Given the difficulty the research staff encountered over months of data collection, it is unreasonable to expect that the probation department serving the Boston Municipal Court would routinely be able to provide full and accurate information to the presiding judge, given the short period of time between arrest and arraignment in municipal court in which this task must be accomplished. This fact of life in the court was underscored in our interviews with the BMC judges and in their responses to questionnaires.

2. Under half of all entering defendants secured release at the booking stage as a result of the decision of the part-time bail commissioner located at the police station. Analysis of the booking-stage bail decision was not able to detect thematic differences between the attributes of defendants held (or their cases) and the attributes of those released. Initial (bivariate) differences based on the race and sex of defendants did not survive multivariate tests. The importance of this finding—that detention versus release at the prearraignment stage could not be well explained—is heightened by the fact that detention at this stage had an impact at subsequent decision stages.

3. Recommendations made by the assistant district attorney at the arraignment stage were recorded in about 11 percent of the cases examined. Consistent patterns in whether or not a recommendation was noted were not found, indicating either difficulty in measuring the recommendation (often not recorded in the file and just orally made) or inconsistency among prosecutorial staff in making the recommendations. The minor patterns that were identified related to the seriousness of a defendant's charges: The more serious the charges, the more likely were recommendations. This finding is consistent with information provided by the prosecutor's staff concerning the purposes of their recommendations at arraignment. Often, the recommendation had more to do with prosecutorial strategy relating to the processing of the case than with estimates of the defendant's risk of flight or crime during pretrial release. The assistant district attorney's recommendation was important in later decisions but was not found statistically to be related to risk of default or rearrest among released defendants.

4. Efforts to explain the judges' choices between nonfinancial (ROR) and financial bail options through multivariate analysis were not very successful. We examined 40 items of information intended to reflect 17 criteria specified in the law as appropriate bail considerations to determine the extent of their influence on the judges' decisionmaking. Our analysis revealed little influence. Overall, knowledge of the kinds of information mentioned as governing criteria in the Massachusetts statute was not very helpful in predicting bail outcomes when conceptualized as an initial choice between nonfinancial and financial bail options. Specifically, only four of the statutory criteria appeared to paly a role: The potential penalty, flight to avoid prosecution (measured as evidence of current bench warrants), the defendant's financial resources, and charges relating to illegal drug distribution. The race or gender of defendants did not appear to change their chances for nonfinancial release, once other factors were considered. The district attorney's recommendation and custody before arraignment contributed to the prospects that judges would choose cash bail over ROR, after the effects of other factors had been taken into consideration. The identity of the presiding judge did not appear to make a notable difference.

Our tentative conclusion is that, overall, the municipal court's use of nonfinancial bail options was inconsistent or disparate when similar kinds of defendants were compared. This conclusion is tempered by the knowledge of the difficulties found in gathering information.

5. When we analyzed the judges' choice of particular cash amounts for defendants who would not receive ROR, we found some patterns of modest strength: Principally, the greater the possible penalty and the more serious the charges, the higher was the likely bail. The defendant's custody prior to arraignment did not make a difference in the choice of bail amounts after controls were exercised; however, the presence of a recommendation by the assistant district attorney and the identity of the judge presiding at arraignment did make differences in the levels of bail likely, after the effects of other factors were considered.

In general, the lack of ability to detect strong patterns governing the choice of bail amounts in financial cases reflected disparity or inconsistency in bail setting when similar defendants were compared.

6. Nearly 80 percent of defendants secured release shortly after arraignment in municipal court. Our analysis was unable to discover strong thematic differences between those held and those released at this stage. Apparently, the prospect of being confined for more than one day was unaffected by a recommendation by the assistant district attorney or the identity of the judge presiding at arraignment. However, the fact that a defendant had been confined prior to arraignment had a notable effect on the prospects for further detention, even after the effects of other

factors were taken into account. Earlier, prearraignment detention seemed to beget later, postarraignment pretrial detention.

7. Boston Municipal Court bail decisions generated a very high rate of pretrial release, roughly 94 percent within a 90-day period measured from the time of arrest. Associated with this rate of release were very high rates of failure to appear (FTAs, or "defaults") and moderately high rearrest rates; nearly one-third of BMC defendants gaining release either had bench warrants issued for defaulting or were rearrested for crimes committed during the pretrial period. We should note that equally high rates are generally found among misdemeanor courts in the United States (and in comparison with the two other court systems studied, the BMC was a predominantly misdemeanor-level court), and that most of the rearrests were not for serious crimes.

8. Predictive analysis was undertaken to identify factors associated with misconduct among released defendants. Development of models of FTA and rearrest separately were successful; however, when the criterion was the prediction of either rearrest or failure to appear, we were unable to develop sufficient statistical models using regression or logit analyses.

9. Knowledge of the judge's choice of nonfinancial over financial bail at the arraignment stage did not prove to be a predictor of defendant defaulting and was only very slightly related to risk of rearrest. When we attempted to predict defendant misconduct more generally (as either flight or crime), whether the person had financial bail or ROR assigned to permit release made no significant difference in the likelihood of subsequent misconduct when other factors were taken into account.

Notes

1. Descriptive analyses and meetings to discuss descriptive findings were conducted in superior court during the first year and a half of the project's work in Boston. The project shifted its energies to concentrate on municipal court for two principal reasons: (a) project resources could not support two independent guidelines-development processes in the same system; and (b) the bulk of bail decisions were made at the arraignment stage in municipal court. This strategy recognized the importance of bail decisionmaking in superior court, however, especially in its bail review and initial bail-determination functions. It was argued that, should guidelines development be successful in the "front-line" court (the Boston Municipal Court), extension of guidelines to the superior court would be a logical next step.
2. Those agencies included the clerk's offices for the municipal and superior courts, the probation offices for each court, the district attorney's office, and the Suffolk County Jail, the Office of the Commissioner of Probation, and the Massachusetts Correctional Institute at Framingham.

3. When information is not obtainable in more than about 15 percent of the cases, its reliability may be open to question. Some items of information were missing in more than half of all cases.
4. In Massachusetts, *commissioners* has a different meaning than in Maricopa County. Although commissioners answer to a chief bail commissioner for the state and that official reports to the chief justice of the superior court, they are not judicial officers in the sense of acting judges. Rather, they are part-time officials authorized to set and accept bail at the police station at the booking stage and retain a fee for each bail posted.
5. We followed the data reduction, regression, and logit procedures described in the earlier analyses and were unable to develop a model that fit the data well.
6. Massachusetts criminal procedure law (C. 276, Sec. 58) listed the following criteria to be taken into account by the bail judge: the nature and circumstances of the offense, the potential penalty, family ties, financial resources, employment record, history of mental illness, reputation, length of residence in the community, record of convictions, illegal drug distribution, present drug dependency, flight to avoid prosecution, use of alias or fraudulent identification, prior failure to appear in court, on release at time of arrest for previous charge, on probation, parole or other release pending completion of sentence, and on release pending sentencing or appeal.
7. A minimally fitting logit model could not be developed.
8. With cash bail amounts transformed to logarithms, we were able to explain 23 percent of the variance using eight independent variables.
9. At the time of our research, the manual cards catalog system was being replaced by a computerized system, but only for new cases entering the system.
10. These cases represented a 20 percent random subsample of the unweighted sample of released Boston defendants. Weighted, they produced estimates for over 900 defendants.
11. Goodness-of-fit chi-squared = 1.93 ($DF = 2$; P value = 0.38; $n = 4{,}318$).
12. Goodness-of-fit chi-squared = 3.86 ($DF = 4$; P value = 0.42; $n = 915$, weighted).

10

Visibility, Equity, Rationality, and Effectiveness in the Three Court Systems

In its investigative stages, the guidelines research in the Maricopa County, Dade County, and Boston courts involved descriptive and analytic case studies. Its descriptive aspect involved a careful mapping of the progress of large samples of defendants through the criminal process in each location. We studied the decisions that produced the release or detention of defendants and that were responsible for the performance of defendants given pretrial release. The analytic aspect of the research was to interpret the descriptive findings with working groups of judges and to evaluate the quality of the decisionmaking performed by the courts. Through an iterative process of data examination, interpretation, and debate, we identified areas of decisionmaking that were troublesome—in their operation or effect—or that should be improved. Our question was whether the undesirable side effects of pretrial release decisionmaking, such as crises of jail overcrowding, crimes, and flight from court by released defendants, could be minimized by the development of the particular decisionmaking and policy resource potentially offered by pretrial release guidelines. Although the challenges faced by each of the courts differed in character and scope, they can be usefully understood from the perspective of several issues they shared: issues relating to the visibility, equity, rationality, and effectiveness of pretrial release decisionmaking. These themes, which have been described elsewhere[1] can serve as a useful evaluative framework for comparing the separate sites.

The Visibility of Pretrial Release Decisionmaking

One of the criticisms of traditional bail practices has been that, through the discretionary manipulation of cash bail, judges have been able to bring about the detention or release of defendants before trial in a nearly *sub rosa* fashion. Thus, the considerations that have played a part in the decision to release or to detain remain mysterious, or at least of very low visibility. As we will describe in the next chapter, the guidelines approach to decisionmaking assumes that there is value in developing a more explicit decisionmaking framework, one in which the goals of the decision task as well as the criteria that come into play in pursuing those goals are known and are reviewable. Evaluation of a court's performance of pretrial release functions is hardly possible without some explicit referents for framing the analysis.

The courts we studied varied in the ways their decisionmaking was governed by explicit themes. The commissioners' choices between secured bond and personal recognizance release in the Maricopa County Superior Court, for example, could, in one sense, be said to have been operating according to a highly predictable criterion: the recommendation of the pretrial services staff. In fact, if we use the language of regression, a very large proportion of the variance of their decision choices could be explained by that single piece of information.

However, what at first appears to be a highly visible form of decisionmaking turns out to be just the opposite upon further analysis. As we noted in Chapter 7, the basis for that recommendation itself was largely inexplicable. Whether our inability to "predict" pretrial services recommendations was due to a lack of reliance on explicit criteria by the staff or by a highly subjective (and varied) use of agreed-upon criteria was difficult to determine. Yet the result was that this important judicial determination, which greatly affected defendants' chances for release or detention before trial, was apparently based on goals and criteria that were not at all clear.

Characterizing the visibility of the pretrial-release-detention decision in the Dade County court system is also problematic, despite the appearances given by the use of the highly explicit and visible bond schedule. In one sense, of course, we would certainly have to agree that a defendant entering the criminal process in Dade County during our study could know a great deal about his or her prospects of pretrial release. After all, merely by knowing the criminal charges, the defendant could determine right at booking what amount of money would be required to post bond according to the bond schedule. Despite this impression, however, our analyses caused us to question how systematic the impact of the bond schedule actually was on pretrial release. First, release via the bond schedule at the booking stage was only partly explainable or predictable in a statistical sense. To the extent that this was true, we conclude that such release is often athematic or random in its occurrence.

Second, to the extent that our analyses did reveal some, although modest, predictable patterns governing the securing of release at this stage, other issues surfaced. We found that the seriousness of the charges affected defendants' chances for booking-stage release (because the more serious the charges, the higher the bond the defendant had to raise), but also that the defendant's ability to pay, possession of a telephone, and living arrangements also figured into the prospects for release or detention. We would argue that the questions to be raised at the booking stage concerning the determination of release or detention do not involve visibility (the bond schedule is very explicit) as much as "rationality" (focusing on the relationship of the criteria employed in release decisions to the goals of the decision process).

The bond hearing in circuit court, however, also raised questions about the visibility of the pretrial release determinations. Empirical study of bond-hearing decisions was unable to identify strong themes governing the judges' choices between nonfinancial and financial bond options. It would be normal to conclude as a result that these decisions were highly subjective and erratic and, therefore, that the process was a very-low-visibility undertaking. However, in-court observation gave us cause to reconsider that inference. Clearly, we had not been able to measure the pretrial services staff's oral recommendation for nonfinancial release, the most important determinant of the judges' nonfinancial versus financial choice. At the time of the study, the recommendation was usually not written on any document. Because it was not recorded, we were not able empirically to determine its impact—which was certainly great—nor were we able to determine how it was arrived at in the first place. In this sense, as in Maricopa County, we concluded that the choices between nonfinancial and financial options at the bond hearing were governed by a knowable criterion, but not in a predictable pattern.

In contrast, the choices of bond amounts at bond hearing (for defendants for whom nonfinancial options had been ruled out) were quite predictable. They were based nearly exclusively on the amounts posited by the bond schedule. Thus, if pretrial services personnel were unable to convince the judge to release the defendant on nonfinancial terms, the bond schedule amount was the preferred choice. In fact, in-court observation confirmed this finding: Before each decision, the bond schedule amount was announced to the judge (and courtroom) over a microphone and/or closed-circuit television sound in a loud voice. The determination of pretrial release or detention in Dade County, then, was partly based on concerns or criteria that were unknowable, of low visibility, and partly based on clear-cut themes linked to the bond schedule's ordering of criminal charges.

We reported in Chapter 9 that our analyses of pretrial-release decisions for defendants entering the Boston Municipal Court (BMC) process failed to reveal strong patterns or themes. This was true at the booking stage, at the BMC arraignment stage (especially in the choice between nonfinancial and financial options), and when release within 48 hours was examined. Although we were often told in our discussions and interviews that bail determinations were based on consideration of the criteria spelled out in the relevant Massachusetts statute, our analyses were not able to demonstrate this. When an effect was found, it was primarily related to the seriousness of the defendant's charges. It is very difficult to conclude, therefore, that bail–pretrial-release decisionmaking in the Boston Municipal Court overall operated according to explicit, "visible" themes.

The Equity of Bail–Pretrial-Release Decisionmaking in the Three Courts

The conceptual ideal of *equitable treatment* of defendants at the pretrial stage is easier to describe than it is to measure in practice. Ideally, equitable decisionmaking would assign roughly comparable decisions to similar kinds of defendants based on appropriate criteria. If the bail decision were not so often a subterranean detention decision (one camouflaged by the use of cash bail and tied to a defendant's assets) but were more forthrightly decided, this would more directly mean that similar defendants would face similar prospects of being detained before trial. The empirical measurement of this concept is somewhat more complicated, however.

The difficulty in assessing the "relative equity" of bail–pretrial-release decisions stems from the lack of an agreed-upon "yardstick" that can be employed to compare outcomes for "similar" defendants.[2] Indeed, this is one of the key issues that pretrial release guidelines seek to address. Traditionally bail has been governed by the seriousness of the alleged offenses (e.g., by bond schedules). Bail reformers of the 1960s argued, alternatively, that considerations of defendants' community ties were the more appropriate standard. The charge standard, when linked to the cash bail system, translated into a detention decision governed by economics. In the next chapter, we will discuss the ways in which the decision guidelines developed in this study offer a different answer to the "yardstick" question. In essence, we argue that some explicit standard related to the purposes of the pretrial-release decision (whether the traditional charge measure, the bail reform criteria, or some other appropriate standard) must organize the decisions made.

Analysis of equity-related problems in the practices of the three court systems we studied ought to include two elements: the determination that decisions about release and detention have followed some noticeable, overall pattern and that the nature of the pattern found is an arguably appropriate one, given the decision goals.

Consideration of the first element is closely related to the visibility question discussed above. If no patterns, or only weak ones, are empirically identified, the decisions can be characterized as being both of low visibility and inequitable. That is, to the extent that decisions are inconsistent or athematic, they cannot be treating comparable defendants in similar ways. When sentencing or paroling practices have been discussed in the past, such "unwarranted variation" was referred to as *disparity* or inconsistent treatment of similar categories of offenders.

To the extent that variability in choices cannot be explained by appropriate factors, we may conclude that choices are disparate, characterized by "unwarranted variation"[3] or randomly produced. From a statistical perspective, inequitable or inconsistent treatment of similar defendants is manifest from our inability to construct models of the decision–outcome that fit the data well (that met minimal statistical standards).

In reviewing the analyses of decisions in each of the court systems, it is generally evident that *pretrial-release decisionmaking was rarely adequately explained by measurable factors of any kind.* Even when some patterns were found to modestly explain decisions, to a substantial extent the variability in bail choices had no explanation other than "unwarranted variation." From this, we conclude that disparity characterizes the treatment of defendants at the first judicial stage.

We can, however, point to two notable exceptions. In superior court in Maricopa County, the nonfinancial versus financial choices were very strongly predictable: They were dominated by the recommendations of the pretrial services staff, who interviewed defendants prior to initial appearance. In Dade County, the judges' selection of bail amounts for defendants not being assigned nonfinancial options corresponded very closely to the appropriate booking-stage bond-schedule amount. Assessment of the implications of these exceptions, however, must be placed in the context of their appropriateness given the aims of the bail task.

In the instance of the superior court commissioners in Maricopa County, we are forced to draw our inferences from multivariate analysis of the recommendations made by pretrial services staff. Furthermore, these recommendations were predicted by a number of community-ties-, charge-, and criminal-history-related factors that could reasonably be related to defendants' risk of flight or crime (if not strongly statistically, at least on an intuitive level). However, the magnitude of the relationship was quite modest. Accordingly, we concluded that it was not possible to discover the themes that brought about the pretrial services recommendations that so influenced the commissioners' choices.

In the example of circuit court in Dade County, we speculated that the recommendation of the pretrial services staff was very important—but we were not able to measure it for use in our analyses. However, the fact that financial bail choices by bond-hearing judges were heavily tied to the bond schedule presents a clearer example of the equity of practices there. Certainly, among defendants who have been awarded financial release options, similar defendants (at least based on the charge criterion) were treated similarly. It is questionable at best, however, that the traditional charge criterion is the appropriate yardstick with which to measure the consistency of decisions.

The long-standing debate has juxtaposed two different interpretations of this custom. Those favoring reliance on the criminal charges as the backbone of bail considerations tend to argue that more seriously charged defendants, because they face more onerous penalties, present greater risks of flight and crime to the court.[4] Others, particularly proponents of bail reform, have argued that the seriousness of the defendant's charges bears little statistical relationship to probable flight or crime during a period of pretrial release and that detention becomes a matter not of weighing criteria reflecting the concerns of flight and crime, but a question of the defendant's ability to afford given amounts of bail. From this perspective, the charge standard is the cornerstone of a system that allocates release or detention in a way that discriminates against those without financial assets. In next chapter, we offer another interpretation of the traditional criminal-charge standard at bail.

The Effectiveness of Pretrial Release in the Three Courts and the Utility of Predictive Classifications

Comparing the Effectiveness of Pretrial Release

In the previous chapters, we reported the failure-to-appear (FTA) rates, the rearrest rates, and the general "failure" rates for defendants released in each of the cities studied. In addition, we reported the results of analyses that sought to identify combinations of variables (descriptive of defendants, their cases, or their histories) that could predict defendant outcomes during pretrial release. In this section, we relate the analysis of defendant "outcomes" to the theme of evaluating the relative effectiveness of pretrial release in each of the courts.

Although usually poorly defined, the concept of effectiveness lies at the heart of public policy related to bail and pretrial release. Some critics of the system argue that bail practices chaotically permit the release of criminals who either abscond or prey upon the public by committing additional crimes during pretrial release. Others contend that bail practices have the opposite effect: They needlessly confine defendants who could safely be released and thereby generate jail overcrowding. Both of these issues are related to the effectiveness of pretrial release. Ineffective bail practices contribute both to crime and flight among released defendants and to jail overcrowding because of inappropriate uses of pretrial detention.

Although both kinds of concerns are often debated, reasonable measures of the system's effectiveness in doing the bail–pretrial-release job are seldom employed. In discussing defendant performance during release, rates of FTAs and rearrests are employed. When jail overcrowding is the concern, levels of the jail population are reported. Although appropriate for some purposes, such measures may be highly misleading.

As a consequence, we have created a measure that attempts to link together the two sides of the "effectiveness" coin: release and detention. To illustrate, we can first consider the defendant performance statistics recorded at each of the sites shown in Table 10.1.

TABLE 10.1
Defendant Performance Summary: Percentage of Released Defendants Failing to Appear, Rearrested for New Crimes, or Both, by Court

	Court system		
Defendant performance	BMC	Dade County	Maricopa County
All released defendants			
FTA	21	11	8
Rearrest	14	6	11
Serious rearrest	1	2	3
Failure (FTA or rearrest)	38	15	17
Index-offense defendants only			
FTA	25	11	7
Rearrest	10	6	10
Failure	30	16	16

This table summarizes the percentage of released defendants engaging in "misconduct," variously measured, at each of the sites. When we use this commonly reported measure, it would appear, for example, that Maricopa County produced the lowest FTA rates, Dade County produced the lowest rearrest rates, and Dade County produced the lowest general "failure" rates. (Roughly the same is shown when just defendants charged with Part I index offenses are examined.)

The problem, of course, is that we have learned that these jurisdictions placed different proportions of their defendant populations at risk. Maricopa, with the lowest FTA rate, released only 55 percent of its defendants within a 90-day period, while Dade County released 80 percent and Boston 94 percent. Surely, these measures do not reflect the overall effectiveness of practices well, because they do not link the performance rates with release or detention rates.

Figure 10.1 illustrates the simple measure of effective pretrial release that we have constructed to better ground performance rates in the context of release rates. Each column in Figure 10.1 represents 100 percent of the defendants entering the criminal process in each system. Each column is divided into three parts: the lowest section (black) represents the percentage of defendants detained (and therefore ineligible to engage in miscon-

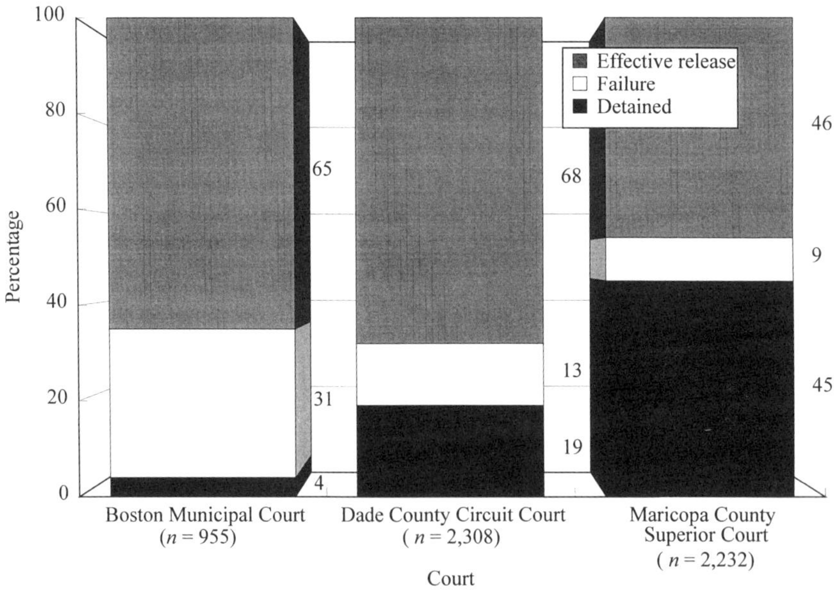

FIGURE 10.1. Comparison of effective pretrial release in Boston Municipal Court, Dade County Circuit Court, and Maricopa County Superior Court: Failure as FTA and/or rearrest.

duct); the middle segment (white) represents the proportion of defendants released but engaging in some form of misconduct; the top portion of each column (gray) represents the percentage of all defendants achieving release and not engaging in misconduct.

Using this key, we can define effective pretrial release as that share of the defendant cohort entering the process in a court system that is released without pretrial misconduct. Or stated another way, effectiveness of a court's pretrial-release practices is reduced for two reasons: (1) the extent that defendants area detained and (2) the extent that defendants are "erroneously" released (they are released but fail to appear or are rearrested).

Figures 10.1 through 10.3, then, throw into question the inferences concerning the effectiveness of practices drawn from consideration of simple defendant performance rates. Far from having the most effective pretrial-release practices from the perspective of FTAs, seen in this light, Maricopa County appears to have been the least effective in overall performance. The Boston Municipal Court produced the largest percentage of "rearrest-free" release when compared to the other jurisdictions. However, when we combine flight and rearrest into one measure of effectiveness (pretrial misconduct generally or just "failure"), Dade County

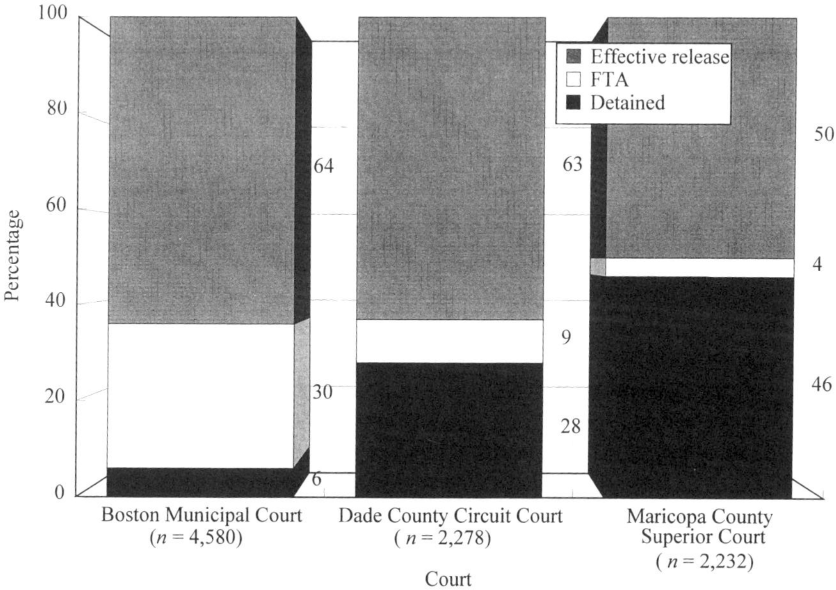

FIGURE 10.2. Comparison of effective pretrial release in Boston Municipal Court, Dade County Circuit Court, and Maricopa County Superior Court: FTA.

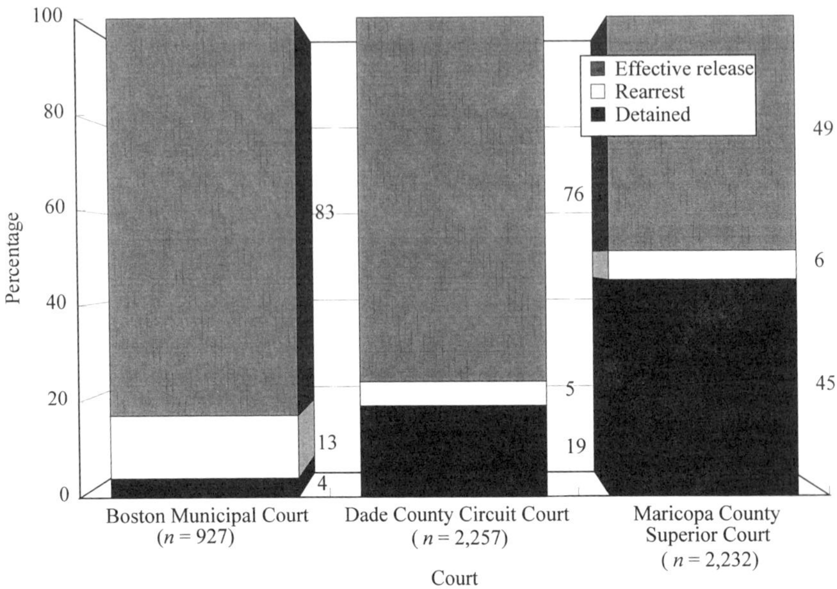

FIGURE 10.3. Comparison of effective pretrial release in Boston Municipal Court, Dade County Circuit Court, and Maricopa County Superior Court: Rearrest.

boasted the greatest effectiveness. This image does not change when we restricted this analysis to serious charges only (not shown in figures).

This performance measure reflects a jurisdiction's release practices and permits analysis of the source of ineffectiveness. For example, despite low rates of defendant misconduct during release, Maricopa County's low effectiveness rating derived form its extensive use of pretrial detention. In contrast, the Boston Municipal Court practices generated very little detention, but a rather large amount of "erroneous" release. The overall effectiveness of Dade County release practices reflected the combined effect of a detention rate roughly one-half that of Maricopa County and an "erroneous" release rate about one-fourth that associated with the practices of the Boston Municipal Court.

Within the context of the guidelines research, this measure of effectiveness is useful because it can help target areas needing improvement which prospective guidelines might be designed to address. For example, the reason for the higher rate of detention in Maricopa County Superior Court could be explored and guidelines development could be oriented to ensure the appropriateness of detention. In Boston, the focus might shift to improving the performance of released defendants, given their high rates of failure. Though pretrial release might be viewed as effective in a more balanced fashion in Dade County, the guidelines development process might be geared toward minimizing the use of detention while maintaining suitably low failure rates.

The Development of Predictive Classifications Relating to Risk of Defendant Misconduct

Critical debate about the bail–pretrial-release function has often centered on questions about prediction. Early advocates of bail reform, for example, in part based their argument that judges should consider a defendant's community ties on their belief that the judges' traditional criterion at bail, the seriousness of the charges, was not a good predictor of defendant risk[5] and that the community ties measure offered a better standard.[6] Opponents of preventive detention laws such as the District of Columbia's code and the Federal Bail Reform Act of 1984 have argued that prediction at the bail stage was not accurate enough to warrant detention decisions based on anticipated future conduct of defendants and that error associated with such prediction would generate a very large amount of erroneous pretrial detention.[7] The U.S. Supreme Court recently stated that judges' ability to make predictions in deciding detention did not need to meet statistical standards.[8]

In response to questions asked by each of the judicial working committees, however, our approach employed statistical prediction, first, as an analytic tool and, ultimately, as a dimension in decision guidelines, again based on the directions given by the courts in development of the decision guidelines. Theoretically, predictive analysis of bail–release outcomes was conducted for two principal reasons. First, the bail–pretrial-release decision is and always has been essentially a predictive decision in which the judge seeks to weigh the likelihood that a defendant, if released, would flee or commit additional crimes and then selects a bail option that matches that risk. Normally he or she does so rather subjectively and with little guidance. Given the importance of the pretrial release decision, if this is true, then it makes sense to evaluate the predictive capacities of courts as they make these predictions. Second, research has demonstrated that, however imperfect, choices resulting from statistical prediction will out perform choices made on the basis of strictly subjective ("clinical") decisionmaking every time.[9] Thus, although decisionmaking based on statistical prediction may not reach the "no-error" ideal, it does more often produce "correct" results than subjective choices. In employing statistical prediction first as an analytic tool and later as one dimension in the guidelines, we recognize that a combination of the two kinds of decisionmaking—the statistical and the subjective—probably produces the most reasonable approach to decisionmaking overall.[10]

In Chapters 7 through 9, we reported some results of multivariate modeling designed to produce predictions of defendant performance: failure to appear in court, rearrest, or both kinds of misconduct. At a later stage, we discussed the utility and appropriateness of statistical prediction as a feature of a prescriptive guidelines system. At the descriptive and developmental stage of the research, however, our aims were illustrative, designed to respond to the judges' questions: How would statistical models of defendant performance help us in making decisions about defendants? Compared to what a statistical approach might say, how do our decisions look?

We noted earlier that the ability to predict defendant performance during pretrial release in the three court systems was constrained by at least three obstacles: (1) sample bias (to the extent that defendants were not released from jail before trial in a jurisdiction, their performance cannot be systematically studied); (2) lack of information or data (some potentially relevant data describing defendants and/or their cases were not available at each of the sites); and (3) the rarity of the outcomes being predicted (statistical prediction is most difficult when the phenomena under study are infrequent, such as pretrial flight and crime). At each of the sites we attempted to model failure to appear (FTA), rearrest, and then "failure" generally construed (as either flight or crime).

Beyond reporting variables that, when taken together, can "predict" or model defendant performance during pretrial release, the purpose for developing predictive classifications was to identify criteria that, when weighted according to the models, could classify defendants into groups characterized by differing probabilities of misconduct. The most satisfactory models derived for the classification of defendants based on flight and crime concerns (taken together) for each site are summarized in Table 10.2.[11] Although the models differ somewhat between Maricopa County and the other two sites, each was based on weightings of charge-related, ties-related, and prior-history-related variables.

By assigning points based on the weights of each of the variables included in the models,[12] each defendant can be assigned a "score" according to a probability of misconduct. A classification of defendants is produced by selecting "cutoff" scores so that several categories can be distinguished based on differing probabilities of flight or crime during pretrial release. The groupings of defendants based on these scores and the probabilities of misconduct associated with them are displayed in

TABLE 10.2
Predictive Classification Models for Misconduct during Pretrial Release, by Site

		Weight
Maricopa County Superior Court		
Prior failures to appear		
One	1 ×	.541
Two or more	2 ×	.273
Police: Risk of flight		1.013
Person victim		−.514
Defendant lives alone		.548
Charges involve robbery		.675
Police: Risk of flight and FTAs		
With one prior FTA	1 ×	.122
With two or more prior FTAs	2 ×	.267
Police: Risk of flight and lives alone		.415
Constant		.012
Dade County Circuit Court		
Lives with spouse or child		1.000
Has telephone		2.000
Property charges only		2.000
Any robbery charges		−2.000
Any drug charges		−1.000
Prior arrests within past three years		
One		−1.000
Two or more		−2.000
Prior failures to appear		
One misdemeanor or one felony FTA		−1.000
One prior felony or misdemeanor FTA		−2.000
Two misdemeanor or two felony FTAs		−2.000
One or more prior felony convictions		−2.000
Two or more prior arrests on drug charges		−2.000
Boston Municipal Court		
Lives with spouse or child		1.000
Has telephone		2.000
Property charges only		2.000
Any robbery charges		−2.000
Any drug charges		−1.000
Prior arrests within past three years		
One		−1.000
Two or more		−2.000
Prior failures to appear		
One		−1.000
Two or more		−2.000
One or more prior felony convictions		−2.000
Two or more prior arrests on drug charges		−2.000

Table 10.3.[13] (Examples of how defendants would be grouped on the basis of these predictive classifications are described in the next chapter.)

The principal uses for classifications based on the probable risk of flight and crime that groups of defendants might pose are to provide a tool for the evaluation of the then-current decision practices in the jurisdictions and for improving future practices. In the next chapter, which describes the development of decision guidelines, we will discuss the applicability of predictive classifications to improving future decisions. The use of these classifications for evaluation of current decisionmaking is illustrated here and in the next section.

Perhaps the simplest way in which the predictive classifications are helpful in the evaluation of current practices is in providing a characterization of the risk attributes of the defendant caseload in each jurisdiction. Using the Boston Municipal Court classification, for example, we see from Table 10.3 above that only about 6 percent of entering defendants fell within the highest-risk grouping (Group 4), in which three in every five

TABLE 10.3

Classification of Defendants According to Probability of Misconduct (Rearrest and/or Flight), 1984, by Site

Risk group	Misconduct points	Number	Percentage	Percentage released	Percentage misconduct
Maricopa County Superior Court					
Total	—	2,232	100	54	17[a]
1	1–34	322	14	59	7
2	35–67	1,130	51	61	15
3	68–107	565	25	43	20
4	107–224	215	10	35	53
Dade County Circuit Court					
Total	—	2,308	100	81	15[a]
1	5–7	442	19	95	6
2	2–4	855	37	88	12
3	−2–1	654	38	76	23
4	−9–−3	356	15	57	30
Boston Municipal Court					
Total	—	4,580	100	94	33[b]
1	5–7	779	17	99	16
2	1–4	2,415	53	95	34
3	−4–0	1,123	24	92	39
4	−10–−5	262	6	82	54

[a]Of released and at-risk defendants.
[b]These numbers are derived from a special subsample of cases ($n = 414$) which, when weighted, total 995, with 40 cases missing.

defendants could be expected to fail to appear in court or to be rearrested for crimes occurring during pretrial release. In Maricopa County, 10 percent were classifiable as of highest risk. In Dade County, 15 percent of entering defendants fell into the highest-risk category.

A second way in which the predictive classifications may provide a useful framework for assessing current practices is in characterizing the risk attributes of defendants held in the local jail facility. Figure 10.4 classifies the populations of pretrial detainees held in the jails of each of the jurisdictions according to their respective four-part risk (flight or crime) rankings.[14]

In Maricopa County, nearly one-fourth (22 percent) of the detained population fell into the highest-risk category, but fully 13 percent were characterized as lowest risk. About one-fifth of the defendants held in the Dade County jail facilities were classifiable in the highest-risk category, and roughly 30 percent of detainees fell within the two lowest-risk groupings. In the Boston jail, under half of detainees were classified within the two lowest-risk groups.

In trying to determine the extent to which portions of the pretrial jail populations might be released as part of strategies to reduce crowding, the risk classifications can provide a rough tool for pinpointing categories of defendants for whom release options might be productively considered.

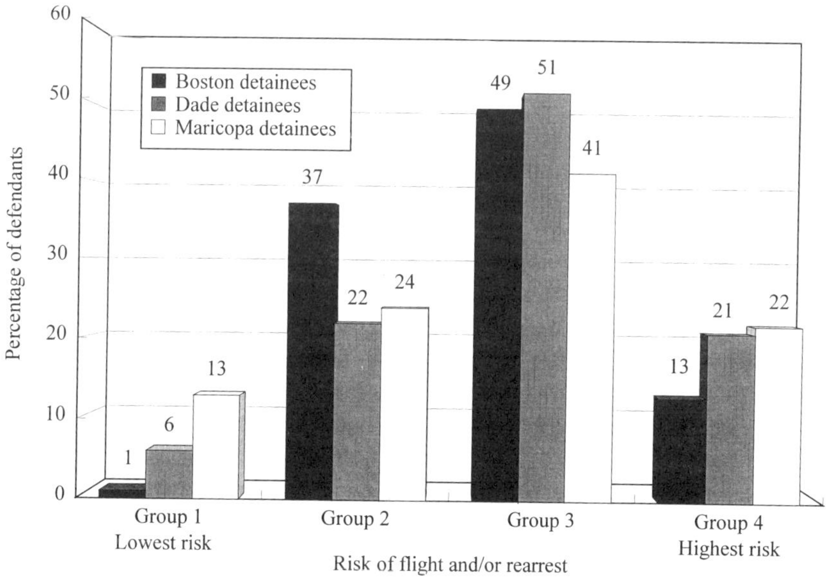

FIGURE 10.4. Risk classification of persons detained in jail facilities, by site, Fall 1985.

Although risk attributes would not be the only criteria considered in weighing alternatives to incarceration, they certainly would provide a useful source of information. Even relatively small percentages of defendants falling within lower risk groupings can translate into large actual numbers of defendants in the larger jails.

Statistically derived classification schemes can also be helpful in assessing the "rationality" of bail–pretrial-release decisionmaking, which is discussed in the next section.

The Rationality of Pretrial Release Decisionmaking in the Three Court Systems

Another analytic theme central to the guidelines research concerns the "rationality" of pretrial release decisionmaking. As we explained earlier,[15] by seeking to improve a decision's rationality, we do not mean to imply that the goal is somehow to combat "irrationality" in decisionmaking (although this might be viewed as a desirable side effect). Rather the task is to evaluate the extent to which the criteria seen to guide the decisionmaking process relate to its legitimate goals. In fact, this approach assumes that the more discretionary a decision, and the broader the scope for unguided decisionmaker subjectivity, the greater is the need for evaluation of the way the decision is made and of its results.

More specifically, if we assume the goals of the bail–pretrial-release decision involve simultaneously minimizing defendant flight from court and crime committed by released defendants, then the criteria relied on by judges ought to bear a relationship to those goals. Of course, it is arguable, given the imperfect state of decisionmakers' predictive skills in criminal justice settings, whether the relationship between decision criteria and decision goals should exhibit a strong statistical relationship or merely an intuitive relationship.[16] Optimally, to be characterized as "rational" within our meaning of the term, a strong statistical relationship should be found between the predictors of judges' choices at bail and the outcomes of flight and crime, for this would signal that judges' pretrial-release decisions are guided by factors related to the decision aims.

In Table 10.4 the relationships between the variables predicting bail decisions as a group at each of the sites and flight and crime are summarized; the measure of multiple correlation (multiple *r*) is used for comparative purposes. In the left-most columns, the variables most predictive of bail–pretrial-release decisions are shown; then, in the next three columns, these same predictors are applied to the prediction of failure-to-appear, rearrest, and failure. In general, we found relationships that range from weak to slight.[17] Given that we earlier found that bail–pretrial-release decisions at each of the sites could be only poorly explained statistically and that poor predictors of bail decisions could predict defendant performance only rather poorly, we conclude that bail–pretrial-release decisionmaking was not convincingly "rational," in the sense that, at each of the sites, it did not appear to optimize bail–pretrial-release choices based on the most appropriate use of the available information.

Using the predictive classification systems we described above, we can also evaluate bail and decisionmaking in a somewhat different fashion, to shed light on the rationality question. If we assume that, to be considered "rational," bail–pretrial-release decisions ought to operate strongly in line with the risk attributes of entering defendants, then, at a simple level, we would expect persons rated as lower risks—based either on risk "points" or on the grouped risk classifications—to receive OR or lower bond amounts generally and to be less often detained than their higher-risk counterparts.

When we did such an analysis (not shown in tabular form), moderate, nearly monotonic relationships were found in the expected directions at each of the sites when the assignment of nonfinancial versus financial choices and the allocation of release within 48 hours were compared (the lower the risk the greater the use of nonfinancial bail and the greater allocation of release). (See Figures 10.5 to 10.7.) Similar relationships did *not* appear when the assignment of financial bail or bond was examined among defendants not receiving OR. One interpretation of these findings might be that straightforward pretrial-release determinations (resulting in personal recognizance release and release within 48 hours) roughly operate under the guidance of risk concerns. The fact that the selection of cash bail amounts does not reinforces the view that case is mainly invoked as an option to cause detention (once high risk has been assumed). Cash is not used to further distinguish among defendants on the basis of risk.

If we wished to compare the jurisdictions on the basis of the strength of the relationships between their decisionmaking and the risk attributes of defendants, it would be difficult to single out an exemplary site. We studied these relationships using Pearson's r and employing both the risk points (ungrouped risk ratings) and risk classifications. The correlations were uniformly low.

In summary, keeping the limitations of our data in mind, our analysis of the relative "rationality" of decisionmaking at the study sites might

TABLE 10.4

Testing Key Predictors of Bail Decisions as Predictors of Defendant Performance during Pretrial Release, by Site

Key predictors of bail decisions[a]	Dependent variables: Possible outcomes		
	Failure to appear	Rearrest	Failure
	Independent variables from prediction of outcomes		
Site: Date County Circuit Court			
Nonfinancial versus financial bail			
Drug trafficking Prior arrests for serious property offense Has a telephone Robbery charge	Has a telephone Prior arrests for serious property offense Robbery charge Drug trafficking	Prior arrests for serious property offense Robbery charge Drug trafficking Has a telephone	Prior arrests for serious property offense Has a telephone Drug trafficking Robbery charge
Cases = 1,818 r^2 = .10	Cases = 1,856 Multiple r = .14 r^2 = .02; p = .000	Cases = 1,856 Multiple r = .16 r^2 = .02; p = .000	Cases = 1,856 Multiple r = .15 r^2 = .02; p = .000
Cash bail amount			
Seriousness of charge based on bail schedule Drug trafficking Prior felony conviction Prior weapons conviction	Prior weapons conviction Prior felony conviction Seriousness of charge based on bail schedule Drug trafficking	Prior felony conviction Prior weapons conviction Seriousness of charge based on bail schedule Drug trafficking	Prior weapons conviction Prior felony conviction Seriousness of charge based on bail schedule Drug trafficking
Cases = 554 r^2 = .82	Cases = 1,856 Multiple r = .10 r^2 = .009; p = .002	Cases = 1,856 Multiple r = .17 r^2 = .03; p = .000	Cases = 1,856 Multiple r = .14 r^2 = .02; p = .000

Site: Maricopa County Superior Court			
Nonfinancial versus financial bail			
Outstanding warrants	Police: Risk of flight	Recent prior arrests	Police: Risk of flight
Length of residence	Outstanding warrants	Outstanding warrants	Outstanding warrants
Recent prior arrests	Length of residence	Police: Risk of flight	Recent prior arrests
Police: Risk of flight	Recent prior arrests	Length of residence	Length of residence
	Multiple r = .26	Multiple r = .10	Multiple r = .17
r^2 = .25	r^2 = .07; p = .000	r^2 = .01; p = .015	r^2 = .03; p = .000
Nonfinancial release recommended	Nonfinancial release recommended	Nonfinancial release recommended	Nonfinancial release recommended
Cases = 2,232	Cases = 1,200	Cases = 1,200	Cases = 1,200
r^2 = .90	Multiple r = .27	Multiple r = .11	Multiple r = .18
—	r^2 = .07; p = .000	r^2 = .02; p = .012	r^2 = .03; p = .000
Cash bail amount			
Severity of most serious charge	Police: Risk of flight	Robbery charge	Police: Risk of flight
Sexual assault	Severity of most serious charge	Sexual assault	Robbery charge
Robbery charge	Sexual assault	Police: Risk of flight	Sexual assault
Police: Risk of flight		Severity of most serious charge	Severity of most serious charge
	Multiple r = .26	Multiple r = .11	Multiple r = .17
r^2 = .59	r^2 = .07; p = .000	r^2 = .01; p = .009	r^2 = .03; p = .000
Nonfinancial release recommended	Nonfinancial release recommended	Nonfinancial release recommended	Nonfinancial release recommended
	Multiple r = .27		
	r^2 = .07; p = .000		
	Robbery charge		
Cases = 1,296	Cases = 1,200	Cases = 1,200	Cases = 1,200
	Multiple r = .27	Multiple r = .12	Multiple r = .19
r^2 = .59	r^2 = .07; p = .000	r^2 = .02; p = .002	r^2 = .04; p = .000

(continued)

TABLE 10.4 *(Continued)*

Key predictors of bail decisions[a]	Dependent variables: Possible outcomes		
	Failure to appear	Rearrest	Failure
	Independent variables from prediction of outcomes		
Site: Boston Municipal Court			
Nonfinancial versus financial bail			
Severity of most serious charges Recent prior arrests Selling drugs, most serious charge Prior pretrial relase	Prior pretrial release Selling drugs, most serious charge Severity of most serious charge Recent prior arrests	Recent prior arrests Prior pretrial release Selling drugs, most serious charge Severity of most serious charge	Selling drugs, most serious charge Recent prior arrests
Cases = 4,580 r^2 = .10	Cases = 4,318 Multiple r = .03 r^2 = .0009; p = .442	Cases = 915 Multiple r = .22 r^2 = .05; p = .000	Cases = 915 Multiple r = .06 r^2 = .003; p = .003; p = .222
Cash bail amount			
Severity of most serious charge Serious personal offense Selling drugs, most serious charge Serious personal offense	Serious personal offense Selling drugs, most serious charge Severity of most serious charge Prior arrests, serious personal offense	Serious personal offense Prior arrests, serious personal offense Severity of most serious charge Selling drugs, most serious charge	Selling drugs, most serious charge Prior arrests, serious personal offense Serious personal offense Severity of most serious charge
Cases = 1,293 r^2 = .18	Cases = 4,318 Multiple r = .06 r^2 = .004; p = .004	Cases = 915 Multiple r = .07 r^2 = .005; p = .331	Cases = 915 Multiple r = .07 r^2 = .006; p = .277

[a]Independent variables from multivariate analysis of judges decisions.

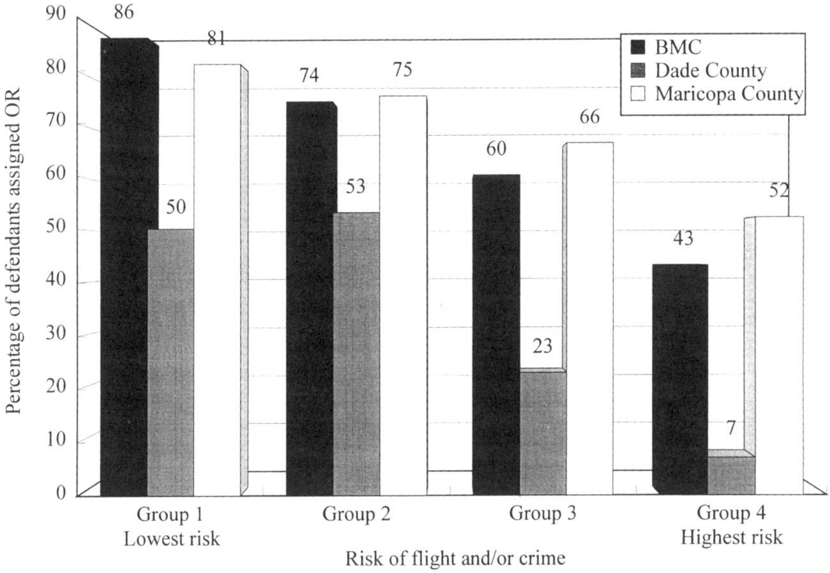

FIGURE 10.5. The relationship between judges' choice of nonfinancial decision and defendant risk of flight and/or crime, by site.
Note: BMC: r = 23; Dade County: r = 20, p = .00; Maricopa County: r = .29, p = .00.

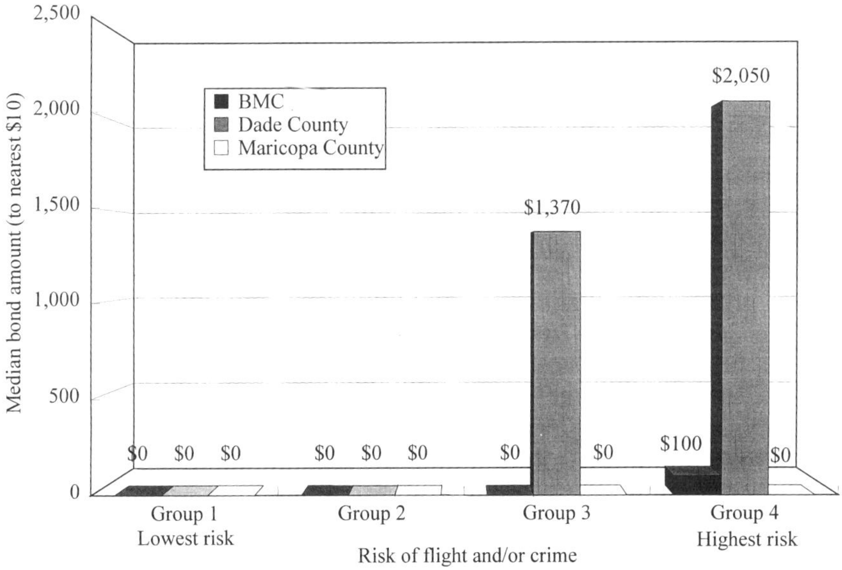

FIGURE 10.6. The relationship between judges' assignment of financial bond and defendant risk of flight and/or crime, by site.
Note: Nonfinancial options are coded as $0 in this analysis.

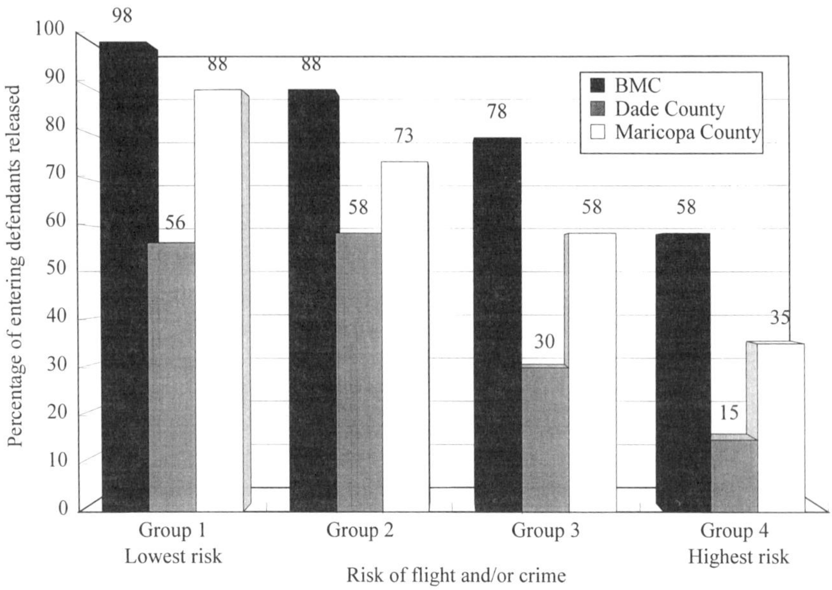

FIGURE 10.7. The relationship between release within 48 hours of arrest and defendant risk of flight and/or crime, by site.
Note: BMC: $r = -.25$, $p = 100$; Dade County: $r = -.35$, $p = .00$; Maricopa: $r = -.28$, $p = .000$.

best be concluded by reporting that pretrial-release decisionmaking was not strongly related to the risk of flight or crime posed by defendants appearing before the court. The simple correlations varied from slight to moderate, however. The findings do present something of a paradox. The use of personal recognizance and the allocation of pretrial release within 48 hours resulting from judges' and commissioners' decisions *did* correspond to risk in a rough sense—even though the predictors of those decisions were shown to be nearly unrelated to predicting defendant misconduct during release. If by *rational* we mean that decisions should be not only logically but empirically related to risk attributes of defendants, the evidence is not strongly supportive.

Notes

1. See e.g., Gottfredson, et al. (1978); Gottfredson and Gottfredson (1988); Goldkamp and Gottfredson (1985).
2. See Goldkamp and Gottfredson (1985).
3. Gottfredson et al. (1978).
4. See, e.g., Mitchell (1969).
5. See, e.g., Schaeffer (1970).

6. Vera Institute of Justice (1972).
7. See, e.g., Angel et al. (1971).
8. See, e.g., Schall v. Martin 467 U.S. 253 (1984); Salerno 481 U.S. 739 (1987).
9. See Meehl (1954); Monahan (1981); Gottfredson and Gottfredson (1986).
10. Dawes (1979).
11. At each of the sites, multivariate analyses proceeded in the same fashion. Burgess models performed better than logit-derived models in both Dade County and the Boston Municipal Court. A model was not viewed as acceptable until the resulting classification was validated—by means of the split-half procedure.
12. The "points" derived from the Maricopa logit formula are divided by a constant and rounded as shown in Table 10.3.
13. Of course, classifications based on just failure to appear or just rearrest could also be (and were) developed. For the sake of brevity we use only the classification based on risk of flight and/or rearrest in this discussion.
14. For discussion of the jail samples studied at each of the sites, see Chapter 2. See Goldkamp and Gottfredson (1988) for standard error tables surrounding the estimates based on each of the samples.
15. Gottfredson and Gottfredson (1980); Goldkamp and Gottfredson (1985); Goldkamp (1987); Gottfredson and Gottfredson (1988).
16. Certainly, the U.S. Supreme Court has not adopted the view that predictive decisionmaking should be evaluated on a statistical basis. See, e.g., Schall v. Martin 104 S.Ct. 2403, 2413 (1984); Salerno 481 U.S. 739 (1987); Barefoot v. Estelle 103 S.Ct. 3383 (1983). See also Morris and Miller (1985).
17. We are seeking to gauge the rationality of judicial decisions by determining the predictive power of the criteria we have inferred as guiding those decisions. Although we can study all decisions made, we can only evaluate the statistical relationship to defendant performance only by using defendants who gained release. In Boston, only 4 percent did not gain release within 90 days; in Dade County, 20 percent did not; in Maricopa County, 45 percent did not.

III

CONSTRUCTION OF DECISION GUIDELINES FOR PRETRIAL RELEASE

11

Consideration of Alternative Decisionmaking Models

Introduction

In each court, descriptive research and group discussions led to the next, more difficult step of trying to devise decision guidelines helpful in establishing an overall policy and as a day-to-day decisionmaking tool. Defining the task in general terms was straightforward: The goal was to devise a decisionmaking aid that would incorporate the particular court's policy aims, that would bring together key pieces of information relating to defendants and to their cases, and that would point to preferred decisions for usual kinds of cases. Arriving at a specific product for each of the three court systems, however, meant addressing a number of important policy and practical questions.

This next stage in our process was difficult because it asked what such guidelines should look like and what kind of an impact they might be expected to have. Thus, as the task for the working committees shifted from examination, interpretation, and critique of findings relating to past bail practices to development of a tool for shaping future practices, the debate became more involved. Thus establishing a policy framework for guiding decisionmaking in the future involved quite different questions from understanding how decisionmaking had been operating in the recent past (the task described in Chapter 7). Moreover, a great deal more was at stake in deciding how to shape future policy than was risked in discussing the strengths and weaknesses of court practices of the past.

At each site, before actual construction of decision guidelines could begin, the judicial working committees first had to agree on the theoretical model of guidelines that would be most suitable to their needs in the future. This involved consideration of what they had learned about their past practices and formulation of how practices should be improved for future processing. In this chapter, we summarize the consideration of alternative models that occurred at each site and illustrate some of the guidelines models that were reviewed by the courts.

Models of Decision Guidelines for Pretrial Release

Perhaps predictably, judges within each of the working committees directly requested that the research staff "show" them what the best version of decision guidelines ought to look like. For example, they asked to see the guidelines that had been developed and implemented in the Philadelphia courts. Because we believed that guidelines should be seen to address the specific needs of each of the courts, we resisted the temptation to make a recommendation regarding the kind of model that might *a priori* be most suitable for each site. Instead, we sought to illustrate the kinds of models the court might find helpful.

In the working group discussions, the research staff reviewed the issues and questions about pretrial release and detention that had been raised in the descriptive research stage, placing them more clearly in the context of "decisionmaking." That is, in order to get to the point of deciding upon the substance of guidelines, questions relating to the goals of the pretrial release decision, the information that should be relied on in meeting those goals, and the decision options that should be available to act on the information in light of the agreed-upon goals had to be addressed.[1]

Depending on how the judges viewed the decisionmaking task and how they viewed questions relating to goals, information, and decision alternatives, a variety of decision guidelines could be conceived. The particular form the guidelines might ultimately take would depend not only on how importantly the courts considered these kinds of questions, but also on the weight that would be given to particular themes (such as crowding or flight, for example) and on the extent of change to be achieved. For example, a court system like Boston's might choose to develop guidelines closely linked to then current practices but might place great weight on the potential benefit of improving the quality and availability of information relied on in making the bail decision. Another jurisdiction, like Maricopa County, might instead wish to bring about more dramatic overall improvement in a more selective and constrained use of pretrial detention.

From a practical perspective, two dimensions were central in decision guidelines the courts considered: a conceptualization of the nature of the decision task and an ideological direction concerning the descriptive versus prescriptive thrust of the guidelines.

The first dimension was critically important if the judges and commissioners who were to employ the resource were to be intuitively comfortable with the guidelines tool. If the decision task were to be represented in a fashion alien to the day-to-day decisionmaker, judges would be unlikely to employ them in the intended fashion. The second dimension was important because of the value that judges may or may not have placed on the fashion in which bail practices then operated. The guidelines could be made to be rooted squarely in past traditions, to the extent that these could be uncovered by empirical analysis, or they could be devised on a purely normative basis, based mostly on judges' visions of how bail ought to operate in an ideal world.

In this chapter, we discuss five examples of types of decision guidelines that we proposed to the judicial working committees: (1) guidelines viewing bail as a two-stage decision; (2) guidelines viewing the decision as a direct choice between detention and release; (3) guidelines based solely on the actuarial classification of defendants according to risk (of flight or crime or both); (4) guidelines based on detention and risk; and (5) guidelines based on risk and the seriousness of the criminal charges (the Philadelphia model). Note that these models for future decisionmaking selectively draw on conceptualizations of how pretrial release decisionmaking had been operating in the descriptive phase of the research—but are not the same. Although we describe each in detail below, they may briefly be characterized as follows. We created these models in an effort to provide a broad array of choice among *principles* that might guide prescriptive guidelines. Thus, the first model reflected the view of most of our judges concerning how they actually made decisions. It was based on "past practice" and did not include *explicit* consideration of the utilitarian function of bail. Its virtues were meant to include greater visibility and consistency of decisionmaking. The second model had a fundamentally different aim: to explicitly acknowledge that the fundamental outcome of the decision was release or detention and to recognize that this threshold outcome should be met head-on in an explicit fashion. The third model represented a radical departure from past practice. It recognized the fundamentally utilitarian purpose of the decision (to minimize flight and pretrial crime) and sought to employ the best available statistical technology in achieving these purposes. The fourth model sought to focus attention simultaneously on detention and on pretrial risk (again, a radical departure from practice). The final model, similar to those commonly used in sentencing and paroling guidelines, combined charge seriousness and risk of failure. The attractiveness of this form is undoubtedly that one judge could consider risk and some notion of harm simultaneously.

Clearly, these models incorporate profoundly different policy choices for the decision. While each could potentially serve to enhance visibility and consistency, they would differ in individual-case decisionmaking. Our purpose is presenting them to our committees was to facilitate the necessary policy debate.

A Two-Step Model

In the two-step model, the judge's task at the first judicial stage involves two choices. First, the judge determines whether financial or nonfinancial bail is appropriate. Second, the judge sets the conditions of (nonfinancial) release or selects an amount of bail. During discussion of the descriptive findings, judges in each of the locations had expressed some comfort with this basic conceptualization of the pretrial release decision. However, even given their evident preference for this model as a point of departure, there remained the determination of whether a relatively descriptive or prescriptive orientation should inform the development of the guidelines.

A "Descriptive" Two-Step Model

One version of guidelines based on this model would seek to formalize traditional practices by employing the criteria that best explained how judges' choices were usually being made in the particular court. To the extent certain variables "explained" judges' decisions in the past, the decision guidelines would be shaped so that the same principal factors would guide judges' choices in the future. Thus, depending on our success in identifying "predictors" of judges' recent decisions, defendants would be scored and placed in groups, each having a presumptive pretrial-release decision option assigned to it.

To illustrate how this kind of two-stage guidelines model might work, we turn to the analysis of commissioners' decisions at initial appearance in superior court in Maricopa County. From our analysis of the commissioners' choices between nonfinancial and secured forms of bond, several characteristics appeared to be central.[2] Using these characteristics and weighting them to reflect their influence on the commissioners' decisions,[3] we can place defendants in two categories: one (Part I) in which defendants in the recent past nearly always received OR and one (Part II) in which they almost never did. (See Figure 11.1.)

The pretrial services staff would classify each defendant first as a "Part I" kind of defendant, destined to receive some nonfinancial form

Part I
Choosing Nonfinancial versus Secured Bond

Nonfinancial 1	2	Nonfinancial 3	4	Secured 5	6
Standard Conditions		Special Conditions		Go to Part II	

Guidelines Category (please check):

_______Nonfinancial -- Standard Conditions
(List: ______________________)

_______Nonfinancial -- Special Conditions
_______Third-party custody
_______Supervision
_______Other (______________)

_______Secured range ($ ______ to ______)

Part II
Choosing Amount of Secured Bond

1	2	3	4	5	6
$1 to $1,000	$1,001 to $1,500	$1,501 to $2,500	$2,501 to $4,000	$4,001 to $7,500	$7,501 to $15,000

Commissioner's Decision: ________________

If exception, give reason: ________________

Commissioner: ________________________

FIGURE 11.1. Hypothetical two-part guidelines: (1) nonfinancial versus secured bond; (2) amount of secured bond.

of release, or as a "Part II" kind of defendant, destined to have financial bond assigned by scoring the defendant on the criteria listed in Table 11.1. The pretrial services staff would interview each defendant to focus on the following kinds of information, which would be used to place them within a suggested decision category: whether there were outstanding warrants, how long each had resided in the area, the record of arrests within the last three years and the seriousness of the charges (using a special scale), and whether the police believed the defendant might flee, for example.

Depending on defendants' ratings on these items, the pretrial services staff could determine whether the suggested decision would fall into the nonfinancial category. If so, the points earned would further differentiate for the commissioner employing this version of guidelines whether the defendant should be released under normal ("standard") conditions of release, or whether more restrictive but still nonfinancial conditions ought to apply. If the defendant's ratings placed her or him out of the range for nonfinancial categories, the staff member would turn to a second rating to determine the appropriate range of cash bond that ought to be assigned.

Table 11.1 classifies the following example of a defendant to illustrate the use of this version of guidelines derived for Maricopa County:

> The defendant is charged with a burglary (second degree). He was in the process of committing the burglary when the police arrived at the scene. Before being apprehended, the defendant fired two shots from a pistol at the officers,

TABLE 11.1
Scoring of Defendants on Part I Factors under the Two-Step Model (Nonfinancial versus Financial Options), Maricopa County

Factor	Part I points	Example's score
Outstanding warrants		
No	0	—
Yes	7	7
Least serious charge		
No	0	0
Yes	−7	
Weapons charge		
None	0	—
One or more	4	4
Defendant lives alone		
No	0	—
Yes	4	4
Wages reported		
No	0	0
Yes	−2	—
Length of residence		
0–3 months	0	0
4–12 months	−7	—
12 or more months	−13	—
Prior arrests in last three years		
No	0	—
Yes	5	5
Police: Risk of flight		
No	0	—
Yes	3	3
Add points	18	18

Decision groupings	Part I points	Number of defendants	Percentage of defendants	Percentage with ROR
1	Lowest to 3	510	22.9	73.9
2	4–6	280	12.5	62.2
3	7	310	13.9	45.9
4	8–11	425	19.0	31.4
5	12–15	334	15.0	13.0
6	16 to highest	373	16.7	9.1
Total	—	2,232	100.0	

Example defendant	
Total Part I points	41
Classification	Group 6: Go to Part II

> without hitting them. The defendant has an outstanding warrant for his arrest on charges in another Arizona county. He has been arrested twice in the past three years and has one felony conviction for which he spent one year in prison. He is currently unemployed, lives alone, and does not yet have a telephone installed. The police have expressed the opinion that he might flee if released before trial.

Table 11.1 shows how pretrial services staff would have rated this defendant under such a "descriptive" system. First, we see that he would have earned 41 points. Second, in looking at the array of all Maricopa felony defendants studied, we learn that this score places him in Part I, Group 6, in which defendants in the past seldom received nonfinancial decisions at initial appearance. Figure 11.1 posits that defendants in Groups 5 or 6 under Part I of the descriptive guidelines should have secured bond be set under financial (Part II) guidelines.

Classification of defendants under the Part II guidelines for secured or financial bond is based on another scoring system derived from the empirical analysis of the Maricopa commissioners' choices of different bond amounts. The criteria on which defendants are scored in this section of the descriptive guidelines include the seriousness of the charges, whether a victim of sexual violence was involved in the charges, whether a robbery charge was included, whether the police indicated a risk of flight, whether a weapon was allegedly involved, and whether the crime involved an alcohol- or drug-related offense.

Table 11.2 demonstrates how Maricopa felony defendants in the study would have been distributed among Part II categories of suggested secured-bond amounts. According to the evaluation scheme outlined in Table 11.2, the defendant in our example rates a total of 61 points, placing him in the second highest bond groups, for which the average bond has been close to $6,850 in the recent past. Given this classification of the defendant by the pretrial services staff, the commissioner's job would be to decide whether an amount within the range suggested by the guidelines would be appropriate, or whether an exceptional decision would be required, and then to follow the procedures discussed in the previous example.

At each of the sites, this descriptively based, two-step model of guidelines was developed and discussed by the members of the judicial working committees. Should any of the courts have chosen to develop further and then to adopt this version of guidelines, several advantages over current practices could have been realized. First, this conceptualization would have structured pretrial release decisions, as nearly as possible, in line with then-current practices. And even though it would not have prescribed decisions very different from those usually seen in superior court, this

TABLE 11.2

Scoring of Defendants on Part II Factors under the Two-Step Model (Amount of Secured Bond)

Factor	Part II points	Example's score
Seriousness of charge		
0	0.0	
1	1.0	
2	2.0	2
3	2.5	
4	3.0	
5	4.0	
6	5.0	
Charges: Sexual assault		
No	0.0	0
Yes	10.0	
Charges: Robbery		
No	0.0	0
Yes	8.0	
Charges: Weapons		
No	0.0	
Yes	4.0	4
Charges: Alcohol- or drug-related		
No	−3.0	
Yes	0.0	0
Number of charges		
1	6.0	6
2	7.0	
3	10.0	
4	13.0	
5 or more	25.0	
Police: Risk of flight		
No	0.0	
Yes	3.0	3
Add points	46.0	46

Decision groups	Part II (bond points)	Number of defendants	Percentage of defendants
1	43–48	179	8.0
2	49–53	1,060	47.5
3	54–57	554	24.8
4	58–60	181	8.1
5	61–67	198	8.9
6	68 to highest	60	2.7
Total	—	2,232	100.0

	Median secured-bond amount ($)	Interquartile range ($)	Range
1	700	245–1,519	1,274
2	1,375	564–2,240	1,676

TABLE 11.2 (Continued)

	Median secured-bond amount ($)	Interquartile range ($)	Range
3	2,050	1,028–3,299	2,271
4	3,425	1,380–9,492	8,112
5	6,850	2,741–12,338	9,597
6	20,750	8,229–33,004	24,775
Total	2,055	—	—

Example defendant	
Total Part II points	61
Classification	Group 5

approach could nevertheless have potentially contributed other enhancements to the decision process. For example, it would make the criteria guiding pretrial please decisions explicit, readily apparent to judges and pretrial services staff. Presumably, in turn, this increased visibility of decisionmaking would lead to a more systematic collection of information and to more consistency among decisions. In enhancing consistency, this framework based on explicit criteria, it was argued, could contribute more equitable pretrial-release decisions in the court as a whole.

Discussion of this version of guidelines, however, uncovered several disadvantages as well. First, although the explicit decision framework would add visibility and consistency to the bail process and reduce the extent to which similar defendants were treated differently, it would not substantially change decisionmaking practices. Thus, if the court felt that particular issues needed to be addressed in guidelines, such as a reduction of flight or rearrests among released defendants, a version based on modeling current practices would not have been likely to have the desired impact. The guidelines would have been aimed rather at preserving and reorganizing the status quo.

Another problem was practical: To the extent that our analyses of the nonfinancial versus financial decisions were not able to identify systematic criteria influencing the judges' choices or, at least, were not able to locate strong themes—and this was true of each of the sites—the descriptive guidelines models would be based on relatively weak criteria. One implication is that the guidelines would treat these (empirically weak) criteria as the dominant criteria. As a result, having weak but detectable criteria institutionalized as the henceforth guiding criteria, it would be difficult to claim that the guidelines were "descriptive" in the sense that they reflected traditional practice. Moreover, to the extent that these criteria were directly or indirectly related to factors considered inappropriate pretrial-release concerns (such as economic status, gender, or race or ethnicity), this approach would have the potential of amplifying some of the most undesirable aspects of past practices to shape future practices.

Modifying the Descriptive Two-Step Approach

Although the two-stage model just described would have the advantages of making the decision criteria explicit and fostering consistency and ease of application, the decision guidelines would be based on a description of then-current practices. And thus they would not dramatically change the court's overall approach, for example, to the use of pretrial detention. In addition, it is unlikely that either the choices of nonfinancial versus secured-bond options (Part I) or the selection of particular amounts of secured bond (Part II) would be more related to prediction of flight or crime in such new guidelines than they had been in the recent past under traditional practices.

Thus, a possible alternative model of guidelines would modify the decisions suggested within particular guidelines categories (under either Part I or Part II) using data relating to detention, flight, crime and so on. For example, perhaps the guidelines falling within the lowest secured-bond group in Part II could be moved to the "special conditions" category under Part I. Or perhaps suggested bond amounts within Part II categories should be lowered to reduce the use of detention in the expectation that, perhaps supplemented by special conditions of reporting or supervision, flight and rearrest rates would not be increased.

Figure 11.2 shows the data pertaining to each of the categories of Part I and Part II guidelines that could prove helpful in taking the prescriptive approach. Figure 11.3 uses the summarized information to suggest changes that might be considered in revising the descriptive approach to arrive at prescriptive guidelines.

A second means of modifying this model of guidelines based on a description-derived approach might be more normative in emphasis, based on discussion and debate of how pretrial release decisions ought to occur. The steering committee might decide, for example, that specific criteria ought to be made central in bail decisions—whether or not research identified them as playing an active role currently—and that guidelines ought to be developed that took them into account. Following this path, the court working group would then merely have to decide which criteria should be important and how they should be emphasized relative to one another.

The difficulty experienced in attempting to model bail decisions in the Boston Municipal Court, for example, suggested that the strictly de-

Part I
Choosing Nonfinancial Versus Secured Bond

	Nonfinancial 1	2	Nonfinancial 3	4	Secured 5	6
N	510	280	310	425	334	373
% OR	74	62	46	31	13	9
% det	23	35	49	64	81	85
% FTA	4	8	5	8	14	19
% rear	10	12	10	12	14	13
% fail	13	19	14	19	22	28

Guidelines Category (please check):

_______Nonfinancial -- Standard Conditions
(List: _______________________)

_______Nonfinancial -- Special Conditions
_______Third party custody
_______Supervision
_______Other (_______________)

_______Secured Range ($ _______ to _____)

Part II
Choosing Amount of Secured Bond

	1	2	3	4	5	6
N	179	1060	554	181	198	60
Med $	685	1370	2055	3425	6849	13814
% det	32	48	61	65	80	82
% FTA	2	6	11	14	11	5
% rear	11	11	10	13	9	24
% fail	13	16	19	21	17	29

Commissioner's Decision: _______________

If Exception, give reason: _______________

Commissioner: _______________

FIGURE 11.2. Hypothetical Maricopa County two-part guidelines: (1) nonfinancial versus secured bond; (2) amount of secured bond.

scriptive approach might not be feasible. In an exercise designed to develop a modified version of bail guidelines, we asked all the sitting judges in the Boston Municipal Court to assign weights (from 1 to 17 points) to each of the 17 criteria listed in the Massachusetts bail statutes based on how important they believed these items should be in bail decisions generally. The average scores assigned to each of the statutory criteria

Part I
Choosing Nonfinancial versus Secured Bond

Nonfinancial 1	2	Nonfinancial 3	4	Secured 5	6
Standard Conditions		Special Conditions		Go to Part II	

Guidelines Category (please check):

_______Nonfinancial -- Standard Conditions
(List: _______________________)

_______Nonfinancial -- Special Conditions
_______Third-party custody
_______Supervision
_______Other (_______________)

_______Secured range ($ _______ to _____)

Part II
Choosing Amount of Secured Bond

Nonfinancial 1	2	Nonfinancial 3	4	Secured 5	6
$1 to $800	$801 to $1,200	$1,300 to $2,000	$2,500 to $3,500	$3,501 to $5,000	$8,000 to $15,000

Commissioner's Decision: _______________

If exception, give reason: _______________

Commissioner: _______________

FIGURE 11.3. Hypothetical Maricopa County two-part guidelines: (1) nonfinancial versus secured bond; (2) amount of secured bond.

for bail decisions by the judges in this fashion are summarized in Table 11.3. A glance at the judges' ratings shows that the Boston judges believed that the "nature and circumstances of the offense" should be the most important factor considered in making the bail decision. In contrast, the item related to defendants' financial resources was rated as the least important to be considered by judges at bail. (In fact, the most important item was given 17 times the weight of the least important item, according to the judges' scoring exercise.) Thus, rather than basing guidelines on what the research has shown (or not shown), this exercise illustrated how a court might devise an approach using statutory or other criteria. In this normative approach, the overall scoring derived through the judicial ranking exercise would be translated into a classificatory scheme that placed defendants in distinct classes for which particular presumptive bail decisions would be specified, such as ROR, ROR with special reporting conditions, or financial bail.

Guidelines for Pretrial Detention

Judges or bail commissioners may not agree with the conceptualization of their decision task at the initial-appearance stage of criminal processing that posits a direct, explicit choice between custody and release of particular defendants. Wishing to be candid and accountable for their decisions, judges might nevertheless argue that guidelines should be fashioned not for a "bail" decision, but for a "detention" decision, using a rationale employed by Congress, for example, to support enactment of the original preventive-detention law for the District of Columbia, of the federal preventive detention law in 1984, or of recent revisions of the District of Columbia law (designed to bring district procedures more in line with the Federal Bail Reform Act).[4] Findings from empirical analysis of bail and release decisions at the sites are consistent with this conceptualization of bail practices (that beneath the useful vagueness of bail decisions lies a *sub rosa* detention decision). For example, analyses demonstrated that, at all sites, when bail was set at any amount over $500, a majority of defendants were not released within 24 hours. In effect, at each of the sites, selection of any financial bail option greater than $500 was tantamount to a decision to detain.

Thus forthright "pretrial-detention" decision guidelines might be structured to place defendants within presumptive release or detention categories. For defendants falling within presumptive release categories, the guidelines might further designate appropriate conditions of release. Like the two-step guidelines described above, detention guidelines might

TABLE 11.3
Scoring of Defendants on Part I Factors under the Two-Step Model (Nonfinancial versus Financial Options), Boston Municipal Court

Statutory criteria	Weight	Defendant score
Nature and circumstances of offense	17	1 (least serious) 17 (most serious)
Prior failure to appear	15	0 (none) 10 (one) 15 (two or more)
Record of convictions	15	0 (none) 5 (one, not serious) 10 (one or more, serious)
On probation, parole, or other release pending completion of sentence	11	0 (none) 11 (yes)
On release pending sentence or appeal	10	0 (none) 10 (yes)
Flight to avoid prosecution	9	0 (no) 9 (yes)
One release for previous charge at time of arrest	8	0 (no) 8 (yes)
Use of alias or fraudulent identification	7	0 (no) 7 (yes)
Present drug dependency	7	0 (no) 7 (yes)
Employment record	6	0 (stable) 6 (not)
Length of residence of community	5	0 (2 years or more) 2 (more than 1 year) 5 (less than 1 year)
Family ties	4	0 (close, verified) 4 (no close ties)
Potential penalty	4	0 (5 years or less) 2 (6–10 years) 4 (more than 10 years)
History of mental illness	4	0 (none) 4 (yes)
Illegal drug distribution	4	0 (none) 4 (yes, alleged)
Reputation	1	0 (reasonably good) 1 (not good)
Financial resources	1	0 (no resources) 1 (has resources)

be developed from an empirical basis, based on descriptive analyses of the "normal" use of pretrial detention at each of the sites, or might be crafted by normative modifications of the empirical model using knowledge of decision outcomes and impact as data to shape the guidelines.

Descriptive Detention Guidelines

Once again, knowledge of the attributes of defendants and their cases associated with their release or detention before adjudication would allow classification of defendants into categories reflecting different probabilities of detention (see Figure 11.4, Version I). Each of the categories would designate whether defendants with like characteristics should be released or detained. If detained, defendants would be scheduled for appropriate reviews and hearings as required by law and placed on expedited calendars. If the defendants were designated for release, the conditions of release would next be specified.

Prescriptive (Preventive?) Detention Guidelines

Descriptive detention guidelines could be designed so that roughly the same level of pretrial detention would result as had been occurring

Probability of Detention

	1	2	3	4	5
Version I	Released (Standard Conditions)	Released (Standard Conditions)	Released (Special Conditions)	Detained	Detained

Current Rate of Detention (45%)

	1	2	3	4	5
Version I					
N	652	342	171	184	883
% ROR	78	59	42	30	7
Med $	$1,650	$1,500	$1,775	$1,650	$2,054
% FTA	21	36	53	63	87
% Rearrest	4	9	4	6	17
% Failure	12	9	9	12	13
	15	17	12	16	25

Current Rate of Detention (45%)

	1	2	3	4	5
Version II	Released (Standard Conditions)	Released (Standard Conditions)	Released (Special Conditions)	Released (Special Conditions)	Detained

Modified Rate of Detention (30%)

FIGURE 11.4. Hypothetical guidelines based on release or detention.

in the particular jurisdiction in the recent past as documented by the descriptive analyses. However, with the kind of information presented above in Figure 11.2 to illustrate the example of superior court in Maricopa County, guidelines for detention could be modified to effect a lower rate of detention, moving, say, from the 45 percent usually held throughout the pretrial period to a substantially lower level, to perhaps 30 percent of felony defendants (Version II in Figure 11.4).

For example, some defendants who would be detained in Group 4 (Version I) seem to have shown reasonably low rates of failure to appear and of rearrest when released in the past. Thus, this category could be transformed to become a presumptive release category, with special or restrictive conditions of release (such as supervision and calling in) to be set. In addition, some of the defendants usually falling into Group 5 would now be identified as suitable for release under special conditions.

Actuarial Guidelines Based on the Defendant's Risk of Flight and Rearrest

Our discussions of models of decision guidelines included a version of pretrial release guidelines based purely on empirical risk—of flight, of crime, or, if desired, of both. If developed for implementation, this version of decision guidelines would posit release conditions and assign bond or detention according to the classifications described in Chapter 10 and would resemble actuarial tables like those insurance companies employ to determine driver premiums.

For Boston Municipal Court, as an example, the BMC probation staff could collect the kinds of information outlined in the discussion of prediction of default and/or rearrest in Chapter 10. They then and would classify defendants into groups according to relative risk of flight or rearrest. Decisions would then be suggested by the guidelines (see Figure 11.5). Actuarial guidelines would therefore place each defendant in a risk class and suggest that in most cases defendants would be treated as if they shared the risk attributes of a particular class. The court might decide that such guidelines could be based only on risk of flight or only on risk of rearrest, or it could decide that both flight and public safety concerns would be appropriately considered, depending on state law or the policy direction of the court.

These guidelines would not mirror current decision practices because, as we have seen, at each of the locations, factors central to judges' decisions were not shown to be strongly related to prediction of flight or crime by defendants during pretrial release. In addition, although it is arguable

Risk of Misconduct		Expected Failure	Suggested Decision
	I Lowest	1 in 6	ROR
	II Medium Low	1 in 3	ROR/Standard Conditions
	III Medium	1 in 2	ROR/Special Conditions (Including Bail $1 to $500)
	IV Highest	3 in 5	Restrictive Conditions (Including Bail $501 to $5,000) Detention

FIGURE 11.5. Pretrial-Release bail guidelines based on risk of flight and/or crime for the Boston Municipal Court.

that empirically derived risk classifications would represent as improvement over the current intuitive approaches taken by judges (from a statistical point of view), they would probably offer marginal improvement when compared to the ideal of "perfect" prediction. A decision by the court to employ guidelines totally governed by useful, though imperfect, risk-related criteria would have represented a dramatic departure from the current practice of any of the courts.

Pretrial Detention Guidelines Based on Defendant Risk

Figure 11.6 illustrates guidelines that combine pretrial detention *and* defendant risk. Such guidelines would seek to address simultaneously the use of pretrial detention and the risks of flight and crime. In this fashion, not only could the use of detention be carefully monitored, but conditions of release responsive to the risks posed by defendants who would be released before trial could be implemented in a systematic

Probability of Detention (Low → High)

Risk of Failure (Low → High)	Certain Release	Release	Release/Detention	Certain Detention
1	Released (Standard Conditions)	Released (Standard Conditions)	Released (Standard Conditions)	Detained
2	Released (Standard Conditions)	Released (Standard Conditions)	Released (Special Conditions)	Detained
3	Released (Standard Conditions)	Released (Special Conditions)	Detained	Detained

FIGURE 11.6. Hypothetical release–detention guidelines based on risk of failure.

fashion. Of course, because of the frank nature of the detention decision and the importance of a risk classification, a court choosing this model of decision guidelines would be embarking on a path of dramatic change.

Guidelines Based on Risk and the Seriousness of the Charge

Our final model of decision guidelines for the pretrial release stage involved a risk dimension and a dimension representing the relative seriousness of defendants' charges (see Figure 11.7). This is the most traditional kind of guidelines format[5] and was the approach taken by the judges in the Philadelphia court in the original experiment. Even though this model of decision guidelines was the last presented for discussion by the judicial working committees, it was the version unanimously selected for further refinement at each of the sites. The rationale—and its variations—employed by the courts in their selection of the risk–charge-seriousness model of decision guidelines for pretrial release are interesting.

Each of the court working groups found appealing the notion that day-to-day decisions could be improved by making information available that would rank defendants according to their relative likelihood of flight from court or of crime during pretrial release. Yet the working groups overall did not express a particular affinity for "statistics" or reveal enthusiasm for a guidelines system to be based solely on the concept of actuarial risk. In fact, their wish to adopt a charge seriousness dimension in the guidelines in large part was explained as an intuitive means to counterbalance the undesirable properties of a risk dimension.

The choice of an offense seriousness dimension was carefully debated. Over the last two decades, part of the criticism of bail practices in the United States has focused on the nearly exclusive reliance by judges on the seriousness of charges in setting bail. Critics have argued that,

Seriousness of Charged Offense (Low → High)

Risk of Failure (Low → High)	1	2	3	4	5	6	7
1 (Low)	Nonfinancial (Standard Conditions)	Nonfinancial (Standard Conditions)	Nonfinancial (Standard Conditions)	Nonfinancial (Standard Conditions)	Nonfinancial (Standard Conditions)	$1,001 to $1,500	$2,001 to $3,000
2	Nonfinancial (Standard Conditions)	Nonfinancial (Standard Conditions)	Nonfinancial (Standard Conditions)	Nonfinancial (Special Conditions)	$1 to $1,000	$1,501 to $2,000	$2,001 to $3,000
3 (High)	Nonfinancial (Standard Conditions)	Nonfinancial (Standard Conditions)	Nonfinancial (Special Conditions)	$1 to $1,000	$1,001 to $1,500	$2,001 to $3,000	$3,001 to $10,000

Nonfinancial — Financial

FIGURE 11.7. Detention guidelines based on offense seriousness and risk of failure.

since the task of the bail decision did not involve punishment (in contrast to the tasks of the sentencing decision), it was not an appropriate bail concern (or, at least, it should not be the sole concern).[6] In addition, reliance on charges has been viewed in the literature as contributing to inequity because release was tied to the defendant's ability to afford given amounts of bail. Moreover, recent research (including this research) has not shown charge seriousness to be a good predictor of defendant misconduct during pretrial release.

Despite these concerns, the argument was made in each of our courts that, despite being a very poor yardstick of likely flight or crime, the severity of a defendant's charges might still serve a useful purpose. It might serve to measure the costs of potential mistakes or of the "stakes" involved in making the "risky" pretrial-release determinations. S. Gottfredson and D. Gottfredson (1986) have employed the notion of "risks" and "stakes" in discussion of strategies for selectively deinstitutionalizing convicted offenders imprisoned in crowded prison systems. They analogize the decision to decarcerate (or incarcerate) particular categories of individuals to the gambler's consideration not only of the probability of winning a bet, but also of the amount of the wager (the stakes involved in a possible win or loss). The notion of a risks–stakes approach to decisionmaking may be especially appropriate to the way the judges and commissioners at the sites described the pretrial release decision.

For example, while the guidelines risk classification alone might suggest that "numbers runners" all be detained (because they would have a very high probability of repeating their crimes), a low charge-severity rating for this offense might suggest comparatively low stakes associated with releasing such defendants. That is, such defendants would pose a relatively low potential cost to the court system and the public safety if the grant of provisional liberty were to be abused during the pretrial period. The stakes involved would be comparatively "low" in the sense that a judge's "mistake" (misjudgment) in releasing this kind of defendant would not result in a major harm to society, to victims, to witnesses, or to the integrity of court processes, if the release were to go awry. In fact, given the seriously overcrowded jails in the study sites, a low costs or "stakes" assessment might strongly suggest that the courts should avoid detaining such "nuisance-level" defendants. Or to cite another illustration, risk alone might indicate that an alleged rapist could be depended on (was classified as very "low-risk") to return to court and not to repeat the alleged crime during the pretrial period. The severity rating of the alleged offense, however, might suggest that—risk aside—the stakes involved (the potential cost of a "mistake") in releasing such a defendant (or releasing such a defendant without sufficient restraints) could be very great indeed, given the possible harm to a victim that might result. By discussing these kinds of decision situations illustrating the stakes and risks aspects of pretrial release determinations, the judges in the working groups rationalized incorporation of a seriousness dimension in a guidelines model. As a result, each of the study courts selected this model as the one with which to proceed.

Notes

1. See Gottfredson (1987).
2. We exclude the role of the recommendation of the pretrial services staff here for the purposes of illustration. Earlier, we pointed out that it was the most important "predictor" of commissioners' choices between nonfinancial and financial release.
3. Parameter estimates from logit analysis were divided by a constant and were rounded to form "points" for scoring defendants.
4. If this model were selected by the judges, of course, an interesting question would present itself: If the decision were to be viewed as a "detention" decision, to what extent would "detention hearings" and other procedures need to be added to the process along with the guidelines?
5. See Gottfredson et al. (1978); Gottfredson and Gottfredson (1986); Gottfredson and Gottfredson (1988).
6. See Foote (1954).

12

The Construction of Pretrial Release Decision Guidelines in the Courts

Structuring the Guidelines

Although it is true that the general model of decision guidelines chosen by each of the judiciaries for further development was essentially the same—a decision matrix defined by a charge-seriousness and defendant-risk dimension—the processes leading to these selections were independent and were shaped by the local concerns of each of the courts. In this section, we briefly describe the special rationales that shaped the choice of a decision guidelines format for pretrial release at each location.

Maricopa County Guidelines: The Role of Police Opinion, a Special Focus on Defendant Danger and Injury to the Victim

Once the leadership of the superior court felt comfortable in opting for a seriousness-risk format for its pretrial release guidelines, it faced several important policy decisions concerning the specific form various components of the guidelines would take. For example, although the court leadership had indicated a preference for a risk classification incorporating risk of crime (defendant rearrest) and risk of failure to appear (FTA) taken together as "risk of misconduct," two risk classifications had been developed and presented to the judges. (Two were presented because neither was clearly more powerful statistically, and each had different themes.) The items and their weights forming the risk scale chosen to be applied by pretrial services staff in classifying defendants for the guidelines are presented in Table 12.1. It included prior failures to appear, property charges, and whether the defendant lived alone, among other factors. The principal difference between the two models was that, in one,

TABLE 12.1
Scoring of Defendants on Risk Factors under Pretrial Release Guidelines, Maricopa County Superior Court

Factor	Weight	Points[a]
Prior failures to appear		
None		0
One	1 × .541	36
Two or more	2 × .273	40[b]
Police: Risk of flight		
No		0
Yes	1.013	67
Charges involve property only		
No		0
Yes	.514[c]	34
Defendant lives alone		
No		0
Yes	.548	37
Charges involve robbery		
No		0
Yes	.675	45
Police: Risk of flight and FTAs		
No		0
With one prior FTA	1 × .122	8
With two or more prior FTAs	2 × .267	17[d]
Police: Risk of flight and lives alone		
No		0
Yes	.415	28
Add points	.012	1

Risk group	Bond points	Number of defendants	Percentage of defendants
1	1–34	322	14.4
2	35–67	1,130	50.6
3	68–107	565	25.3
4	108 and over	215	9.6
Total	—	2,232	100.0

[a]Points are calculated by dividing the weight by a constant, .015, and rounding.
[b]By agreement, the value for two or more failures to appear was doubled and rounded to 40 points to enhance its negative impact.
[c]To keep the points all positive, rather than subtracting 34 points for crimes against the person (associated with lower risk), 34 positive points were given for the appropriate category: charges involving no crimes against the person.
[d]This value was deemphasized slightly (by half) when it was learned that the police measure was based in large part on a record check of the first FTA measure.

pretrial services would consider whether the police had indicated in the arrest paperwork whether they believed the defendant might flee, while, in the other, the question would be more factual, asking instead whether the police indicated that the defendant had been arrested with evidence of the crime in his or her possession. (Depending on the model, defendants with police indications that they might flee or that they had evidence in their possession would be ranked as higher risk.)

Because some members of the working committee suspected that, if given the chance, police officers would describe most defendants as likely to flee, the risk model employing this item was seriously debated. There was a feeling among one or two commissioners, for example, that, in their arrest paperwork, the police almost always reported that the defendant might flee. Upon consulting the data, the research staff was able to report that, to the contrary, police had noted a concern about defendant flight in only about 25 percent of the cases in the defendant cohort studied. However, there was also some feeling among the commissioners that, once the police became aware of the weight that would be given to their comments in scoring defendants for the guidelines, they might manipulate the information in the hope of increasing defendants' risk rankings (thus lowering the chances of pretrial release). After considering the two models and the questions being raised, the judicial leadership opted for the model including the police comments reflecting their belief that defendants might flee. The leadership argued that the prospects of success of the guidelines system would be enhanced only if other parties, such as the police, could see that their cooperation was considered important by the superior court.

Beyond their agreement with the general rationale for its inclusion in the pretrial release guidelines, the judges had other policy-related questions to decide regarding the charge seriousness dimension. The first, seemingly simple problem was to select a definition of *charge seriousness.* Should defendants' charges be ranked according the felony–misdemeanor grading outlined in Arizona's criminal code? Should all charges be ranked cumulatively, or should just the most serious charge be employed for the purposes of classifying a defendant?

Finally, a two-part seriousness approach was decided upon which resulted in six groupings of charge seriousness. First, the severity of defendants' charges would be ranked according to a seriousness classification based on empirical analysis of how commissioners differentiated among criminal charges (in contrast to how the state penal code might have classified the charges).[1] Second, a checklist of "special severity factors" would adjust the initial ranking of charges upward in instances involving weapons use, injury to victims, or repeated counts of especially serious offenses (see Figure 12.1).

PRETRIAL SERVICES AGENCY

State of Arizona vs.____________________Defendant
Court:____________________
Date:____________________

Attorney Appointment
❑ PD
❑ PVT
❑ NE

	(Enter)
Risk Group	
Severity Level before Factors	

Special Severity Factors Considered (check)

Not applicable		No change
Weapon used		Add 1 level
Injury to victim		Add 1 level
Serious counts: 2 or more at 5 or higher		Add 1 level

	(Enter)
Final Severity Level	

Charge Severity: Least Serious ← → Most Serious

Probability of Failure: Lowest ↑ ↓ Highest

	1	2	3	4	5	6
1	OR/ Standard Conditions	OR/ Standard Conditions	OR/ Standard Conditions	OR/ Standard Conditions	OR/ Special Conditions to $685	$1,507 to $6,850
2	OR/ Standard Conditions	OR/ Standard Conditions	OR/ Standard Conditions	OR/ Special Conditions	$685 to $1,507	$4,110 to $8,220
3	OR/ Standard Conditions	OR/ Standard Conditions	OR/ Special Conditions to $685	$685 to $1,507	$1,507 to $2,740	$6,850 to $13,700
4	OR/ Special Conditions	OR/ Special Conditions to $685	$685 to $1,507	$1,507 to $3,425	$2,740 to $6,850	$10,960 to $20,550

FIGURE 12.1. Guidelines classification for Maricopa County Superior Court.

The commissioner-based part of the severity ranking was decided upon partly so that the decision guidelines would incorporate a measure reflecting the practices of the decisionmakers who would be the ultimate consumers and partly so that, as consumers, they would feel intuitively at home in employing the guidelines. The second part of the severity classification of defendants' charges was to highlight the court's public concern for victims of serious crimes, for weapons use, and for cases in which a number of very serious charges were involved. In fact, because the commissioner-based ranking also reflected the commissioners' individual-level concerns for precisely these kinds of dimensions of defendants' criminal charges, the severity scale sharply weighted defendants alleged to have used weapons, to have injured a victim, or to be charged with repetitive counts of serious charges in a more restrictive direction. The severity dimension represented a "double whammy" where these kinds of charges were concerned.

Reconciling Pretrial-Release Guidelines with the Traditional Bond Schedule in Dade County

In Dade County, the judicial working committee probably felt comfortable with a charge seriousness dimension in the proposed guidelines because of the long tradition of relying on a bond schedule ("standard bond") at the system's earliest processing stages. Although their comfort was not as great with a risk dimension, two factors may have contributed to their acceptance of it. First, the judicial leadership felt determined to learn whether a more objective system for effecting pretrial release could reduce the pressures of jail overcrowding which were continually at the crisis stage. Secondly, the circuit and county courts were accustomed to transferring the "risks" of their bond decisions to the pretrial services agency itself.

This interesting practice was demonstrated by the way in which unsupervised ROR was usually decided: Although it is true that outright ROR would occasionally be assigned, more often the sitting judge would assign the defendant to PTS (pretrial services) or to the responsibility of that agency as a form of nonfinancial pretrial release. In fact, assignment to PTS was usually preceded in court by the judge's asking of the pretrial services staff member if the agency "wanted" a particular defendant. The implication was that, once transferred to pretrial services, a defendant on pretrial release was not the court's responsibility. Thus, the court could view the guidelines as a more objective system for pretrial services to employ in deciding whether or not to "take" defendants entering the criminal process. Not surprisingly, then, the adoption and shape of the risk and seriousness dimensions were determined largely by the concerns and responsibilities of the leadership of the pretrial services agency. The four-group risk classification that was adopted for the guidelines is depicted in Figure 12.2. The design of a charge seriousness dimension was guided by the need to answer questions similar to those addressed by the court in Maricopa County.

In attempting to resolve the first question regarding the organization of the seriousness dimension, the developmental process in Dade County could not avoid coming to grips with the strong traditional role of the bond schedule. Our research had revealed that roughly 20 percent of entering felony defendants secured release by posting the amounts of bond specified by the court bond schedule immediately at the booking stage. Our research had also revealed that judges were very often influenced by the bond schedule in selecting bond amounts at the bond-hearing stage. We also knew that the bond schedule was based primarily on the statutory ranking of offenses in the Florida penal code but was also modified occasionally by the court's bond-schedule committee. As a result, and unlike in our experience in Philadelphia, Maricopa County, and Boston, there would be no need to develop an "individualized" measure of charge seriousness through empirical analysis of judges' decisions.

CORRECTIONS & REHABILITATION DEPARTMENT
METROPOLITAN DADE COUNTY, FLORIDA
PRETRIAL SERVICES

UNIFORM BOND STANDARDS: CLASSIFICATION

DATE______________

DEFENDANT'S NAME________________________________ JAIL #______________

STEP 1

Risk Group Classification

IF ANSWER IS "NO", ENTER 0 IN BOX IF ANSWER IS "YES", ENTER NUMERICAL VALUE		Value	Column N	Column P
			The Proper Column Below	
Ties:	Lives with spouse and/or child	1		
	Has a telephone	2		
Charges:	Property charge	2		
	Drug-related charges	1		
	Robbery charges	2		
Prior History:	Not arrested within 3 yrs.	1		
	One arrest	1		
	Two or more	2		
	Prior arrests: drug charges (two or more)	2		
	Has one or more prior felony convictions	2		
	No prior FTAs	1		
	1 prior FTA	1		
	2 or more FTAs	2		
TOTAL POINTS			N Total	P Total

STEP 2

Complete only if N total is larger or equal to P total

N	
P	

(Enter and find difference)

Complete only if P total is larger than N total

P	
N	

(Enter and find difference)

STEP 3

RISK GROUP	POINTS
I	5 or more
II	2 to 4
III	1 to -2
IV	-3 or less

Circle Risk Group.
Enter on Judge's Form.

STEP 4
Charge Severity Classification

Bond Schedule	Severity Ranking
$1 - 1,000	1
1,001 - 1,500	2
1,501 - 2,000	3
2,001 - 3,000	4
3,001 - 4,000	5
4,001 - 5,000	6
5,001 - 7,500	7
7,501 or higher	8

Total defendant's bond and circle Severity Ranking. Enter Ranking on Judge's Form.

STEP 5
Additional Information

PRETRIAL SERVICES OFFICER________________________
NAME

FIGURE 12.2. Pretrial services worksheet for Dade County Circuit Court.

Because the guidelines system would not replace or abolish use of the bond schedule—when this prospect was discussed by the working committee, it was dismissed with a roll of the judges' eyes—it seemed important to have the guidelines' seriousness dimension linked conceptually to the ranking of charges employed by the standard bond schedule.

Thus, it was decided to use the ranking of offenses (and all offenses were ranked, not just the single most serious) implicit in the bond schedule, given its status as a "holy cow." Because, under then existing court practices, all of a defendant's criminal charges were classified and assigned a dollar bond by the standard bond schedule, the guidelines for the circuit and county courts treated the defendants' bond-schedule bond (the total dollars designated by the schedule) as tantamount to the assignment of seriousness "points." The reasoning was that the courts' bond schedule (which considered only the seriousness of charges) was really a seriousness scoring device.

The Dade County guidelines, then, used the bond schedule "score" (amount of dollars) as the means of classifying defendants within one of eight severity groupings: Bond schedule bond falling between $1 and $1,000 placed a defendant's charges within the least seriously ranked group (Group 1); bond schedule bond higher than $7,500 placed a defendant in the group with the most seriously charged defendants (Group 8). (Note that although the ranking of offenses was therefore borrowed directly from the bond schedule, the presumption that defendants would be required to post a designated amount of bond was not.)

An advantage to this system, of course, was that, since the bond-schedule bond amount was known and recorded right at the booking stage, pretrial services staff had to do no severity classification of their own. Rather, the staff member selected a severity ranking based on the bond schedule amount. A potential disadvantage was the fact that all of the defendants' charges would figure into the classification of severity, not just the most serious—for this was the practice in effect in the court's bond schedule. The problem with this practice was that defendants charged with a gamut of charges of lesser seriousness might end up ranked more seriously than defendants charged with a single but serious felony offense.

Flight, Crime, and Crowding in the Boston Municipal Court Guidelines

As the research described various aspects of bail decisionmaking and the use of pretrial release and detention in Boston, there was a great deal of discussion of the meaning of the findings among the judges of the Boston Municipal Court. There seemed to be little doubt in the court that something had to be done about crowding at the Charles Street Jail, for example, but there also seemed to be a growing feeling (growing with presentation of findings showing that BMC judges caused the release of about 94 percent of incoming defendants) that the BMC was not responsible for the jail problem. Certainly, there seemed to be some dismay expressed by the BMC judges, when reviewing the findings showing that roughly 1 in 3 of released defendants either subsequently failed to appear in court as required or were rearrested for new crimes allegedly committed during their periods of pretrial release. However, they expressed reservations about implementing a system that might even slightly affect the low rate of pretrial detention—given the crowded jail facilities. The judges complained about the poor quality of information available at the arraignment stage but seemed to believe that little could be done to change the situation.

Against this background, the development and discussion of decision guidelines seemed marked by uncertainty and indecision. In contrast to the ambivalence shown by the committee of judges itself, the court's chief justice argued that the Boston Municipal Court needed to try to improve its bail practices and requested that guidelines be developed for eventual implementation by the court. In a letter to the research staff, the chief justice requested that the design of the guidelines reflect a number of concerns, such as the seriousness of the defendants' charges and the risk they pose of defaulting and/or being rearrested. In addition, he requested that the following factors be taken into account: (1) a defendant's ties; (2) the safety of victims or witnesses; and (3) the impact of guidelines on the jail population. In response to his request, the staff proceeded to draft the guidelines shown in Figure 12.3.

Like the Arizona model, the Boston version employed a decision-maker-based measure of charge seriousness that was derived from study of the judges' assignment of ROR. The severity classification resulted in only four offense rankings—in contrast to six in Maricopa County and eight in Dade County—because of the large number of offense-specific categories in which the large majority of defendants received ROR. (Remember that, in comparison with the other two court systems, the Boston Municipal Court processed a large number of misdemeanor defendants, most of whom gained ROR at arraignment.)

The development of a defendant risk dimension, which included factors relating to community ties, injury to the victim, and other concerns raised by the court's leader, faced a number of obstacles: First, potentially relevant information was sometimes not available in Boston Court data, and, in contrast with court appearance data, rearrest data were difficult to come by[2] (see our discussions in earlier chapters). The model of risk ultimately chosen (and validated on the Boston data) was the simple model originally developed for the Florida pretrial-release guidelines.

SECTION I: GUIDELINES DECISION MATRIX

Charge Severity (Least Serious → Most Serious); Probability of failure (Lower → Higher)

Probability of failure	1	2	3	4
1 (Lower)	ROR	ROR	ROR	\$100 to \$300 B
2	ROR	ROR/ Conditions	ROR/ Conditions B D	\$250 to \$450 D B
3	ROR/ Conditions	ROR/ Conditions	ROR/ Conditions to \$200 B D	\$300 to \$600 D B
4 (Higher)	ROR/ Conditions	ROR/ Conditions to \$200 B	\$300 to \$600 B	\$500 to \$1,000 B

Key:

B = higher than average probability of bindover

D = higher than average dropout rate

SECTION II: GUIDELINES SUMMARY

Classification: Severity Level__________ Risk Group__________

Suggested Decision: Nonfinancial (ROR) Yes _________ No__________

Financial \$__________to __________ Specify Conditions (if yes):____________________

Unusual Circumstances (check): Not Applicable: _________ Applicable: __________

Specify:____

SECTION III: JUDGE'S DECISION

Nonfinancial (ROR) Yes _________ No__________ Conditions:____________________

Financial \$______________________________

Departs from Guidelines: No_________ Yes_________

(If yes, note reasons)

- ❑ The nature and circumstances of the offense charged.
- ❑ The potential penalty the defendant faces.
- ❑ The defendant's family ties.
- ❑ The defendant's financial resources and employment record.
- ❑ The defendant's history of mental illness.
- ❑ The defendant's reputation and length of residence in the community.
- ❑ The defendant's record of convictions.
- ❑ The defendant's present drug dependancy or record of illegal drug distribution.
- ❑ The defendant's record of flight to avoid prosecution.
- ❑ The defendant's fraudulent use of an alias or false identification.
- ❑ The defendant's failure to appear at a court proceeding to answer an offense.
- ❑ The defendant's status of being on bail pending adjudication of a prior charge.
- ❑ The defendant's status of being on probation, parole, or other release pending completion of sentence for any conviction.
- ❑ The defendant's status of being on release pending sentence on appeal for any conviction.
- ❑ Other: ______________________________

Judge: ____ Date: ____________________

FIGURE 12.3. Pretrial release guidelines for Boston Municipal Court.

Shaping Future Practice: Establishing the Guidelines Choices

The Process of Drafting Presumptive Decision Choices for Pretrial Release

By designating that two dimensions would govern the formulation of guidelines, the individual courts had made important policy decisions regarding future bail practices: first, that pretrial release decisions would be guided by concerns for defendant dangerousness as well as likelihood of flight; second, that the seriousness of charges and the relative risk of flight and rearrest would be the overall themes organizing judges' daily bail decisions; and, third, that the information required to classify defendants according to these two dimensions was the information to be given the highest priority in pretrial release decisionmaking. Given the diversity of views expressed by judges on each of these matters, the choice by each of the courts of these defining dimensions represented important steps toward clarification of pretrial-release policy. Thus far, therefore, the courts had said that defendants would be classified into categories defined by seriousness of charges and relative risk for the purposes of pretrial release decisions. In Maricopa County, 24 "classes" in Dade County, 32 classes; and in Boston, 16 classes of defendants were defined by dimensions shaping the decision grid.

The next major step in constructing the decision guidelines was to put substance into the overall structure suggested by the courts' choices of guidelines dimensions by determining the decision options to be suggested for each category of defendants. Thus the court policy represented by the goals and themes inherent in the dimensions of the guidelines would be put into action by, in a sense, announcing that defendants with X charge characteristics and Y risk attributes would usually be assigned Z conditions of release.

Designation of the presumptive decisions to be suggested for each of the categories of defendants, however, also involved important policy decisions by each of the courts. The way the presumptive decision ranges would be specified would depend on the reasons the courts had decided to become involved in the guidelines research in the first place. It was in the establishment of the presumptive release options ultimately designated by the courts that each court would be making progress (or not) toward realization of its original goals.

For example, having decided on the governing dimensions and the information needed to support those dimensions operationally, one of the courts could have decided that important accomplishments had already been realized: Goals for pretrial release had been clarified, information to be employed by judges in pursuing those goals had been specified, and a fair classification of defendants in light of these goals had been devised. In many courts in the United States, these steps would, in themselves, represent a major policy advance away from the totally discretionary bail systems of the past. A court satisfied with guidelines development for these purposes might then devise suggested decision ranges based on what defendants in each of the classes had usually received as decisions in the recent past. This could be determined through simple empirical analysis. Other courts might start at this point—having acknowledged the advances in policy and clarification of goals and information—and devise presumptive decisions that would bring about a degree of change in decision practices among judges that would be intended to accomplish certain goals, such as the reduction of pretrial detention or of defendant flight.

In each of the courts, the research task then turned to postulating a range of decision options and estimating their likely impact: Most simply stated, the courts wanted to know if decision ranges could be established that would reduce the use of pretrial detention without increasing misconduct of defendants during pretrial release. Superior court in Maricopa County and circuit court in Dade County were under a great deal of pressure to consider the likely impact of guidelines on detention and public safety. (In fact, the presiding criminal judge in Dade County stated that guidelines would not be considered if there were a chance that guidelines would add to the use of pretrial detention.) In Boston, assuming that it would be difficult to expect to reduce the already extremely low rate of detention (only 6 percent of defendants were being detained), the question was more whether the extremely high rate of flight and rearrest among defendants (occurring in one-third of all released defendants) could be lowered noticeably without adversely affecting the jail population.

Beginning with Descriptive Data

Once the dimensions structuring the decision grids had been agreed upon, the next task was for the research staff to draft suggested decision ranges for the guidelines for review and revision by the judicial working committees. The drafting process, which was a policymaking exercise informed by descriptive data, began by examining defendants within each of the categories formed by the charge seriousness and defendant risk dimensions according to the decisions made in the past, the courts' use of detention, and the performance of each category of defendants during pretrial release. (These kinds of data have been simply summarized in Tables A.1, A.2, and A.3 in the Appendix.)

From these data, a first version of decision zones could be produced that generally reflected what the court's past practices had been. For example, we could adopt the rule that the guidelines would suggest decisions that had been designated because they represented the "average" past range of decisions made for defendants with attributes in given categories. Or we could say that categories of defendants showing ROR assigned in a majority of past decisions should have ROR suggested as the presumptive decision for future decisions under the guidelines. Referring to the data for Maricopa County, for example, we found that defendants in Categories or "Cells" 1, 3, 4, 7, 8, 9, and 19 had had ROR assigned a majority of the time. In cells having nonfinancial release assigned in a minority of instances, we could designate the median bail or bond amount—or perhaps the interquartile range or values of the 50 percent of cases surrounding the median bond amount—as the preferred decision for like cases in the future.

Modifying the Suggested Decisions Based on the Policy Dimensions

With this approach, decision ranges (of bond) could have been developed for all defendant categories, with the result that the pretrial-release guidelines would be based on an averaged picture of a court's past practices. Even if this "descriptive" version of decision guidelines was the express goal of a particular court, this first-draft method would encounter some limitations that would have to be corrected by policy decisions.

For example, certain categories of defendants would turn out to be relatively rare. (Only 6 Maricopa defendants of roughly 2,000 fell into Category 1, for example.) Thus basing decision ranges on an average of past decisions could prove unreliable over the long run. Further, the averaged-past-decisions method could also produce guidelines that would be illogical given a court's choice of policy dimensions. For example, if categories were defined by rankings of seriousness and risk, it would be illogical to posit ROR as the presumptive decision for future defendants falling into Categories 1 and 3 in Maricopa County, while suggesting a financial bond amount for Category 2 defendants.

In fact, selection by the courts of the explicit policy orientations represented by the charge seriousness and risk dimensions of the guidelines preordained conflict with a purely averaged, or status quo, approach to decision guidelines—at least to the extent that these dimensions did not govern past decisionmaking implicitly. That is, by choosing the severity and risk emphases, the courts had determined that the restrictiveness of decisions suggested by the guidelines ought to correspond with the relative severity of the charges and relative risk posed by the defendant. Thus formulation of suggested decision ranges became a little more complex with the requirement that presumptive decision ranges be made to vary with the two dimensions conjointly.

Considering these policy requirements, the research staff then proceeded away from the strictly averaged approach and began again by choosing key matrix categories as points of reference. So, for example, a first point of reference in the development of the Maricopa guidelines might be Cell 1, because according to the logic of the guidelines dimensions this category included defendants with the lowest severity and lowest risk rankings. A look at the data suggested that an appropriate suggested decision would be the least restrictive available; nonfinancial release (it had been assigned in the past virtually 100 percent of the time).

A second key point of reference might be the cell at the other extreme of both dimensions, representing the most seriously charged and highest-risk defendants. The median bond assigned by superior court commissioners in the past for defendants with attributes placing them within this category had been $9,042. If the research staff employed the interquartile range around the median, for example, as its method of designating a range for future decisions within the guidelines, the data showed that the 25th percentile case had had bond set at $2,055, and the 75th percentile case had had bond set at $21,920. With suggested decisions for these two categories—theoretically the least and most serious extremes—thus posited, the research staff could then turn to other key cells that ought to serve as points of reference. The guiding principle was that the restrictiveness of suggested decisions correspond with both relative severity and risk rankings. This was the procedure followed in beginning to draft the "suggested decisions" (the presumptive bail–pretrial-release decisions) that would provide the central substance of the decision guidelines at each of the sites.

Consideration of Other Policy Goals: Equity

Once such a draft had been completed by the research staff, other policy goals of the court working groups also had to be taken into consideration. In each of the courts, for example, the judges had expressed a desire to bring about more equitable decisionmaking. If the notion of equity for the purposes of pretrial release could be translated as somehow ensuring that like defendants would be treated with more similar decisions than previously, then guidelines ranges should also reflect a concern for consistency. In some categories, then, basing the range on the middle 50 percent of amounts from past decisions would have the effect of centering future decisions toward the value of the former median case within each category. In some instances, in which former decisions were extremely disparate, however, the middle 50 percent approach might not accomplish this goal. In a sense, having a suggested decision range varying from $2,000 to $22,000, as in the example from Maricopa just described, might be little better than having no range at all. In this kind of situation, it was argued, the participating court might wish to establish a range more closely centered on the median value of $9,000.

To this point, the drafting process had considered mainly past decisions in light of the policy dimensions that the courts had selected to serve as the overall structure of the guidelines. However, data describing a court's past use of pretrial detention and the performance of defendants who had gained pretrial release were also considered important in suggesting modifications to the suggested decisions within each guidelines category. For example, it would be illogical to discover that past decisions had detained lower-risk and lower-severity defendants more often than their higher-severity and higher-risk counterparts. Thus, part of the drafting process took such anomalies into consideration and "corrected" suggested decisions in order to align the likely use of pretrial detention with the seriousness and risk dimensions, where detention patterns had differed from decisionmaking patterns in past cases.

Similarly, at each of the sites, the research staff identified categories of defendants in which failures to appear and rearrests had seldom been recorded, but in which detention had often been employed. These categories then became candidates for establishing presumptive decisions that would be clearly less restrictive than in the past—to encourage greater pretrial release in the lower risk categories. Or the opposite was also encountered: Categories of defendants generally showing low rates of detention in the past but having undesirably high rates of flight and crime associated with them became candidates for presumptive decisions of a more restrictive sort.

Decision Choices Suggested by the Guidelines

So far, we have summarized the guidelines construction process as if the decision options to be employed were limited to nonfinancial release

(ROR) or financial bail or bond in some amount. The use of cash bond, however, has long been criticized on a number of grounds. Although we will not review them in detail here,[3] they have included concerns that a cash-based bail system discriminates against the poor, that the use of cash camouflages a *sub rosa* system of preventive detention, and that it has invited corruption (through the resort to profit-oriented bondsmen in brokering the release process). Another criticism of the use of financial options at bail is that cash fails to serve adequately as a condition of release likely to minimize either propensity toward flight or threat of additional crime by released defendants.

It was interesting that, in each of the jurisdictions, none of the judges working on the development of guidelines expressed satisfaction with cash bail as the principal currency of the pretrial-release decision. Discussion in each of the judicial working committees questioned the judges' routine reliance on cash bond. Each court agreed that a range of decision options was needed but saw some difficulty in thinking that guidelines could merely eliminate the use of cash bond.

As a result of these kinds of concerns about the centrality of financial bail or bond in the pretrial release practices at the study sites, the guidelines development process sought to discover more directly the implications of the judges' use of cash bail and to devise additional release conditions that did not involve financial assets but responded more practically to the goals of the bail process. First, the empirical analysis had shown that at each of the sites, certain amounts of bond served to define boundaries between release and detention. When bond amounts were set over $500 at each site, the bail decision was tantamount to a decision to hold the defendant in jail. Thus, in adjusting suggested ranges of bonds in the construction of the guidelines, the research staff and court could be made aware of the implications of amounts of bond for the resulting likely use of pretrial detention.

Second, the guidelines at each of the locations sought to make use of an additional category of suggested decision option for middle-risk, middle-severity cases, an option not leading to detention but providing more restrictive conditions on the release of these categories of defendants. For lack of a better term, the guidelines at each of the locations posited that specified categories of defendants be assigned *special conditions of release,* as opposed to standard conditions (ROR with agreement to refrain from crime and to attend court) or financial conditions (amounts of bond). To a certain extent, particularly in Dade County, these kinds of conditions already existed; however, to a degree they would also have to be developed for the first time, particularly in Maricopa County.

PRETRIAL SERVICES AGENCY

State of Arizona vs.________________________Defendant
Court:____________________
Date:____________________

Attorney Appointment
❑ PD
❑ PVT
❑ NE

	(Enter)
Risk Group	
Severity Level before Factors	

Special Severity Factors Considered (check)

Not applicable		No change
Weapon used		Add 1 level
Injury to victim		Add 1 level
Serious counts: 2 or more at 5 or higher		Add 1 level

	(Enter)
Final Severity Level	

Charge Severity (Least Serious → Most Serious); Probability of Failure (Lowest → Highest)

Probability of Failure	1	2	3	4	5	6
1 (Lowest)	OR/ Standard Conditions	OR/ Standard Conditions	OR/ Standard Conditions	OR/ Standard Conditions	OR/ Special Conditions to $685	$1,507 to $6,850
2	OR/ Standard Conditions	OR/ Standard Conditions	OR/ Standard Conditions	OR/ Special Conditions	$685 to $1,507	$4,110 to $8,220
3	OR/ Standard Conditions	OR/ Standard Conditions	OR/ Special Conditions to $685	$685 to $1,507	$1,507 to $2,740	$6,850 to $13,700
4 (Highest)	OR/ Special Conditions	OR/ Special Conditions to $685	$685 to $1,507	$1,507 to $3,425	$2,740 to $6,850	$10,960 to $20,550

UNUSUAL CIRCUMSTANCES: PRETRIAL SERVICES	SPECIAL CONDITIONS: PRETRIAL RELEASE	
____________	PTS - supervision____________	THIRD PARTY Name/Relationship
____________	Third party____________	____________
____________	Other (specify)____________	____________

OTHER CONDITIONS AND RESTRICTIONS

- ❑ The defendant is not to return to the scene of the alleged crime.
- ❑ The defendant is not to initiate contact of any nature with the alleged victim(s) and/or witnesses, including arresting officers.
- ❑ The defendant is not to possess any weapons.
- ❑ The defendant is not to drink alcoholic beverages and drive, or drive without a valid driver's license.
- ❑ The defendant is to continue to reside at the present address.
- ❑ The defendant is to contact the probation/parole officer____________.
- ❑ The defendant is to reside with____________ at ____________.
- ❑ Other *(specify)*: ____________

COMMISSIONER'S DECISION

Nonfinancial/standard conditions____________	**GUIDELINES FOLLOWED:** ❑ YES ❑ NO ❑ NA
Nonfinancial/special conditions____________	If no, indicate reason:
Secured bond (amount)____________	❑ Defendant nonbondable-Murder 1/Felony while on release
	❑ Defendant has Probation/Parole Hold
	❑ Defendant serving other sentence
	❑ Fugitive of justice
	❑ Other: ____________

FIGURE 12.4. Pretrial release guidelines for Maricopa County Superior Court.

CORRECTIONS & REHABILITATION DEPARTMENT
METROPOLITAN DADE COUNTY, FLORIDA
PRETRIAL SERVICES

UNIFORM BOND STANDARDS - DADE COUNTY CIRCUIT COURT

DATE:____________

DEFENDANT'S NAME____________________________ JAIL #____________

SECTION A: SUGGESTED DECISION

Least Serious ← Severity Ranking → Most Serious

Relative Risk (Lowest → Highest)	1	2	3	4	5	6	7	8
I	PTS/ Nonfinancial	PTS/ Nonfinancial	PTS/ Nonfinancial B D	PTS/ Nonfinancial	PTS/ Nonfinancial	PTS/ Nonfinancial	PTS/ Nonfinancial D	500 to 2,000
II	PTS/ Nonfinancial	PTS/ Nonfinancial B D	PTS/ Nonfinancial B	PTS/ Nonfinancial B	PTS/ Nonfinancial	PTS/ Special	PTS/ Special	1,500 to 3,000
III	PTS/ Special D	PTS/ Special D	PTS/ Special B X	PTS/ Special B X	PTS/ Special B	PTS/Special to 500 B	PTS/Special to 1,000	2,500 to 5,000
IV	PTS/ Special B D	PTS/ Special D	PTS/ Special to 750	PTS/ Special to 1,500	1,500 to 3,500	2,500 to 4,500	3,000 to 5,000	6,000 to 11,000

Note: X = higher risk
B = higher than average probability of bind down
D = higher than average dropout rate

SECTION B: UNUSUAL CIRCUMSTANCES	SECTION C: SUGGESTED SPECIAL CONDITIONS

SECTION D: JUDGE'S DECISION

Check
- ❑ PTS/Nonfinancial *or*
- ❑ Financial $____________ (amount of bond)
- ❑ Falls within Uniform Bond Standards (UBS) *or*
- ❑ Differs from Suggested Decision
- ❑ PTS/Conditions:____________

Reasons (for deciding out of UBS range):
- ❑ Currently on Felony Bond
- ❑ Probation/Parole Hold
- ❑ Fugitive
- ❑ A/C, Outstanding Warrants or Detainers
- ❑ Physical or Mental Health
- ❑ Added Charges
- ❑ Other (please specify)

____
(Judge's Signature)

FIGURE 12.5. Pretrial release guidelines for Dade County Circuit Court.

These kinds of concerns guided the drafting and redrafting of the suggested decisions for each category of defendants in the guidelines and for each of the court systems. Based on input from the judicial working committees, the draft guidelines were revised until it appeared that they met the policy concerns the courts had articulated. The final products are shown in Figures 12.3, 12.4, and 12.5.

Notes

1. The analysis simply subdivided defendants' charges into their smallest generic groups and, assuming a minimum number of cases existed for the analysis, determined the proportions awarded ROR (personal recognizance release). The reasoning was that (a) commissioners were very influenced by the seriousness of defendants' charges in making their choices between nonfinancial and financial options—though this influence was not measurable merely through the penal code ranking, and (b) charge categories more often assigned ROR were viewed by commissioners as less serious.
2. The bench warrant information was kept very accurately in manual records by the Boston Municipal Court clerk's office; however, arrest data were kept in manual files in the state offices of the commissioner of probation. Because of the labor involved in manually checking the records of 2,000 defendants, we were required to gather this information for a small subsample (414 cases) instead. This meant that the modeling of risk of flight and/or crime was based on only the small sample; thus the power of the statistical solutions was limited.
3. For a detailed review, see Beeley (1927); Foote (1954); Goldfarb (1967); Thomas (1976); NAPSA (1978); Goldkamp (1979); Goldkamp and Gottfredson (1985).

13

Estimating the Impact of the Guidelines

It is critical that a jurisdiction have the opportunity to anticipate a guidelines system well in advance of actual implementation. The criminal justice system should assess the utility and consider the resource implications of guidelines without having already committed to implementation on faith or, as one Boston judge aptly phrased it, by "buying a pig in a poke." How well will the innovation achieve the goals the court leadership had in mind in its design? Will more or less confinement result? Will new forms of supervision be required for particular categories of defendants? Even if the analysis of impact suffers from a number of limitations, these can be made explicit and can form part of the discussion of the resources implications attendant on implementation. Thus this stage of the guidelines process gives the judiciaries an opportunity to reconsider the substance of the guidelines they have designed and the desirability of their likely impact. Estimates of the likely effect of the pretrial release guidelines can result in encouraging the redesign of guidelines in advance of implementation, thus preventing a costly mistake, or can even lead the court leadership to abandon plans for implementation because of anticipated undesirable consequences.

To assist the courts in deciding whether to implement the pretrial release decision guidelines that had been drafted, the research staff conducted analyses aimed at estimating the impact that the guidelines would have on existing practices. The courts in Dade County and Boston requested an analysis of impact on the use of pretrial detention both in the hope that guidelines might reduce the use of detention and in the fear that guidelines might increase the use of detention, given the jail crises at those locations. In Maricopa County, the court wished to learn whether the guidelines could help reduce the court's use of pretrial detention, which the descriptive analyses had revealed to be considerable. To estimate the impact that guidelines might have on the three court systems, we asked a simple question: To what extent would the decisions in our samples of past cases be different had they been made according to the newly drafted pretrial-release guidelines?

Analysis of the likely impact of the guidelines amounted to trying to predict how decisionmaking would be affected by use of the guidelines in the future. As in all predictive analyses, the analysis of the future impact of guidelines was constrained by certain limitations and assumptions. The first limitation was that such analyses would be tied to the characteristics of the particular defendant samples employed. To the degree that the composition of the future criminal caseloads would differ from those studied during the development of pretrial release guidelines, estimates of likely impact might be misleading.

A second limitation concerned the fact that, in principle, decision guidelines of the voluntary sort we had been developing were not intended to be followed by judges in 100 percent of the cases. They were intended primarily as a policy resource in two ways. First, they were designed to reflect the broad policy directions a court wished to pursue in its decisionmaking. Second, they were conceived to provide a case-by case decision aid based on the policy aims of the particular court. Depending on a particular court's need to revise its then-current practices, to be useful the guidelines should foster compliance a majority of the time, but by no means in all cases. The guidelines approach is premised on the assumption that a minority of cases will be decided as exceptions to the guidelines, for acknowledged reasons which the judges or commissioners would record. Thus, even in a jurisdiction seeking to effect marked change in practices, it would be unlikely to see judges' decisions agreeing with the guidelines 100 percent of the time. Rather, it would be more likely to find judicial choices agreeing with those suggested by the guidelines in closer to, say, 75 percent of the cases.

This expectation, unfortunately, made estimating the impact of guidelines on future decisions more problematic. We could not estimate a 75 percent effect as soundly as we could estimate the effect that the guidelines would have if they were to be followed 100 percent of the time. To avoid making the task needlessly complicated—and because we could not know how often judges would actually follow the guidelines—we chose to describe the impact that could be expected if guidelines were to be followed literally. This approach resulted in an exaggeration or an overstatement of what the actual impact of guidelines might be because judges and commissioners would make decisions conforming to the guidelines at an unknown rate of less than 100 percent.

We present the following analysis to illustrate the manner in which such an exercise can be carried out. Of course, the projections of impact made prior to implementation also serve as a basis for later comparison, when the guidelines systems have been implemented. Such projections allow comparison of how the guidelines were expected to affect decisions and outcomes with how they actually did affect court practices.

The Likely Impact of Decision Guidelines in Maricopa County

In constructing decision guidelines for use by superior court commissioners in Maricopa County, the special characteristics of the final model obviously would determine the nature of the impact of guidelines on decision practices. For example, if the court had preferred a model of pretrial release guidelines based primarily on mirroring current practices (devising essentially descriptive guidelines), dramatic change would be unlikely to result, except that many fewer atypical decisions would be produced. The explicit format would have helped the commissioners to center their decisions in certain categories on a range defined by the way they had made decisions in like cases in the recent past. But because the model finally chosen in Maricopa County departed considerably from that purely descriptive orientation, the likelihood that it would restructure future decisionmaking notably increased. In short, because commissioners' recent past decisions had been governed exclusively neither by charge severity nor by defendant risk, the final version of guidelines which would seek to do this could be expected to produce decisions that differed from those practiced in the past.

Aligning the decisions suggested by the guidelines according to the severity of a defendant's charges presented the least amount of change in future decision patterns because the severity measure used as one of the guidelines dimensions in the Maricopa County guidelines was derived from study of the relative use of nonfinancial conditions for given offense types by the commissioners as a group. (Of course, commissioners did not always agree in their ranking of offenses; thus the resulting ranking of offenses was a generalized measure.) To the extent that in future decisionmaking this theme would become one of two primary emphases—as opposed to one of several in the past—the severity dimension in the guidelines would represent a more structured use of severity. Consideration of special-emphasis "severity factors" would also accentuate this theme a bit more than in the recent past.

Greater change in practices would be posed by use of the risk dimension in the Maricopa guidelines. Clearly, commissioners weighed the risk of flight and crime posed by defendants in making their decisions at initial appearance. But as a group, their diverse, subjective approaches to assessing defendant risk appeared to have relied on factors *not* strongly predictive of flight and crime in a statistical sense. In fact, to the extent that (and because) commissioners' decisions had conformed to severity concerns in the past (and thus would not differ much from the severity ranking developed for use in the pretrial release guidelines), they did not conform to predictors of risk. Our research showed that, in Maricopa County, the severity of offenses was almost unrelated to the prospects of pretrial flight or crime among Maricopa (and other) defendants.

We could estimate the nature of the impact of some of the projected changes by applying the draft Maricopa County guidelines to the defendants we had studied from the summer of 1984. In addition, we could apply the guidelines to data describing persons held in pretrial detention in Maricopa County on one day in the fall of 1985 and determine whether they had received different decisions under the guidelines.

The Likely Impact of Guidelines on Decisions in Maricopa County

We present these implementation analyses in tabular form in the Appendix (Tables A.4 to A.13). Here, we summarize the principle findings and illustrate our technique. First, we summarized the decisions and outcomes characterizing the defendants in our sample in terms of how they fell within given categories of the guidelines. By contrasting actual decisions with the decisions suggested by the guidelines for each category, we could approximate in a rough way how different decisions under the guidelines might or might not be made. In other words, by superimposing the guidelines grid over the actual data, we tried to draw conclusions about differences that could be understood as estimates of the *maximum possible effect*. As noted above, the actual impact of the guidelines would be something less than indicated because, for the sake of simplicity, this comparison assumed 100 percent compliance by superior court commissioners with the guidelines.

To begin assessment of the differences that would be produced through use of the guidelines, it was useful to consider how defendants would be distributed within the guidelines "grid." We did this first by examining the effects of the grid used alone and then of the grid as modified by the court's "special severity factors."

We found that, by superimposing the guidelines decision grid over the data, 11 categories would involve some form of nonfinancial release, and 3 categories would permit nonfinancial options (or low amounts of secured bond). Approximately 69 percent of the felony defendants we studied would now fall into these presumptive nonfinancial-release categories. This compares with 40 percent of the studied defendants who actually did receive some version of nonfinancial release. An estimate of the maximum possible effect was that nonfinancial release would be increased by 29 percent under the guidelines—before taking into account the extra severity factors also included in the guidelines. When we adjusted the guidelines decisions to take into account whether a weapon had been used in the offense, whether a victim had suffered any injury, and whether there had been repetitive serious counts, the maximum projected use of nonfinancial options at initial appearance dropped to 64 percent.

Again, though the impact was overestimated (because we did not expect commissioners to follow guidelines in 100 percent of the cases), this finding was important because any increase in the use of nonfinancial release would translate into a reduction in the use of pretrial detention, an important goal in a jurisdiction experiencing crowded jail facilities.

One explanation for the projected greater use of OR and reduced use of detention was the guidelines' reliance on more restrictive or "special" conditions of release for targeted categories of defendants (defendants who would have been detained in the past). Formerly, under the practices we had recently studied, what we called *special conditions* (which we roughly measured as either third-party custody or supervision by pretrial services) were assigned in 16 percent of all cases and were not focused on a small number of categories. Under these guidelines, the proportion would be 25 percent, the middle severity and middle risk kinds of cases.

Secured bond would be permitted in 13 categories (though it would be presumed in only 10 of these). We compared the bonds that would be suggested under the guidelines with those received by defendants in these categories in the past. Assuming that all secured-bond defendants would receive the middle bond suggested for their category, the average bond for all defendants raised by the guidelines would be approximately $500. The impact this was likely to have was uncertain because, when bonds were set over $500 in the first place, they usually caused the detention of the defendant.

Because detention is not decided directly in all cases (release is a direct outcome of a nonfinancial release decision, but when bond is set release depends on the defendant's unknown ability to afford bond), it is somewhat more difficult to estimate the impact of guidelines on the use of pretrial detention. As an outside estimate, we can begin with the knowledge that if we expect nonfinancial release in 66 percent of the cases (up from 40 percent), we cannot expect detention to result in more cases than the number having bond set—or 33 percent of the cases. This compares with 54 percent of defendants in the sample who were held at least more than one day.[1] So, assuming very conservatively that all financial defendants would be detained, this measure estimates that the number detained would be reduced at least 21 percent.

Because of the importance of questions about the impact of pretrial release guidelines on the use of pretrial detention, we tried to estimate their effects a little more thoroughly. The "projected" rate of detention for each guideline cell was arrived at from the suggested decisions in the guidelines. In categories in which the guidelines suggested OR, the projected impact was that 0 percent of defendants would be detained (either longer than one day or throughout the pretrial period). In categories with a range of cash bond suggested, we determined a probability of detention (for detention measured as more than one day and for detention throughout the pretrial period) associated with given levels of financial bond[2] and made the assumption that defendants falling into each of these categories would receive the highest amount of bond within the suggested range.[3]

Cell-by-cell analysis showed that, in the middle and lower severity and risk categories, the use of pretrial detention would be decreased, while, in the more seriously charged and higher-risk categories, greater use of detention would occur. Overall, however, we estimated that detention for longer than one day should decrease at least 10 percent[4] but perhaps as much as 20 percent,[5] with almost comparable reductions in detention throughout the pretrial period.

We did a similar analysis to estimate the impact of guidelines on the number of "jail days" associated with bail practices. Briefly, the actual total number of days spent in jail by defendants in each of the categories in 1984 was calculated. Then jail days values associated with the decision ranges suggested by the guidelines were determined. For example, in categories suggesting nonfinancial release, the expected number of jail days was assigned as 0. Analysis was conducted to determine an average number of jail days associated with given levels of financial bail. Assuming again that commissioners would select the highest bond in the suggested bond ranges, the number of jail days associated with that bond level was assigned to all defendants falling in given categories.

The results show that, under guidelines, the sample defendants would have been detained for 22,245 fewer jail days, a reduction of 24 percent. Or stated another way, bail practices under the 1984 procedures in Maricopa County produced an average of 42.7 jail days per entering felony defendant compared to an estimated 32.6 expected under the guidelines system. This estimate suggests that the cost of housing inmates in the jail could be considerably reduced by use of the guidelines system.

Another way to estimate the impact of guidelines on detention was to examine data describing a sample of defendants detained in the Maricopa County jail. The approach was simple: We merely classified defendants held in Maricopa County on a given day as if they were to have bond decided under the draft pretrial-release guidelines.

To do this, we were not able to take fully into consideration the effect of the special severity factors, because our jail information was not as complete as our information describing the sample of 1984 felony defendants. On the basis of the guidelines matrix alone, however, we were able to classify defendants detained in Maricopa County on September 21, 1985, according to severity and risk.

Of the detained defendants, 43 percent were ranked within the two lowest risk categories; 30 percent fell within the two least severe charge categories. Remarkably, without considering th especial severity factors which were part of the guidelines approach, 44 percent of those held would be suggested OR releases under the guidelines: 31 percent OR with standard conditions and 13 percent OR with special conditions of release.

This comparison, of course, exaggerates the releasability of the detainees in three ways. First, it does not consider the effects of the special severity enhancements (weapons use, injury to victim, and repetitive serious counts),[6] and it takes the guidelines too literally. Further, we were making the unlikely assumption in this estimate that none of the detainees were "unusual cases," the kind likely to be treated as exceptions under the guidelines. Finally, this estimate did not consider the extent to which defendants previously not held in jail might be confined as a result of the guidelines.

The Likely Impact of the Guidelines on Decisions in Dade County

A similar analysis of the likely effect of guidelines was carried out for the circuit court in Dade County. So concerned was the court leadership about the possible side-effects of a guidelines approach on the critically crowded jail facilities in Dade County that the research staff worked closely with the pretrial services program to draft two versions of guidelines with varying impact for the committee's review. The difference between Version I and Version II was in the decisions suggested for high-risk low-severity cases. In Version I, these categories offered a choice between nonfinancial release with special conditions and low amounts of bond; in Version II, the suggested decisions involved only nonfinancial release with special conditions.

Like the Maricopa analysis, the analysis began by superimposing the draft guidelines over the data describing the decisions and outcomes characterizing the defendants in the 1984 sample we studied. For Version I, we estimated that the use of nonfinancial release would increase 7 percent, from 69 to 76 percent. For Version II, the estimated increase in the use of nonfinancial release would be 12 percent.

A rough estimate of bond-hearing defendants assigned in 1984 the equivalent of what we now call "special" conditions of release might include those assigned to pretrial services and then supervised and those released to ADAP (alcohol drug abuse program) or DIP (domestic intervention program). Approximately 20 percent of the 1984 defendants fell into those categories. From the guidelines, we estimated that from 8 to 11 percent more of entering felony defendants would be classified within "special" conditions ranges.

In striking contrast to the slight increase in average bond amount projected under the guidelines in Maricopa County, our estimates pointed to a sharp drop in the average bond amount in Dade County among bond defendants under guidelines, from $6,264 to $2,575.

Using the same procedure outlined above in the discussion of Maricopa County, we estimated the likely detention associated with each category of the proposed guidelines and for defendants overall (here we limit our discussion to Version II, the one with the greater likely impact). The data suggested that the effect of the guidelines would be to reduce the use of pretrial detention noticeably in the lower-risk, lower-seriousness categories of defendants and would increase the use of detention in the higher-risk, higher-severity kinds of categories. Overall, assuming full compliance with guidelines (which we knew to be unlikely), the use of detention for more than two days would be reduced from 42 to 24 percentage points (depending on assumptions about what judges would do in the categories giving choices between nonfinancial special conditions and low amounts of cash bond).

We also analyzed the likely impact of the guidelines decision on the number of jail days associated with bail practices. If the 1984 sample of defendants had had the decisions suggested by the (Version II) guidelines—rather than their actual decisions—the total number of jail days generated by the court's bond decisions would have been cut roughly in half. The average of 11.2 jail days per defendant characteristic of bond practices in 1984 would be reduced to 4.2 jail days per defendants.

Assuming (unrealistically) full compliance with the guidelines, a remarkable 40 percent of Dade County's detainees would fall within nonfinancial release categories when the Fall 1985 detainees were classified according to the Version I guidelines.

The Likely Impact of Bail Guidelines on the Boston Municipal Court

By superimposing the draft Boston Municipal Court guidelines on the Boston defendant sample, we compared the likely decisions under the proposed guidelines with what municipal court judges had actually assigned, assuming that judges in the future would follow the guidelines 100 percent of the time.

In 1984, the population of defendants studied entering the Boston Municipal Court received ROR approximately 71 percent of the time. Under the version of guidelines proposed, defendants would receive ROR between 92 percent of the time (assuming that no defendants in the ROR–special-to-low-bond amounts categories would actually receive ROR) and 95 percent of the time (if we assumed the opposite).

We were unable to identify use of the equivalent of "special" conditions of release in the BMC data (there was no pretrial services program or equivalent supervisory program). The draft guidelines would propose that from 36 to 39 percent of the cases—or slightly more than one-third of all the cases in nonfinancial categories—would be targeted for restrictive conditions of release. This focused use of "special" conditions was intended to respond to the research findings that roughly one-third of all BMC defendants would either fail to appear or would be rearrested during the pretrial period.

Since the BMC guidelines would increase the use of ROR notably and would target special conditions of release on a large number of medium-risk defendants, we projected that the average bond amount for the (now smaller) category of defendants receiving bond would increase slightly, from approximately $200 to $350—an increment that was unlikely to affect the use of pretrial detention.

Using the procedures described above in the Maricopa County and Dade County discussions, we used the decisions suggested by the BMC draft guidelines to project a level of pretrial detention. (See Tables A.12 and A.13 in the Appendix.) We estimated that the rate of detention for longer than one day would be reduced from 21 percent of defendants entering the BMC to 13 percent, and that the length of stay in detention would be reduced by 80 percent—from a total of 19,825 jail days, or 4.3 jail days per defendant, to 3,963 jail days, or an average of 0.7 jail days per defendant.

When the population of defendants held in the Suffolk County Jail on the date of the jail study was classified according to the draft bail guidelines, the result was that approximately 8 percent would be classified as appropriate for outright release on OR (standard). At least another 40 percent would be classified as candidates for release under restrictive nonfinancial conditions (OR special). Thus, even if this estimate based on an unrealistic 100 percent compliance with guidelines were cut in half, nearly one in four of defendants held on a given day would be released under some version of nonfinancial release.

A Concluding Note: Limitations of the Estimates of Impact

It is worth reiterating some of the limitations to the estimates being made of the possible impact of initial-appearance guidelines on release practices. First, when we apply the guidelines to the sample of felony defendants we studied, we make two fundamental assumptions: (1) that future defendants will not differ significantly from 1984 defendants; and (2) that guidelines will be followed in 100 percent of the cases.

The first assumption provides few problems. The defendant population is stable in composition, though the proportions falling into specific categories might vary over time and thereby affect the use of nonfinancial and secured-bond options, as well as pretrial release and detention. For that reason, cell-specific estimates, because they deal with specific categories of defendants rather than defendants overall, will prove most valuable.

We have repeatedly noted that our estimates represent a maximum possible effect, even though we acknowledge that guidelines are not intended to be followed in all cases. In practice, rather than total compliance among decisionmakers, we would expect guidelines to be invoked (i.e., the suggested decisions followed) in from 70 to 80 percent of cases. Because we cannot estimate well the nature of the likely departures from guidelines, we cannot meaningfully project the impact of guidelines under any other set of assumptions. We imagine, for example, that judges or commissioners will wish to set nonfinancial bond in categories suggesting secured bond upon occasion and that they will employ secured bond from time to time when the guidelines suggest nonfinancial options as a rule of thumb.

Finally, we should stress the limitations of our estimates of the effects of guidelines on the jail populations. While it is evident that detention may be reduced by guidelines (and refocused according to risk and severity concerns), our application of guidelines to the local populations of detainees overestimates the likely impact for two reasons:

1. Once again, we "pretended" that guidelines would be applied literally in 100 percent of the cases; we have explained why this is not a practical assumption.

2. Similarly, the estimate of the impact on the jail population may be exaggerated. Recall that a minority of cases decided under guidelines will be decided as "exceptions." One could argue that, in a jurisdiction which has been sifting through the detention population to find suitable candidates for "emergency" release to alleviate crowded conditions, those remaining in jail might all be appropriately classified as special exceptions. In fact, many of the defendants who fall into nonfinancial decision categories may have special holds or other unusual circumstances that we do not examine when placing them in the guidelines.

Even considering the limitations of our analyses, we conclude that (1) the net effect—though less than the maximum effects reported here—will be in the direction of more release; and (2) the guidelines may be adjusted to adapt to release effects as they are used.

Notes

1. Again, this assumes that guidelines would be followed in 100 percent of the cases and that defendants in cells specifying choices between ROR and low bond amounts all would be given ROR.
2. The probabilities of pretrial detention associated with given amounts of bond were the following in Maricopa County:

Bond range ($)	Percentage detained more than one day	Percentage detained more than two days	Percentage detained throughout
1–500	65.7	63.4	53.7
501–1,000	87.0	85.5	77.8
1,001–5,000	92.1	90.6	77.8
>5,000	97.8	96.0	78.1

3. Of course, we could have assumed that commissioners would usually set bond at the midpoint of the guidelines ranges, thus lowering the bonds and decreasing the estimates of detention somewhat.
4. This estimate assumes that defendants in categories with a choice of OR "special" or low bond would all be detained.
5. This estimate assumes that defendants in categories with a choice of OR "special" or a low bond would all be released.
6. We do know that at least 18 percent were charged with weapons offenses; however, we could not determine if weapons were alleged to have been used as the guidelines would require. We also know that a victim suffered some harm in 17 percent of the cases.

IV

IMPLEMENTATION AND EVALUATION OF JUDICIAL DECISION GUIDELINES

14

Implementation and Evaluation

In earlier chapters, we described the issues surrounding pretrial release decisionmaking in the United States and our research in three urban court systems leading to the development of decision guidelines. In this chapter, we consider the implementation of the guidelines, as the courts considered the practical questions involved in moving from developmental stages to adopting a new approach.

When the research team first met with the judiciaries in the three selected sites, we explained that the "guidelines" idea involved a process of self-examination in which the judiciary would explore difficult policy questions related to the bail function, pretrial release, and detention using a collaborative approach "staffed" by the research team. We stressed the fact that we were not interested in transplanting a finished product that had been developed for application elsewhere; instead, we were interested in applying the lessons learned earlier in Philadelphia and building on those promising results. Any final product would be tailor-made to the concerns of each particular jurisdiction and would bear the imprint of each judiciary's policy objectives and priorities.

The challenges posed for the guidelines in the courts varied considerably. The process of data collection, group discussion of findings, and construction of guidelines—not to mention their implementation and evaluation—proceeded at a different pace at each site, depending on the issues that surfaced, the problems encountered, and the difficulties associated with data collection. The three processes did not begin at the same time, nor—sometimes to the dismay of the research team (and project funders)—were they completed within a comparable or neatly predictable timetable. Yet each of the processes accomplished many of the goals originally set forth.

In each jurisdiction, the guidelines process proceeded through the early stages of descriptive research and problem identification to the development of decision guidelines. Large samples representative of recent bail decisions in the five courts at the three sites were carefully collected. Once final refinements were worked out in Maricopa County

Superior Court and in Dade County Circuit Court, the guidelines process proceeded to implementation of guidelines. Although the research was productive in many respects in Boston, the process did not successfully reach the implementation stage there for a variety of reasons. (We discuss the specific lessons of the Boston experience in Chapter 17). The remainder of the book therefore examines the experience gained in the guidelines process in the three court systems but necessarily focuses on the implementation and impact of the guidelines at the two sites where they were implemented.

A Review of the Pretrial Release Guidelines Produced: Form and Substance

It may be most helpful to conceive of voluntary guidelines as simultaneously a process and a product. The guidelines process is collaborative in its investigative and problem-solving approach, mixing rigorous empirical study of decisionmaking and its consequences with critical discussions of findings and normative debate about appropriate policy for pretrial release. It is a process of self-study that moves from the theoretical to the practical and that grounds judicial debate about bail procedures in hard empirical evidence. It is a normative process in that the aim of the inquiry is to produce a prescriptive framework to guide a court's future policy in the performance of its pretrial-release-related duties. The guidelines framework, then, is founded on a study of "what is" but is shaped by a court's formulation of "what ought to be," not only as a general statement of policy, but as a practical decisionmaking resource for the judges who decide bail on a daily basis.

As a representation of the court's general policy and a daily tool for decisionmakers, the product—the guidelines—is itself temporary, because it can be further shaped by the process to adapt to new realities. Guidelines are meant to facilitate generation of management information—feedback data similar to the data used in their construction—to allow the court periodically to review their fit and appropriateness, as well as the performance of the decisionmakers.

In appearance, the guidelines have turned out to be variations on a theme (or themes). After having facilitated the guidelines development process in four urban court systems over a 10-year period (including Philadelphia), we were surprised to discover that each of the courts had selected the same basic model of pretrial release guidelines to prepare. The surprise resulted from the fact that great steps had been taken in the developmental process to introduce a variety of conceptualizations of decision guidelines and because strong emphasis had been placed on the need to tailor the guidelines to the needs and preferences of the particular jurisdiction.

The popularity of the charge-severity–relative-risk-of-misconduct matrix over other possible formats is understandable; the reasoning of the judicial working groups is by now familiar and convincing. Each of the courts valued the development of an empirical risk classification; yet none valued it so highly as to allow it to dominate the guidelines constructed. Instead, each preferred inclusion of a counterbalancing perspective to increase the "safety" of the predictive decisions that would be made. On the one hand, the risk dimension summarized the odds that the categories of defendants would pose of failing to appear in court or of being rearrested before trial if released. On the other, the severity dimension of the guidelines served as a crude yardstick of the "stakes"—the potential costs—involved in release decisions within specific categories of defendants. The judicial decisionmakers felt that the juxtaposition of risk and severity dimensions fairly depicted the two-dimensional aspect of pretrial release determinations.

Although the development of the pretrial release guidelines has been traced in detail in earlier chapters, it may be helpful here to display the three "final"[1] (preliminary working versions) of the decision guidelines in question and describe their central features and purposes. Figures 12.3, 12.4 and 12.5 are the guidelines forms that were designed for use in the three jurisdictions. These are the "decision forms" that would be seen by the judges or commissioners presiding at the bail stage.

The key to the guidelines is the decision matrix or grid which designates suggested decisions for specified categories of defendants. The important features of the grid are the *dimensions* that determine the categories and the *decision ranges* that are framed within the categories. The idea behind the use of the guidelines is that, because they had been designed after careful study of decision practices and debate about preferred policy, they should be relied on in most cases. In a minority of cases—in cases presenting unusual circumstances—judges or commissioners would want to make decisions departing from those suggested by the guidelines. Once the working groups in each of the courts had indicated a preference for guidelines that were based on counterbalancing the severity of defendants' charges with their relative risk of misconduct, the next task was to define each of those notions operationally.

Ranking the Severity of Charges

A number of approaches to ranking the seriousness of defendants' charges for the purposes of classification according to the guidelines were possible. We could have polled the court to develop a purely subjective measure of seriousness; we could have adopted the felony misdemeanor or other grading scheme found in the penal codes of each of the states for purposes of sentencing. Because the penal codes had overly broad categories of offenses, and because judicial decisionmakers drew distinctions among offenses in pretrial release determinations (that sometimes differed with the penal codes' overall gradings), we ultimately derived a seriousness measure tailored to each of the sites based on study of the way decisionmakers appeared to rank offenses in their assignment of pretrial release options.

In Boston, charge categories were rank-ordered according to the relative proportions of defendants assigned ROR (release on own recognizance); offense categories with higher proportions of cases receiving ROR were considered less serious than offense categories with smaller proportions. In Maricopa County Superior Court, the guidelines dimension was based on a similar ROR-based ranking which was "corrected" for special "severity factors" (whether there was injury to a victim, whether a weapon was used, and whether the charges were in serious categories and involved multiple serious counts).

In Dade County, the circuit court already had an elaborate severity ranking in its bond schedule. Under that bond schedule, each possible criminal charge was assigned a dollar amount by a committee of judges. Under the then-current practice there, the bond that a defendant would have to pay to gain release at booking (and later at the bond hearing if the judge used the bond schedule to make his or her decision) consisted of the total bonds associated with each of the specified charges. We decided to build on the bond schedule's inherent ranking system, viewing bond schedule dollars as tantamount to "severity points" assigned to charges by the Dade judiciary. Thus, using the Dade County bond schedule as a charge-scoring mechanism, we identified eight grouped rankings of the charges in the large 1984 sample of felony defendants studied, each of the groups being defined by total ranges of bond assigned by the bond schedule right at the booking stage. As simple as this was, and as purposely linked to the bond schedule tradition as it was, the Dade County guidelines (named "Uniform Bond Standards" by the chief judge) borrowed only the severity ranking implicit in the jurisdiction's traditional bond schedule, not the presumptions about reliance on cash bail and bondsmen that were associated with it.

Classifying Defendants According to Risk of Flight or Rearrest

The criteria ultimately used in the risk classifications were not identical at the sites (although in Dade County and Boston, similar risk items could be employed reasonably well). This was so because of differences in the defendant samples on which analyses were based, because of the differences in the availability of information in each of the systems, and because of the different proportions of released defendants "failing" at each site. These classifications differed in content from the classification developed for the Philadelphia Municipal Court guidelines.[2]

Despite the differences in their detail (see Figures 12.2 and 14.1 showing the pretrial services worksheets used to compute risk), the risk classifications in the different sites did share a similar function. Based on the classification criteria, they could place defendants in one of four risk

PRETRIAL SERVICES AGENCY
MARICOPA COUNTY SUPERIOR COURT
PRETRIAL RELEASE GUIDELINES

CLASSIFICATION WORKSHEET

Name of Defendant ____ Court ____

Date ____ Calculated by ____

Charge Severity Calculations:

Charges: (list by Code Section Number)	Severity level
____	____
____	____
____	____
____	____
____	____
____	____
____	____

* For lesser included offenses enter "L10"

* Enter highest charge severity level from above ____

* Enter name of this offense (full) ____

Check the Applicable Categories Below		Enter Below	
Beginning Score of . . .		1	1
☐ Prior FTAs	☐ One.......... ☐ Two or more..........	36 40	
☐ Police: Flight Risk Facts	☐ Police note facts defendant might flee.....	67	
☐ Property Offense	☐ Charges involve property..........	34	
☐ Defendant Lives Alone	☐ Lives alone..........	37	
☐ Robbery Offense	☐ Charges involve robbery..........	45	
☐ Police Risk with FTAs	☐ With one prior FTA..... ☐ With two or more.........	8 17	
☐ Police Risk and Lives Alone	☐ Police: flight risk and lives alone..........	28	
Total column in space at right			

Points	Risk Group
1 to 34	Group 1 [ ]
35 to 67	Group 2 [ ]
68 to 107	Group 3 [ ]
108 or more	Group 4 [ ]

☐ Indicating Charge Severity Level has been circled on Commissioner's Matrix

☐ Indicating Risk Group has been circled on Commissioner's Matrix

FIGURE 14.1. Pretrial services worksheet for Maricopa County Superior Court.

categories associated with differing probabilities of flight or crime during pretrial release, ranging from relatively low likelihoods to relatively high likelihoods of misconduct. In the Boston classification, for example, the risk categories could be interpreted in the following fashion: defendants in Risk Group 1 would be expected to flee or to be rearrested in about one of six cases (a rather low probability); defendants in Risk Group 4 would be expected to engage in pretrial misconduct in about three of every five cases (a rather high probability). The proposed risk dimensions thus were intended not to provide a statement of certainty as to the defendant's anticipated behavior, but to capsulize an amalgamation of information dealing with the track record of defendants with given attributes.

The Decision Choices Suggested by Guidelines

In each of the 24 or 32 "cells" (subcategories) of the guidelines designated by the intersection of risk and charge-severity dimensions—depending on the site—the guidelines posit a suggested or "presumptive" decision or range of decision options. Because many of the judges we worked with expressed strong reservations regarding the concept of guidelines initially and were resistant to the notion of presumptions implicit in the guidelines, it is worth taking a moment to clarify what is meant by suggested or presumptive pretrial-release choices.

An important distinction must be drawn between the self-help, court-based approach to decision guidelines that we have been describing in the context of pretrial release determinations and the legislative, presumptive sentencing versions of guidelines with which judges are much more familiar. In the former approach, individual courts worked with a research team to develop an outline of a policy intended to be a reasonable approach to the goals of pretrial release decisionmaking and the associated problems. Thus, according to the court-based approach, the judges who would be using the pretrial release guidelines (directly or indirectly) played a part in the problem-solving process that generated the guidelines "product." If that process was well-carried out, then the final guidelines should reflect an in-depth examination of evidence concerning bail practices as well as a thorough debate and formulation of desirable court policy.

Taking Exception to the Guidelines: Unusual Circumstances

As an information resource for decisionmaking, the guidelines tool was designed to characterize defendants and their cases along the pertinent dimensions (as determined by the judicial working group) in a compact, shorthand fashion that judges could understand at a glance. Implicit in the judicial suggestions of decisions was the message that, considering these (guidelines charge- and risk-related) criteria, defendants should usually be assigned one of the decision choices suggested by the guidelines and that, usually or in most cases, the guidelines would point to the optimal decision.

However, in a minority of cases, other kinds of information about the defendant could be so important as to cause the judge to set aside the guidelines suggestion and to select another release option. Out-of-the-ordinary circumstances were to be noted on the guidelines form by pretrial services staff preparing the guidelines. Thus, a defendant's history of escape from penal institutions, his or her mental-health history of suicide attempts, or the willingness of an organization to guarantee supervision and custody of the defendant might, beyond the usual guidelines classification, persuade the judge that a more or less restrictive condition of pretrial release might be appropriate.

When these exceptional decisions were taken by the judge or commissioner, however, the guidelines system counted on the notation of reasons for the departure by the judge, so that when the use of guidelines was reviewed periodically, appropriate modifications could be made. The judges' practice of taking exceptions could also be reviewed for appropriateness in light of the overall court policy and of data describing the experience of defendants in each of the guidelines categories.

Additional Special Features: Caseflow-Processing Indicators

Guidelines might also be devised to provide information that placed cases in the larger context of caseflow-processing concerns. For example, particular defendant categories could be highlighted to indicate that these type of defendants in the recent past had experienced higher than ordinary *dropout* rates (see the Maricopa and Dade guidelines), meaning that defendants in these categories were unusually likely to have their cases dropped, dismissed, withdrawn, or nolle prossed. Similarly, the guidelines could indicate categories of defendants in which higher than average *binddown* rates, rates at which felonies had been transferred to be processed as misdemeanors, had been experienced in the recent past (see the Dade guidelines). Guidelines categories could also flag defendants presumptively eligible for diversion processing (for example, for drug treatment) or could point to defendants whose case history attributes would make them good candidates for fast-track adjudication or early disposition. In the face of the pressures of jail overcrowding or crowded dockets, the guidelines could thus also incorporate information linking pretrial release determinations to a number of related processing concerns and could be used to set procedures for enhancing expeditious case-flow management.

A Note about the Evaluation of Decision Guidelines

From a scientific point of view, the impact of an innovation is best measured through experimentation. That is, under ideal conditions, some method of randomly allocating defendants to guidelines decisionmaking and to traditional decisionmaking during the same period in time would best show the strengths and weaknesses of the approaches being compared. This is the approach we followed successfully in the first test of the concept in the Philadelphia Municipal Court. Given the resource and time constraints of the demonstration project, however, we adopted instead a more feasible pre-post approach, in which we compared practices before the use of decision guidelines at initial appearance with practices after their adoption. Two factors argued in favor of this approach: (a) an experimental design would have been too disruptive to implementation efforts in Dade and Maricopa counties; and (b) funding resources for evaluation were modest. Despite the methodological issues associated with the pre-post method of evaluation,[3] we believed that a great deal still could be learned about the effects of the pretrial release guidelines on the outcomes of interest. We noted above that the leadership of the Boston Municipal Court was unsuccessful in implementing the guidelines that had been developed, although it had expressed a desire to do so. To attempt to learn more about the impact of the guidelines, therefore, our research strategy was to evaluate the guidelines implemented in the felony courts in Maricopa County and Dade County within the means then available.

Notes

1. Of course, no guidelines can be "final," certainly not in their first version. They are meant to evolve, to be revised and updated as experience may warrant.
2. See Goldkamp and Gottfredson (1985).
3. The principal question that arises using this approach is the possible effects on the later outcomes of phenomena other than the one being investigated. For example, if greater use of OR and pretrial release was found generally in 1987 when compared to 1984, we would want to be assured that something other than the guidelines had not caused the change.

15

The Implementation of Pretrial Release Guidelines in Maricopa County

During the period between November 1984 and December 1986, the leadership of the superior court of Arizona in Maricopa County worked with the researchers to examine its pretrial release and detention practices and to devise pretrial release guidelines[1] for use by pretrial services and commissioners at initial appearance. The initial version of the court's pretrial release guidelines was put into use during January 1987. During the descriptive research which led to the design of decision guidelines, the court focused on a number of concerns related to the conduct of pretrial-release and detention decisionmaking in superior court. For the sake of brevity, these concerns can be divided into two groupings: those relating to the pretrial-release-decisionmaking process and those relating to the possible impact of the guidelines.

Concerns related to the pretrial release process included a wish to clarify the pretrial-services-recommendation function, to encourage greater consistency among the decisions of the commissioners presiding at initial appearance, and to consider implementing a program of supervised release as well as a case review procedure for eliminating unnecessary cases from the court caseload and from the jail population. Questions about the impact of pretrial release decisionmaking in superior court were raised because of the history of jail overcrowding in Maricopa County.[2] The county's recently completed jail facility opened its doors to discover a second generation of crowding problems. Concerns about the effect of pretrial release practices on minimizing flight and crime among defendants granted release before adjudication were also a high priority principally because of occasional and relatively rare episodes of crimes committed by released defendants that received a great deal of publicity, even though large numbers of released defendants were not shown to fail to appear in court or to be rearrested during the study period.

Given the press of these kinds of concerns, it was logical for the court to review its decisionmaking processes. Thus the research examined the procedures employed by the pretrial services agency responsible for interviewing defendants prior to their initial appearance in court and for preparing recommendations concerning pretrial release for submission to the commissioners who presided at that stage. In addition, large numbers of pretrial release decisions and conditions assigned to defendants were studied, and their outcomes (in terms of release and subsequent misconduct) were contrasted.

One of the special features of the Maricopa County guidelines was that neither the severity of a defendant's current charges nor the categorization of a defendant within the empirically derived risk classification served as the sole emphasis in suggesting pretrial release options. Because of the court's special concerns about cases involving victims of crime, particularly victims who had been injured, and about crimes involving weapons use or repetitive serious criminal charges, these attributes of defendants' cases were given special structural prominence within superior court's guidelines framework.

The court's concern about minimizing the use of unnecessary pretrial detention of defendants while maintaining very low rates of misconduct among released defendants was further reflected by the designation of suggested decisions (ranges and options) within each of the guidelines categories. To the extent that the guidelines could be implemented and employed appropriately by the commissioners at initial appearance, the court's policy goal of achieving equitable pretrial-release and detention decisions would also have been realized in the sense that similarly situated defendants (defendants with similar guidelines classifications) would be receiving reasonably comparable decisions.

The Implementation of the Guidelines at Initial Appearance

The development of decision guidelines for pretrial release in superior court sought to bring about improvement in a number of areas, including the reduction of unnecessary pretrial detention. Accordingly, their implementation involved change on the part of pretrial services staff and the superior court commissioners who decided pretrial release. The required changes ranged from seemingly (but not always) minor new procedures and paperwork to more substantive differences.

Changes Required of Pretrial Services Staff

For the pretrial services program, the implementation of the pretrial release guidelines would require a fairly notable change. Under the former preguidelines procedures, pretrial services customarily considered the defendant's background and criminal history information and then recommended to the commissioners that a defendant should be released under nonfinancial conditions; otherwise, they made no recommendation, from which the commissioners were free to conclude that the defendant was a better candidate for secured (financial) bond. Earlier we described the very influential part played by the subjectively formulated pretrial services recommendation in the commissioners' choices and the defendants' prospects for pretrial release or detention.

Under the guidelines approach, the pretrial services staff would no longer make subjective recommendations to the commissioners regarding pretrial release. Instead, they would "classify" defendants according to the guidelines criteria—based on risk of misconduct, the severity of criminal charges, and the "special" severity factors—and indicate for the commissioner the decision options usually suggested in similar cases. Thus the "recommendation" function under the guidelines would be eliminated and would be replaced by an objective fact-gathering and information-prioritizing scheme.

This change was not minor for the pretrial services staff for at least two reasons. First, pretrial services might have felt deprived of an important decisionmaking role (making a subjective recommendation regarding nonfinancial release to the commissioners). Second, the new "objective" procedures eliminated discretion in choosing which kind of defendant information was most important. Instead, items were to be ranked, scored and summed. Thus a successful implementation of the guidelines system would require an adjustment in the attitude or outlook of the staff as well as training in the new procedures. On a smaller scale, therefore, it would be natural for pretrial services staff to feel what commissioners or judges might fear, that the key part of their role was being replaced by a cold, "computerized" decision process.

The Court Commissioners and the Guidelines

It is fair to say that the commissioners, who had been participating in the research process throughout, viewed the advent of implementation of decision guidelines with some trepidation. The guidelines development process to that point may have seemed academic—the meaning of various findings were freely debated at the many meetings—but as the date of implementation approached, some of the commissioners clearly became uncomfortable. The procedures and forms were revised a number of times to incorporate suggestions from the commissioners and the pretrial services staff so that the guidelines would be as simple, understandable, and practical as possible. Finally, the process of preparation came to an end when one of the commissioners argued that the suggested decisions were too lenient and the ranges of secured bond "were just too low" and recommended that the upper limit of guidelines be left open-ended. What the commissioner was expressing, in fact, was his feeling of discomfort with the guidelines, with the idea of an explicit policy that would constrain his exercise of discretion.

At this last meeting, the operation of the guidelines was reviewed, and the intent was reiterated and reclarified that the guidelines were designed to be a useful reference in most cases, not all cases; that commissioners were free to depart from the guidelines, and were only asked to note reasons for their departures; and so forth. Finally, the presiding judge set a date for their implementation and urged the commissioners to make the best use of them, noting that we would study their use and come up with recommendations for change after an initial period, if change seemed appropriate.

For the commissioners, some change was indeed involved. Formerly, they had considered the recommendation of the pretrial services staff and had often agreed with it, though they had not been bound by it in the slightest. In this instance, a "presumptive," usual case decision or choice of decision options would be pointed out. The guidelines were a more explicit representation of court policy; though they were not binding, they required reasons for exceptional decisions and fostered the feeling that commissioners were accountable for their decisions.

Proposed Procedural Innovation

Just as the implementation of the guidelines strategy required individuals to cooperate in trying out the new procedures, the implementation plan also called for the "system" to do some new things—though perhaps not all of them at once. Two of the court's most important planned innovations involved (1) establishing a more forceful program of supervised release and targeting its use to particular categories of defendants (those falling within the "special-conditions" guidelines cells) and (2) instituting a review of the status of defendants' situations from three to five days after the initial-appearance decision.

The first proposed innovation, developing a supervision program for medium-risk defendants, was problematic because additional resources would need to be deployed to keep track of defendants falling into the "OR/Special Conditions" part of the guidelines matrix. Although commissioners had previously been releasing defendants on conditions involving supervision, the pretrial services program did not have the resources to mount an effective program, and very little supervision had generally been involved in "supervised release." However, a meaningful program of supervised release would clearly be pivotal under the guidelines, since guidelines were designed to reduce unnecessary detention through targeting formerly detained categories of defendants (medium-risk–medium-severity) for nonfinancial release under restrictive conditions, for example, supervised release.

The second suggested innovation was based on the recognition that improvements at the initial-appearance stage alone could not accomplish some of the court's goals in the areas of pretrial release and detention. It was felt that a second-stage consideration of the defendants' custody and case status should be closely linked to implementation of the guidelines. The developmental research had produced several findings supporting this recommendation, including the fact that once a defendant had failed to secure release at the initial-appearance stage in Maricopa County, there was little likelihood and/or chance for change of his or her custody status throughout the remainder of the case. The research also pointed to categories of defendants who, although they had not been released at initial appearance, could well have been released later (within the next couple of days) without posing higher risks than defendants gaining immediate release.

Often the explanation was that additional information needed to be obtained by pretrial services (perhaps regarding residence or employment or out-of-state warrants) before a favorable recommendation could be made, but because of the short period between arrest and initial appearance, it was sometimes impossible. In analyzing the processing of entering felony cases, we found that a large proportion were dropped or dismissed within the first 90 days, including large numbers of defendants held in detention.

In short, linked with the implementation of the guidelines system at initial appearance, the court sought to establish complementary procedures that would address the use of pretrial detention and release in other ways. Taken together, decision guidelines and the related procedures had the dual goals of ensuring that appropriately restrictive conditions of release would be applied to cases posing the most serious risks of crime and flight and preventing unwarranted and wasteful confinement in the other cases.

The Evaluation Design in Maricopa County

Given the strict constraints of limited resources and time (we wanted to give prompt feedback to the superior court judges who were concerned about correcting any possible negative impact the implementation period might have), we decided to collect data describing the use of guidelines at the very beginning of their implementation and to collect a smaller, later sample to indicate the nature of guidelines use after several months of operation. Data describing pretrial release decisions and a 90-day follow-up were collected for roughly the first 500 cases entering superior court during the months of January 1987 (the first month of guidelines use) and February 1987 ($n = 991$). Defendants securing release within 48 hours were followed up for a period of 90 days to determine whether any failures to appear in court (FTAs) or rearrests for crimes occurring during pretrial release were recorded.[3] In addition, data describing the use of guidelines for 436 cases entering the process during a two-week period beginning September 23, 1987, and ending October 4, 1987, were also collected. The purpose of this later sample was limited to examining the use of guidelines at a point subsequent to the initial start-up, when the problems associated with new programs had had more chance to work themselves out. It was not possible to follow the progress of these cases during pretrial release. The preliminary evaluation of the use of the pretrial release guidelines was thus limited to these samples and did not address their use throughout 1987.[4]

The press of time in this project required that we evaluate new programs at an early stage of their development. Ideally, it would be preferable to allow some time for implementation difficulties to be identified and sorted out before measuring the performance of a complex innovation. Indeed, it would be understandable for a court system implementing guidelines to take several months of testing and adjusting before the program could be tested fairly. However, research time tables are often shaped by very pragmatic concerns such as funding and deadlines. We simply did not have the time (especially given the length of the necessary follow-up that would be required) to follow a lengthier data collection strategy. In all likelihood, a year-long study may well have shown fluctuations in the effects of the guidelines strategy and would have offered a greater base of experience from which to draw conclusions. To address some of these longer-term questions, at least to the extent feasible, we added the September–October sample to capture practices at a more seasoned stage of their development.

The research team was aware of the need to exercise great caution in the interpretation of findings generated from a pre-post comparison of the effects of an intervention. The samples of defendants entering superior court in 1984 and during the two periods in 1987 were not precisely similar (they differed somewhat in the severity and risk attributes of their respective defendants), and it was necessary to make comparisons with great care.[5] Fortunately, the guidelines themselves offered a vehicle for making comparisons across two sample periods. By contrasting subcategories of defendants with similar characteristics, such as defendants classified within the same guidelines "zones" or "cells," we were, in effect, able to "control" for variations in the composition of the entire sample.

Preparation of the Guidelines by Pretrial Services

Just as the staff of the superior court's pretrial services agency played a central role in the development of the guidelines, they carried a major share of the burden for implementing the system at the initial-appearance stage. To prepare the guidelines and to summarize relevant information for the commissioners who presided over initial appearance in superior court, pretrial services staff interviewed each defendant and reviewed other potentially important case- or history-related information. To situate each defendant within the guidelines—and thus to indicate the pretrial release option suggested by the guidelines for like defendants—the pretrial services staff was required correctly to classify the defendant's criminal charges and to determine the risk category in which the defendant belonged. To determine the charge severity level, the interviewer followed procedures for designating the most serious criminal charge facing the defendant and reviewed the relevance of the special severity factors relating to victim injury, weapons use, and repetitive serious charges. If the "special" factors were in evidence, the restrictiveness of the defendant's guidelines classification was increased. To place the defendant within the appropriate risk group, with choices ranging from Group 1 (the lowest risk) to Group 4 (the highest risk), the pretrial services staff member would score the defendant according to the items shown on the pretrial services worksheet. Ordinarily, the risk and charge classifications would permit the interviewer to indicate for the commissioner in which guidelines category the defendant belonged. When that category was circled on the commissioner's guidelines form, the commissioner would be able to see the pretrial release option usually suggested for defendants with given charge and risk attributes.

When relevant, however, the pretrial services staff member would also indicate other unusual aspects of the case or of the defendant's background that the commissioner would need to know to make the most appropriate decision at initial appearance. Thus, even before the commissioner could make the pretrial release decision, the pretrial services agency would already have performed several key functions.

The data describing our evaluation is provided in the Appendix (Figures A.1 to A.7). Here we can highlight some of the notable results. More than half of the 1987 defendants were classified within categories not calling for financial conditions (secured bond), and most of these (45 percent of the January–February defendants and 48 percent of the September defendants) fell into the least restrictive categories involving only "standard" conditions of release.[6]

The patterns of the January, February, and September defendants were quite similar. In particular, although 1987 defendants were scattered among many guidelines "cells," there were three particularly important clusters. Fully one-fifth (22 percent) of the 1987 defendants fell in the cell designated by severity Level 3 and risk Group 2 of the guidelines. A further one-fifth of the 1987 defendants were equally divided among two other cells. With nearly half of all entering criminal defendants in these three categories, it became clear that the utility of the pretrial release guidelines would depend heavily on the decisions made within these categories.

Errors in Classifying Defendants According to the Guidelines

It was to be expected that persons employing new procedures and completing new paperwork during implementation of the guidelines system would make mistakes in classifying defendants, in ranking their criminal charges, or in scoring them according to the risk dimension. Indeed, it would be very unusual to discover few or no inaccuracies during the first few months of a new program. (In the first use of decision guidelines during the Philadelphia experiment, for example, simple math mistakes were found in completing risk classifications in about 5 percent of the cases.) Because of the importance of accurate classification of defendants within the guidelines for achieving the policy goals of the guidelines, we examined the classification of superior court defendants during the two sample periods.

The review of the risk classification adopted two approaches: It examined the way defendants were scored (comparing defendant and case information with the ratings given by pretrial services) and verified the computation of the risk scores and the subsequent placement of defendants in risk groups for the guidelines.[7] The computational check of points assigned by the pretrial services interviewer revealed an error rate of roughly 6 percent. When we more thoroughly reviewed the scoring of items for the 991 defendants entering during the January–February period sample, we found errors in 135 cases (or about 14 percent of the time). Of these errors, about half (7 percent) were of a magnitude leading to an erroneous classification under the pretrial release guidelines. The majority of these (58 percent) placed the defendant within a less restrictive suggested decision category, while the remainder (42 percent) led mistakenly to more restrictive suggested decisions.[8]

The Notation of Unusual Circumstances

In completing the "Unusual Circumstances" section of the commissioner's guidelines decision form, the pretrial services interviewer was indicating that there were special features of the defendant's case or situation that ought to be included among the other kinds of information the commissioner considered. The *unusual* in the title was purposely intended to denote restricted use of this section; it was not designed, for example, to include general biographical data or notes about employment status and so on. Review of the use of this section in the January–February cases revealed that "unusual circumstances" were reported in roughly one-third (36 percent) of the cases. Although the level of use was low, it most certainly was not "rare." Analysis of the September–October cases showed that "unusual" factors were reported less frequently, in only one-fourth (26 percent) of all cases.

The importance of the proper use of this section of the guidelines was underscored when its relationship to the commissioners' decisions was examined. When any unusual circumstance was noted by pretrial services, it doubled the chance that the commissioner would make a decision that departed from the guidelines. The most common circumstances found to be unusual were "in Arizona only a short time," defendant had "open" or "pending cases," the defendant was "on probation or parole," or "other holds or warrants" were indicated. Thus, for this section to be of practical use to the commissioners, its use would need to be carefully monitored.

Suggestions for Special Conditions of Release

According to the guidelines classifications of the 1987 sample of defendants, just under 10 percent of defendants fell within guidelines categories calling for OR with special conditions of release to be assigned. Between 13 and 18 percent of defendants (depending upon the month) fell within categories suggesting either OR with special conditions to be assigned or a low secured bond. Theoretically, pretrial services should have specified which restrictive conditions would be most appropriate in these cases (and would be unlikely to specify special conditions for cases falling in other categories). Suggestion of special conditions occurred in less than 20 percent of the cases, a level closely in line with the goals of the guidelines classification.

Use of the Pretrial Release Guidelines by Superior Court Commissioners

In designing the decision guidelines for use at initial appearance by the commissioners, the court did not propose or expect that the guidelines would be followed unquestioningly by commissioners in all cases. Rather, the idea was to provide general guidance which would be appropriate in most cases and yet provide the flexibility to accommodate unusual cases. Thus, while the guidelines were to provide a strong compass for general bearings in pretrial release decisionmaking, they also provided the information through the work of the pretrial services agency on the basis of which commissioners could decide to make decisions different from those suggested by the guidelines.

By definition, though, departures from the suggested decisions were expected to occur relatively infrequently. Moreover, departures should ideally be equally divided among those involving more restrictive and those involving less restrictive options. Overall, we expected commissioners' choices to agree with guidelines suggestions in roughly 75 percent of the cases. Finally, our evaluation of the initial use of the guidelines would also examine the notation of reasons by the commissioners in the exceptional cases to provide important feedback to the court in its review of guidelines and consideration of possible modifications.

In the first two months of the guidelines, commissioners agreed in about 70 percent of the cases, a level of agreement very close to the ideal. By September, however, the level of agreement by commissioners had slipped noticeably to 62 percent. While this still represented agreement in a majority of cases, it represented a much weaker degree of compliance than an effective system would look for. Departures from the guidelines were five times more likely to be in the direction of more restrictive than less restrictive choices. In short, decisions were increasingly being made outside the guidelines and were generally moving in the direction of more restrictive decisions overall.

To evaluate the guidelines more closely—either with the aim of modifying the suggested decisions or of encouraging greater compliance among the decisionmakers—examination of specific guidelines categories (cells) may be more helpful (see Figure A.4 and A.5).[9] Reasonably high levels of agreement were seen for January–February decisions across most cells, with the exceptions of three cells. While it was not unusual to see frequent departures in the highest risk, highest severity categories (one of the exceptions), disagreement in middle cells (also the case) was more problematic since, combined, they accounted for roughly 20 percent of all entering defendants. High levels of disagreement in these categories resulted in a disproportionate effect on the overall use of the guidelines. On the other side of the ledger, the cell containing the largest number of defendants produced one of the highest levels of commissioner agreement during January–February. Among the September–October 1987 sample decisions, some slippage occurred across cells.

Agreement from Commissioner to Commissioner

We also studied the extent to which individual commissioners' decisions agreed with those posited by the pretrial release guidelines.[10] In comparison with the expected level of general agreement (about 75 percent), three commissioners were making use of guidelines during the January–February period in the fashion envisaged. Three commissioners agreed with guidelines at notably lower levels. By October, the decisions of only one commissioner showed the expected level of agreement with guidelines.

Notation of Reasons by Decisionmakers Making Exceptions

In a well-implemented program of pretrial release guidelines, the decisionmakers are asked to provide notation of reasons when the decisions they make depart from those suggested by the guidelines. During subsequent review of the use of guidelines, the reasons commissioners noted could help determine whether the guidelines should be modified or, perhaps, whether the decisionmakers should be encouraged to follow the guidelines more frequently. During the initial use of guidelines in superior court, commissioners departed from guideline suggestions 30 percent of the time. In the great majority of these instances (75 percent), the commissioners did note reasons for the exceptions. In the Fall 1987 sample, commissioners were slightly less likely to give reasons for departures from the guidelines (65 percent). Generally, the reasons cited by the commissioners were appropriate, given the goals of the guidelines. However, a couple of reasons were not of the variety envisaged by the guidelines system. For example, prior failures to appear would not be viewed as appropriate reasons for departures generally, given the pronounced role of that criterion in the guidelines in the first place. "Guidelines too low" was also not the kind of reason useful to the court in reviewing the use of the guidelines; rather more useful would have been an explanation of why, in the particular instance, the guidelines appeared "too low" to the commissioner.

Pretrial Release Decisions before and during the Guidelines

Examination of the preparation and use of pretrial release guidelines set the stage for consideration of the extent to which decisionmaking at initial appearance and its outcomes had changed in the desired directions as a result of the guidelines program. This section first briefly compares decisionmaking in 1984 and 1987, focusing on the use of nonfinancial release, secured bond, and detention. Subsequently, we will examine the consequences of the decisions in terms of the performance of defendants given pretrial release.

Analysis of the use of nonfinancial conditions was central to evaluation of the impact of the guidelines because of the earlier findings showing that resort to secured bond by commissioners in Maricopa County was tantamount to detaining defendants. Thus, to the extent that personal recognizance release (with or without conditions) could be increased in appropriate areas, for example, pretrial release would be increased.

For clarity, we also studied the guidelines after dividing the matrix into four zones (i.e., presumptive OR cells, special release cells, low bond, and high bond). Two conclusions can be drawn from this procedure. First, guidelines appear to have contributed to a dramatic increase in the use of nonfinancial release in three of the four decision zones. This is particularly important when we recall that more than half of the 1987 defendants fell within these sections of the guidelines. Second, by the fall—at least as shown by the September–October sample—this progress was eroding, particularly within the "OR/Special Conditions" groups.[11]

The Use of Pretrial Detention: 1984–1987

Perhaps the outcome of greatest concern in the superior court's review of the initial use of pretrial release guidelines was the impact on the use of pretrial release and detention. Because of time constraints, we measured pretrial detention as whether a defendant gained release within two days for the purposes of studying release in the January–February 1987 sample (see Figure 15.1). Overall, the use of pretrial detention dropped noticeably and significantly during the initial guidelines period: 54 percent of the 1984 defendants had been held longer than two days; only 42 percent of the January–February 1987 defendants had been so held.

The use of pretrial detention was cut in half among defendants classified within the "OR/Standard Conditions" zone: In 1984, 35 percent of defendants with these attributes had been held more than two days; in January–February 1987, 16 percent had been held. The same figure also shows a halving of detention in the "OR/Special Conditions" zone and a 17 percentage-point reduction in the "OR/Special to Low Bond" categories. Detention for more than two days was increased 4 percentage points among the "Secured Bond" defendants.

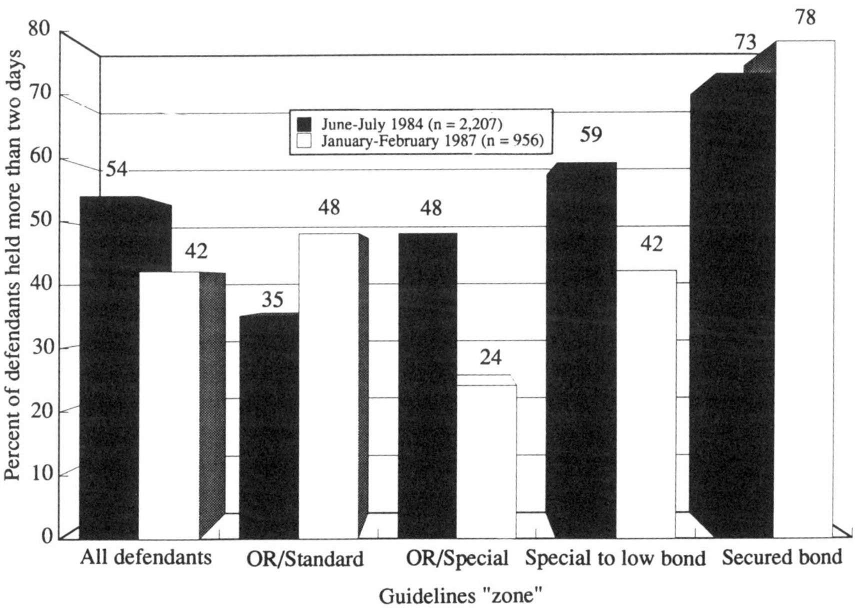

FIGURE 15.1. Change in use of pretrial detention (held more than two days) among entering felony defendants in Maricopa County Superior Court from 1984 to 1987, by guidelines "zone," by sample. (Chi-squares were not significant, at .05, in the "Secured Bond" zone.)

The Performance of Defendants during Pretrial Release: Comparing the Effectiveness of Practices, 1984–1987

Of FTA, Rearrest, Felony Rearrest, and "Failure" Rates

We compared the rates of misconduct recorded by released defendants in the June–July 1984 and January–February 1987 samples.[12] The slightly lower failure-to-appear rate recorded by the 1987 defendants over all was not statistically significant. A slightly higher rearrest rate (6 percentage points) was shown by the defendants released in the 1987 sample. However, when rearrest for felonies (as opposed to rearrest for any offense) was analyzed, no difference in the two samples was shown. When rearrest and FTA rates were combined as one measure—to indicate "failure" during pretrial release—an increase of 4 percentage points in 1987 was shown.

Earlier, we indicated that simple rearrest–FTA statistics such as those just reported are quite misleading and, though popular, are not very helpful. Comparing "failure" rates without paying attention to release and detention rates at the same time is not fully informative. We can illustrate this point best by recalling our comparison of what we termed the *effectiveness* of release practices in the three cities we studied. To be effective, practices must release as many defendants as possible and, then, minimize "errors" (defendants who abscond or commit crimes) among those released. The formula for effectiveness then "marks off" for (1) not releasing defendants and (2) releasing defendants who record misconduct. Using this definition, we found in Chapter 10 that, compared to Boston Municipal Court and Dade County Circuit Court defendants, Maricopa County Superior Court was the least effective jurisdiction we studied, primarily because of its dramatically high rate of pretrial detention.

The same measure, taking into account the different release and detention rates, is useful to apply to the analysis of defendant performance in superior court over time, between 1984 and 1987. When this measure was calculated to compare both years, it was seen that the overall "effectiveness" of pretrial release increased noticeably under guidelines during the initial period, moving from 39 percent in 1984 to 47 percent of defendants in 1987. The guidelines framework allows for a more detailed cell-by-cell analysis of effectiveness as well.[13]

The effectiveness of release increased in 6 of the 11 cells we could compare. The effectiveness was increased most in the cell containing the largest number of defendants. In considering cell-by-cell effectiveness ratings, it is essential to keep in mind the following:

- Effectiveness of pretrial release can be improved by increasing pretrial release, decreasing failure among released defendants, or both.
- Increased release can be brought about by greater compliance with guidelines suggestions or by modifying the guidelines suggestions to permit greater release.
- Reduced "failure" can be brought about by application of more restrictive conditions of release.
- Some cells falling within the "Secured Bond" zone of the guidelines have lower rates of effectiveness because of the high amounts of bond set by the commissioners and the higher rates of pretrial detention that accompany that practice. (It was in these areas where agreement with guidelines was lowest.) Thus, greater agreement with the guidelines might bring bond levels down, encourage greater release, and hence promote increased effectiveness.

For example, improved effectiveness might occur both by encouraging greater compliance and by changing the guidelines suggestion to include "special" conditions of release. Alternatively, in some cells including defendants with the highest risk and the most serious criminal-charge attributes, it might be argued that because detention is expected to be at a higher level, the effectiveness of pretrial "release" is expected to be low. The standard in these kinds of cells should at least be that we do no worse under guidelines than before (in 1984).

One could easily argue that the overall effectiveness of pretrial release in a court system can be no more than the aggregate of the effectiveness of the practices of each of its pretrial-release decisionmakers. One of the goals of the guidelines tool would be to increase the overall effectiveness of pretrial release by improving the effectiveness of the decisions generated by each individual decisionmaker, so we compared the effectiveness of pretrial release associated with each of the commissioners presiding over initial appearance during the January–February study. Although a much larger sample covering longer periods throughout the year would be more desirable, rather divergent rates of effectiveness can be seen when commissioners are compared, ranging from a low of 25 percent effective release (Commissioner 6) to a high of 51 percent (Commissioner 4). (See Figure A.7, p. 319.)

The Equitable Treatment of Defendants, 1984–1987

In response to research findings showing disparity to be as much a characteristic of pretrial-release decisionmaking as of sentencing, one of the hypothesized goals of decision guidelines for pretrial release decisionmaking is to encourage more equitable treatment of defendants. One way guidelines can contribute to this end is in the establishment of a policy yardstick by which the decisions given to defendants can be evaluated. By building the guidelines around acknowledged goals—such as the minimization of flight and crime and unnecessary pretrial detention—and setting forth criteria for pursuing those goals in an explicit decision framework, a mechanism is set in place that can encourage greater equity (to the extent guidelines are followed by the decisionmakers).

Formerly, answering the question "Are similarly situated defendants treated similarly at the bail stage?" was complicated by the problems of defining *similarity*. Often it focused vaguely on the single criterion, seriousness of defendants' charges (hence the rationale for the traditional bond schedule, for example). Because guidelines represent the culmination of policy decisions about why and how the pretrial release decision should henceforth be conducted, the guidelines represent a fuller and more relevant gauge by which equity can be evaluated.

Simply put, defendants with characteristics like defendants falling in the "OR/Standard Conditions" zone should usually receive "OR with Standard Conditions." Defendants with attributes placing them within guidelines Cell 9 should usually receive decisions like other defendants in Cell 9. One measurement of improvement in the equity of decisions between the 1984 and 1987 study periods involves comparison of the numbers of defendants with given characteristics (as defined by the guidelines dimensions) having similar (guidelines-suggested) decisions. That is, we should find more consistency in the treatment of given categories of defendants under the guidelines system.

Using guidelines zone as the frame of reference, we compared the percentages of defendants receiving specified decisions between June–July 1984, January–February 1987, and September–October 1987. Substantially more defendants (14 percentage points) with traits placing them within the "OR/Standard" zone received OR in January–February 1987 than in the 1984 period. A somewhat greater share (7 percentage points more) of September–October defendants than their 1984 counterparts received OR.

Very few 1984 defendants falling in the "OR/Special Conditions" zone received OR with special conditions (partly because the 1987 definition of "special" or restrictive conditions did not translate perfectly to 1984 practices). Sixty-eight percent of such defendants in January–February received OR with special conditions. However, nearly a third less of similar defendants in the September–October sample received OR with special conditions. We can see that, compared to like defendants in 1984, greater shares of 1987 defendants falling within the remaining two zones received the specified decisions.

Summary of the Maricopa County Evaluation Findings

We collected two relatively small samples of data reflecting pretrial release decisionmaking at initial appearance in superior court in Maricopa County to evaluate the effect of the then recently implemented decision guidelines on key aspects of release practices. The first sample described decisions in felony cases entering the criminal process in January and February of 1987 during the very first weeks of the new guidelines program. We also collected a small sample reflecting initial-appearance decisionmaking during September and October of that year so that we could obtain a reading on the functioning of guidelines once the new program had had a chance to ripen and become more routine. Because time and funding did not allow, we were unable to collect follow-up data describing the release and performance during pretrial release of the fall defendants.

Pretrial Services

In a short period, the pretrial services agency set in motion the procedures necessary to the successful implementation of the guidelines system. Certainly, the kinds of errors by pretrial services staff we detected in employing the guidelines for the very first time were normal and easily correctable with a little experience. Our review suggests that in other respects the agency had implemented the program reasonably well. The policy of pointing out unusual circumstances to the commissioners was appropriately performed but should be carefully monitored in the future. Perhaps the major difficulty we found was in the area of "special conditions of release." In the January and February samples, suggestions for special supervision were made for the appropriate categories of defendants, but no resources were in place for the supervised release option; a new program of supervision has been set in place since.

The Use of Guidelines by the Commissioners at Initial Appearance

During the first two months of the new program, the overall agreement between the commissioners' decisions and those suggested by the guidelines almost reached the desired level. (The guidelines were designed so that they should be viewed as appropriate suggestions in a majority of cases—with an ideal goal of about 75 percent of the cases; 70

percent of the commissioners' decisions agreed with the guidelines during the January–February samples.) By fall, however, the use of the guidelines by the commissioners appeared to have declined noticeably to only 62 percent of the cases. Moreover, this decline appeared to be systematic, applying across guidelines categories.

When the decisions of the six commissioners were examined, it was found that use of guidelines varied noticeably from commissioner to commissioner. Initially, two were strong consumers of the guidelines, and a third commissioner was not far behind. In our fall study, only one commissioner maintained his consistently frequent agreement with the guidelines suggestions, and a second became less consistent in his utilization of the guidelines. By the time of the fall sample, agreement with guidelines in the decisions of the other commissioners had dropped off dramatically or had lowered an already low rate of agreement.

Changes in Pretrial Release Decisionmaking

Although the overall use of nonfinancial release (OR) increased from the 1984 levels somewhat, use within several important subcategories of defendants increased dramatically. Among the highest risk most seriously charged defendant groups, its use was reduced. When secured bond was employed, its average level was reduced somewhat as well. Where agreement with the guidelines was strong, use of nonfinancial release was strong. Where departures from guidelines became more pronounced—as was particularly the case during the September–October study—the use of nonfinancial release was set back, in some instances to levels slightly lower than the 1984 baseline comparison.

Changes in Pretrial Release and Detention

Overall, pretrial detention as measured at the 48-hour mark dropped approximately 11 percent during the initial use of guidelines. In some categories of defendants, larger and more dramatic drops in detention were observed. These strong and positive findings from the January and February samples of decisions were threatened, however, by the findings of lower use of guidelines and lower assignment of nonfinancial conditions evident in the September–October study. Although we were unable to follow up the subsequent release and performance of defendants in the September study, our analysis of the decisions made during that period suggests that the detention rate may have been moving back up toward its former high levels.

Rates of Misconduct among Released Defendants

Release of an additional 11 percent of the entering felony defendants resulted in an overall FTA rate that was no higher than the previous norm for Maricopa defendants and a rearrest rate that was slightly higher. However, the rearrest rate for "serious" offenses (i.e., felony offenses specifically) among the 1987 releasees was no higher than among the 1984 releasees.

Changes in the Effectiveness of Pretrial Release

Rates of misconduct during pretrial release are very misleading because they do not take into account the use of release and detention. (Recall that superior court in Maricopa County and circuit court in Dade County showed similar rates of misconduct among released defendants—only circuit court released roughly 50 percent more felony defendants.) The effectiveness of pretrial release can be measured as the percentage of all entering defendants put on release and not "failing" (through FTA or rearrest).

The overall effectiveness of pretrial release increased under the guidelines during their initial use. Substantial improvement in "mistake-free" release was noted among defendants falling within the nonfinancial sections of the guidelines. Effectiveness appeared to be best when agreement with the guidelines was most frequent.

Equitable Decisionmaking

Decisions were more consistent within categories during the January–February sample period—although analysis of individual cells reveals some exceptions. This at first dramatic effect appeared to have begun dissipating by the time of the September–October sample.

In summary, we found a number of positive outcomes and promising directions associated with the initial use of the pretrial-release-decision guidelines at initial appearance in superior court. Perhaps most troublesome are the findings that (1) agreement of guidelines fell just a little bit short of the intended goal in January and February of 1987, and (2) agreement was decreasing substantially by the time of the September–October defendant sample. It appears that important improvements were within reach, but only as long as the guidelines were employed effectively.

Notes

1. As we pointed out earlier, the terminology describing bail proceedings differed in each of the courts—as ultimately did the name of the decision guidelines developed. In Maricopa County, bail was referred to as *bond,* financial bail as *secured bond,* and first appearance as *initial appearance.* At one of the earliest project meetings, the then criminal presiding judge insisted that the decision guidelines to be developed be called *pretrial release guidelines* to emphasize the overall importance of the decision at initial appearance and to distinguish the guidelines from a bond schedule, which is what he believed the term *bail guidelines* conjured up.
2. In fact, one of the reasons the court invited the research was to discover whether development of a guidelines resource might serve as a resource in addressing crowding problems. When the research began in 1984, the old jail was seriously crowded. By the time the research was completed, a new jail had been opened and filled to capacity, and the county was again facing overcrowding crises.
3. This represents a shortened method of studying defendants' performance during pretrial release when compared to the 1984 study, upon which guidelines development was based. In that study, we followed cases for up to 90 days first to determine whether they had been released. If they had been released during that period, we then followed the cases for up to 90 days of pretrial release (or until adjudication of the case). Thus nearly six months of follow-up was required for the study of cases released late in the process. Because we did not have that amount of time or the necessary staffing available, we chose to study release as an immediate result of the initial-appearance decision. Thus we determined whether or not a defendant had secured release within 2 days and then conducted a 90-day follow-up to determine whether rearrests or failures to appear had occurred.
4. However, the pretrial services agency produced a report for the second half of 1987 that summarized information relating to the use of guidelines during the latter period, although the agency report employed a different methodology.
5. What is evident is that the January–February and September 1987 samples of entering defendants differed little from one another in the areas of risk and charge severity. The severity of the defendants' charges seemed to differ between 1984 and 1987 in one area: The final severity ratings (the defendants' classification once the victim injury, weapons, and repetitive serious counts criteria were taken into account) showed that more 1984 defendants were charged with offenses placing them at severity Level 4, while the 1987 defendants were more often placed within severity Level 3. Yet the proportions of defendants at the highest severity levels were reasonably similar in the two years.
6. By "standard" conditions of release are meant conditions such as returning to court and refraining from criminal activity, which did not seriously restrict a defendant's activities.
7. We were unable to review the accuracy of rankings of criminal charges according to the guidelines severity dimension because we collected only the pretrial services worksheet (we did not see the police forms with the initial charges). Thus we can only assume that this part of the guidelines classification went mostly well.
8. Review of the use of the police item during the January–February sample showed that 26 percent of defendants received negative ratings on this item. In the September–October sample, only 11 percent of defendants were so rated. Thus it appears that negative ratings by the police regarding the flight risk posed by defendants had been restricted. Although the use of this item did not appear to be widespread among arresting officers as some had feared, examination of the kind of responses the police were giving

in the release questionnaire may raise some questions about just how this item should be used. For example, the police "facts" often took one or more of the following forms: the defendant was "transient"; "transient and very mobile"; "unemployed"; had "no work address"; had "no community ties"; had "only temporary work"; "nature of the charge"; "prior FTAs"; "prior criminal history"; "subject attempted to avoid arrest by fleeing."

Two problems are raised by this risk item. First, the form of police response had become increasingly factual, and the substance of the response had changed. Second, as the substance had changed, sometimes replicating the kinds of information pretrial services would use to assign risk categories to defendants, scoring problems resulted.

Consider, for example, the impact on a defendant's risk rating of a police "nature-of-the-charge" response. First, at a minimum, the defendant would be assigned the 67 points under the guidelines risk scheme because the police response was completed, what ever it said. (Note that accumulation of points increased the likelihood of a higher risk classification and, ultimately, a more restrictive release decision.) Then, if the charge was a property offense or involved robbery charges, additional points would be assigned by pretrial services on separate items. Furthermore, the severity dimension of the guidelines would also place the defendant in a more restrictive category because it was based wholly on the notion of the "nature of the charge." In other words, because of the police officer's notation, aspects of the defendant's charges would be given inordinate weight.

A more extreme example was seen when the police officer noted that his or her "fact" for believing the defendant might flee was the defendant's prior record of FTAs. The defendant received the 67 risk classification points because of this police "facts" response, received at least an additional 8 risk points under the "Police facts and prior FTA" risk item, and received at least 36 additional points under the item "Prior FTAs." One way to avoid the inherent problems of double or triple counting was to exclude the "police facts" item when the police were merely replicating facts that pretrial services would be recording elsewhere, such as under prior FTAs.

9. We can discuss only cells within which a sufficient number of defendants were found for analysis.
10. Note that all commissioners were not necessarily represented by the same numbers and kinds of cases. For example, data for Commissioners 2 and 6 did not produce sufficient numbers of cases during the September–October sample period to be included in part of the analysis.
11. The guidelines system provided even more specific feedback concerning pretrial release decisions by examining decisions within guidelines cells. For example, earlier (in Figure A.2), we noted that the three most influential "cells" of defendants among our 1987 decisions were Cells 9, 7, and 15.

Among the Cell 9 defendants (making up roughly one-fifth of the 1987 defendants), the use of nonfinancial release went up 24 percentage points (from 56 percent to 80 percent) in the January–February 1987 sample. By September–October, however, the use of OR in that category had begun dropping back (down to 74 percent of defendants).

Among Cell 7 defendants, nonfinancial release went down slightly among January–February defendants (4 percentage points) and went back up to the 1984 rate in the fall of 1987 (the difference was not statistically significant). Among Cell 15 defendants, in the January–February sample OR increased 8 percentage points over the level in the 1984 sample and 13 percentage points in the September–October sample (the difference was not statistically significant).

For purposes of brevity, we do not review the changes occurring in each of the defendant categories but hope to illustrate how the cell-specific analysis could identify areas needing attention. For example, one might argue particularly that OR release should not be allowed to decrease even slightly from previous (preguidelines) levels among Cell 7 defendants (who accounted for 10 percent of the defendant population) given their low-risk, low-severity attributes. Examination of the rates of agreement with guidelines suggestions within this category might point to a need for stressing action in this area.

12. A follow-up study of defendants in the September–October sample was not conducted.
13. The greatest increases in the effectiveness of release occurred in Cells 8 (16 percent), 9 (15 percent), 10 (13 percent), and 15 (10 percent). Decreased effectiveness was found in Cells 11 (12 percent) and 7 (6 percent).

16

The Implementation of Pretrial Release Guidelines ("Uniform Bond Standards") in Dade County

Two years of research in the Dade County criminal courts revealed a very challenging situation: The criminal caseload was large and growing and was characterized by more serious criminal charges than the other courts participating in the research, and the jail facilities were critically overburdened. The bail process was very traditional in the sense that a bond schedule dominated the release prospects of defendants, both at the booking and at the bond-hearing stage, and bondsmen were routinely involved in the process. A single county court judge usually presided over bond hearing during the twice-daily sessions on weekdays, while on weekends circuit court judges would sit on a rotating basis, not more than one or two weekends a year. Thus, for most of the week, felony bond hearings were handled by a county court judge who reported to the presiding judge of that court.

Yet it was clear to us from the beginning of the project that, as concerned as it was with the public safety, the leadership of the circuit court was greatly preoccupied with the seriously overcrowded condition of the Dade County jail facilities. Just prior to the project's start, the court had replaced the director of the pretrial services program that operated from within the county corrections department. The search was given high priority because of the jurisdiction's need to strengthen and upgrade the then fledgling pretrial-services agency to play a greater role in addressing the crowding crises. It was against this background of unrelenting jail crowding that the chief judge agreed to participate in the guidelines research and asked the administrative judge for the criminal division to supervise the project, hoping, though perhaps not expecting, that some new ameliorative strategies might result.

Those two years of descriptive research had revealed some interesting results. Despite the challenging caseload of the felony court and the dominance of the bond schedule in pretrial release determinations, the reorganizing pretrial-services program managed to facilitate the release of a large share of felony defendants with no worse than "average" misconduct rates (i.e., rates of rearrests and FTAs). (Given the composition of the criminal caseload, in fact, in comparison with the other sites, overall release practices were somewhat more "effective.") However, our findings suggested that several factors, such as the central role given the bond schedule and the reliance on one or two judges to decide bond, combined to minimize the prospects of releasing more and different categories of defendants. Despite the efforts of a variety of officials in the jurisdiction, a critical state of overcrowding had been reached; nonetheless, the guidelines analyses and discussions within the judicial working group suggested that a guidelines system—and all the changes that would imply—could make an important difference in Dade County.

In fact, in our estimate of the theoretical maximum impact that the final version of guidelines was likely to have if successfully implemented in circuit court, we projected that rather dramatic changes could be facilitated through guidelines: Nonfinancial release could be increased as much as 12 percent among incoming felony defendants (much of this by focusing use of special or restrictive conditions of release on medium-risk defendants ordinarily detained); the average financial bond could be cut in half and the resulting detention (for more than 48 hours) could be reduced approximately 18 to 25 percentage points; and the average jail days per entering defendant could be more than cut in half.[1]

Key Roles of Pretrial Services and the Judges

In practice the impact that decision guidelines could have in Dade County would fall short of the theoretical maximum to the extent that the guidelines (dubbed "Uniform Bond Standards" by the chief judge) were implemented. As explained in Chapter 13, one of the limitations of the analyses of the likely impact of the bond-hearing guidelines was that they overstated their likely effect because for purposes of calculating estimates they had to assume that judges would comply with the guidelines 100 percent of the time. In reality a guidelines system aims for a lower level of compliance, say, around 75 percent.[2]

For the guidelines to be successful in obtaining the desired 75 percent compliance rate initially achieved in the Philadelphia experiment and quite nearly reached in the Maricopa County Superior Court program, two seemingly small innovations in procedure would have to be accomplished during the implementation. First, pretrial services would have to reorganize the collection of background information and alter its method of presenting the information and "recommendation" (now to be guidelines "suggestion") to the judge in court at the bond hearing. Second, the judges would have to cooperate in operationalizing the new arrangements at bond hearing and to consider the information and suggestions offered by the guidelines.

In a general sense, the substance of the pretrial services role would not change under the guidelines program. The pretrial services staff would continue to collect and to prepare information relating to defendants, their backgrounds, and their cases that would enable the judge at bond hearing to make an informed pretrial-release decision. The focus of the information collection and the form of its summary would change as pretrial services would classify defendants under the guidelines by following specific policy-defined procedures for weighting the information and preparing recommendations for conditional release.

Rather than using the results of a wide-ranging defendant interview as the basis of a subjective in-court recommendation to the bond-hearing judge as was normally done, the guidelines would require pretrial services staff to interview each defendant and immediately complete the information required to rank the defendant on the severity and then the risk dimension. In Chapter 13, we reviewed the bond schedule derivation of the charge-severity ranking. The advantage of relying on the severity ranking of charges inherent in the Dade bond schedule was that it was a ready-made charge-severity scoring system under the supervision of the court and was available at the booking stage. The pretrial services staff merely needed to determine what the total "bond schedule bond" was to place the defendant's charges in one of eight severity categories.[3]

The adoption of the risk classification of the guidelines was more involved, however. It clearly represented conflict between the former, subjective ways of evaluating defendant background information and the newer, guidelines scoring checklist that was objective and empirically derived. The new system meant that staff would need to set aside their intuition concerning certain kinds of information to score the defendant on each item correctly, and then to add the defendant's scores to arrive at one total score placing the defendant in one of four risk groups, just as the Maricopa pretrial services staff had learned to do earlier.

During the training sessions conducted with the Dade pretrial services staff, it was clear that some workers felt that something vital and important, the role of their own personal judgment, was being eliminated by these procedures. A great deal of discussion centered on the value, goals, and limitations of the empirical risk classification. In part, the new guidelines procedures were telling the pretrial services staff that it was not appropriate for them to be acting as "judges" in formulating subjective impressions as to the releasability of defendants, that their responsibility was instead to marshal and present factual information in a manner designed to assist the bond-hearing judge in making his or her judgment. A common fear shared by some of the pretrial services staff in the process of learning the new procedures was that the guidelines would be too restrictive, that they would not allow release of defendants typically already being released as a result of pretrial services recommendations, subjective as they may have been.

That is not to say that the pretrial services role under the guidelines did not call for judgment at all. The classification of defendants according to the charge severity and risk dimensions that served as the basis of the guidelines was accompanied by pretrial staff determinations of "unusual circumstances" that the bond-hearing judge ought to be aware of in considering the appropriateness of the guidelines suggestion. In training sessions, every effort was made to make clear the difference between "unusual circumstances" and other, general background information that pretrial services staff were used to noting, such as employment and ties to the community.

The working definition of *unusual* was information so important as to be "mind changingly important" to the judge or so essential that, without it, the judge would make an inappropriate decision. Examples of "unusual" aspects of the defendant or of his or her case discussed during the pretrial services preparation included having an obvious history of drug addiction, of domestic violence, or of escape from custody. So that the concept could be made as clear as possible, the director of pretrial services developed a list of the kinds of information that would qualify as "unusual."

Transforming the Role of Pretrial Services Staff in Court

Although these requirements challenged the pretrial services staff to relinquish "old habits" and institute new guidelines procedures, perhaps the most significant change in pretrial services practices created by the implementation of pretrial release guidelines lay in the presentation of the guidelines information and decision suggestions in court. No longer would pretrial services staff make a subjective formulation—an oral argument—as to the defendant's releasability at the bond hearing. Rather, the agency representative would present the guidelines classification indicating the suggested decision for the relevant category of defendants and any unusual circumstances or special release recommendations to the judge presiding. The oral presentation would clarify information or explain the special conditions that could be proposed. Theoretically, the judge would review the guidelines form (see Figure 12.5), make a decision to follow the guidelines suggestion or not, and note a reason in cases in which guidelines were not followed.

To understand just how much this represented a departure from normal practice and, thus, more of a "major" innovation than a "minor" change, it may be useful to review how bond hearings usually transpired in circuit court prior to the guidelines. Rather than presenting the judge with a written summary of the information and the recommendation for pretrial release, as might occur in other jurisdictions, the Dade County pretrial services staff would speak in court mainly to respond to the bond-hearing judge when he would ask whether "pretrial services will take him." (The nature of the interaction in court varied depending on the judge presiding. Some judges would take more time to inquire of pretrial services concerning particular facts related to the defendant's background or prospects for support during release.) Pretrial services staff soon became familiar with the prejudices and preferences of the judges with whom they worked most often. Some, for example, particularly abhorred drunken-driver-related charges; others reacted strongly to drug-related charges or other charges that might attract special notice of the news media.

Over time, this kind of interaction served to put pretrial services staff "in their place." The bond hearing, often dominated by what had been specified by the booking-stage bond schedule, resembled a competition in which the pretrial services representative was thrust into the position of being an advocate for pretrial release against a presumption in favor of the dictates of the bond schedule. Given the pressures of the jail crisis toward avoiding all unnecessary pretrial detention (pretrial services is a division of the corrections department), the end result would often be that the pretrial services staff might agree to "take" defendants they would not have recommended, and they might not have had assigned to them by the judge many defendants considered appropriate risks for some form of nonfinancial pretrial release.

In short, the presumption appeared to be (and this is supported by the empirical research) that pretrial services had the job of convincing the judge why he or she should not go along with the amount suggested by the bond schedule. When pretrial services did persuade the judge to assign a defendant to the agency's care, the implications were clear: Pretrial services (i.e., corrections), not the court, accepted the risks and responsibilities for that defendant's pretrial release and any blame that might come from the defendant's misbehavior during pretrial release.

To emphasize the provisional nature of the arrangement (the assignment of a defendant to pretrial services for nonfinancial release or supervision), the judge routinely set "alternate bond." Alternate bond—again usually exactly the amount of bond designated by the booking-stage bond schedule—seemed to be the court's way of saying that, had the court not given pretrial services the benefit of the doubt in a particular case, the defendant would have had the specified amount of bond assigned. Alternate bond, similar to "unsecured bond" in other jurisdictions, had the effect of serving as the "backup" bond decision for defendants taken back into custody, but it also had the odd effect of permitting defendants preferring not to be supervised by pretrial services to bond out via a bondsman or, sometimes, their own pocketbooks.

Taken most seriously, implementation of the guidelines system would result in a shift in focus (and in burden) from the pretrial services agency back to the judge as the pretrial-release decisionmaker. Looked at one way, the guidelines were designed to improve on the unidimensional thrust of the bond schedule by adding and compactly organizing key information for the judge's bond-hearing decision that went beyond just the criminal charges. The idea was that pretrial services would collect and prepare relevant information that would classify defendants according to the guidelines and that the presumption would be that judges would want to follow the court's judicial guidelines rather than the court's booking-stage bond schedule, which had originally been designed as a crude release mechanism for booking-stage release—except when information gathered by pretrial services demonstrated that other approaches should perhaps be taken.

In short, not only would the former pretrial services' recommending function be made objective, but the recommendation function would be eliminated. The pretrial services' job at the bond-hearing stage would involve factual classification of defendants according to the guidelines and summary of pertinent information for the judge that might assist the judge in deciding whether or not to go along with the guidelines suggestion.

The Role of the Judges under the Circuit Court Guidelines System: Responsibility and Accountability

The principal aim of the circuit court's Uniform Bond Standards was to provide a practical resource that would assist individual judges presiding over bond hearing in making bond and pretrial-release decisions, while also serving as a vehicle for the court as a whole to manage and review bail policy. Two years of collaborative research supervised by the court's working committee demonstrated empirically that, despite the court's efforts in meeting the demands of an increasing and serious felony caseload and of extreme jail crowding, there was room for improvement at the initial pretrial-release (bond-hearing) stage. Although the court could congratulate itself for performing better than might be expected under the circumstances—better in some respects than other comparable jurisdictions—the presiding judge determined that it was worth exploring whether bond-hearing practices could be improved further by means of the voluntary guidelines decision resource.

Ideally, introduction of the Uniform Bond Standards would create little change in the normal routine of the judge presiding at bond hearing but would bring to bear a fully developed informational resource. The guidelines would be prepared by pretrial services staff, would indicate the relative risk posed by the defendant of risk of flight or crime during pretrial release, and would point to a suggested decision that would "in most cases" serve the multiple goals of the bond-hearing decision: minimizing risk to public safety and court processing of criminal cases, making decisions more equitable, and avoiding unnecessary pretrial detention (as mandated in Florida's bail law). The judge would consider the information (including the severity of the charges and the relative risk posed by the defendant) and the guidelines suggestion and make the decision. The difference would be that judges would note briefly the reasons for taking exception to the guidelines.

Depending on one's perspective, one could argue that the Uniform Bond Standards would basically replace the bond schedule as the "rule-of-thumb" yardstick for bond-hearing decisions. If the Uniform Bond Standards were looked at this way, the most noticeable change would be in asking the judge to review (at a glance) the summary paperwork and to note reasons in cases in which the guidelines were not followed. This proposed guidelines routine in reality called for two innovations in the judge's role: first, reviewing the information describing a defendant (at least understanding the implications of the severity and risk classifications) hitherto left totally to the pretrial services staff, and second, deciding on the appropriateness of decisions suggested by the guidelines as well as providing reasons for exceptional decisions.

Prior to the implementation of the guidelines, the bond judges had shown little interest in knowing the reasons for pretrial services' recommendations (preferring only to know whether pretrial services would accept a defendant). They showed little interest in reviewing descriptive information relating to the defendant's background, no matter how briefly summarized. They had never been asked to provide reasons for decisions they made.

Just as the ultimate contribution of the guidelines could be measured only if the daily bond-hearing judges cooperated in the effort to implement the new program, the overall success of the innovation would be determined chiefly by the role played by the judicial working committee, which supervised the development of the guidelines, and by the leadership of the court in their implementation. The working committee supervised by the administrative justice for the criminal division of the court certainly left its mark on the guidelines, in directing the empirical investigation of bail-decisionmaking practices and their effects on the system and in shaping the decision guidelines ultimately for use by the judges.

Unfortunately, just as the project reached the implementation stage, the strong committee dissolved. Its supervising judge was appointed to a higher Florida court by the governor, and one of the most active judges, the one most versed in the issues and practicalities of reform in the area of bail in the United States, decided to step down from the bench. Suddenly, the guidelines effort was without its principal sources of support and leadership. The working committee was to have been an important springboard for introducing the new approach to the judges in the two Dade courts who would be deciding bond in the near future. It was left to the presiding judge to set the guidelines in motion. He appointed a new head of the criminal division who was not familiar with the guidelines research or the needs it sought to address. Unfortunately, before the new criminal chief could learn about the project and guide its implementation, he died.

The chief judge then decided to expedite plans for implementation by emphasizing the role of the pretrial services agency. The agency was required to implement the new system and to educate and engage new bond-hearing judges as the court schedule dictated. The chief judge assisted the pretrial services director in making judges aware of the new program, but the introduction of the guidelines inevitably lacked the systematic introduction that was originally planned. This turned out to be important for the entire guidelines experience in Dade, at least through the evaluation period, and explains in part why decision guidelines did not serve as the decisionmaking resource they were designed to be.

Implementation of the Guidelines, June–July 1987

Once the general version of decision guidelines had been decided upon by the working committee, the research staff worked closely with the director of pretrial services to produce a refined set of guidelines ready for implementation. This involved working with pretrial services to develop procedures and to conduct training so that the agency could be primed for its new responsibilities. The chief judge asked the research staff and pretrial services director to introduce the guidelines at a meeting of the Criminal Justice Coordinating Council for Dade County. At the meeting, the concepts and procedures were explained to heads of the relevant justice agencies (such as the state attorney's office, the public defender's office, and the police and probation departments). Individual visits were made to the state attorney's staff and the public defender's staff to review the program and to answer questions. The research staff and pretrial services director prepared explanatory materials for and met with the weekday bond-hearing judge who would be the first to employ the guidelines to review the guidelines goals and procedures.

The guidelines were first used in mid-June 1987 at the bond hearing. Initially, the pretrial services staff complained that completing the guidelines took more time than the former procedures and caused backups in presenting defendants at bond hearing. As these problems were being addressed, it was clear that other challenges had to be faced. Despite the implementation of guidelines, the bond schedule continued to be announced formally at the beginning of each defendant's appearance, clearly influencing the judge's considerations at the hearings. Furthermore, the bond-hearing judge, though well briefed on the operation of guidelines, instructed the pretrial services staff not to show him any of the guidelines information. He continued his practice of asking pretrial services if they would "take" or "wanted" the defendant, and they responded that the court's Uniform Bond Standards *suggested* a certain decision option or range of options. When he responded, "I am asking if you will take this defendant or not," the pretrial services staff would either say, "yes," (reverting to the preguidelines custom) or would steadfastly repeat the guidelines suggestions, risking the judge's ire. Next, when the judge made a decision that departed from the guidelines (which he had scarcely considered), the judge would not agree to give a reason for the departure and certainly would not note one in writing. (The more courageous of the pretrial services staff asked the judge to give the reasons orally and then noted the information on the form.)

The lack of judicial working committee was clearly a major impediment to the successful implementation of the guidelines. Without a committee to educate, engage, and prompt their own colleagues, the "minor" changes in procedure initially practiced by the newly trained pretrial services staff appeared more like major reform. Accordingly, early efforts were made to obtain feedback from the pretrial services staff, to offer additional training and problem-solving sessions, and to work vigorously with the court to acclimate the judges to the new routine.

The Evaluation Design in Dade County

To conduct a pre-post analysis, we compared results for the sample of over 2,000 felony defendants entering between April and October 1984 and a sample of 2,995 felony defendants entering Dade County Circuit Court during June and July 1987 (the first two, "shakedown" months of guidelines use).[4] All cases involving defendants securing release within 90 days (or a shorter period if adjudication of the charges had occurred) were followed for a period of 90 days to determine whether any failures to appear in court (FTAs) or rearrests for crimes occurring during pretrial release were recorded. In addition, we collected data for a smaller sample of 366 defendants entering the criminal process several months later, between November 9 and November 13, 1988, to permit a more limited view of decisions under a guidelines system which ought to have become more routine.

The Limits of the Evaluation: Comparability of the Samples

An important caveat must necessarily precede a discussion of the results. Although defendants in each sample were likely to be reasonably comparable, it is important that sample differences be identified and assessed. The data indicate general similarity, with a few notable exceptions. For example, cases in the 1987 samples involved more serious charges. Also, the risk characteristics of the three samples differed slightly.[5] Even such minor differences prompt caution in the assessment of overall comparisons reported. Differences may be due in part to sample variations rather than actual differences in decision practices or their outcomes. However, the guidelines context provides an important control for intersample variation, and we have more confidence in comparisons made between similar subcategories of defendants, where key (risk and severity "zone" or "cell") characteristics of cases are controlled for.

Our review of the overall use of decision guidelines will be complemented by examination of the decisions assigned to defendants within specific "zones" and "cells" of the guidelines (at least, where sufficient numbers of cases permit such comparisons). In general, the only notable difference among the samples seems to be that greater proportions of defendants in the 1984 sample were classified within the "OR/Standard

Conditions'' zone of guidelines (i.e., were lower-risk, less seriously charged defendants) than 1987 defendants.[6]

The Preparation of Guidelines and Classification of Defendants by Pretrial Services

The first and most important guidelines task performed by pretrial services involved the classification of defendants along the severity and risk dimensions of the guidelines, so that the appropriate presumptive guidelines decision could be indicated for the judge. Each of these dimensions involved new procedures, although the risk scoring was likely to involve more mistakes in the early going.

The guidelines system sought to classify all defendants entering the court process at the bond-hearing stage within the guidelines. Given the large volume of cases in the Dade courts and the extra time the new procedures initially required of the pretrial services staff, this idea was not initially reached. The strain of the high volume of cases waiting to be interviewed before bond hearing, as well as the limited number of pretrial services staff available, caused supervisors to occasionally suspend full guidelines ''workups'' on defendants. For example, sting operations by police brought in a large number of defendants at once, and pretrial services were frequently required to release a large number of defendants in a short time to bring the population level down to court-imposed capacity limits. At such times, guidelines might not be completed, and we found that guidelines materials had not been attempted in about 29 percent of the cases in both 1987 samples.

In addition to these crisis situations, there were other periods when guidelines appeared not to be completed. Guidelines forms were begun but left incomplete (lacking full risk and charge-related information) in 10 percent of the June–July 1987 sample and 37 percent of the one-week November sample.

Comparisons of complete and incomplete guidelines cases revealed several themes governing the preparation of pretrial services guidelines. These themes indicate court policies limiting the applicability of guidelines (or of eligibility for release generally) that were clarified as the guidelines were being implemented. Because they were potentially non-bondable, defendants entering the process on new charges in addition to prior pretrial release for open felony charges were often not classified within the guidelines framework nor were defendants in jail having new felony charges lodged. Similarly, guidelines information was often not prepared for defendants who were discovered to be on probation or parole at the time of their recent arrest because of the court's policy of denying bond to these individuals until the former sentencing judge could review the case. Defendants who had been previously supervised by pretrial services and who had been rearrested usually did not have the guidelines information prepared, for the simple reason that pretrial services representatives would be requesting the judge to rescind pretrial release for noncompliance at bond hearing because of the new arrest.

In addition to these situations, guidelines were not completed in cases in which the bond schedule amount was exceedingly high, because the pretrial services staff saw little potential that judges would consider guidelines options in very seriously charged cases. In addition, heavy caseloads on weekends sometimes resulted in expedited release procedures by the judge, who would grant nonfinancial release to numbers of defendants in court prior to completion of the usual paperwork by pretrial services.

The fact that guidelines were not prepared at all for some defendants was a predictable outcome of an evaluation conducted in the early stages of program implementation. However, it is clear that the numbers of incomplete cases can be explained by established court policies that impact categories of generally nonbondable cases that ordinarily would not have been included in our analysis of the effect of guidelines on decisions in the cases of bondable felony defendants. The initial idealistic aim of the leadership of pretrial services was to make use of the guidelines framework to foster the release of defendants not ordinarily released at the bond-hearing stage. The no-release policy for defendants on active probation or parole status had been targeted by the staff, as was the bond-hearing judges' informal policy of not considering nonfinancial release (or anything but a very high bond) in drug-trafficking cases. However, in attempting to build acceptance of the guidelines approach among the bond-hearing judges, the director of the pretrial services program tempered the broad-based strategy—in a sense, giving up on these more difficult categories of releases—to focus on kinds of defendants that might be more acceptable, at least to begin with. The early results show that, in addition to their general resistance to the innovation, judges did not adjust their positions regarding these kinds of more difficult cases, causing pretrial services to drop plans to prepare guidelines on "all" defendants and contributing to a general growing feeling that guidelines preparation was probably not going to be a worthwhile activity. This also reflects the disappointment experienced by pretrial services staff when county court judges essentially opted to ignore the guidelines innovation.

This phenomenon was partly a consequence of the lack of judicial support for the implementation of the guidelines system, and it had a major limiting effect on the ability to analyze the impact of guidelines. If the pretrial release "guidelines" were not successfully implemented, they could not possibly have an impact. The following description of the pretrial release guidelines experiment in Dade County is inevitably constrained by the fact that implementation was, at best, partial.

The Ranking of Defendants' Charges According to Severity

The total bond-schedule bond noted in each defendant's case enabled pretrial services to locate each defendant within one of the eight severity categories shown in Figure 12.2. This bond schedule information permitted us to validate the severity level indicated by pretrial services, and the results suggested that selection of the correct severity classification was not as straightforward as initially supposed.

In roughly 15 percent of the June–July cases and 19 percent of the November cases for which pretrial services classifications were found, pretrial services had not correctly ranked the severity of defendants' charges. More than one-third (37 percent) of the errors in the June–July sample and one-half (48 percent) in the November sample resulted in placing the defendant at a lower severity level. Two-thirds of the misclassified June–July and nearly one-half of the misclassified November defendants had their charges ranked too seriously. Obviously, mistakes in the ranking of defendants' charges meant that the final guidelines designation was likely to be inappropriate and might have translated into unfair treatment of defendants in the event judges consider the guidelines.

The Classification of Defendants According to Risk of Misconduct

The calculation of the defendant risk group required the pretrial services staff to score defendants on a series of nine risk items. The individual scores were added to yield a total score, which was used to locate defendants in one of the four risk groups. In "degree of difficulty," the classification of risk offered greater potential for error than the ranking of criminal charges. Our experience in reviewing the initial preparation of guidelines in Philadelphia and in Maricopa County had shown us that a certain margin of error initially is to be expected in this area.

We were able to observe three kinds of errors in the risk classification of Dade felony defendants. A first kind of error was produced when pretrial services staff did not correctly score the presence or absence of an attribute. For example, when robbery charges were present, the defendant was scored as if they were not. Second, the staff member may have correctly noted the presence of the attribute (yes, there were robbery charges), but may have assigned an incorrect or invalid score. For example, the only valid risk codes for "robbery charge" are "0" (no robbery charges present) or "2" (robbery charges present), but in a number of cases a "1" or other number was recorded. The third kind of error involved the incorrect addition of scores, which resulted, in some cases, in the selection of an incorrect risk-group classification for the defendant.

With the exception of "living arrangements," each of the individual risk items could be directly checked for accuracy against a comparable variable. One or more items were wrongly scored (shown as not involving robbery when robbery was involved, for example) in a total of 71 percent of the classified cases. One or more items were assigned invalid scores (scores that did not exist) in 10 percent of the classified cases. Overall, we found errors associated with at least one individual risk item in 75 percent of the cases for which the risk classification had been completed.[7]

Overall, only 50 percent of the June–July felony defendants and only 48 percent of the November defendants whose guidelines risk classification contained errors were assigned to the correct risk category. Furthermore, the classifications of risk were not evenly divided; the majority resulted in rating defendants in higher risk categories than they should have been: Of incorrectly assigned defendants in the June–July sample, 59 percent were placed in a more serious risk category. Among those incorrectly classified in the November sample, 73 percent were placed mistakenly in a higher risk category. At no other site was such a strikingly high error rate observed.

The errors in ranking the severity of defendants' charges and in scoring them on the various risk attributes inevitably translate into overall misclassification of defendants within the guidelines. Among June–July 1987 defendants, only 44 percent were correctly classified by pretrial services into the appropriate guidelines cells. When the broader decision zone designation ("OR/Standard," "OR/Special," "OR/Special to Low Bond," and "bond") are used, the overall agreement rate was 64 percent. The classification of defendants in the November sample showed an even lower rate of correct placement within the guidelines: Only 40 percent of defendants were placed in the correct guidelines cells and 61 percent in the correct decision zones. Unfortunately, the misclassification of defendants by pretrial services according to severity of criminal charges and risk of flight or rearrest was more often in the direction of a more restrictive guidelines-decision category. In a system in which judges relied heavily on the guidelines to inform their bail choices, this magnitude of misclassification may have translated into a sizable number of inappropriate decisions. Obviously, such a level of misclassification limits *a priori* the ability of the guidelines to affect the problems they were designed to address.

In addition to placing the defendant within the appropriate guidelines subcategory based on the severity and risk rankings, the pretrial services task also included pointing out to the judge special circumstances about a defendant or his or her case that might shed extra light on the appropriateness of the decision choices suggested by the guidelines. The aim of this feature of the Uniform Bond Standards was to call attention to critically important, unusual features of a case. It was not to be an opportunity for pretrial services to add other biographical data of general interest. Properly employed, this feature would be found in a small number of cases (for example, to be "unusual," these circumstances ought to appear in a minority of cases).

During June and July, among the defendants having guidelines information prepared, pretrial services staff noted "unusual circumstances" over one third of the time (34 percent). During the November sampling period, a smaller proportion of cases had unusual circumstances recorded: one-sixth (16 percent). Interestingly, these findings come very close to the findings in Maricopa County regarding the notation of unusual circumstances. By definition, especially at the very beginning of the guidelines implementation period, it appears that the "unusual" notation was somewhat too "usual," given its intended use.

Among the most common reasons noted by the staff under the heading of "unusual circumstances" were that the defendant was on probation or parole at the time of arrest, the defendant was on release on felony bond (a potentially nonbondable situation), the defendant was on pretrial release in other matters, the current charge was an added charge (meaning the defendant was in jail already for failing to post bond in an earlier felony matter), the defendant had no immediate ties to the area, the defendant was a "high-bond" defendant (meaning the bond was likely to be so high that guidelines were not realistic), and the defendant refused the interview. Other reasons of questionable appropriateness included "drug charge," "bench warrant," "uses drugs," "alcohol problem," "not arrested before," and "scored outside guidelines."

A final task in the preparation of the Uniform Bond Standards classification for the bond-hearing judge was to complete the section of the guidelines designating special conditions of release recommended by pretrial services in relevant cases. Special conditions were to be provided for defendants falling within Zones 2 ("OR/Special") or 3 ("OR/Special to Low Bond") of the guidelines. The purpose was to provide the bond-hearing judge with an option permitting the release of medium-risk–medium-severity defendants while minimizing the risks of flight or crime. Such special conditions might include supervision by pretrial services, drug or alcohol treatment, and domestic violence treatment.

By design, special conditions were not intended to be dispersed throughout the guidelines categories at the discretion of the pretrial services staff. They were to be targeted in the "special-conditions" categories of the guidelines.

As we have noted earlier, the corrected classification of defendants would have placed approximately one-third of the June–July defendants and of the November defendants in Zone 2, which included cells suggesting "OR/Special Conditions," and located roughly 15 percent of each sample in Zone 3, which suggested either "OR/Special Conditions" or some low bond amount. In the cases actually classified by pretrial services (the only ones we could study in this regard), the picture was not very different, except that the November sample placed more defendants in Zone 3 (16 percent) and fewer defendants in Zone 2 (25 percent).

In all, special conditions were suggested for 49 percent of the June–July sample and 71 percent of the November sample; both rates are higher than a policy of restricted and targeted use of special conditions of release would suggest. Moreover, special conditions were specified for kinds of cases not associated with use of special conditions: In the June–July sample, 40 percent of special conditions were attached to cases classified within Zones 1 and 4 of the guidelines, zones which did not require any special conditions. In the November sample, 54 percent of special conditions were assigned in those inappropriate zones.

Conclusions: Problem Areas in Preparation of the Guidelines by Pretrial Services

Although an immediate evaluation of the guidelines innovation in Dade County may not provide the best opportunity to view the program, it nevertheless offered the advantage of uncovering some of the problems areas that would require attention during an initial implementation phase. In a large urban court system, the first problem is trying to reach the full target population entering the judicial process in the short period before the initial appearance or bond hearing. In Dade County, the continuing jail-overcrowding crisis periodically produced the need for expedited release procedures, often not allowing time for defendant interviews or guidelines classification. Ironically, had the guidelines been fully and effectively implemented, the need for emergency release procedures could have been greatly diminished.

Another difficulty reflected in these early data concerns the mastery of the guidelines classification processes by pretrial services, not only in the severity rankings of the criminal charges, but in the scoring of defendant risk groupings. While error-free implementation of the guidelines classification was not expected, the amount of error and the resulting misclassification of defendants within the guidelines ensured ineffective implementation of the system. The overutilization of special conditions of release and the notation of unusual circumstances were also issues of major concern. Inevitably, these problems seriously limited the ability of the guidelines system to deliver on its promise to address the problems of public safety, jail crowding, and equity that were of such great concern to the court system in the design phase.

Judicial Use of the Guidelines

Because decision guidelines are intended ultimately as a resource for judicial policy and decisionmaking in pretrial release determinations, a key aspect of evaluation of the guidelines must be their use by the circuit and county court judges. However, it is not possible to gauge the impact of the judicial guidelines on areas of concern if guidelines were simply not utilized by the judges.

Given the limited and imprecise preparation of the guidelines by pretrial services staff, any analysis of judicial utilization is constrained in two ways. First, we can analyze the effects of the guidelines approach only in cases that were prepared by pretrial services for the judges. Second, when guidelines materials were prepared for the judges, many defendants were incorrectly classified.

It is difficult to guess whether the initial classification errors by the pretrial services staff had any effect on the judges' use of the guidelines. For example, we do not know whether defendants may have seemed too often placed in less or more restrictive decision categories than seemed appropriate to the judges, thus adding to their impression that guidelines suggestions seemed inappropriate or "off base." For the purposes of analysis, we can assume that the misclassifications by pretrial services were largely invisible to the judges, who were mainly reacting to the fact of a new procedure, not its details—at least at first.

The two most important questions in examining the impact of the guidelines on the judges' role in the pretrial release determinations focus on the rate of agreement with the guidelines represented by the judges' decisions and the differences in decisions that may have been produced as a result (see Figure 16.1). Examination of the first question is framed in terms of the presumption that guidelines were designed to achieve a rate of agreement by judges in a sizable majority of cases. Examination of the second question requires a comparison of decisions made using the guidelines during 1987 with decisions made before guidelines went

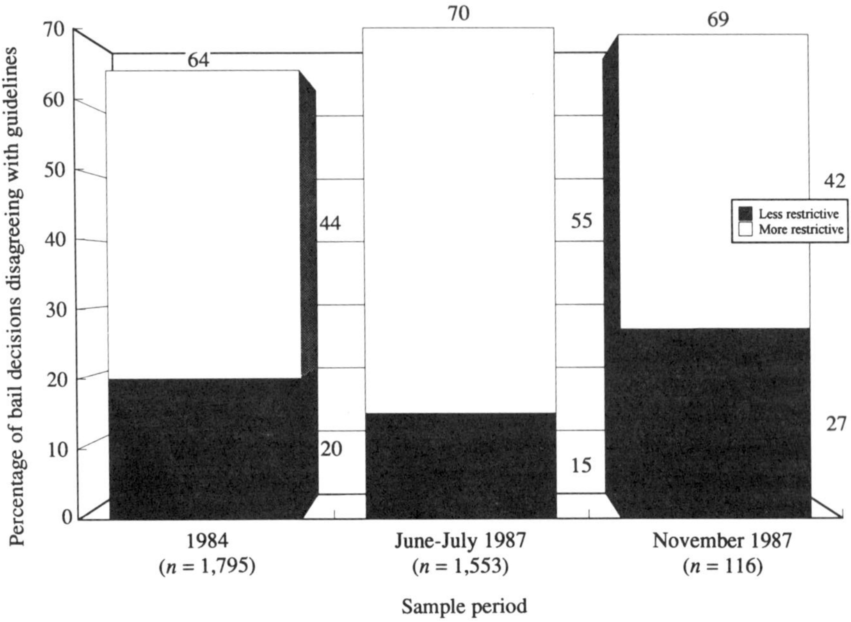

FIGURE 16.1. Disagreement between judicial decisions at bond hearing and the guidelines suggestions among felony defendants entering Dade County Circuit Court, by sample.

into effect (i.e., we would compare the guidelines-based decisions to the 1984 pretrial release decisions, as a base rate for assessing the extent of change in decisions).

The finding regarding the use of guidelines by the judges was dramatic. Instead of agreement in a "sizable majority" of bond-hearing decisions, a majority of decisions disagreed with the guidelines ranges. During June–July, agreement between judicial decisions and the guidelines was 30 percent; in November, judges agreed in only 31 percent of the cases. When comparing this rate of agreement with the extent to which 1984 bond decisions would have agreed had guidelines been in effect—36 percent of the time—we can conclude that overall judges did not change their decision practices to make use of the newly developed Uniform Bond Standards. In fact, their decisions gravitated further away from the policy directions implicit in the court's pretrial release guidelines. In short, this finding suggests that the Dade County judges seldom referred to the guidelines or that, if they did, they were largely uninfluenced by them.

Agreement with Guidelines by Judge

In trying to understand the court's initial experience with the guidelines, it is informative to consider the practices of individual judges who decided bond during the periods studied. Unfortunately, the evaluative component of the research was not specifically designed to investigate judge-by-judge variation in use of the guidelines. (The guidelines samples could not guarantee that equal kinds and numbers of cases representing each judge would be included because our focus was on the effect of court bond practices overall.) In fact, 45 different judges were involved in deciding bond during the two 1987 sample periods studied, many presided over just a handful of cases. In examining the degree to which individual judges agreed with the decisions suggested by the guidelines, we have restricted the analysis to 9 judges hearing a minimum of 30 cases during the 1987 guidelines sample periods.

Our study revealed that not one judge even approached the hoped-for agreement rate of a "sizeable majority" of decisions (about 75 percent). Indeed, the decisions of none of the judges agreed with the guidelines even 50 percent of the time. Of special note is the experience of the initial guidelines judge, who had been specially briefed about the guidelines program. As the summer schedule happened to dictate, he decided a disproportionate share of the June–July 1987 cases. In cases in which pretrial services had prepared the guidelines, he selected decisions agreeing with the guidelines less than one-third of the time[8] (87 percent of his "disagreements" were in the direction of more restrictive bond decisions).

Reasons for Departures from Guidelines

An important feature of the guidelines, designed to provide feedback to the court about their use, was the provision of reasons by judges when they made decisions which departed from the guidelines. Such reasons were seldom provided by the judges presiding over bond hearing in Dade County: During the June and July sample, reasons were noted only 48 percent of the time; reasons were provided for only 34 percent of the exceptions made to guidelines in the November sample. The notation of reasons for exceptional decisions varied considerably by the particular bond-hearing judge, from a low of 24 percent to a high of 72 percent.

Conclusion: The Judges' Failure to Use the Guidelines

The evidence presented above suggests strongly that the guidelines made little impression on the judges presiding at the bond hearings in

Dade County. Their very low rate of agreement and their failure to cooperate in the notation of reasons when making decisions departing from the guidelines create the impression that the guidelines program had failed to engage the judges in circuit court during the period of the research.

The Impact of Bond-Hearing Guidelines on Pretrial Release Decisions

Had the guidelines been successfully implemented, a number of other goals could have been achieved, relating to changes in the use of nonfinancial pretrial release, in detention, and in defendant misconduct during pretrial release. Given the judges' failure to make use of the guidelines during the initial period, however, one could expect little impact in these areas stemming from the guidelines themselves. Contrasting decisionmaking during the 1984 and 1987 sample periods is nevertheless useful in documenting trends in the use of pretrial release and its impact in Dade County and in showing, in a sense, what guidelines could have helped address.

Nonfinancial Release, 1984 and 1987

Our investigation of bond decisions in Dade County in 1984 showed that, when judges resorted to bond in making their decisions, a substantial majority of defendants were detained as a result. Thus the use of nonfinancial release (ROR) of any form under the guidelines—irrespective of whether routine or restrictive conditions were attached—would have had an important impact on the overall rate of release or detention.

Overall, judges' decisions during the two sample periods in 1987 revealed a substantially reduced use of nonfinancial pretrial release (ROR). In the period immediately following implementation of the guidelines, we found that nonfinancial release had dropped from 69 percent in the 1984 sample to 47 percent during the June–July 1987, and then returned to 1984 levels once again by the November sample (65 percent). The use of nonfinancial release dropped in each zone of the guidelines between 1984 and the June–July 1987 sample. Interestingly, as the overall rate of nonfinancial release began to move back up to the previous levels in the November 1987 sample, it moved to even higher than 1984 levels among Zones 2 and 3. However, the results are a far cry from the levels that would have been expected had guidelines been employed by the Dade County judges in the fashion originally intended.

The Use of Financial Bond, 1984 and 1987

As the assignment of ROR by bond-hearing judges dropped in the 1987 samples, the use of financial bond increased notably from 31 percent of defendants in the 1984 study to 53 percent in the June–July 1987 sample. The use of bond had nearly returned in the 1984 level in the November 1987 sample (35 percent). The overall cost of pretrial release as measured by the levels of bond set increased also, from a median of $0 in 1984 (nonfinancial release) to a median of $1,000 in 1987.

The Use of Pretrial Detention, 1984 and 1987

One of the primary concerns of the guidelines strategy in Dade was its potential impact on the use of pretrial detention. To reflect the immediate impact of bond-hearing decisions, we measured release and detention of defendants after a 48-hour period, although we also collected data looking at release occurring up to 90 days from booking. Use of pretrial detention among felony defendants entering circuit court appeared to increase quite dramatically during the June–July 1987 guidelines period, when contrasted to the 1984 levels. Overall, detention moved from 36 percent of the 1984 sample to 53 percent among guidelines-prepared cases during June–July 1987, then almost returned to the 1984 rate during the November period (39 percent).[9] Had we reported above that the guidelines were employed routinely by the Dade judges, we would infer that an effect of the guidelines had been to increase the use of pretrial detention. Because we found instead that the Dade judges did not rely on guidelines, we conclude that this increase in detention is explained instead by two factors: the differences in the composition of the 1984 and 1987 samples and an apparent trend toward more restrictive bond decisions among Dade judges during the study period.[10]

The Performance of Defendants during Pretrial Release: Comparing the Effectiveness of Practices, 1984–1987

Of FTA, Rearrest, Felony Rearrest, and "Failure" Rates

If the pretrial release guidelines designed for Dade County had been strictly based on a risk classification and did not include the severity dimension, we might have expected to find that the guidelines had had an impact on the rate of misconduct of defendants who gained pretrial release—had the guidelines been effectively implemented. At least, the guidelines would have identified categories with high rates of misconduct during pretrial release that could be targeted with special conditions of release. Since the severity dimension, which was not related to risk of flight or rearrest, was purposely incorporated into the guidelines to counterbalance the risk dimension, the use of guidelines did not offer a straightforward test of an ability to reduce defendant misconduct. When we add to this the fact that the guidelines were not influential in judges' decisions in Dade County, the strength of the risk classification in reducing misconduct rates cannot be said to have been tested at all.

We compared the failure-to-appear and rearrest rates for defendants released within two days of booking in the 1984 and the 1987 samples, respectively.[11] It appears that overall defendant misconduct rates—however measured—were higher in the 1987 samples.[12] Failure-to-appear rates increased from 12 to 17 percent between the two sample periods, while rearrests increased from 7 to 17 percent. When defendant performance was examined by guidelines zone, however, we found that FTA rates decreased among Zone 4 defendants, increased only slightly among Zone 2 and 3 defendants, and increased notably among Zone 1 defendants. Rearrest rates among released defendants increased within each zone.

Just as the comparison of overall failure rates has to be viewed with some caution (and therefore comparison of subcategories is more appropriate), there are limitations on the use of these kinds of misconduct rates in the first place. Because rates of defendant misconduct are so dependent on the proportions and kinds of defendants released during each sample period, their comparison has little value other than to document that increased rates of pretrial detention were compounded by higher misconduct rates during the period in which guidelines were intended to be implemented.

Comparison of the Effectiveness of Pretrial Release

An appropriate measure of the effectiveness of pretrial release decisionmaking takes into account the use of both pretrial detention and pretrial release. Given the legal presumption favoring release under the least restrictive alternatives in many jurisdictions and the concerns about jail crowding, court systems releasing as many defendants as possible while not increasing the threat to public safety or the risk of defendant flight are considered "effective." When 100 percent of a court's entering caseload is considered the frame of reference, "ineffectiveness" is generated in two ways: (1) by not releasing defendants and (2) by "mistakenly" releasing defendants who commit new crimes or who fail to appear in court. The effectiveness measure is therefore equivalent to the proportion of all defendants released and not engaging in misconduct.

From the perspective of FTAs, the effectiveness of pretrial release dropped from 55 percent of defendants in 1984 to only 40 percent of defendants during 1987. Roughly similar findings are found when rearrest and "failure" are the focus. Note that if the guidelines had been implemented in the proposed fashion, a cell-by-cell analysis of release and misconduct rates would be valuable in assisting the jurisdiction in further targeting categories of defendants with above-average misconduct rates. The major indicators of difficulties with bail, pretrial release, and detention worsened considerably in Dade County during the period when the guidelines were not effectively implemented.

The Initial Impact of the Guidelines: Summary

Incomplete Implementation: A Glass Half Full

The results of our comparison of 1984 and 1987 bond-hearing decisions and their consequences raise the question of whether it can be said that the guidelines developed for Dade County were indeed implemented. Certainly, the pretrial services staff invested considerable effort in the preparation and implementation of the guidelines program. However, as we have shown, their classification of defendants according to guidelines criteria resulted—at least, in the very earliest stages of implementation—in a very high rate of error, such a high rate of error that, had judges relied on the guidelines suggestions, inappropriate bond-hearing decisions would have resulted in a large number of cases. Had this been the only difficulty, however, it would have been viewed as correctable and partly attributable to the learning curve of the early implementation phase associated with any innovation. In fact, if we were limiting ourselves to the efforts of pretrial services, we could be confident in concluding that the first major steps toward implementation of guidelines had indeed taken place. The second difficulty, however, was more fundamental, considering the aim of the entire innovation was to provide a judicial policy and decisionmaking tool—in the fashion achieved earlier in Philadelphia and Maricopa County. The new policy was never effectively introduced to the judges in Dade County and, as a result, was not taken seriously or taken advantage of by them when they took their turns presiding at the bond hearings.

We believe that the difficulties identified in the attempted implementation of the Dade guidelines are important in learning about the requisites of implementation of such an approach and where and how pretrial release guidelines may work best. When placed in the context of the body of experience gained in Maricopa County, Boston, and Philadelphia, these admittedly limited evaluation results suggest the importance of centralized authority and modern, well-funded pretrial-services organizations under the direction of the court—or at least having a close working relationship with the court. For the most part, the guidelines were not implemented in line with the original intention to provide a judicial resource, although perhaps they were implemented enough to allow us to learn better what the effects of well-run guidelines could have been, if they had been fully implemented in Dade County.

Pretrial Services: Problem Areas Surfacing in the Early Stages of Implementation

The difficulties associated with pretrial services were largely explained by the challenge of very quickly training a large staff working on shifts around the clock to perform new procedures. In the first weeks of the guidelines program, the principal difficulties had to do with perfecting the preparation of the guidelines for the judges, particularly in accurately completing the criminal-charge and defendant-risk information. Given the large volume of cases entering the jail and the limited staff, it was difficult on normal days to process the full number of defendants entering the criminal process. The extra time initially required for the staff to learn and streamline new guidelines procedures was not always available. Consequently, the new procedures had to be dropped on the busiest of days so that defendants could be brought to court on time for the bond hearing. Within the context of a very busy urban court, the leadership of the program and its supervisory staff put in many extra hours to make the transition to the guidelines procedures as effective was practically possible.

During the research in Dade County, we observed the hard work and dedication of that agency in planning and carrying out the new program against the background of the continuing jail-crowding crisis. Nevertheless, the guidelines strategy was envisaged as a judicial resource—and it is on those terms that its potential for improving pretrial release decisionmaking must be gauged.

The Failure of the Guidelines to Engage the Judges

The findings describing the use of guidelines by the Dade judges are unmistakable: They were seldom relied on. Because the judges rarely employed the guidelines in the expected fashion, few of the hoped-for results—like those relating to greater use of nonfinancial release and reduced use of pretrial detention produced in Maricopa County Superior Court—were in evidence. Moreover, the poor reception by the judges of the pretrial services presentations of guidelines information may ultimately have served as a disincentive to pretrial services to implement the program forcefully.

Normally, the purpose of a first and very early review of the use of guidelines in a court is to provide direction for improving the initial implementation effort and suggestions for modification of the guidelines system. In fact, the description of the research findings in this book is intended to illustrate the use of the informational "feedback" function of the guidelines. Thus evaluation of the earliest stages of implementation supports and shapes the next stages of implementation, in an iterative fashion, fostering an evolutionary rather than a discrete approach to problem solving and improvement.

In this light, our primary difficulty was the guidelines' failure to engage the judges in the fashion intended, even for a trial period. Indeed, we are unable to move beyond this finding to address specific recommendations regarding particular categories of defendants showing very positive or very negative results. It follows that the most important task in improving the operation of the guidelines is to determine why judges did not participate in the guidelines program to the extent anticipated.

At this stage, several explanations might productively be considered. First, having lost our supervising group of key judges just prior to the implementation phase, we may have failed to work sufficiently with the court to "educate" the other judges about the goals and advantages of the bond-hearing guidelines. Although we are aware of the court's efforts in this area,[13] as well as the efforts of the pretrial services program and the research staff, judges may not have been made familiar with the program in a practical fashion.

Second, the Dade County judges may have understood quite well the implications of the guidelines and simply rejected them as undesirable on an individual basis. Certainly, because of frustrating experiences with sentencing guidelines, we were made aware at an early stage that many judges had a strong reaction against the notion of guidelines of any sort. Thus our attempts to explain the difference between the legislative variety of guidelines and the court-developed self-help version with which we worked may have fallen on deaf ears.

Finally, we may also have underestimated the power of tradition and inertia in the Dade County court. The bond schedule dominated decisionmaking in Dade in two principal ways. First, a large number of entering felony defendants (about 20 percent) gained release immediately after the booking stage by posting the bond designated by the bond schedule, often by making use of the services of bondsmen. Second, the bond schedule amount influenced the judges strongly at the bond-hearing stage, almost to the point where it was assumed that the bond schedule should be followed almost blindly at the bond hearing—unless pretrial services could offer a good argument for nonfinancial release and would accept responsibility for the defendant during pretrial release.

Thus, during the initial use of the guidelines, because of the court's decision to place the responsibility for the innovation with pretrial services, judges may have seen the guidelines strictly as something that pretrial services employed for its own internal defendant-classification purposes, rather than as a new, modernized version of the bond schedule based on more comprehensive information. Instead of a new presumption that the Uniform Bond Standards should usually be followed, the old assumption that the bond schedule showed the appropriate option seemed to remain firmly in place. In attempts to improve the use of the guidelines—or bond decisions generally in circuit court—the implications of the bond schedule for the improvement of pretrial release will need to be faced candidly.

Notes

1. As we explained earlier, these estimates represent a maximum possible effect, depending on the extent to which judges would agree with the guidelines.
2. Statistically, of course, we could not estimate which 25 percent of the cases would be the exceptions—hence the necessity to begin with the 100 percent compliance yardstick.
3. See Figure 12.2.
4. All defendants entering the felony court process during this period who were charged with bondable offenses were included. Thus the sample is a complete sample of felony defendants entering circuit court from June 9 through July 24, 1987.
5. The large number of missing cases in the risk classification results from the failure of pretrial services staff to classify all defendants in the June–July 1987 sample and also in the later, November sample. Because the purpose here is to contrast the samples for similarity, we employ a "corrected" measure of these variables. See the discussion of pretrial services preparation of the guidelines below.
6. If defendants were equally distributed throughout the guidelines, we would expect roughly 3 percent to fall within each cell. With this as a basis for comparison, defendants are found half as often or less than expected in six cells across samples: Rarely evident are defendants in Cell 1 ("PTS/Standard"), Cell 3 ("PTS/Standard"), Cell 4 ("PTS/Standard"), Cell 5 ("PTS/Standard"), Cell 8 ("Financial Bond"), and Cell 25 ("PTS/Special"). In only Cell 22 were defendants found in each of the samples consistently to include twice the proportion of defendants expected (6 percent) or more. In four cells (10, 13, 14, and 18), more than 5 percent of all defendants were classified in each sample.

In general, the 1987 samples appeared to be somewhat more heterogeneous, that is, more evenly distributed among all guidelines cells.

7. In more than one-third (37 percent) of the cases, pretrial services did not correctly score the "property charges" item, which asked them to assign 0 points if a crime against the person was involved and 2 points if no crime against the person was included in any of the defendants' charges. Recent prior arrests were incorrectly indicated in 30 percent of the cases, and other aspects of a defendant's prior record also appeared troublesome. Simply invalid scores were less common but still troublesome. Addition errors were found in about 10 percent of the cases, about one-third resulting in lower and two-third in higher risk classifications. This rate of addition error is relatively consistent with error rates found in other jurisdictions during initial implementation periods and has been shown to diminish as new procedures become more routine. Indeed, there was a slight diminution of addition errors from the June–July sample (10 percent error rate) to the November sample (4 percent error rate), but not much of a change in the other kinds of risk classification errors.
8. Two other judges together heard as many as 18 percent of cases. No other single judge in either of the 1987 samples heard as many as 5 percent of the cases.
9. See Chapter 6 to contrast the experience of Maricopa County with Dade County regarding pretrial detention.
10. This view is supported when data from cases decided during the same period but not processed for the guidelines are contrasted with the guidelines cases.
11. Note that the 1987 samples were combined in this analysis because of the small number of cases in the November sample.
12. The comparisons are misleading, for one thing because of the problems involved in comparing samples that may have been dissimilar. Again, that these samples were related to an overall trend not linked to guidelines cases is supported by analysis of the companion data collected during the same period.
13. In fact, at one point in response to the continuing crowding crisis in the Dade jail facilities, the leadership of circuit court even drafted an administrative order authorizing the pretrial services staff to release defendants falling within the zone of the guidelines suggesting outright nonfinancial release (under the auspices of pretrial services) prior to a bond-hearing appearance. This draft was superseded by more expansive emergency-release procedures before ever going into effect.

V

CONCLUSION: THE PROMISE OF PRETRIAL RELEASE GUIDELINES

17

The Promise of Decision Guidelines for Pretrial Release

> Explicit recognition of uncertainty can save you from deluding yourself.
>
> —HOGARTH (1980:12)

Lessons from the Guidelines Development Process

The overriding purpose of the research presented in this book has been to discover the extent to which a court-based self-help guidelines methodology first developed in connection with parole and sentencing decisions[1] and, implemented successfully in one large urban court system for bail,[2] could find application in more diverse court settings. The three court systems we studied differed both in law and custom guiding their procedures, in decisionmakers, in support staffs, in goals, and in the adequacy of the information available at the first court-release-decision point. This latter point was perhaps most striking and of considerable consequence as our research progressed. In Boston, for example, in one out of five cases, the judge could not know from the information supplied to him or her what the prior criminal record of the arrestee was or even the current pretrial-release status. With respect to the structure of decisionmaking at our study sites, diversity was the hallmark. The structures ranged from a system in which a single judge made most of the decisions most of the time with the assistance of an organized pretrial staff working under the department of corrections (Dade County) to a system in which numerous judges rotated the assignment in the absence of a modern pretrial-service-agency (Boston). Maricopa County, with its system of several commissioners (who doubled as city court pro tem judges) and a large and modern pretrial-services agency working as an arm of the court, represented yet another model.

In sheer numbers of defendants alone, the study sites differed substantially, reminding us that even in the largest cities in the country the size and scope of the criminal court system can themselves vary dramatically. Dade County's court processed over three times the number of defendants at the bail stage that did the other two courts. The relevant pretrial-detention facilities in Maricopa and Dade Counties held about 1,500 defendants, while the jail serving the Boston court we studied held only about 300. Our study courts had differing caseloads, with respect to both the characteristics of the defendants and the criminal charges. Seriously charged felony defendants were in a small minority in the Boston Municipal Court in comparison to the other sites. Drug cases more frequently came before the Dade court.

The range of options with respect to release or detention before trial employed by the decisionmakers at the sites reflected the diversity of procedures found in American courts. The proportion released before booking, the use of bond schedules, the use of ROR, the relative amounts of money bail required to be released, the detention rates, and the misconduct rates all varied enormously among the demonstration sites. We discovered that the role of the pretrial services agency (at the two sites having one) and the form of their recommendations played a large role in the process of allocating release or detention before trial. At one site the recommendations of the pretrial staff were, for all practical purposes, indistinguishable from the decision of the commissioner; at another site, agency representatives "agreed" to take clients from court at the bond hearing; at the third, no agency existed. We discovered that, despite considerable variation in detention practices early in the process, the majority of defendants did gain release before their trial and that the misconduct rates before trial were generally quite low. In particular, serious crimes committed by the pretrial population of released defendants at the sites was quite rare.

Despite this important variability, at all sites common factors were important in the initial bail decisions. Overwhelmingly, the seriousness of the charges facing the defendant determined the form and prospects of release. Beyond this, however, it was difficult to discover much consistency in pretrial release decisionmaking, either within or between the courts in the study. In fact, our empirical analysis (informed by discussions with the pretrial release decisionmakers) led us to conclude that bail decisions were disparate; they could not systematically be explained by the objective factors available to us. (In Boston, at the request of the judiciary, we even constructed an empirical model based on the criteria suggested by the statute, since the municipal court judiciary told us that they followed these "guidelines." This "legal" model failed to show a correspondence with the actual decisions of the Boston judges, contrary to the judges' predictions but consistent with the expectations of the guidelines approach.) On this basis alone, the need for explicit decisionmaking guidelines was evident.

With respect to the effectiveness of the decisions made in the three courts studied, we discovered that, here, too, the courts varied substantially. With respect to misconduct rates generally, they ranged from 16 percent of released felony defendants in Dade and Maricopa to 30 percent of all defendants in Boston. In terms of *effective* releases, (effectiveness being defined as the proportion of all defendants entering the process who were not detained and not released later to fail to appear as required or to be rearrested), the study courts also differed dramatically. Maricopa County Superior Court displayed the lowest effectiveness because of its frequent resort to detention, although its proportion of released defendants engaging in misconduct was comparatively low. Again, there was considerable evidence of the need for explicit guidelines to provide decisionmakers with systematic knowledge of the consequences of their decisions.

The Guidelines Development Process

At each site we worked with a steering and policy committee formed expressly to aid in the collaborative work. After the descriptive work resulting in the findings described in earlier chapters, each site began the process of thinking through the various forms that guidelines might take and the implications of adopting different models. The research team developed several models for the consideration of each committee, and a series of meetings was held at each site to discuss the virtues and defects of each model. The models had different assumptions and radically different forms. One was a strictly "actuarial" approach that would take the best of the predictors of pretrial flight and rearrest and combine them into guidelines that would consider nothing but these two classical aims of the decision. Another was a two-staged model, in which first the decision about release or detention was made and then, for those released, the method of release was considered. Considerable empirical work was involved in this phase of the research, with the project team developing models at the suggestion of the court committees, constructing appropriate forms, and fitting the models to the data for the particular site.

In many respects, this phase of the collaborative research was most stimulating to the policy committee. The choices were real choices, each embodying a different vision of the pretrial process. The research staff not only presented the models but developed material about their likely effects. Also, the research staff briefed the steering and policy committees about the social scientific literature and debates about such relevant topics as the consequences of prediction, the bail-setting practices of other courts, and the guideline models in use elsewhere in the criminal justice system. The process was iterative, with the site committees sending the researchers back to the drawing board for additional models and more data, time and time again. In every case, prescriptive, descriptive, actuarial, and legalistic guideline models were built, examined empirically, critiqued, and modified.

In the end, an important finding emerged: despite the diversity of organization, staffing, legal codes, resources, and caseloads, all three sites opted for some form of matrix guideline system of the now-classic form that considered simultaneously the seriousness of the case and the actuarial probability of misconduct. Of course, the details of the models differed substantially; the predictors of risk differed on grounds of both availability and efficiency of defendant information, and the jurisdictions had different notions of "severity" of the offense. Much work had to be done to tailor the classic guidelines form to the needs and preferences of the specific jurisdictions. But the general discovery should not be lost in this detail (however time-consuming and difficult the detail was): the judicial working groups saw virtue in an explicit policy that tempered the actual risk the defendant posed if released with the seriousness of the crime bringing the defendant to the court to begin with.

After the selection of the matrix—risks and stakes-type—model, site-specific goals began to play a more prominent role. In Maricopa, the judiciary was especially concerned about crimes in which weapons were used and in which persons had been injured. Similar concerns were shared by Dade County judges; at both sites, public reaction was an important concern. In Dade County, the tradition of relying on a bond schedule had to be reckoned with. In Boston, the judges wished to reduce the remarkably high failure-to-appear ("default") rate without decreasing the use of pretrial release among defendants.

Thus another important finding emerged from this study: Although the classic matrix model was apparently the most popular among judges, it would not be possible to develop a "generic" guidelines model and simply mail it to jurisdictions throughout the country. Significant local and situational modifications are vital components in an acceptable pretrial guidelines model, as is the participation of the decisionmakers in the development of the model itself. Put together with what has been learned in other settings, the conclusion seems inescapable that all criminal-justice decisionmakers making decisions involving the deprivation of liberty are greatly attracted to a system that considers their *own* risk in making an error (seriousness of offense) and the objective risk to the community of wrongful releases and a system that allows such concerns to be applied more equitably than is generally the case. Other considerations are clearly subordinate to these, including the overcrowded state of the local correctional facilities.

Constructing a Policy Tool

Once the sites had settled in principle on the matrix model, and once the research team had given operational meaning to the concepts of risk and seriousness, hard work had yet to be done on the precise nature of the matrices and how they might actually be implemented in the ongoing court processes in some of the busiest court systems in the country. One important task was to establish presumptive decisions and decision ranges for the cells of the guidelines matrix, a normative task given that the combination of empirical risk and charge seriousness was novel at each of the study sites. This process was truly as much a part of the development of pretrial policy as the adoption of the matrix form itself. Whatever constituted the presumptions in these cells was to be the new policy of the court. Thus preferred cash bail sums, alternative modes of release (supervised or ROR) had to be inserted into this new form. To assist the policymakers with this task, the research team "fit the data" pertinent to each site to various presumptions for each cell (i.e., that the cell would be an ROR cell, a cell in which special, more restrictive conditions of release would apply, or that the presumption would be for cash bail of, say, $500), seeking misconduct and detention rates that would be expected under various decisions. Throughout all of this, the research staff presented data about equity and about the potential impact of various scenarios on the fairness of the guidelines.

Once the steering and policy committees at each site settled on the specific nature of their matrices, and once presumptive decisions had been established (both Maricopa and Dade forced the guidelines toward greater use of nonfinancial release options because of jail overcrowding), the research team used the models to estimate their likely impact on the jails, misconduct rates, and releases. Not surprisingly, given that the matrices had been established to optimize these goals, the guidelines seemed to have a plausible chance of reducing jail populations, lowering or keeping constant the misconduct rates, and enhancing the consistency of decisionmaking in the pretrial process.

The Adaptability of Guidelines and the Decision of the Boston Municipal Court Judges Not to Implement Guidelines

In undertaking the research we have described in this book, our goal was to learn—through case study and by illustration—whether and how the positive lessons of the Philadelphia experience with bail guidelines could be brought to bear on other jurisdictions similarly concerned about bail- and pretrial-detention-related issues. The study provided us with the first glimpse of the adaptability of guidelines to varied circumstance. At each of the sites, our agreement with the participating courts was to work with the steering committees to examine bail practices and to develop decision guidelines to address the issues that surfaced. We did not ask for or receive a commitment in advance from any of the courts to adopt a particular end product—such as decision guidelines—but we obtained their agreement to participate in the collaborative research process to determine whether such a resource might be useful. The fact that the guidelines process resulted in implementation of guidelines in three jurisdictions (if we include Philadelphia, the first jurisdiction to devise and implement bail guidelines) may leave the misleading impression that adoption of decision guidelines for pretrial release was a preordained fact.

Our experience in the Boston courts serves as a reminder that courts may participate fully in the guidelines process only to exercise their option not to proceed further. In fact, after two and a half years of research, reports, meetings, interviews, and guidelines development, and after a formal request from the presiding judge to prepare guidelines for implementation, the Boston Municipal Court judges decided not to go forward to implement the guidelines or arraignment. In explaining their wish to postpone implementation of a guidelines system, the municipal court judges cited a range of arguments, including doubts about the impact that guidelines would have on the jail-crowding situation (because many other courts were "more" responsible for the makeup of the jail population), beliefs that other problems—such as information management—needed to be addressed before guidelines would be appropriate, questions about the additional court resources that would be needed to mount a guidelines program (Would the existing probation department be upgraded to serve a more developed pretrial-services role?), and opinions among some judges that—despite the research findings—bail decisionmaking was operating quite well in its current state.

Although some might regard the decision of the Boston Municipal Court judges not to implement the guidelines as a failure of the voluntary guidelines approach, in other respects the guidelines research process played a positive role for the courts and related agencies in Boston. The process was productive particularly in identifying several areas of concern relating to bail practices.

Overcrowding in the Charles Street Jail

A continual theme in our studies and discussions in Boston was the constant state of crisis caused by crowding at the Charles Street Jail, which served as the repository of the bail decisions made by Boston area courts. Unlike in other jails with which we had been working, the crowding problem in Boston was almost solely a "pretrial" problem. Throughout the study, we observed a number of crisis-oriented procedures being implemented to relieve pressures on the jail until some more long-term and systematic relief could be found. Our analysis of the potential impact of the Boston guidelines suggested strongly that the use of and the length of detention could be notably reduced through guidelines.

"Defaulting" Defendants

When we first visited the courts in Boston to discuss participation in the study, the *Boston Globe* was in the midst of a series describing the large number of "defaults" (failures to appear) from court hearings among BMC defendants. In many ways, our study confirmed an exceptionally high rate of defaults. While it is common to see higher rates of absconding among misdemeanor cases (and the BMC caseload was predominantly misdemeanor-like), the high rate of defaults was found among the more seriously charged defendants as well. Default (FTA) rates among BMC defendants charged with "index" crimes—at 25 percent—was more than twice as high as the rates shown by similar Dade County and Maricopa County defendants. This was another area squarely addressed by the guidelines framework developed for the Boston Municipal Court.

Inconsistency in the Application of Bail

To be fair and effective, bail decisions should be influenced by concerns and factors appropriately related to the goals of the bail task. Statistical analyses of bail decisions in our study, however, were hard put to detect patterns or themes governing judges' decisions rationally related to the concerns of the bail task. Lack of overriding patterns (e.g., concerns about community ties and prior defaults) suggests inconsistency in the treatment of similar defendants. This raises questions about the criteria that do and/or should govern pretrial release as well as about the equitable treatment of defendants at the pretrial release stage. A central rationale for guidelines is to devise a policy framework that can enhance the equitable treatment of defendants at the pretrial-release-decision stage.

Problems with the Availability and Reliability of Potentially Useful Information about the Arraignment Bail Stage

The apparently inconsistent nature of BMC decisions may have been traceable to the highly subjective and discretionary nature of the judge's task at bail (and our interviews with judges lent support to this view) and/or by the fact that the information judges had to rely on was often rather poor or incomplete. While it is also true that, even with a wealth of sound information available about defendants and their cases, judges may take very different approaches to defendants at bail, it is certainly true that inadequate information will accentuate the subjective nature of the decisions and the diversity of approaches. The result was a lack of evenhandedness in the application of bail and the use of pretrial release and detention. Again, the development, collection, organization, and presentation of relevant information is at the backbone of the guidelines strategy.

Although we believe the guidelines process in Boston was productive, nevertheless, implementation did not take place. Interestingly, we do not regard the level of collegial disagreement or of concern about the utility of guidelines among the judges to have been any greater than in any of the other courts we have studied. What did differ was the eventual sense (perhaps realistic) that there was not any way guidelines *could* be implemented in the Boston court. The municipal court lacked staff and lacked control over the staff it did have (e.g., its probation department reported to the state commissioner of probation). It also lacked funds. Finally, its chief judge lacked centralized decisionmaking authority over the judiciary as a whole. In each of the other courts, we studied the judge was, fundamentally, independent; in Boston, we found the least evident "line-authority" administrative and decisionmaking judicial structure.

Lessons from the Implementation of Decision Guidelines for Pretrial Release

This book has described the results of developmental and evaluative research designed to throw light on the potential and the "success" of decision guidelines in realizing goals in American court systems under very different kinds of conditions. In a number of ways, our conclusions are tentative. For example, we conducted a "small" evaluation in Maricopa County, a "large" evaluation in Dade County, and no evaluation in Boston. In our evaluations, we were forced by circumstances to study the implementation of the new programs at their outset rather than after an appropriate period of months when stability and routinization could occur. As a result, we have reported both positive and negative findings that might have been mediated with the passage of time as program procedures matured. We emphasize this point particularly because guidelines systems are intended to be evolutionary and are designed to accommodate adjustments and corrections. In fact, rather than producing "evaluations" designed to make pronouncements concerning the "failure" or "success" of the guidelines at this point, normally we would be reporting these findings back to the respective courts for review so that they could consider appropriate action.

In concluding this review, we believe it would be useful to use a measuring stick of the experiences at each of our sites the definition of the guidelines development process described in M. Gottfredson and D. Gottfredson (1988:11) in their discussion of the essential aspects of guidelines as a "specific method of policy control." They specify the following components in the development of voluntary decision guidelines:

1. *A general policy for decisionmaking, including a statement of the goals sought, articulated in explicit terms, within which individual case decisions are made.* At each of the three sites, the guidelines development process was grounded in discussion and clarification of bail and pretrial release policy in explicit terms. In Maricopa County, the court made explicit several policy objectives, including more evenhanded and predictable decisions and the use of a risk dimension in the guidelines grid that classified defendants based on probabilities of flight and crime during pretrial release. This was not unusual as it both reflected the concerns of Arizona law and continued in the tradition of the Philadelphia bail guidelines. In addition, however, the severity dimension of the superior court guidelines incorporated specific crime-related concerns, including special provisions for persons charged with crimes involving injury to victims, use of weapons, or repeated counts of serious charges. These explicit policy concerns were juxtaposed to another of the court's specific policy objectives: to minimize unnecessary pretrial detention.

In Dade County, the concerns of the court's steering committee were quite similar. Public safety concerns—mirroring those expressed in Florida law—as well as concerns about defendants' failure to appear were at the heart of the guidelines structure. However, in Dade, an emphatic policy constraint upon which the circuit court conditioned development of its decision guidelines for bond was that the guidelines should not increase the use of pretrial detention over its then current level; in fact, if the other goals could be realized, the court expressed a preference for a guidelines model that would reduce the use of pretrial detention.

In Boston, clear policy aims of the municipal court were reflected in the guidelines that were drafted. There was a focus on defendant misconduct—on the likelihood of both defendant flight and crime—but special emphasis was placed on the implications of the pretrial release guidelines for jail overcrowding.

2. *Explicitly defined criteria for decisionmaking, with the specific weights to be given to these criteria also explicitly defined.* In each of the jurisdictions, guidelines were developed through an explicit format based on the ranking of criminal charges according to severity and on dimensions differentiating defendants according to probability of flight or rearrest during pretrial release. Each of these dimensions was based on very specifically defined criteria with explicit weighting schemes.

3. *Within the general policy model, guidelines in the form of a chart (matrix or grid) are used in the process of arriving at a particular decision. The most important policy concerns, decided by those responsible for the decisionmaking policy, are reflected in the dimensions of the grid. In most models, one axis reflects the seriousness of the offense, and the other reflects the characteristics of the offender. The intersection of the appropriate columns and rows of the two axes provides an expected decision for cases possessing the attributes used in classifications on the chart.* The guidelines development process at each site not only successfully formulated overall policy aims for the pretrial-release-decision process and outlined specific criteria to guide decisions, but also constructed suggested or "presumptive" decision options to achieve those aims. Thus the guidelines-drafting process within each working group arrived at decision choices that counterbalanced the various policy objectives of each court. The result was that, assuming the guidelines would be employed in the way intended, each court had constructed a framework for orienting day-to-day decisionmaking and for reviewing the performance of court decisionmakers in reaching policy goals on a periodic basis.

4. *The guidelines grid is intended to structure the use of discretion, but not to eliminate it. There are two ways in which discretionary judgments are required of the decisionmaker: (a) some discretion must be exercised within the cells of the two-dimensional grid, and (b) considering the facts of the case, the decisionmaker is expected sometimes to reach a decision that is a departure (that is, an exception) from the suggested decision outcome.*

5. *When departures occur, the decisionmaker must provide explicit reasons for the exception to the usual decision.* Once the guidelines were finalized in each of the courts, they were put into use in two of the jurisdictions. In both, the superior court in Maricopa County and the circuit court in Dade County, guidelines were conceived of as a decisionmaking resource that offered guided decisionmaking—reflecting notions of equity, defendant misconduct, and the use of pretrial detention. They were never presented as, or conceived of as, some sort of ironclad, computerized mandatory bail scheme. Each court emphasized the voluntariness of the resources and explained that the guidelines were based on a long process, including rigorous empirical study of bail practices and informed debate about desirable policy directions.

The requirement for judges to note reasons when they chose to depart from the options suggested by the guidelines was designed to establish a system of accountability in decisionmaking as well as to provide important data for reviewing the use and appropriateness of guidelines at periodic intervals. In the first use of the guidelines at the two sites, we found that a majority of initial-appearance commissioners in Maricopa County but less than half of the judges in Dade County noted reasons when making exceptions.

6. *There is an established system of monitoring to provide periodic feedback to the authorities responsible for the decision policy, giving the percentage of decisions falling outside each guideline category and the reasons given for those decisions.* An important and often overlooked feature of the decision guidelines strategy involves monitoring the use of guidelines and periodic review of their impact by the judicial leadership. This requires a procedure for collecting data describing the use of guidelines by the judges, the kinds of reasons given by them when making decisions outside the suggested alternatives, and the consequences of decisions (such as the use of nonfinancial release and bond, pretrial detention, and failure to appear and rearrest among released defendants). Since our evaluation of the early use of the guidelines in Arizona and Florida, the respective pretrial services agencies have initiated procedures that will allow them to report to the courts on the use of guidelines.

The pretrial services agency in Maricopa County, for example, has incorporated data using guidelines categories, decisionmakers, and outcomes into its quarterly, semiannual, and annual reports. The initial statistics tended to confirm the directions suggested in our evaluation of the initial use of guidelines and have been employed by the court to monitor developments and to plan meetings based on the issues raised. In Dade County, such systematic reports were not developed, but information relating to the use of guidelines was included in a new court-based computer-information system, thereby providing the opportunity for reports to be routinely made available to pretrial services and the court.

7. *The authorities may modify the guidelines at any time.*

8. *The general policy, including the guidelines incorporated within it, is not regarded as a "once-and-for-all" statement of "right" policy; rather, the policy statement and the procedures are designed to facilitate an evolutionary system of policy development, changing in response to experience, resultant learning, and social change.*

9. *The policy in general and the guidelines specifically are open and available for public review.* The purpose of these data is to allow the court to consider modifications in the guidelines or to be made aware of use of the guidelines that may be falling below the desired level. Such modifications have occurred in Philadelphia and Maricopa County. However, having the reporting procedures in place guarantees that data will be available to permit continual review of the guidelines and encourage flexibility and accountability.

Conclusion: Addressing the Judicial Dilemma at Bail: Personal Liberty and Community Safety

Despite decades of reform in the pretrial process that has indeed made for a fairer and more rational process, the general picture of pretrial decisionmaking is still one that departs substantially from what is desirable. The responsibility lies principally with the judiciary. By and large, pretrial decisionmakers have neither a clarity of purpose marked by focused goals nor an explicit policy for how various goals of the decision might be simultaneously considered. They do not have adequate information concerning how the data they receive (when they receive them at all) are related to the achievement of those goals. They do not receive systematic feedback about the outcome of cases in the system. They do not have the means to ensure that equally situated cases will be treated equally, and they generally have inadequate resources (jails are full, pretrial supervision staff are too few, and time is too short). The criminal court judges responsible for pretrial release decisionmaking do have discretion. The decision guidelines strategy seeks to assist judges in addressing the problems associated with such discretionary decisionmaking.

We now have experience with the development, implementation, and evaluation of pretrial release guidelines in four large urban court systems (Philadelphia, Maricopa, Boston, and Dade). Although by ordinary research standards these systems represent a small sample, we believe that this body of work permits some general inferences about the problems of implementation and the prospects for this type of system to structure the discretion of an important decisionmaking body. Therefore, keeping in mind the tentative nature of these conclusions, we offer these findings as road signs for future research and reform in the area.

The Ubiquity of the Matrix Form

The original guidelines work in parole and sentencing[3] settled on a two-dimensional "grid" form of guidelines, with one dimension relating to the current offense or to its seriousness and the other dimension relating to the risk, however established, posed by the person. In Philadelphia, the original bail judges adopted a similar set of concerns, even though the stage in the criminal justice process was profoundly different.[4]

In this set of studies, we presented to the various advisory bodies an array of possible decisionmaking approaches, critiqued them together, and sought, the best we could, to assess their potential consequences if adopted. We never "pushed" one set of concerns over another, and we always tried to pay strict attention to the ideas and desires of the judiciary. Nevertheless, each site saw the "grid" form as the most appropriate for it and selected some version of the two-dimensional structure to try out. The conclusion seems inescapable that the issues of the seriousness of the conduct for which the defendant is being considered and the potential risk to the community posed by the defendant simply overwhelm all other concerns. Incidentally, this seems to be true at all stages of the criminal process.[5] Even the U.S. Sentencing Commission, which initially sought other models, has settled on this established form.

There are, of course, a variety of reasons why the interplay between risk and seriousness may dominate the criminal justice system. Issues of desert, incapacitation, and deterrence all come into play. But whatever the theoretical rationale for the empirically established regularity, it is highly noteworthy that it does seem to be an empirically established regularity. Guidelines and the matrix form seem to go hand in hand, judging by the work described here.

Successful Implementation Requires Strong Judicial Leadership

In every court we have studied, there has been a majority of the judiciary who, in the end, believed that the voluntary guidelines would be a good idea for their court. They participated fully in the development of the guidelines, putting in long hours and engaging in serious, sustained policy debate. Yet full implementation has taken place only in Philadelphia and Maricopa, with partial implementation in Dade.

Clearly, belief in the appropriateness of the guidelines and willingness to work toward that idea are not sufficient. Guidelines seek to make justice more evenhanded and more rational; as a consequence, they also seek to remove some judicial discretion and force accountability in the giving of reasons for decisions. Because every such decision is a critical one from the perspectives of accountability, community safety, and the deprivation of individual liberty, proponents of guidelines believe that these intrusions on judicial discretion are justifiable. After all, compliance is still voluntary, and judges always retain the right to go their own way. But from the point of view of some judges, guidelines go too far. From the point of view of others, they defeat the principal of individual responsibility for decisions and relegate these tasks to the group. Such debates are long-standing in criminal justice and will forever be argued.

The consequence of all this, it seems to us, is that the implementation and maintenance of voluntary guidelines of the type we have studied depend on the extent to which there is a centralization of authority within the court, so that, once the collective decision to implement has been made, it can be carried out. This condition was particularly present in Maricopa County during this research and in the Philadelphia Municipal Court during the first guidelines experiment.

Centralized authority is necessary but not sufficient to establish the required types of discretion-structuring systems. It is the experience of these studies that large urban court systems require modern data collection and retrieval systems and a staff of sufficient numbers and quality, directly reporting to the authority of the court, for implementation. Where modern, "data-ready" pretrial-services agencies have been in place, guidelines seem to have worked well. In their absence, there appears to be little promise of an effective system.

Urban court systems, surely, have plenty to do to occupy their attention. Guidelines and the issues of fairness and rationality with which they attempt to deal compete with a host of other pressing problems confronting court leadership. Staffing problems, overcrowded dockets, scheduling changes, press coverage of sensational cases, the current focus on drug crime, jail overcrowding, and the like are more than enough to keep any court administrator busy. The agenda that guidelines seek to bring into focus is an important one, more important for some jurisdictions than for others perhaps, and the success of guidelines implementation rests in no small measure on the centrality of this agenda to the court and to the court leadership. In recent times, this agenda has become less of a concern of the judiciary than other agendas in the political world in which courts operate.

Equity and Safety Are Not Incompatible Goals in a Good Pretrial-Release System

Our findings in Maricopa County and in Philadelphia indicate that, when implemented, voluntary guidelines can enhance the equity of the process and can do so without increasing the risk posed to the community by the pretrial population.

When the term *similarly situated defendants* is taken operationally to mean defendants within cells of the guidelines matrix and *equal treatment* refers to the extent of liberty deprivation or the conditions of release, our research strongly suggests that the guidelines increase equity of treatment at the bail stage. Similar results have been shown to hold for parole guidelines.[6] In both Philadelphia and the Maricopa experiences, this increase in equity came without an increase in felony-level rearrests. In fact, it came with overall increases in the proportion of defendants given the least restrictive release conditions at the bail stage. In Maricopa County, it also came with a substantial decrease in the rate of pretrial detention. It seems fair to conclude, at this stage of guidelines evaluation research, that voluntary guidelines properly implemented can achieve a substantial disparity-reduction function. And when the definition of *equally situated* includes a judgment of risk, an objective risk instrument as part of voluntary guidelines can ensure that equity and less restrictive conditions of release will not have to be sacrificed to "community safety."

The Need to Monitor the Guidelines

It has been said that measurement creates improvement. When people have a firm idea of what they are doing and cannot be led astray by the unusual or idiosyncratic cases, things will get better. As in all other aspects of human affairs bound by rules, those who decide cases under guidelines will soon drift from them if there is no enforcement of the rules. In this case, the enforcement is meant to be part of the guidelines themselves through the provision of the giving of reasons for departures and systematic empirical feedback to the decisionmakers of recent past experience.

But evidence from this research suggests that the "reason-giving" provision of guidelines remains problematic. There is the tendency to make exceptions to the guidelines and to cite as a reason factors already incorporated into the guidelines structure. The evidence from Maricopa County suggests that the departures from the guidelines norm are much more frequently in directions more restrictive than in the less restrictive directions. Furthermore, there is evidence that individual judges differ considerably in their compliance with the guidelines, a finding again suggesting that the feedback and monitoring function that is part and parcel of the guidelines system must be taken as central to any operating system. This in turn reemphasizes the importance of centralized authority and an effective pretrial services agency.

The Urge for Subjectivity

Guidelines increase the objectivity of criminal justice decisionmaking by stating the rules openly and applying them as uniformly as possible. In the pretrial arena, as at most criminal-justice decision points, the common practice is to attempt to individualize decisionmaking and to take into consideration the "totality of the circumstances" of any given case. Guidelines remove discretion; decisionmakers seek to restore it. This tension was exhibited time and again in our evaluation of pretrial guidelines systems; it appeared in the initial and strong reaction against any formalized rules by pretrial services staff (and may account in part for implementation problems) and the resistance to guidelines shown initially by the commissioners in Maricopa County and bond judges in Dade County. It surfaced as well in the concern about empirical risk measures used by guidelines in lieu of the subjective or more "clinical" methods used by pretrial services agencies. In any event, our experience in evaluating this process of development and implementation of guidelines serves to underscore for us the constant tension in the system to individualize and to make "sensible" decisions. For those who subscribe to explicit decision rules based on the best available experience, the drive toward subjectivity reinforces the belief that such guidelines are necessary.

Notes

1. Gottfredson et al. (1978).
2. Goldkamp and Gottfredson (1985).
3. Gottfredson et al. (1978).
4. Goldkamp and Gottfredson (1985).
5. Gottfredson and Gottfredson (1988).
6. Gottfredson (1979).

18

Postscript: Pretrial Release Guidelines and the Passage of Time

The first pretrial-release-decision guidelines—then referred to as *bail guidelines*—were introduced experimentally in Philadelphia's Municipal Court in 1981. This book has described the experiences of three "second-generation" jurisdictions that tested the pretrial release guidelines approach. It is fair to say that the pretrial release concept has not transformed bail and release practices in the United States. It is also fair to say that the need to focus on judicial responsibility in pretrial-release and detention determinations has also not gone away.

Rather, the challenges to fair and effective practices have grown. In the time since the first experimental research in Philadelphia, the personal computer (PC) made its first appearance and has evolved into powerful pentium-based technology that can be carried in a small brief case. Similar innovation and reform has not characterized pretrial-release and detention practices. The war against drugs has been waged and redefined across three presidential administrations. All sorts of preventive detention laws have been enacted to respond to the concerns we have described in this book. Localities have continued to struggle with correctional crowding crises, some having carried out two or three cycles of jail construction, with great cost and little hope of long-term relief. The potential of rational, planned approaches focusing on criminal justice decisionmakers, the legitimate goals of the decisions they must make, judicial policy, and their consequences still remains simply a potential. There are nevertheless positive signs in some court systems that the judiciary may be breaking out of its traditional "hands-off" role to develop more active and collaborative approaches to crime and criminal justice problems.[1]

As fate and research would have it, we have had occasion to stay in touch with the three court systems—Philadelphia, Miami, and Phoenix—in which implementation of pretrial guidelines was attempted. (Recall that the Boston judges stopped short of implementing the system, once it had been designed.) In concluding this book, we believed that it would be informative to provide a less formal update on what has become of the pretrial-release-guidelines systems at these sites. In our view, such a retrospective of the considerably different experiences of these jurisdictions illustrates the potential and actual utility of the court-based self-help guidelines approach to pretrial release determinations and management—as well as the challenges any like judicial innovation faces.

Dade County, Florida: The Eleventh Judicial Circuit

As detailed in earlier chapters, our attempt to implement guidelines in the Dade County Circuit Court met with a number of unfortunate occurrences just as the effort reached the critical implementation stage. These involved changes in the judicial leadership responsible for project oversight, including, for example, the sudden ascension to the Florida Supreme Court of the chief criminal judge who had been supervising the guidelines development process and the untimely death of his successor as criminal chief, who was also a formidable leader. As the project concluded in 1988 in the midst of these events, the chief judge sought to implement the system as best he could in the time available, relying by necessity (and by default) on the strength and reputation of the pretrial services agency to mount the program, as well as on the strong support of its parent organization, the Metropolitan Dade County Department of Corrections and Rehabilitation.

This strategy relied on the hope that, as pretrial services implemented the program, participation by the judges could be achieved as they were more fully apprised of the purposes and advantages of the pretrial-release-guidelines approach. However, efforts to involve other circuit and county court judges who would be responsible for pretrial release determinations were not successful over the longer term. These dynamics—reliance on the central role of pretrial services and the lack of ownership on the part of the judiciary—continued to devolve over the next years and set the guidelines approach on an unpromising path. Ironically, as the pretrial services approach weakened, the pressures of the growing felony caseload in circuit court continued to grow, further exacerbating the jail-crowding crisis.

In the spring of 1991, the chief judge requested our assistance in examining the impact of court-related practices on the correctional population, as part of his efforts to address overcrowding in the county facilities and to respond in good faith to the federal court overseeing the crowding litigation. Our report (Goldkamp and Weiland 1991) identified a greatly weakened pretrial-release-decisionmaking function as a principal factor in the jail crowding situation. The nature of the interaction between judges and pretrial services staff had not improved, and the preparation of guidelines information for the judges by pretrial services had atrophied notably. We discovered that, in our brief absence from the Dade County courts, the leadership of the corrections department had changed, as had the leadership of pretrial services itself. More significantly, the philosophical orientation of the new leadership and its view of the importance of pretrial services appeared to have undergone a dramatic change. In fact, the new leadership emphasized issues relating to confinement and security and deemphasized community-based programs and pretrial supervision. Together with the diminished standing of the pretrial services function within the judiciary, the effect of this shift in correctional direction on the pretrial services agency (and on the principles of justice informing its mission) was crippling. In essence, pretrial services and pretrial release guidelines had been relegated to the status of unwanted stepchildren.

We pointed out in earlier chapters that pretrial release guidelines were designed to offer a day-to-day decisionmaking tool as well as an overall policy resource *for the judiciary* in managing its pretrial release functions. The fact that the implementation efforts never succeeded in having the Dade County judges take ownership of the innovation foreshadowed the likelihood that the system would ultimately fail to achieve its original purposes. Clearly, pretrial release guidelines were meant to affect pretrial release decisions; they were never meant to be employed by the pretrial services staff alone. They were certainly not meant to be ignored or resisted by the very judges they had been developed to assist. (Such a stance on the part of the judiciary clearly indicates that important aims of the development process were not achieved.) In short, the hoped-for impact on the responsible and safe use of pretrial release and detention was not in evidence in 1991.

By the end of 1994, the news had not improved. It is clear to us as we now write that, since the 1991 court study, the state of the pretrial release function in Dade County has worsened in many important respects. The pretrial services agency shows signs of "forgetting" its mission, disappearing as a key agency, or, sadly, becoming altogether irrelevant. Most recently, despite an enormous criminal caseload, continued strains on the county correctional facilities, and ongoing jail-crowding litigation that shows no signs of going away soon, pretrial services in Dade County appear to have been unable even to respond to criticisms and lobbying efforts orchestrated by organized bail bondsmen, the traditional adversaries of bail reform and pretrial services initiatives.[2] That the entreaties of bail bondsmen could be seriously considered by judicial leaders—if, in fact, they have been—is a symptom of a judicial environment that has failed to move forward to improve pretrial release decisionmaking or to address the critical issues associated with its poor transaction, such as public safety, defendant flight, and institutional crowding. At this time, it is apparent that pretrial services and pretrial release guidelines together have been relegated to a low-priority status. By default or design, the pretrial release mechanism now risks returning to "pre-modern" days, when pretrial release determinations were made on the basis of the "bond schedule," an offense-ranking scheme tracing its roots to the bail-bonding industry and to the profit motives of bondsmen. From the perspectives of personal liberty and community safety, then, pretrial-release-decision guidelines failed to replace—or finally even to budge—reliance on the archaic bond schedule by circuit and county court judges in Dade County and the *sub rosa*, idiosyncratic, and unfocused use of pretrial detention it has generated.

Maricopa County, Arizona: Superior Court

The pretrial release guidelines described in earlier chapters have been used continuously in Maricopa County since their inception. Of the original bail commissioners, all but one are new (as of Spring 1994), and the chief presiding judge and criminal presiding judge have been replaced, as has the administrator of the pretrial services agency. The principal staff for the agency remains largely the same as when the implementation took place. The original overcrowded jail that was in use in the beginning phases of our research had been replaced with a modern facility, which in its turn has also become overcrowded.

In the fall of 1992 and early spring of 1993, we had occasion to revisit the operation of the bail guidelines in Maricopa courts in conjunction with a class-action lawsuit filed on behalf of the inmates of the jail (see discussion in Chapter 4 of *Hart v. Hill*). The consent decree in the suit (involving as defendants the county sheriff and the county board of supervisors) regarding the management of population growth and the consequences of overcrowding in the new jail was clearly in trouble in the fall of 1992. The jail population in Maricopa County had continued to grow, causing serious overcrowding, so that, by November 1992, the population stood in excess of 5,300, of whom 3,400 were being held, at least in part, as pretrial detainees. The county offered a bond election in the spring of 1991 to build new facilities for the second time in a decade to help resolve overcrowding and the lawsuit, and the voters turned it down, stimulating the federal court to once again intervene to require the county to alleviate the unconstitutional conditions that had developed.

At the request of the board of supervisors and the sheriff, we returned to Maricopa and studied the jail, sentencing, and bail practices, with the aim of describing various options to reduce the overcrowding problem. This gave us the opportunity to study data concerning the use of the pretrial release guidelines and to consider the question of whether the guidelines themselves could play an important part in a coordinated policy to reduce the numbers of people incarcerated in the Maricopa County jails.

It is significant that, several years after their implementation, bail guidelines have been fully integrated into the operations of the superior court and continue to be used in all of the pretrial release decisions by the commissioners. Routine reports on compliance with the guidelines, FTA and rearrest rates, and cell-by-cell analyses are generated by pretrial supervision staff. Because only one of the bail commissioners involved in the original study was still performing this job in 1994, it seemed as though the guidelines method had successfully been transferred to a second generation of decisionmakers.

It is also significant that, in all important respects, the guidelines had not been changed since their initial adoption. Some minor modification of variables had taken place, essentially in the form of clarification of variables and labels on the operating forms. Both the pretrial services staff and the superior court judicial leadership (who, as noted above, had also changed since the project) expressed strong satisfaction concerning the performance and utility of the guidelines.

Because such a large portion of the jail population continues to be in pretrial detention status, considerable attention was focused in our overcrowding project on the identification of ways in which judicial activities in the pretrial area could be altered to reduce incarceration. In this context, the policy that the superior court had adopted via the guidelines provided important guidance. The court had, after all, been explicit in deciding that the dimensions of defendant risk and offense seriousness should guide presumptive pretrial release decisions. Within that policy, however, there was left the substantial question of whether the presumptive bail decisions (e.g., the amount of cash bail required for release) could be altered in such a way that greater release was achieved without undue risk to the community. That is, the overcrowding project sought to discover whether the guidelines themselves could be used as a mechanism to study the overcrowding problem and to design a solution. This is, of course, precisely one of the original intents of the guidelines.

The project proceeded in several steps. First, compliance figures, by individual decisionmaker, were computed for the recent past, and departures from the matrix were studied in an effort to determine whether unusual patterns were contributing needlessly to the detention problem. Second, attention focused on the presumptions within the cells themselves with the aim of reducing the presumptions in cells that caused significant detention to the extent that such reductions were acceptable to the superior court. Third, the empirically derived risk scale was once again studied, in an effort to determine whether it continued to have reasonable validity in predicting pretrial misconduct several years after it was developed and to see whether an alternative scale could be developed that would both have validity and cause less detention.

Examination of compliance rates in the fall of 1992 indicated good overall compliance by the five bail commissioners. For the month of September, 78 percent of the decisions were being made within the guidelines ranges. However, one commissioner, who was responsible for a disproportionate share (about one-third) of the pretrial release decisions was "outside" the guidelines significantly more frequently than others (64% of decisions were within the guidelines). For this individual, the departures were most frequently in a more restrictive direction (i.e., setting financial release conditions where the guidelines called for OR, or setting higher bail than provided for by the guidelines). Thus there was some evidence that one decisionmaker was not conforming to the court's policy to use the guidelines and that such noncompliance was raising the rates of pretrial detention.

The first step in the project to use the guidelines to manage the overcrowding situation was thus to request that the superior court investigate whether the compliance of this decisionmaker could be increased. The court did this, indicating to all commissioners that it was the *superior court's policy* that the guidelines be followed most of the time and that exceptions were expected to be infrequent. Compliance rates were computed again in January of 1993 and found to be 85 percent, with a corresponding decrease in detention.[3]

The second step in the project focused on a consideration of the presumptions within the cells of the matrix, in collaboration with the court leadership, with the aim of making the presumptions less restrictive on a trial basis. Overcrowding had become such an important issue—both in terms of cost and in terms of a reduction of options for sentencing convicted offenders—that the court was willing to test whether the presumptions could be lowered without a substantial reduction in pretrial misconduct.

The guidelines themselves provided the policy tool enabling the project. It was agreed that greater release should be sought within the context of empirical risk measures and offense severity. Thus, for six cells in the matrix, the bail presumptions were shifted to match the presumption in the adjacent category across the seriousness dimension (leaving the risk classification alone). At the same time, it was agreed that the court would adhere to the policy that in excess of 80 percent of the decisions should be consistent with the guidelines, an agreement necessary to ensure that the guidelines shift would not simply be "overruled" by the commissioners by a lowering of their compliance rates. The court adopted this new policy in the spring of 1993 with apparently positive results. However, whatever the outcome of this new policy, it is highly significant to learn that it was undertaken directly within the context and theory of guidelines.

The third step was to assess the current validity of the risk scale and to seek its modification, if possible, in a way that would yield less detention. On an independent project in the same court, we had, in 1990, collected risk and follow-up data for several random samples of several hundred felony defendants. These samples allowed the application of the risk scale and study of its predictive validity for pretrial misconduct.

Of interest in the present work is our funding that the risk scale continued to have substantial predictive validity for pretrial misconduct several years after its development. When cases were classified into risk groups and the pretrial misconduct rates (either FTA or rearrest) computed for those released prior to trial, they were found to range from about 12 percent in the lowest risk category to about 55 percent in the highest risk category. The continuing predictive validity of the risk scale is impressive; apparently those factors of risk, such as age, prior FTAs, and property offenses, are highly robust indicators of failure during the pretrial period.

As was the case in the original risk scale, a substantial proportion of the cases in the risk scale fell into the middle groups in the revalidation study. Our efforts on behalf of the overcrowding project to further discriminate risk for the middle categories—and thereby include more defendants in the lowest risk group and increase the release rates—was not successful. Although we can achieve a stable risk instrument with modest discrimination in risk, we are not able to produce an instrument that permits greater separation of defendants on risk alone.

Our return to Maricopa in the context of jail overcrowding taught us several things about pretrial release guidelines: (1) they can become integrated into the routine operations of courts; (2) they can be transferred from one generation of decisionmakers to another without the active involvement of outside researchers or consultants; (3) compliance rates can remain very high for extended periods of time; (4) empirically derived risk scales can have validity for extended periods of time; and (5) guidelines can indeed serve the policy-review and reformulation function they were hypothesized to allow when circumstances within the court change.

Philadelphia, Pennsylvania: Municipal and Common Pleas Courts

More than 17 years have elapsed since we made our first overtures to the Philadelphia judiciary to discuss the guidelines idea and the possibility of conducting research to explore its feasibility in municipal court at the preliminary arraignment (initial-appearance) stage. After reviewing the results of the experimental research, the court leadership recommended that pretrial release guidelines be formally adopted as court policy, and the municipal court bench approved the recommendation. The chief judge and his court administrator set in place procedures to monitor the use of the guidelines as planned and to provide periodic feedback to the court as to their impact. Nearly immediately after the pretrial release guidelines were instituted, the judicial leadership successfully gained legislative authorization to create the position of "bail commissioner" to replace judges at the preliminary arraignment stage. The chief judge of municipal court argued for a law-trained position that would essentially employ the guidelines as designed, all under the supervision of the chief judge and his administrative staff.

Although the bail commissioner position was approved and implemented, the requirements that commissioners should be lawyers did not survive the legislative and political process. The strict control that the chief judge would exercise over appointing commissioners also did not survive considerations of political patronage in the Philadelphia courts. The result was the appointment of five or six commissioners, some of whom had excellent credentials and common sense, and some of whom had political connections. Nevertheless, the chief judge created a mechanism for monitoring their decisions carefully and enforcing the appropriate use of the guidelines. This included appointment of an administrative official whose major responsibility was to collect data relating to pretrial release decisions, the use of exceptions, the commissioner departures. There was a tendency for some appointees to choose to "go their own way" upon occasion, particularly in cases which they perceived to be likely to be highly publicized. Yet the administrative mechanism designed to monitor the guidelines seemed to be workable and allowed the chief judge to exercise supervision, particularly through the vehicle of periodic meetings with bail commissioners to review the guidelines use data. During this period, the pretrial services division became proficient in the guidelines information functions and has effectively continued those functions (even to this day). All in all, the implementation of the pretrial-release-guidelines system in municipal court seemed to approach the ideal.

In the mid-1980s, however, the ideal approach was severely tested by side effects of the changing crime picture, the war against drugs, and other unforeseen conditions in the Philadelphia's historically overcrowded correctional institutions and the backlog in its criminal courts. Institutional populations reached historical highs; the average length of time in confinement increased as criminal processing in the courts bogged down under the impact of the drug-related caseload. (Dispositions of felony drug cases in the court of common please increased more than 1500 percent between 1978 and 1990.) Crowding and conditions of confinement worsened to the point where, by the late 1986, the effectiveness of the pretrial-release-guidelines mechanism was nearly submerged by emergency release procedures ordered in a consent decree supervised by the federal court presiding over Philadelphia's crowding litigation.[4] In effect, the rules and release programs imposed by the consent decree in *Harris v. Reeves* superseded decisions made by the bail commissioners at the preliminary arraignment stage and rendered their efforts nearly meaningless. The rational approach to pretrial release innovated in the bail guidelines was submerged somewhere beneath layers of *ad hoc* emergency approaches. The moratorium on admissions also meant that, when the Philadelphia courts did set conditions of pretrial release for defendants, they lacked the ability to enforce those conditions with the threat that release could be revoked and defendants could be detained upon violation.

We maintained our involvement in Philadelphia after the completion of the original guidelines experiment in 1983 by conducting an evaluation of emergency release with the use of the bail guidelines framework[5] and by studying the jail population and sources of crowding in the mid-1980s.[6] At the close of the 1980s, the crowding situation had not improved, and, in response to the federal litigation, the City of Philadelphia agreed to develop a plan for alternatives to incarceration that would address conditions of confinement, that would adopt practices that would permit the justice system to live within the available confinement capacity, and that would construct a rational framework for managing the very large numbers of defendants and offenders who would be supervised at large in the community. In working with city and court officials on the plan,[7] we found that the processes responsible for pretrial release and detention once again became a central focus.

As part of our work in developing the alternatives plan, we conducted two studies of pretrial release, the most recent one nearing completion at the time of this writing. In doing so, we made several discoveries. One was that, despite many obstacles presented by the emergency release procedures, the pretrial services staff had continued steadfastly—and on faith—to prepare guidelines information for the commissioners at the preliminary arraignment stage, even though many of the decisions were overridden by emergency release procedures. Second, although the proportion of defendants released at the initial stage had changed little over time (about three-fourths were still released), the failure-to-appear rate had skyrocketed since the last time it had been studied, reaching roughly 50 percent of all defendants, and upwards of 80 percent of those gaining release under emergency release procedures. Third, the risk dimension of the original guidelines, which had not been validated since they were designed a decade ago, still classified Philadelphia defendants according to their probabilities of misconduct during pretrial release very well. Finally, the makeup of the criminal caseload of the Philadelphia courts and of the correctional populations in Philadelphia's jail system had become much more difficult. They involved much more serious cases, persons with more extensive criminal histories, and defendants who, according to the guidelines measure of risk, posed higher risks than previous populations.

In November 1992, Philadelphia's mayor appointed a task force chaired by the chief criminal judge in the Court of Common Pleas to redevelop and implement pretrial release guidelines as a first step toward implementing the plan for alternatives to incarceration. The task force included representatives of the mayor's office, court administrators, judges from the common pleas and municipal courts, representatives of the prosecutor's office, the public defender, pretrial services, and probation. Since its inception, we have assisted the task force in reexamining the issues associated with pretrial release and have drafted and revised a number of working models of new pretrial-release guidelines. The redrafting of the guidelines has focused on problems of public safety, attendance in court, and the impact of guidelines on the correctional population in Philadelphia's facilities. As of this writing, an analysis of the resource implications of the revised guidelines is underway prior to implementation planned for mid-1995. There is systemwide support for the implementation of a new guidelines system for improving release practices and as a centerpiece for resolving institutional crowding issues. The current process in Philadelphia coincides not only with the modernizing of jail space, but with the design and construction of a new criminal justice center (criminal courthouse). Thus the recent emphasis on pretrial release processing focuses on integration with related court processes and functions, management information needs related to court activities and the status of the correctional population, and the overall gatekeeping information-processing role to be played by Philadelphia's pretrial services agency in the future. In short, the current guidelines process in Philadelphia is addressing pretrial release and detention concerns in a much larger context than when the idea was first examined in the early 1980s and will be an important building block in efforts to manage the institutional population more effectively.

Some of the Lessons from the Pretrial-Release-Guidelines Experience

We have enjoyed a unique opportunity to pursue and examine an innovative idea in diverse settings and to observe its evolution over time. We have seen many developments affect the operation of pretrial release and detention and the supporting role of pretrial services agencies that have their roots in the bail reform efforts of the Vera Institute from the 1960s. Preventive detention laws of all sorts have become fairly widespread. The original law passed by Congress establishing preventive detention procedures for the District of Columbia in 1970 has been imitated, adapted, and, in some instances, "bastardized" in many states, with the result that we now see a wide range of approaches fostering a greater emphasis on the public safety implications of release and detention. In reviewing the federal preventive-detention law (the Federal Bail Reform Act of 1984), the U.S. Supreme Court has let it be known that public safety is an appropriate concern at the pretrial-release-decision stage. During the same period, we have seen an emphasis on drug testing at pretrial stages (tied to public safety concerns linking drugs to crime) advocated by two administrations. Despite its sponsorship by the U.S. Department of Justice, we have seen research fail to provide support for the claims that drug testing offers both an indispensable type of information for predicting the likelihood of defendant misconduct and an effective deterrent to crime by drug-involved defendants.[8] While pretrial services programs have prospered during this time in some locations, they have withered in many others, as the original aims of bail reform seem as elusive as ever, or even forgotten. Finally, bondsmen still play too large a role in the justice process and are, quite unbelievably, still a powerful lobby to be reckoned with.

With the luxury now of hindsight to assist our analysis, the following seem still to be true:

• Even after decades of bail reform, serious questions about the fairness and effectiveness of pretrial release in the United States have not been resolved. Continued reliance on financial bail as the currency of release decisions is a major reason. *Sub rosa* pretrial detention is the continued result, and the profiteering role of the bondsman still an unexplainable anachronism.

• Improvement in pretrial release and detention practices is in large part the responsibility of the judiciary. Chronic problems with pretrial release and detention in the United States will never be effectively addressed without judicial leadership and accountability in the pretrial release function.

• Either the judiciary will develop court-based approaches to improving management of the pretrial release function, or others (i.e., legislatures) will mandate their own versions of system improvements (and the history of such measures is not encouraging).

• The pretrial services mission is to "staff" the judicial pretrial release function and to provide the wherewithal to manage the fair and effective use of pretrial release and detention.

• As courts try to enter the information age, pretrial services agencies have a major responsibility to redefine their roles to serve as the gatekeepers of information for the criminal process as well as for pretrial-release and detention decisionmaking.

Given all this, the guidelines method appears to offer an important tool to criminal courts in their efforts to address pretrial release and detention problems.

Notes

1. The development of treatment drug courts in Miami, Portland, Seattle, Los Angeles, Las Vegas, Washington, and other cities, of domestic violence treatment courts in Miami and Seattle, and of other "multidisciplinary" community courts, such as the Midtown Manhattan misdemeanor court, suggests a new activism on the part of an increasingly involved judiciary.
2. Given the sordid history of bail bonding in the United States and the major repudiation of the use of compensated sureties by authorities as diverse as the U.S. Supreme Court, the American Bar Association, and not a few state legislatures, it is astounding to discover that bondsmen still thrive and take profit from the criminal process—and still form a powerful political lobby—at many locations. Bondsmen have always resisted efforts to reform bail and pretrial release practices because of the advocacy of release under nonfinancial conditions. Bondsmen saw early that successful bail reform would reduce the use of cash bail in the determination of pretrial release and hence their potential for profit.
3. All compliance data are from personal communication with Tom Morrison, head of pretrial services.
4. For a description of the crowding litigation in the court of common pleas and the federal district court in Philadelphia during the 1970s and 1980s, see Babcock (1990).

5. Goldkamp (1983).
6. Harris, Goldkamp, and Harland (1984).
7. Goldkamp and Harris (1992).
8. See, for example, Belenko and Mara-Drita (1988); Goldkamp, Gottfredson, and Weiland (1990); Britt et al. (1992); Goldkamp and Jones (1992); Jones and Goldkamp (1993); Kapsch and Sweeney (1990).

APPENDIX: Supplemental Tables and Figures

TABLE A.1

Background Data for Guidelines Formulation: Classification of Maricopa Felony Defendants According to Draft Release Guidelines, by Bail Decisions, Detention, Defendants' Performance, and Case-Processing Outcomes, June–July 1984

	Charge Severity: Least serious 1	2	3	4	5	Most serious 6
Lowest risk	Cell 1 (n = 6)	Cell 2 (n = 14)	Cell 3 (n = 28)	Cell 4 (n = 157)	Cell 5 (n = 67)	Cell 6 (n = 34)
	%ROR 100	%ROR 43	%ROR 64	%ROR 61	%ROR 24	%ROR 50
	Mdn $ (0)[a] 0	Mdn $ (0)[a] 68	Mdn $ (0)[a] 0	Mdn $ (0)[a] 0	Mdn $ (0)[a] 1507	Mdn $ (0)[a] 0
	IQ (0, 0) 0	IQ (0, 1781) 1781	IQ (0, 1096) 1096	IQ (0, 1370) 1370	IQ (0, 2740) 2740	IQ (0, 13700) 13700
	%Det > 1 day 0	%Det > 1 day 50	%Det > 1 day 32	%Det > 1 day 36	%Det > 1 day 60	%Det > 1 day 47
	%FTA 17	%FTA 0	%FTA 0	%FTA 1	%FTA 3	%FTA 0
	%Rearrest 0	%Rearrest 25	%Rearrest 10	%Rearrest 5	%Rearrest 0	%Rearrest 5
	%Failure 17	%Failure 25	%Failure 10	%Failure 6	%Failure 3	%Failure 5
	%Dropped 67	%Dropped 79	%Dropped 79	%Dropped 77	%Dropped 70	%Dropped 82
	Cell 7 (n = 30)	Cell 8 (n = 229)	Cell 9 (n = 328)	Cell 10 (n = 369)	Cell 11 (n = 143)	Cell 12 (n = 116)
	%ROR 80	%ROR 62	%ROR 55	%ROR 48	%ROR 41	%ROR 20
	Mdn $ (0)[a] 0	Mdn $ (0)[a] 0	Mdn $ (0)[a] 0	Mdn $ (0)[a] 206	Mdn $ (0)[a] 822	Mdn $ (0)[a] 3425
	IQ (0, 0) 0	IQ (0, 411) 411	IQ (0, 842) 842	IQ (0, 1370) 1370	IQ (0, 2740) 2740	IQ (685,12330) 11645
	%Det > 1 day 13	%Det > 1 day 30	%Det > 1 day 38	%Det > 1 day 48	%Det > 1 day 55	%Det > 1 day 76
	%FTA 4	%FTA 4	%FTA 4	%FTA 5	%FTA 5	%FTA 10
	%Rearrest 8	%Rearrest 10	%Rearrest 10	%Rearrest 12	%Rearrest 8	%Rearrest 15
	%Failure 11	%Failure 13	%Failure 13	%Failure 16	%Failure 13	%Failure 20
Probability	%Dropped 60	%Dropped 65	%Dropped 65	%Dropped 69	%Dropped 51	%Dropped 59
of flight and/or crime	Cell 13 (n = 4)	Cell 14 (n = 60)	Cell 15 (n = 110)	Cell 16 (n = 163)	Cell 17 (n = 71)	Cell 18 (n = 68)
	%ROR 25	%ROR 35	%ROR 26	%ROR 22	%ROR 18	%ROR 13
	Mdn $ (0)[a] 685	Mdn $ (0)[a] 500	Mdn $ (0)[a] 959	Mdn $ (0)[a] 1370	Mdn $ (0)[a] 1791	Mdn $ (0)[a] 4110
	IQ (0, 959) 959	IQ (0, 1370) 1370	IQ (0, 2055) 2055	IQ (274, 3000) 2726	IQ (479, 3836) 3357	IQ (1100, 20550)19450
	%Det > 1 day 75	%Det > 1 day 52	%Det > 1 day 64	%Det > 1 day 71	%Det > 1 day 77	%Det > 1 day 85
	%FTA 33	%FTA 3	%FTA 10	%FTA 20	%FTA 28	%FTA 5
	%Rearrest 68	%Rearrest 9	%Rearrest 12	%Rearrest 13	%Rearrest 21	%Rearrest 0
	%Failure 68	%Failure 9	%Failure 79	%Failure 29	%Failure 38	%Failure 5
	%Dropped 25	%Dropped 33	%Dropped 24	%Dropped 34	%Dropped 28	%Dropped 35
	Cell 19 (n = 1)	Cell 20 (n = 18)	Cell 21 (n = 31)	Cell 22 (n= 73)	Cell 23 (n = 36)	Cell 24 (n = 76)
	%ROR 100	%ROR 33	%ROR 10	%ROR 3	%ROR 6	%ROR 4
	Mdn $ (0)[a] 0	Mdn $ (0)[a] 548	Mdn $ (0)[a] 1370	Mdn $ (0)[a] 2740	Mdn $ (0)[a] 2055	Mdn $ (0)[a] 9042
	IQ (0, 0) 0	IQ (0, 1370) 1370	IQ (411, 2055) 1644	IQ (1370, 3425) 2055	IQ (1027, 5480) 4453	IQ (2055, 21920)19865
	%Det > 1 day 0	%Det > 1 day 50	%Det > 1 day 84	%Det > 1 day 92	%Det > 1 day 86	%Det > 1 day 85
	%FTA 100	%FTA 46	%FTA 27	%FTA 44	%FTA 50	%FTA 18
	%Rearrest 0	%Rearrest 39	%Rearrest 27	%Rearrest 22	%Rearrest 20	%Rearrest 29
	%Failure 100	%Failure 62	%Failure 54	%Failure 56	%Failure 45	%Failure 39
Highest risk	%Dropped 0	%Dropped 28	%Dropped 10	%Dropped 10	%Dropped 3	%Dropped 22

[a] Median bail calculated including $0.

TABLE A.2

Background Data for Guidelines Formulation: Classification of Dade Felony Defendants According to Draft Release Guidelines, by Bail Decisions, Detention, Defendants' Performance, and Case-Processing Outcomes, 1984

Probability of flight and/or crime	Charge Severity: Least serious 1	2	3	4	5	6	7	Most serious 8
Lowest risk	Cell 1 (n = 31)	Cell 2 (n = 67)	Cell 3 (n = 29)	Cell 4 (n = 28)	Cell 5 (n = 32)	Cell 6 (n = 39)	Cell 7 (n = 39)	Cell 8 (n = 28)
%Nonfinancial	90	87	79	93	91	87	88	22
Mdn $ (0)[a]	0	0	0	0	0	0	0	50000
%Det > 2 days	15	9	16	6	19	16	20	44
%FTA	12	2	6	6	11	0	5	6
%Rearrest	0	0	0	6	10	5	0	0
%Failure	11	2	6	11	15	5	5	6
%Bound down	10	23	32	22	10	0	12	0
%Dropped	45	35	58	44	52	56	36	33
	Cell 9 (n = 45)	Cell 10 (n = 131)	Cell 11 (n = 70)	Cell 12 (n = 71)	Cell 13 (n = 127)	Cell 14 (n = 79)	Cell 15 (n = 56)	Cell 16 (n = 63)
%Nonfinancial	89	77	78	72	76	86	77	40
Mdn $ (0)[a]	0	0	0	0	0	0	0	20000
%Det > 2 days	28	31	42	33	34	29	31	58
%FTA	15	6	11	11	8	11	9	14
%Rearrest	4	4	6	6	8	4	6	0
%Failure	19	10	14	16	15	13	13	14
%Bound down	17	28	42	37	21	8	14	5
%Dropped	45	57	51	54	56	51	39	20
	Cell 17 (n = 37)	Cell 18 (n = 105)	Cell 19 (n = 67)	Cell 20 (n = 67)	Cell 21 (n = 102)	Cell 22 (n = 50)	Cell 23 (n = 73)	Cell 24 (n = 73)
%Nonfinancial	59	64	76	67	69	72	66	50
Mdn $ (0)[a]	0	0	0	0	0	0	0	0
%Det > 2 days	54	47	46	49	45	37	47	47
%FTA	22	8	31	27	11	13	16	13
%Rearrest	18	10	10	13	9	4	3	3
%Failure	39	18	40	37	17	17	16	16
%Bound down	8	13	37	30	29	31	13	9
%Dropped	58	60	40	42	53	41	62	51
Highest risk	Cell 25 (n = 17)	Cell 26 (n = 42)	Cell 27 (n = 39)	Cell 28 (n = 42)	Cell 29 (n = 67)	Cell 30 (n = 31)	Cell 31 (n = 34)	Cell 2 (n = 59)
%Nonfinancial	64	70	56	65	48	37	48	36
Mdn $ (0)[a]	0	0	0	0	2000	4500	1500	9000
%Det > 2 days	64	44	84	74	72	70	64	81
%FTA	67	6	40	23	19	29	11	14
%Rearrest	40	18	40	15	12	14	22	0
%Failure	83	18	53	31	26	36	33	13
%Bound down	46	15	44	19	16	10	5	3
%Dropped	55	59	36	30	56	35	68	41

[a] Median bail calculated including $0.

TABLE A.3

Background Data for Guidelines Formulation: Classification of Boston Municipal Court Defendants According to Draft Release Guidelines, by Bail Decisions, Detention, Defendants' Performance, and Case-Processing Outcomes, April–October 1984

	Charge Severity: Least serious 1		2		3		Most serious 4	
Lowest risk	Cell 1 (n = 668)		Cell 2 (n = 95)		Cell 3 (n = 10)		Cell 4 (n = 7)	
	%Nonfinancial	89	%Nonfinancial	70	%Nonfinancial	100	%Nonfinancial	0
	Mdn $	100	Mdn $	100	Mdn $	---	Mdn $	300
	Mdn $ (0)[a]	0	Mdn $ (0)[a]	0	Mdn $ (0)[a]	0	Mdn $ (0)[a]	300
	%Det > 1 day	7	%Det > 1 day	25	%Det > 1 day	0	%Det > 1 day	15
	%FTA	16	%FTA	17	%FTA	30	%FTA	42
	%DA Rec.	3	%DA Rec.	27	%DA Rec.	0	%DA Rec.	44
	%Bindover	0	%Bindover	6	%Bindover	0	%Bindover	44
	%Dropped (90 days)	14	%Dropped (90 days)	8	%Dropped (90 days)	30	%Dropped (90 days)	15
	Cell 5 (n = 1800)		Cell 6 (n = 470)		Cell 7 (n = 53)		Cell 8 (n = 77)	
	%Nonfinancial	81	%Nonfinancial	61	%Nonfinancial	36	%Nonfinancial	18
	Mdn $	100	Mdn $	200	Mdn $	200	Mdn $	250
	Mdn $ (0)[a]	0	Mdn $ (0)[a]	0	Mdn $ (0)[a]	100	Mdn $ (0)[a]	200
	%Det > 1 day	13	%Det > 1 day	25	%Det > 1 day	35	%Det > 1 day	40
	%FTA	28	%FTA	31	%FTA	19	%FTA	24
	%DA Rec.	6	%DA Rec.	26	%DA Rec.	27	%DA Rec.	43
	%Bindover	0	%Bindover	4	%Bindover	15	%Bindover	45
Probability of flight and/or crime	%Dropped (90 days)	13	%Dropped (90 days)	12	%Dropped (90 days)	28	%Dropped (90 days)	21
	Cell 9 (n = 780)		Cell 10 (n = 199)		Cell 11 (n = 76)		Cell 12 (n = 64)	
	%Nonfinancial	69	%Nonfinancial	41	%Nonfinancial	40	%Nonfinancial	41
	Mdn $	100	Mdn $	200	Mdn $	100	Mdn $	300
	Mdn $ (0)[a]	0	Mdn $ (0)[a]	100	Mdn $ (0)[a]	100	Mdn $ (0)[a]	100
	%Det > 1 day	27	%Det > 1 day	41	%Det > 1 day	43	%Det > 1 day	45
	%FTA	44	%FTA	33	%FTA	29	%FTA	33
	%DA Rec.	11	%DA Rec.	28	%DA Rec.	43	%DA Rec.	53
	%Bindover	1	%Bindover	10	%Bindover	12	%Bindover	32
	%Dropped (90 days)	9	%Dropped (90 days)	18	%Dropped (90 days)	21	%Dropped (90 days)	21
	Cell 13 (n = 125)		Cell 14 (n = 66)		Cell 15 (n = 29)		Cell 16 (n = 43)	
	%Nonfinancial	68	%Nonfinancial	37	%Nonfinancial	15	%Nonfinancial	3
	Mdn $	250	Mdn $	150	Mdn $	300	Mdn $	500
	Mdn $ (0)[a]	0	Mdn $ (0)[a]	100	Mdn $ (0)[a]	300	Mdn $ (0)[a]	500
	%Det > 1 day	32	%Det > 1 day	41	%Det > 1 day	69	%Det > 1 day	79
	%FTA	2	%FTA	36	%FTA	41	%FTA	30
	%DA Rec.	13	%DA Rec.	16	%DA Rec.	34	%DA Rec.	49
	%Bindover	2	%Bindover	12	%Bindover	31	%Bindover	58
Highest risk	%Dropped (90 days)	13	%Dropped (90 days)	14	%Dropped (90 days)	10	%Dropped (90 days)	9

[a] Median bail is calculated including $0.

TABLE A.4

The Distribution of 1984 Maricopa County Felony Defendants within Guidelines Categories: Without Taking into Account Special Severity Factors

Charge severity: Least serious ⟷ Most serious

Probability of flight and/or crime: Lowest risk (1) ⟷ Highest risk (4)

	1	2	3	4	5	6
1 (Lowest risk)	0.3 % (n=7) OR/ Standard	0.7% (n=15) OR/ Standard	1.2% (n=26) OR/ Standard	10.0% (n=222) OR/ Standard	**0.4% (n=9) OR/Special to $750**	1.9% (n=43) $1,000 to 5,000
2	1.7% (n=38) OR/ Standard	10.4% (n=232) OR/ Standard	15.6% (n=348) OR/ Standard	19.4 (n=431) OR/ Special	3.7% (n=83) $500 to $1,500	4.9% (n=109) $3,000 to $7,500
3	0.2% (n=5) OR/ Standard	3.0% (n=66) OR/ Standard	**5.6% (n=125) OR/Special to $750**	7.7% (n=171) $500 to $1,500	2.4% (n=53) $1,000 to $2,500	1.3% (n=29) $5,000 to $10,000
4 (Highest risk)	0% (n=1) OR/ Special	**0.9% (n=19) OR/ Special to $500**	1.6% (n=35) $500 to $3,500	3.8% (n=85) $1,500 to $3,500	1.3% (n=29) $2,000 to $5,000	2.1% (n=46) $10,000 to $15,000

Total n=2,232

TABLE A.5

The Distribution of 1984 Maricopa County Defendants within Guidelines Categories: Taking into Account Special Severity Factors

Probability of flight and/or crime (Lowest risk → Highest risk)	Charge severity (Least serious → Most serious): 1	2	3	4	5	6
1	0.3 % (n=6) OR/ Standard	0.6% (n=14) OR/ Standard	1.2% (n=28) OR/ Standard	7.0% (n=157) OR/ Standard	**3.0% (n=67) OR/Special to $750**	1.5% (n=34) $1,000 to 5,000
2	1.3% (n=30) OR/ Standard	10.3% (n=229) OR/ Standard	14.7% (n=328) OR/ Standard	16.5% (n=369) OR/ Special	6.4% (n=143) $500 to $1,500	5.2% (n=116) $3,000 to $7,500
3	0.2% (n=4) OR/ Standard	2.7% (n=60) OR/ Standard	**4.9% (n=110) OR/Special to $750**	7.3% (n=163) $500 to $1,500	3.2% (n=71) $1,000 to $2,500	3.0% (n=68) $5,000 to $10,000
4	0% (n=1) OR/ Special	**0.8% (n=18) OR/ Special to $500**	1.4% (n=31) $500 to $1,500	3.3% (n=73) $1,500 to $3,500	1.6% (n=36) $2,000 to $5,000	3.4% (n=76) $10,000 to $15,000

Total n=2,232

TABLE A.6

Estimating the Impact of Guidelines: Comparison of Initial-Appearance Decisions Projected under Guidelines with Past Decisions for Maricopa County Felony Defendants, 1984

	Decision category			
Decision approach	Financial (%)[a]	Nonfinancial total (%)[b]	Nonfinancial standard (%)	Nonfinancial special (%)
Past (1984)[c]	60	40	24	16
Guidelines without special severity	31	69	45	24
Guidelines with special severity	36	64	39	25

[a]Cases bondable by law but denied bond in practice are included in this category.

[b]This category represents the total of cases receiving or possibly receiving nonfinancial bond, whether "special" or "standard." Included as well are the guidelines categories which suggest a choice of either special conditions of release or low amounts of bond. In practice, in these categories bond could be decided as either nonfinancial or secured financial.

[c]This category reports what the actual bond decisions were for defendants in our study of 1984 felony defendants looked at using the guidelines categories for comparison. Thus, this table shows what defendants in the past received in given guidelines categories compared to what they would receive if guidelines had been in effect at the time.

TABLE A.7

Estimating the Impact of Guidelines on the Use of Pretrial Detention among Felony Defendants in Maricopa County Superior Court

	N	Percent	N	Percent	N	Percent	N	Percent	N	Percent	N	Percent
1984	>1 day (0)	0	>1 day (7)	50.0	>1 day (9)	32.1	>1 day (57)	37.0	>1 day (40)	59.7	>1 day (16)	47.1
	>2 days (0)	0	>2 days (7)	50.0	>2 days (9)	32.1	>2 days (56)	36.4	>2 days (38)	56.7	>2 days (16)	47.1
	90 days (0)	0	90 days (6)	42.9	90 days (9)	32.1	90 days (52)	33.8	90 days (35)	52.2	90 days (14)	41.2
Projected	>1 day (0)	0	>1 day (0)	0	>1 day (0)	0	>1 day (0)	0	>1 day (58.3)	87.0	>1 day (31.3)	92.1
	>2 days (0)	0	>2 days (0)	0	>2 days (0)	0	>2 days (0)	0	>2 days (57.3)	85.5	>2 days (30.8)	90.6
	90 days (0)	0	90 days (0)	0	90 days (0)	0	90 days (0)	0	90 days (52.1)	77.8	90 days (26.1)	77.8
	Cell (6)	100.0	Cell (14)	100.0	Cell (28)	100.0	Cell (154)	100.0	Cell (67)	100.0	Cell (34)	100.0
		OR/Standard		OR/Standard		OR/Standard		OR/Standard		OR/Special to $750		$5,000
1984	>1 day (4)	13.3	>1 day (68)	30.1	>1 day (124)	38.0	>1 day (179)	49.4	>1 day (78)	55.3	>1 day (88)	75.9
	>2 days (4)	13.3	>2 days (67)	29.6	>2 days (121)	37.1	>2 days (176)	48.6	>2 days (76)	53.9	>2 days (88)	75.9
	90 days (4)	13.3	90 days (58)	25.7	90 days (110)	33.7	90 days (159)	43.9	90 days (65)	46.1	90 days (76)	65.5
Projected	>1 day (0)	0	>1 day (0)	0	>1 day (0)	0	>1 day (0)	0	>1 day (129.9)	92.1	>1 day (113.4)	97.8
	>2 days (0)	0	>2 days (0)	0	>2 days (0)	0	>2 days (0)	0	>2 days (127.7)	90.6	>2 days (111.4)	96.0
	90 days (0)	0	90 days (0)	0	90 days (0)	0	90 days (0)	0	90 days (109.7)	77.8	90 days (90.6)	78.1
	Cell (30)	100.0	Cell (226)	100.0	Cell (326)	100.0	Cell (362)	100.0	Cell (141)	100.0	Cell (116)	100.0
		OR/Standard		OR/Standard		OR/Standard		OR/Special		$1,500		$7,500
1984	>1 day (3)	75.0	>1 day (31)	51.7	>1 day (71)	65.1	>1 day (116)	71.2	>1 day (54)	77.1	>1 day (58)	86.6
	>2 days (3)	75.0	>2 days (31)	51.7	>2 days (68)	62.4	>2 days (115)	70.6	>2 days (54)	77.1	>2 days (56)	83.6
	90 days (1)	25.0	90 days (26)	43.3	90 days (62)	56.9	90 days (93)	57.1	90 days (41)	58.6	90 days (47)	70.1
Projected	>1 day (0)	0	>1 day (0)	0	>1 day (94.8)	87.0	>1 day (150.1)	92.1	>1 day (64.5)	92.1	>1 day (65.5)	97.8
	>2 days (0)	0	>2 days (0)	0	>2 days (93.2)	85.5	>2 days (147.7)	90.6	>2 days (63.4)	90.6	>2 days (64.3)	96.0
	90 days (0)	0	90 days (0)	0	90 days (84.8)	77.8	90 days (126.9)	77.8	90 days (54.5)	77.8	90 days (52.3)	78.1
	Cell (4)	100.0	Cell (60)	100.0	Cell (109)	100.0	Cell (163)	100.0	Cell (70)	100.0	Cell (67)	100.0
		OR/Standard		OR/Standard		OR/Special to $750		$1,500		$2,500		$10,000
1984	>1 day (0)	0	>1 day (9)	52.9	>1 day (26)	86.7	>1 day (67)	91.8	>1 day (31)	86.1	>1 day (65)	89.0
	>2 days (0)	0	>2 days (9)	52.9	>2 days (25)	83.3	>2 days (67)	91.8	>2 days (31)	86.1	>2 days (63)	86.3
	90 days (0)	0	90 days (5)	29.4	90 days (20)	66.7	90 days (55)	75.3	90 days (26)	64.9	90 days (45)	61.6
Projected	>1 day (0)	0	>1 day (11.2)	65.7	>1 day (27.6)	92.1	>1 day (67.2)	92.1	>1 day (33.2)	92.1	>1 day (71.4)	97.8
	>2 days (0)	0	>2 days (10.8)	63.4	>2 days (27.2)	90.6	>2 days (66.1)	90.6	>2 days (32.6)	90.6	>2 days (70.1)	96.0
	90 days (0)	0	90 days (9.1)	53.7	90 days (23.3)	77.8	90 days (56.8)	77.8	90 days (28.0)	77.8	90 days (57.0)	78.1
	Cell (1)	100.0	Cell (17)	100.0	Cell (30)	100.0	Cell (73)	100.0	Cell (36)	100.0	Cell (73)	100.0
		OR/Special		OR/Special to $500		$1,500		$3,500		$5,000		$15,000

	N	Percent
1984 total	(2,207)	100.0
Det >1 day	(1,201)	54.4
Det >2 days	(1,180)	53.5
Det 90 days	(1,008)	45.7

	N	Percent
Projected total	(2,207)	100.0
Det >1 day	(918.4)	41.6
Det >2 days	(902.6)	40.9
Det 90 days	(771.4)	34.9

Treating 3 OR/Special to cash cells as non-cash	N	Percent
Det >1 day	(754.1)	34.2
Det >2 days	(741.1)	33.6
Det 90 days	(625.4)	28.3

Key

- >1 day = Detained more than 1 day
- >2 days = Detained more than 2 days
- 90 days = Detained throughout

Guidelines ranges

- OR/Standard = OR with routine conditions
- OR/Special = OR with restrictive conditions
- OR/Special to $750 = choice: OR or low bond
- Cash amount = Upper limit guidelines range

Note: The estimates of the impact of guidelines assumes 100 percent compliance with guidelines and assumes that judges would select maximum bail amounts permitted in each category.

TABLE A.8

Estimating the Impact of Guidelines on Jail Days Associated with the Processing of Entering Felony Defendants in Maricopa County Superior Court

1984 Projected	Mn = 0.3, Sum = 2.0 Mn = 0, Sum = 0 (n=7) OR/Standard	Mn = 41.5, Sum = 581.0 Mn = 0, Sum = 0 (n=14) OR/Standard	Mn = 29.1, Sum = 816.0 Mn = 0, Sum = 0 (n=28) OR/Standard	Mn = 30.8, Sum = 4,748.0 Mn = 0, Sum = 0 (n= 154) OR/Standard	Mn = 47.9, Sum = 3,208.0 Mn = 71.0, Sum = 4,757.3 (n=67) OR/Special to $750	Mn = 38.2, Sum = 1,299.0 Mn = 72.2, Sum = 2,455.7 (n=34) $5,000
1984 Projected	Mn = 12.2, Sum = 367.0 Mn = 0, Sum = 0 (n=30) OR/Standard	Mn = 23.7, Sum = 5,348.0 Mn = 0, Sum = 0 (n=226) OR/Standard	Mn = 30.7, Sum = 9,996.0 Mn = 0, Sum = 0 (n=326) OR/Standard	Mn = 40.3, Sum = 14,594.0 Mn = 0, Sum = 0 (n=362) OR/Special	Mn = 43.1, Sum = 6,075.0 Mn = 72.2, Sum = 10,184.1 (n=141) $1,500	Mn = 62.6, Sum = 7,264.0 Mn = 74.5, Sum = 8,639.0 (n=116) $7,500
1984 Projected	Mn = 26.0, Sum = 104.0 Mn = 0, Sum = 0 (n=4) OR/Standard	Mn = 40.8, Sum = 2,451.0 Mn = 0, Sum = 0 (n=60) OR/Standard	Mn = 52.3, Sum = 5,702.0 Mn = 71.0, Sum = 7,739.5 (n=109) OR/Special to $750	Mn = 54.2, Sum = 8,832.0 Mn = 72.2, Sum = 11,773.2 (n=163) $1,500	Mn = 57.3, Sum = 4,012.0 Mn = 72.2, Sum = 5,056.0 (n=70) $2,500	Mn = 65.0, Sum = 4,355.0 Mn = 74.5, Sum = 989.8 (n=67) $10,000
1984 Projected	Mn = 1.0, Sum = 1.0 Mn = 0, Sum = 0 (n=1) OR/Special	Mn = 28.5, Sum = 485.0 Mn = 49.7, Sum = 844.3 (n=17) OR/Special to $500	Mn = 62.3, Sum = 1,869.0 Mn = 72.2, Sum = 2,166.8 (n=30) $1,500	Mn = 71.9, Sum = 5,252.0 Mn = 72.2, Sum = 5, 272.6 (n=73) $3,500	Mn = 67.2, Sum = 2,420.0 Mn = 72.2, Sum = 2,600.2 (n=36) $5,000	Mn = 60.7, Sum = 4,431.0 Mn = 74.5, Sum = 5,436.6 (n=73) $15,000

1984 total defendants (n=2,207)
Total jail days = 94,211
Mean jail days = 42.7

Projected total defendants (n=2,207)
Projected total jail days = 71,915.1
Projected mean jail days = 32.6

Using 3 OR/Special to cash categories as non-cash
Projected total jail days = 58,574.0
Projected mean jail days = 26.5

Note: The estimates of the impact of guidelines assumes 100 percent compliance with guidelines and assumes that judges would select maximum bail amounts permitted in each category. Sums of jail days were calculated on unrounded means.

TABLE A.9

Estimating the Impact of Guidelines: Comparison of Bond-Hearing Decisions Projected under Versions of Guidelines with Past Decisions for Dade County Felony Defendants, 1984

	Decision category				
Decision approach	Financial (%)	Nonfinancial total[a] (%)	Nonfinancial standard (%)	Nonfinancial special (%)	Special to bond (%)
Past (1984)[b]	31	69	49	20	n/a
Version I guidelines[b]	23	77	39	28	10
Version II guidelines[b]	19	81	39	31	11
Detention population (1985) under Version I guidelines[c]	50	50	12	25	13

[a]This category represents the total of cases receiving or possibly receiving nonfinancial bond, whether "special" or "standard." Included as well are the guidelines categories which suggest a choice of either special conditions of release or low amounts of bond. In practice, in these categories, bond could be decided as either nonfinancial or secured financial.

[b]$n = 1840$.

[c]$n = 203$.

TABLE A.10

Estimating the Impact of Guidelines (Version II) on the Use of Pretrial Detention among Entering Felony Defendants in Dade County Circuit Court

	N	Percent	N	Percent	N	Percent	N	Percent	N	Percent	N	Percent	N	Percent	N	Percent
1984	>1 day (8)	25.0	>1 day (12)	18.6	>1 day (8)	26.3	>1 day (3)	11.1	>1 day (9)	28.6	>1 day (11)	28.0	>1 day (11)	28.0	>1 day (14)	50.0
	>2 days (5)	15.0	>2 days (6)	9.3	>2 days (5)	15.8	>2 days (2)	5.6	>2 days (6)	19.0	>2 days (6)	16.0	>2 days (8)	20.0	>2 days (12)	44.4
	90 days (3)	10.0	90 days (3)	4.7	90 days (5)	15.8	90 days (0)	0	90 days (2)	4.8	90 days (5)	12.0	90 days (5)	12.0	90 days (2)	5.6
Projected	>1 day (0)	0	>1 day (0)	0	>1 day (0)	0	>1 day (0)	0	>1 day (0)	0	>1 day (0)	0	>1 day (11.4)	29.3	>1 day (25.3)	90.2
	>2 days (0)	0	>2 days (0)	0	>2 days (0)	0	>2 days (0)	0	>2 days (0)	0	>2 days (0)	0	>2 days (8.3)	21.3	>2 days (24.3)	86.8
	90 days (0)	0	90 days (0)	0	90 days (0)	0	90 days (0)	0	90 days (0)	0	90 days (0)	0	90 days (0)	0	90 days (13.9)	49.6
	Cell (31)	100.0	Cell (67)	100.0	Cell (29)	100.0	Cell (28)	100.0	Cell (32)	100.0	Cell (39)	100.0	Cell (39)	100.0	Cell (28)	100.0
	PTS/Standard		PTS/Standard		PTS/Standard		PTS/Standard		PTS/Standard		PTS/Standard		PTS/Standard		$2,000	
1984	>1 day (15)	34.5	>1 day (48)	36.5	>1 day (32)	46.7	>1 day (26)	37.0	>1 day (50)	39.0	>1 day (28)	35.3	>1 day (20)	36.1	>1 day (40)	63.4
	>2 days (12)	27.6	>2 days (40)	30.6	>2 days (29)	42.2	>2 days (23)	32.6	>2 days (43)	34.1	>2 days (23	29.4	>2 days (17)	30.6	>2 days (37)	58.5
	90 days (5)	10.3	90 days (22)	16.5	90 days (15)	22.2	90 days (12)	17.4	90 days (26)	20.7	90 days (8)	9.8	90 days (6)	11.1	90 days (9)	14.6
Projected	>1 day (0)	0	>1 day (0)	0	>1 day (0)	0	>1 day (0)	0	>1 day (0)	0	>1 day (0)	0	>1 day (0)	0	>1 day (56.8)	90.2
	>2 days (0)	0	>2 days (0)	0	>2 days (0)	0	>2 days (0)	0	>2 days (0)	0	>2 days (0)	0	>2 days (0)	0	>2 days (54.7)	86.8
	90 days (0)	0	90 days (0)	0	90 days (0)	0	90 days (0)	0	90 days (0)	0	90 days (0)	0	90 days (0)	0	90 days (31.2)	49.6
	Cell (45)	100.0	Cell (131)	100.0	Cell (70)	100.0	Cell (71)	100.0	Cell (127)	100.0	Cell (79)	100.0	Cell (56)	100.0	Cell (63)	100.0
	PTS/Standard		PTS/Standard		PTS/Standard		PTS/Standard		PTS/Standard		PTS/Special		PTS/Special		$3,00	
1984	>1 day (20)	54.2	>1 day (53)	50.0	>1 day (34)	51.2	>1 day (40)	60.5	>1 day (56)	54.5	>1 day (23)	46.9	>1 day (40)	55.3	>1 day (43)	59.6
	>2 days (20)	54.2	>2 days (50)	47.1	>2 days (31)	46.2	>2 days (32)	48.8	>2 days (46)	45.5	>2 days (19)	37.5	>2 days (34)	46.8	>2 days (39)	53.2
	90 days (9)	25.0	90 days (28)	26.5	90 days (20)	30.2	90 days (20)	30.2	90 days (29)	28.8	90 days (12)	25.0	90 days (15)	21.3	90 days (25)	34.0
Projected	>1 day (0)	0	>1 day (0)	0	>1 day (0)	0	>1 day (0)	92.1	>1 day (0)	0	>1 day (25)	50.0	>1 day (47.2)	64.7	>1 day (65.9)	90.2
	>2 days (0)	0	>2 days (0)	0	>2 days (0)	0	>2 days (0)	90.6	>2 days (0)	0	>2 days (25)	50.0	>2 days (42.9)	58.8	>2 days (63.4)	86.8
	90 days (0)	0	90 days (0)	0	90 days (0)	0	90 days (0)	77.8	90 days (0)	0	90 days (12.5)	25.0	90 days (25.8)	35.3	90 days (36.2)	49.6
	Cell (37)	100.0	Cell (105)	100.0	Cell (67)	100.0	Cell (67)	100.0	Cell (102)	100.0	Cell (50)	100.0	Cell (73)	100.0	Cell (73)	100.0
	PTS/Special		PTS/Special		PTS/Special		PTS/Special		PTS/Special		PTS/Special to $500		PTS/Special to $1,000		$5,000	
1984	>1 day (11)	63.6	>1 day (19)	44.4	>1 day (26)	68.0	>1 day (34)	81.5	>1 day (51)	76.7	>1 day (23)	75.0	>1 day (25)	72.7	>1 day (50)	84.2
	>2 days (11)	63.6	>2 days (19)	44.4	>2 days (25)	64.0	>2 days (31)	74.1	>2 days (48)	72.1	>2 days (22)	70.0	>2 days (22)	63.6	>2 days (48)	81.6
	90 days (8)	45.5	90 days (15)	37.0	90 days (15)	40.0	90 days (20)	51.9	90 days (25)	37.2	90 days (9)	30.0	90 days (20)	59.1	90 days (36)	60.5
Projected	>1 day (0)	0	>1 day (0)	0	>1 day (25.2)	64.7	>1 day (37.9)	90.2	>1 day (60.4)	90.2	>1 day (28.0)	90.2	>1 day (30.7)	90.2	>1 day (53.2)	90.2
	>2 days (0)	0	>2 days (0)	0	>2 days (22.9)	58.8	>2 days (36.5)	86.8	>2 days (58.2)	86.8	>2 days (26.9)	86.8	>2 days (29.5)	86.8	>2 days (52.3)	88.7
	90 days (0)	0	90 days (0)	0	90 days (13.8)	35.3	90 days (20.8)	49.6	90 days (33.2)	49.6	90 days (33.2)	49.6	90 days (16.9)	49.6	90 days (29.3)	49.6
	Cell (17)	100.0	Cell (42)	100.0	Cell (39)	100.0	Cell (42)	100.0	Cell (67)	100.0	Cell (31)	100.0	Cell (34)	100.0	Cell (59)	100.0
	PTS/Special		PTS/Special		PTS/Special to $750		PTS/Special to $1,500		$3,500		$4,500		$5,000		$11,000	

	N	Percent
1984 total	(1,840)	100.0
Det >1 day	(883)	48.0
Det >2 days	(771)	41.9
Det 90 days	(434)	23.6

	N	Percent
Projected total	(1,840)	100.0
Det >1 day	(455.6)	24.8
Det >2 days	(436.6)	23.7
Det 90 days	(248.9)	13.5

Treating 4 PTS/Special to cash cells as non-cash	N	Percent
Det >1 day	(320.3)	17.4
Det >2 days	(309.3)	16.8
Det 90 days	(176.0)	9.6

Key

>1 day = Detained more than 1 day
>2 days = Detained more than 2 days
90 days = Detained throughout

Guidelines ranges

PTS/Standard = OR with routine conditions
PTS/Special = OR with restrictive conditions
PTS/Special to $750 = choice: OR or low bond

Note: The estimates of the impact of guidelines assumes 100 percent compliance with guidelines and assumes that judges would select maximum bail amounts permitted in each category. The 1984 Dade sample includes 88 cases (136 weighted) of defendants who received OR ($0 bond) but were released to programs from which they were subsequently rejected. They appear, therefore, as not having been released.

TABLE A.11

Estimating the Impact of Guidelines: Comparison of Arraignment Decisions Projected under Guidelines with Past Decisions for Boston Municipal Court Defendants, 1984

	Decision category			
Decisions approach	Financial (%)	Nonfinancial total (%)	Nonfinancial standard (%)	Nonfinancial special (%)
Past (1984)	29	71	71	0
Guidelines (Version I)	5	95	56	39
(Version II)	8	92	56	36[a]

[a]Percentages treating ROR/special to low bail categories as financial.

TABLE A.12

Estimating the Impact of Guidelines on the Use of Pretrial Detention among Entering Defendants

	N	Percent	N	Percent	N	Percent	N	Percent
1984	>1 day (45)	6.8	>1 day (23)	24.5	>1 day (0)	0	>1 day (1)	14.5
	>2 days (7)	2	>2 days (3)	3.0	>2 days (0)	0	>2 days (0)	0
	90 days (4)	1	90 days (3)	3.0	90 days (0)	0	90 days (0)	0
Projected	>1 day (0)	0	>1 day (0)	0	>1 day (0)	0	>1 day (2.7)	39.1
	>2 days (0)	0	>2 days (0)	0	>2 days (0)	0	>2 days (0.9)	12.2
	90 days (0)	0	90 days (0)	0	90 days (0)	0	90 days (2.1)	30.6
	Cell (668)	100.0	Cell (95)	100.0	Cell (10)	100.0	Cell (7)	100.0
	ROR/Standard		ROR/Standard		ROR/Standard		$300	
1984	>1 day (238)	13.2	>1 day (119)	25.3	>1 day (19)	35.1	>1 day (31)	39.9
	>2 days (150)	8.3	>2 days (92)	19.5	>2 days (12)	22.3	>2 days (24)	30.9
	90 days (60)	3.6	90 days (26)	5.6	90 days (7)	12.8	90 days (6)	7.8
Projected	>1 day (0)	0	>1 day (0)	0	>1 day (0)	0	>1 day (30.1)	39.1
	>2 days (0)	0	>2 days (0)	0	>2 days (0)	0	>2 days (23.6)	30.6
	90 days (0)	0	90 days (0)	0	90 days (0)	0	90 days (9.4)	12.2
	Cell (1800)	100.0	Cell (470)	100.0	Cell (53)	100.0	Cell (77)	100.0
	ROR/Standard		ROR/Special		ROR/Special		$450	
1984	>1 day (214)	27.4	>1 day (81)	40.7	>1 day (33)	42.9	>1 day (29)	44.7
	>2 days (139)	17.8	>2 days (55)	27.5	>2 days (27)	35.0	>2 days (27)	41.6
	90 days (58)	7.4	90 days (18)	8.8	90 days (11)	14.4	90 days (8)	12.4
	>1 day (0)	0						
	>2 days (0)	0	>1 day (0)	0	>1 day (29.7)	39.1	>1 day (44.5)	69.6
Projected	90 days (0)	0	>2 days (0)	0	>2 days (23.3)	30.6	>2 days (42.2)	65.9
	Cell (780)	100.0	90 days (0)	0	90 days (9.3)	12.2	90 days (20.3)	31.7
			Cell (199)	100.0	Cell (76)	100.0	Cell (64)	100.0
	ROR/Special		ROR/Special		ROR/Special to $200		$600	
1984	>1 day (40)	31.8	>1 day (27)	40.5	>1 day (20)	68.8	>1 day (34)	79.2
	>2 days (34)	27.2	>2 days (27)	40.5	>2 days (17)	58.5	>2 days (33)	76.8
	90 days (15)	11.7	90 days (12)	18.0	90 days (7)	24.2	90 days (13)	30.5
Projected	>1 day (0)	0	>1 day (25.8)	39.1	>1 day (20.2)	69.6	>1 day (29.9)	69.6
	>2 days (0)	0	>2 days (20.2)	30.6	>2 days (19.1)	65.9	>2 days (28.3)	65.9
	90 days (0)	0	90 days (8.1)	12.2	90 days (9.2)	31.7	90 days (13.6)	31.7
	Cell (125)	100.0	Cell (66)	100.0	Cell (29)	100.0	Cell (43)	100.0
	ROR/Special		ROR/Special to $200		$600		$1,000	

	N	Percent
1984 total	(4,562)	100.0
Det >1 day	(954)	20.9
Det >2 days	(647)	14.2
Det 90 days	(248)	5.4

	N	Percent
Projected total	(4,562)	100.0
Det >1 day	(182.9)	4.0
Det >2 days	(158.8)	3.5
Det 90 days	(70.8)	1.6

Treating 2 ROR/Special to cash cells as non-cash	N	Percent
Det >1 day	(127.4)	2.8
Det >2 days	(115.3)	2.6
Det 90 days	(53.4)	1.2

Key

>1 day = Detained more than 1 day
>2 days = Detained more than 2 days
90 days = Detained throughout

Guidelines ranges
ROR/Standard = OR with routine conditions
ROR/Special = OR with restrictive conditions
ROR/Special to $750 = choice: OR or low bond

Note: The estimates of the impact of guidelines assumes 100 percent compliance with guidelines and assumes that judges would select maximum bail amounts permitted in each category.

TABLE A.13

Estimating the Impact of Guidelines on Jail Days Associated with the Processing of Entering Defendants in Boston Municipal Court

1984	Mn = 1.3 Sum = 889.1	Mn = 0.6 Sum = 57.0	Mn = 0.3 Sum = 2.9	Mn = 0.4 Sum = 3.0
Projected	Mn = 0 Sum = 0	Mn = 0 Sum = 0	Mn = 0 Sum = 0	Mn = 5.7 Sum = 40.6
	(n=668) ROR/Standard	(n=95) ROR/Standard	(n=10) ROR/Standard	(n=7) $300
1984	Mn = 3.3 Sum = 5,938.3	Mn = 5.2 Sum = 2,462.1	Mn = 3.2 Sum = 168.9	Mn = 7.6 Sum = 582.3
Projected	Mn = 0 Sum = 0	Mn = 0 Sum = 0	Mn = 0 Sum = 0	Mn = 5.7 Sum = 446.6
	(n=1,800) ROR/Standard	(n=470) ROR/Special	(n=53) ROR/Special	(n=77) $450
1984	Mn = 3.7 Sum = 2,880.6	Mn = 6.8 Sum = 1,347.9	Mn = 10.1 Sum = 768.4	Mn = 15.6 Sum = 1,003.9
Projected	Mn = 0 Sum = 0	Mn = 0 Sum = 0	Mn = 5.7 Sum = 440.8	Mn = 19.5 Sum = 1,248.0
	(n=125) ROR/Special	(n=199) ROR/Special	(n=76) ROR/Special to $200	(n=64) $600
1984	Mn = 8.8 Sum = 1,101.2	Mn = 9.8 Sum = 642.0	Mn = 14.3 Sum = 414.2	Mn = 36.7 Sum = 1,563.9
Projected	Mn = 0 Sum = 0	Mn = 5.7 Sum = 382.8	Mn = 19.5 Sum = 565.5	Mn = 19.5 Sum = 838.5
	(n=125) ROR/Special	(n=66) ROR/Special to $200	(n=29) $600	(n=43) $1,000

1984 total defendants (n=4,562)
Total jail days = 19,825.7
Mean jail days = 4.3

Projected total defendants (n=4,562)
Projected total jail days = 3,962.8
Projected mean jail days = 0.9

Using ROR/Special to cash categories as non-cash
Projected total jail days = 3,139.2
Projected mean jail days = 0.7

Note: The estimates of the impact of guidelines assumes 100 percent compliance with guidelines and assumes that judges would select maximum bail amounts permitted in each category. Sums of jail days were calculated on unrounded means.

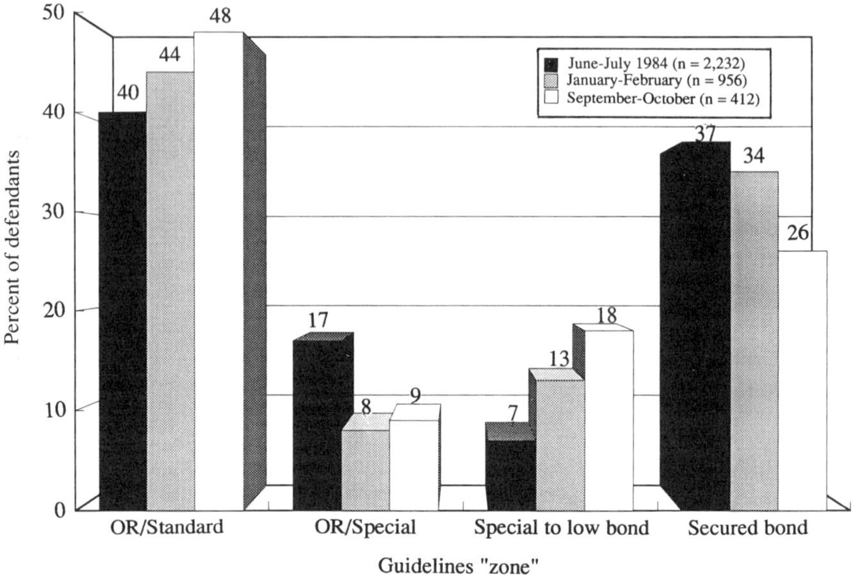

FIGURE A.1. The classification of felony defendants entering Maricopa Superior Court, by guidelines "zone," by sample.

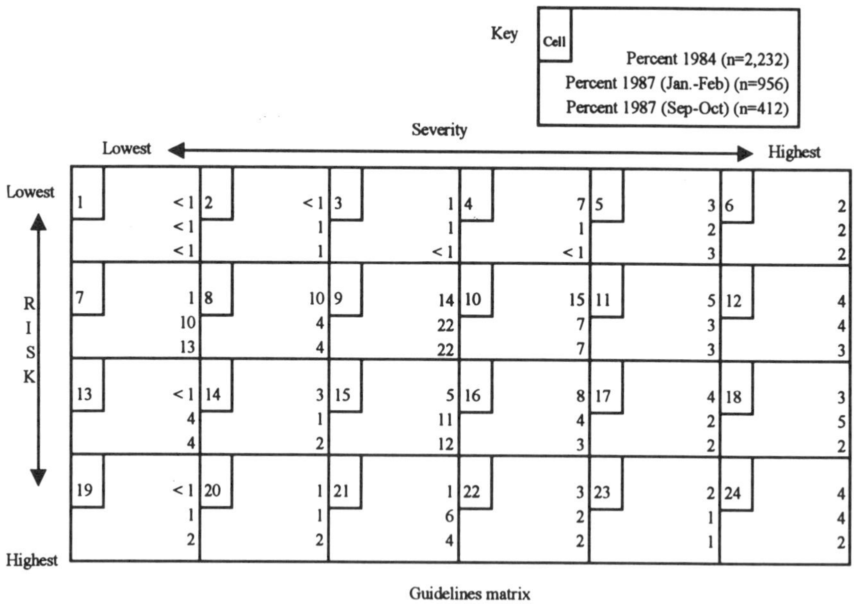

FIGURE A.2. The classification of entering felony defendants in Maricopa County according to guidelines, by sample.

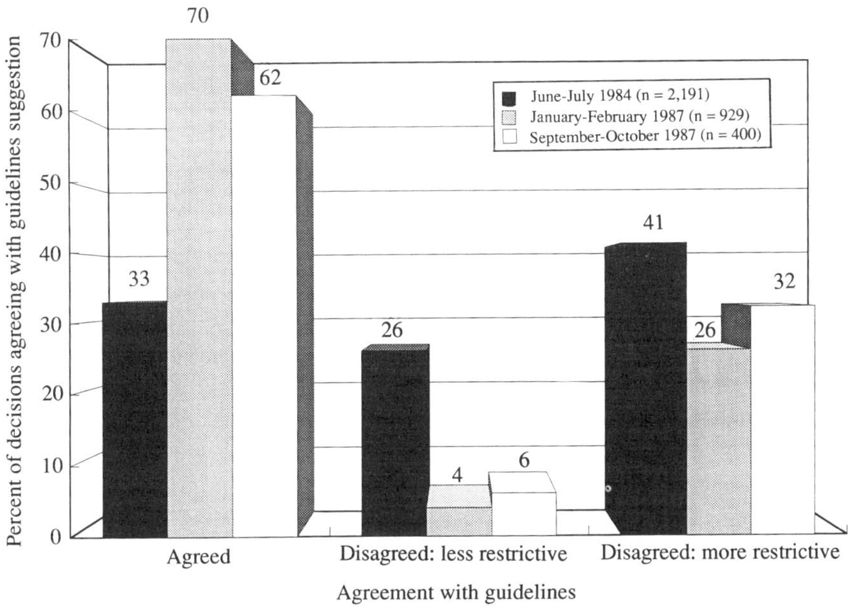

FIGURE A.3. Agreement between commissioners' decisions at initial appearance and the guidelines suggestions in the cases of felony defendants entering Maricopa County Superior Court, by sample. Samples are not strictly comparable.

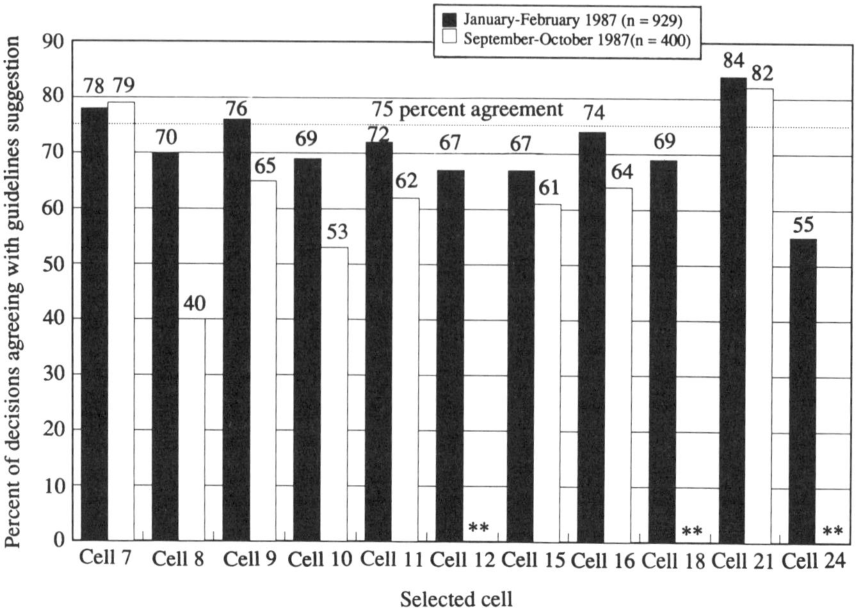

(Note: Asterisks indicate insufficient data.)

	Highest agreement cells	Lowest agreement cells
January-February 1987	7, 9, 16, 21	12, 15, 24
September-October 1987	21	8, 53

FIGURE A.4. Agreement between commissioners' decisions at initial appearance and the guidelines suggestions in the cases of felony defendants entering Maricopa County Superior Court, by selected guidelines cell, by sample.

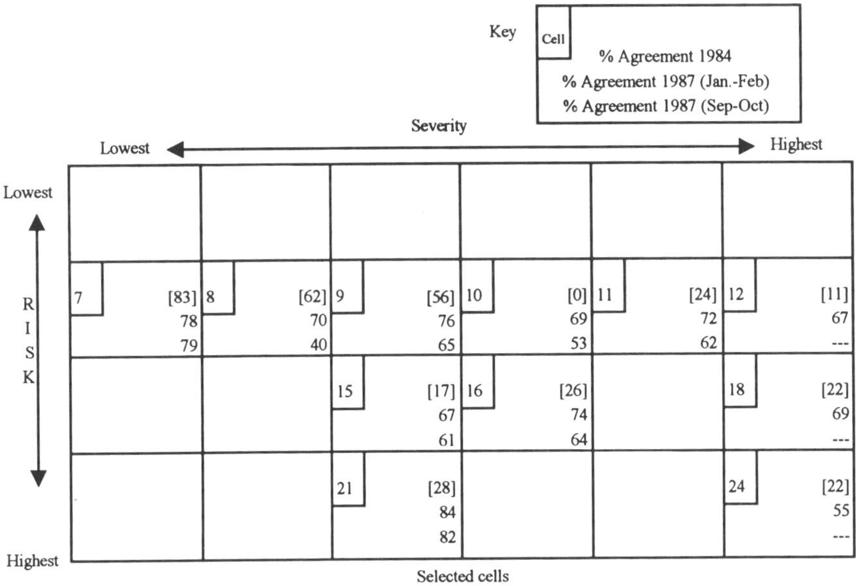

FIGURE A.5. Agreement with decisions suggested by guidelines, by selected cell, by sample. Ideal agreement is 75 percent. Only cells with sufficient numbers of cases are included in the table.

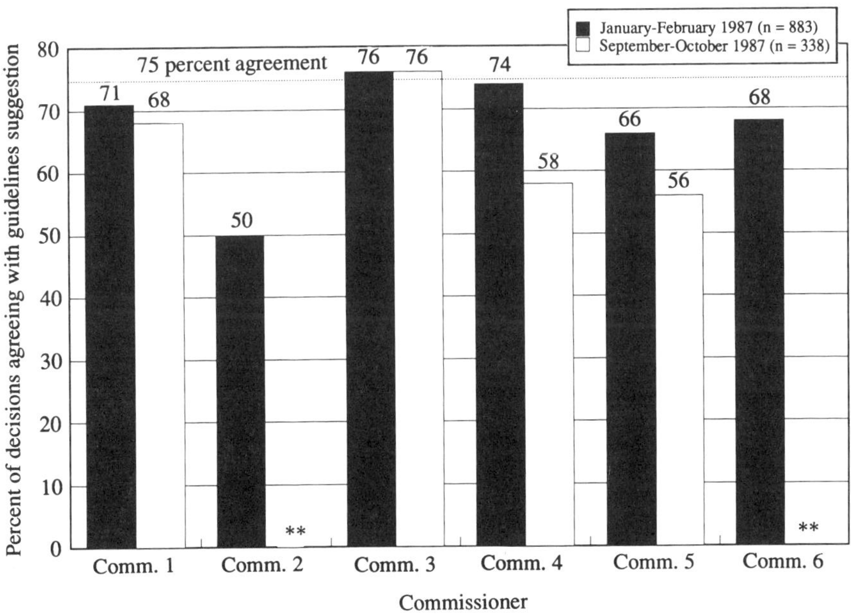

FIGURE A.6. Agreement with decisions suggested by guidelines, by commissioner, by sample. Asterisks indicate insufficient data.

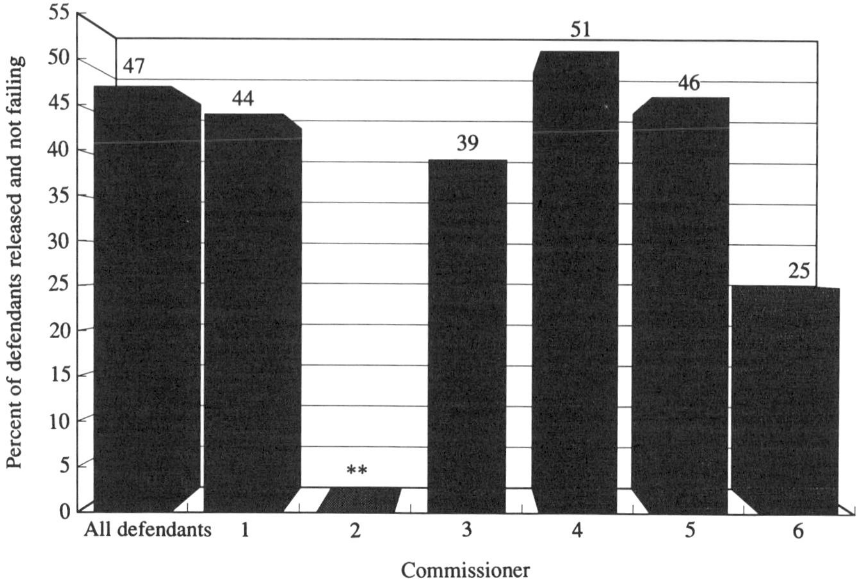

FIGURE A.7. The "effectiveness" of pretrial release among decisions for entering felony defendants in Maricopa County Superior Court during January–February 1987, by commissioner. Asterisks indicate insufficient data.

References

American Bar Association. (1968). *Standards Relating to Pretrial Release.* Washington, DC: American Bar Association.

Angel, A., E. Green, H. Kaufman, and E. van Loon. (1971). "Preventive Detention: An Empirical Analysis." *Harvard Civil Rights Civil Liberties Law Review* 6:301–396.

Ares, C. E., A. Rankin, and H. Sturz. (1963). "The Manhattan Bail Project: An Interim Report on the Use of Pre-Trial Parole." *New York University Law Review* 38:67–92.

Bastion, L. D. (1993). "Criminal Victimization, 1992." *Bureau of Justice Statistics Bulletin.* Washington, DC: U.S. Department of Justice, Office of Justice Programs, Bureau of Justice Statistics.

Beeley, A. L. (1927). *The Bail System in Chicago.* University of Chicago Press (reprint ed.). Chicago: University of Chicago Press, 1966.

Belenko, S., and I. Mara-Drita. (1987). *Drug Use and Pretrial Misconduct: The Utility of Pre-Arraignment Drug Tests as a Predictor of Failure-to-Appear.* New York: New York City Criminal Justice Agency.

Bick, A. J., T. P. Bonazar, and D. K. Gillard. "Jail Inmates, 1992." *Bureau of Justice Statistics Bulletin.* Washington, DC: U.S. Department of Justice, Office of Justice Programs, Bureau of Justice Statistics.

Blumstein, A., J. Cohen, S. Martin, and M. Tonry. (1983). *Research on Sentencing: The Search for Reform,* Vols. 1–2. Washington, DC: National Academy Press.

Britt, C. L., M. R. Gottfredson, and J. S. Goldkamp. (1992). "Drug Testing and Pretrial Misconduct: An Experiment on the Specific Deterrent Effects of Drug Monitoring Defendants on Pretrial Release." *Journal of Crime and Delinquency* 29/1:62–78.

Bureau of Justice Statistics. (1992). *National Update.* Washington, DC: U.S. Department of Justice, Office of Justice Programs, Bureau of Justice Statistics. 1/4.

Carrow, D. M. (1984). "Judicial Sentencing Guidelines: Hazards of the Middle Ground." *Judicature* 68:161–171.

Carrow, D. M., J. Feins, B. Lee, and L. Olinger. (1985). *Guidelines without Force: An Evaluation of the Multijurisdiction Sentencing Guidelines Field Test.* Cambridge, MA: Abt Associates.

Carver, J. A. (1986). "Drugs and Crime: Controlling Use and Reducing Risk through Testing." *NIJ Reports.* Washington, DC: U.S. Department of Justice, National Institute of Justice, September–October.

Carver, J. A. (1993). "Using Drug Testing to Reduce Detention." *Federal Probation* 57/1:42–47.

Clarke, S. H., J. L. Freeman, and G. G. Koch. (1976). "Bail Risk: A Multivariate Analysis." *Journal of Legal Studies* 5:341.

Cohen, J. (1983). "Incapacitation as a Strategy for Crime Control: Possibilities and Pitfalls." In M. Tonry and N. Morris (Eds.), *Crime and Justice: An Annual Review of Research,* Vol. 5. Chicago: University of Chicago Press.

Dawes, R. M. (1979). "The Robust Beauty of Improper Linear Models in Decision Making." *American Psychologist* 34/7:571–582.

Ervin, S. J., Jr. (1971). "Forward: Preventive Detention, A Step Backward for Criminal Justice." *Harvard Civil Rights Civil Liberties Law Review* 6:291–299.

Feeley, M. M. (1979). *The Process Is the Punishment.* New York: Russell Sage Foundation.

Feeley, M. M. (1983). *Court Reform on Trial: Why Simple Solutions Fail.* New York: Basic Books.

Fisher, F. M., and J. B. Kadane. (1983). "Empirically Based Sentencing Guidelines and Ethical Considerations." In A. Blumstein, J. Cohen, S. Martin, and M. Tonry (eds.), *Research on Sentencing: The Search for Reform,* Vol. 2. Washington, DC: National Academy Press.

Flanagan, T. J., and K. Maguire (eds.). *Sourcebook of Criminal Justice Statistics—1991.* U.S. Department of Justice, Bureau of Justice Statistics. Washington, DC: Government Printing Office.

Foote, C. (1954). "Compelling Appearance in Court: Administration of Bail in Philadelphia." *University of Pennsylvania Law Review* 102:1031–1079.

Frankfurter, F., and R. Pound. (1922). *Criminal Justice in Cleveland: Cleveland Foundation* (reprint ed.). Montclair, NJ: Patterson Smith, 1968.

Freed, D., and P. Wald. (1964). *Bail in the United States: 1964.* National Conference on Bail and Criminal Justice, May 1964 (Working papers).

Galegher, J., and J. Carroll. (1983). "Voluntary Sentencing Guidelines: Prescription for Justice or Patent Medicine?" *Law and Human Behavior* 7:361–400.

Goldfarb, R. (1967). *Ransom.* New York: Wiley.

Goldkamp, J. S. (1979). *Two Classes of Accused.* Cambridge, MA: Ballinger.

Goldkamp, J. S. (1983). "Questioning the Practice of Pretrial Detention: Some Empirical Evidence from Philadelphia." *Journal of Criminal Law and Criminology* 74:1556–1588.

Goldkamp, J. S. (1985). "Danger and Detention: A Second Generation of Bail Reform." *Journal of Criminal Law and Criminology* 76:1–74.

Goldkamp, J. S. (1987). "Prediction in Criminal Justice Policy Development." In D. M. Gottfredson and M. Tonry (eds.), *Prediction and Classification.* Chicago: University of Chicago Press.

Goldkamp, J. S., and M. R. Gottfredson. (1984). *Judicial Guidelines for Bail: The Philadelphia Experiment.* United Sates Department of Justice, National Institute of Justice. Washington, DC: Government Printing Office.

Goldkamp, J. S., and M. R. Gottfredson. (1985). *Policy Guidelines for Bail: An Experiment in Court Reform.* Philadelphia: Temple University Press.

Goldkamp, J. S., and M. R. Gottfredson. (1988). *Guidelines for Bail and Pretrial Release in Three Urban Courts: Volume 1. The Development of Bail/Pretrial Release Guidelines in Maricopa County Superior Court, Dade County Circuit Court and Boston Municipal Court.* Philadelphia: Department of Criminal Justice, Temple University.

Goldkamp, J. S., M. R. Gottfredson, and S. Mitchell-Herzfeld. (1981). *Bail Decisionmaking: A Study of Policy Guidelines.* U.S. Department of Justice, National Institute of Corrections. Washington, DC: Government Printing Office.

Goldkamp, J. S., M. R. Gottfredson, and D. Weiland. (1990). "Pretrial Drug Testing and Defendant Risk." *The Journal of Criminal Law and Criminology* 81/3:585–652.

Goldkamp, J. S., and M. K. Harris. (1992). *An Alternatives-to-Incarceration Plan for Philadelphia: Findings and Proposed Strategies.* Philadelphia: Crime and Justice Research Institute.

Goldkamp, J. S., and P. R. Jones. (1992). "Pretrial Drug-Testing Experiments in Milwaukee and Prince George's County: The Context of Implementation." *Journal of Research in Crime and Delinquency* 29/4:430–465.

Goldkamp, J. S., P. R. Jones, M. R. Gottfredson, and D. Weiland. (1990). *Assessing the Impact of Drug-Related Criminal Cases on the Judicial Process, Crowding and Public Safety: Summary and Implications.* Philadelphia: Department of Criminal Justice, Temple University.

Goldkamp, J. S., and D. Weiland. (1991). *The Impact of Court-Related Practices on the Correctional Population in Dade County.* Philadelphia: Crime and Justice Research Institute.

Gottfredson, D. M. (1992). "Selective Deinstitutionalization: Stakes and Risks in Confinement Decisions." 2/1 *CDC Criminal Justice Bulletin* 1.

Gottfredson, D. M., and M. R. Gottfredson. (1980). *Decisionmaking in Criminal Justice.* Cambridge, MA: Ballinger.

Gottfredson, D. M., L. T. Wilkins, and P. B. Hoffman. (1978). *Guidelines for Parole and Sentencing.* Lexington, MA, and Toronto: Lexington Books.

Gottfredson, M. R. (1974). "An Empirical Analysis of Pretrial Release Decisions." *Journal of Criminal Justice* 2:287.

Gottfredson, M. R. (1979). "Parole Board Decision Making: A Study of Disparity Reduction and the Impact of Institutional Behavior." *Journal of Criminal Law and Criminology* 70/1:77–88.

Gottfredson, M. R., and D. M. Gottfredson. (1984). "Guidelines for Incarceration Decisions: A Partisan Review." *University of Illinois Law Review* 2:291.

Gottfredson, M. R., and D. M. Gottfredson. (1988). *Decisionmaking in Criminal Justice: Toward the Rational Exercise of Discretion.* New York: Plenum.

Gottfredson, S. D. (1987). "Prediction: An Overview of Methodological Issues." In D. M. Gottfredson and M. Tonry (eds.), *Prediction and Classification.* Chicago: University of Chicago Press.

Gottfredson, S. D., and D. M. Gottfredson. (1979). *Screening for Risk: A Comparison of Methods.* Washington, DC: National Institute of Corrections.

Gottfredson, S. D., and D. M. Gottfredson. (1985). "Selective Incapacitation?" *Annals, AAPSS* 478(March):135–149.

Gottfredson, S. D., and D. M. Gottfredson. (1986). "Accuracy of Prediction Models." In A. Blumstein et al. (Eds.), *Criminal Careers and "Career Criminals."* Washington, DC: National Academy Press.

Harris, M. K., J. S. Goldkamp, and A. T. Harland. (1984). *Final Report of the Philadelphia Correction Project.* Philadelphia: Department of Criminal Justice, Temple University, Philadelphia, Pennsylvania.

Jones, P. R., and J. S. Goldkamp. (1993). "Implementing Pretrial Drug Testing Programs in Two Experimental Sites: Some Deterrence and Jail Bed Implications." *The Prison Journal* 73/2:199–219.

Knapp, K. A. (1984*a*). *The Impact of the Minnesota Sentencing Guidelines—Three Year Evaluation.* St. Paul: Minnesota Sentencing Guidelines Commission.

Knapp, K. A. (1984*b*). "What Sentencing Reform in Minnesota Has and Has Not Accomplished." *Judicature* 68:181–189.

Kress, J. M. (1980). *Prescription for Justice: The Theory and Practice of Sentencing Guidelines.* Cambridge, MA: Ballinger.

Landes, W. (1974). "Legality and Reality: Some Evidence on Criminal Proceedings." *Journal of Legal Studies* 3:287–337.

Maguire, K., and A. Pastore. (1994). *Sourcebook of Criminal Justice Statistics—1993.* U.S. Department of Justice, Bureau of Justice Assistance. Washington, DC: Government Printing Office.

Meehl, P. E. (1954). *Clinical versus Statistical Prediction: A Theoretical Analysis and a Review of the Evidence.* Minneapolis: University of Minnesota Press.

Mitchell, J. (1969). "Bail Reform and the Constitutionality of Pretrial Detention." *Virginia Law Review* 55:1223.

Moley, R. (1933). "The Administration of Justice." *The Annals* 167:1–143.

Monahan, J. (1981). *Predicting Violent Behavior: An Assessment of Clinical Techniques*. Beverly Hills, CA: Sage.

Morris, N., and M. Miller. (1985). "Predictions of Dangerousness." In M. Tonry and N. Morris (Eds.), *Crime and Justice: An Annual Review of Research*, Vol. 6. Chicago: University of Chicago Press.

National Association of Pretrial Services Agencies. (1978). *Performance Standards and Goals for Pretrial Release and Diversion: Pretrial Diversion*. Washington, DC: National Association of Pretrial Services Agencies.

National Commission on Law Observance and Enforcement. (1931*a*). *Report on Criminal Procedure*. National Commission on Law Observance and Enforcement. Washington, DC: U.S. Government Printing Office.

National Commission on Law Observance and Enforcement. (1931*b*). *Report on Penal Institutions, Probation and Parole*. National Commission on Law Observance and Enforcement. Washington, DC: U.S. Government Printing Office.

Petersilia, J., and S. Truner. (1987). "Guideline-Based Justice: Prediction and Racial Minorities." In D. M. Gottfredson and M. Tonry (eds.). *Prediction and Classification: Criminal Justice Decision Making*, pp. 151–182. Crime and Justice Series, Vol. 9. Chicago: University of Chicago Press.

Pryor, D. E., and T. Murray. (1981). "Maricopa County, Arizona On Site Technical Report." Washington, DC: Pretrial Services Resource Center.

Reaves, B. A. (1992). "Pretrial Release of Felony Defendants, 1990." *Bureau of Justice Statistics Bulletin*. Washington, DC: U.S. Department of Justice, Office of Justice Programs, Bureau of Justice Statistics.

Rhodes, W. (1985). "The Adequacy of Statistically Derived Prediction Instruments in the Face of Sample Selectivity: Criminal Justice as an Example." *Evaluation Review* 9/3:369–382.

Rich, W. L., P. Sutton, T. R. Clear, and M. J. Saks. (1982). *Sentencing by Mathematics: An Evaluation of the Early Attempts to Develop and Implement Sentencing Guidelines*. Williamsburg, VA: National Center for State Courts.

Roth, J., and P. Wice. (1978). "Pretrial Release and Misconduct in the District of Columbia." PROMIS Research Project Publication 16. Washington, DC: Institute for Law and Social Research.

Schaeffer, S. A. (1970). *Bail and Parole Jumping in Manhattan in 1967*. New York: Vera Institute of Justice (Mimeograph).

Smith, D. A., E. D. Wish, and G. R. Jarjoura. (1989). "Drug Use and Pretrial Misconduct in New York City." *Journal of Quantitative Criminology* 5/2:101–126.

Smith, P. Z. (1993). *Felon Defendants in Large Urban Counties, 1990*. Washington, DC: U.S. Department of Justice Office of Justice Programs, Bureau of Justice Statistics.

Sparks, R. (1983). "The Construction of Sentencing Guidelines: A Methodological Critique." In A. Blumstein, J. Cohen, S. Martin, and M. Tonry (Eds.), *Research on Sentencing: The Search for Reform*, Vol. 2. Washington, DC: National Academy Press.

Thomas, W. J., Jr. (1976). *Bail Reform in America*. Los Angeles: University of California Press.

Toborg, M. A., and J. Bellasai. (1988). *Assessment of Pretrial Urine Drug Testing in the District of Columbia: The Views of Judicial Officers*. Unpublished final report. Washington, DC: National Institute of Justice.

Toborg, M. A., A. M. J. Yezer, and J. P. Bellasai. (1987). *Analysis of Drug Use among Arrestees*, Monograph No. 4. Assessment of Pretrial Urine-Testing in the District of Columbia. Washington, DC: Toborg Associates, Inc.

Underwood, B. D. (1979). "Law and the Crystal Ball: Predicting Behavior with Statistical Inference and Individualized Judgment." *Yale Law Journal* 88:1408–1448.

Vera Institute of Justice. (1972). *Programs in Criminal Justice Reform: Vera Institute of Justice Ten-Year Report 1961–1971*. New York: Vera Institute of Justice.
Vischer, C. (1992). *Pretrial Drug Testing*. Washington, DC: U.S. Department of Justice, National Institute of Justice.
von Hirsch, A. (1982). "Constructing Guidelines for Sentencing: The Critical Choices for the Minnesota Sentencing Guidelines Commission." *Hamline Law Review* 5:164–215.
von Hirsch, A., and D. M. Gottfredson. (1984). "Selective Incapacitation: Some Queries about Research Design." *New York University Review of Law and Social Change* 33:11–52.
Welsh, W. N., and S. Smith. (1992). "Correlates of Count Orders against County Jails: A National Sample." Presented at the Annual Meeting of the American Society of Criminology, New Orleans, LA, November, 1992.
Wice, P. B. (1973). *Bail and Its Reform: A National Survey*. Washington, DC: U.S. Government Printing Office.
Wilkins, L. T. (1981). *The Principles of Guidelines for Sentencing Methodological and Philosophical Issues in Their Development*. Washington, DC: National Institute of Justice.
Wilkins, L., J. Kress, D. M. Gottfredson, J. Calpin, and A. Gelman. (1976). *Sentencing Guidelines: Structuring Judicial Discretion*. Albany, NY: Criminal Justice Research Center.
Wish, E. D., and Johnson, B. D. (1986). "The Impact of Substance Abuse on Criminal Careers." In A. Blumstein, J. Cohen, J. Roth, and C. Visher (eds.), *Criminal Careers and "Career Criminals."* Washington, DC: National Academy Press.
Yezer, A., R. P. Trost, M. A. Toborg, J. Bellasai, and C. Quintos. (1987*a*). *The Efficiency of Using Urine Test Results in Risk Classification of Arrestees*, Monograph No. 6. Washington, DC: U.S. Department of Justice, National Institute of Justice.
Yezer, A., R. P. Trost, M. A. Toborg, J. Bellasai, and C. Quintos. (1987*b*). *Periodic Urine Testing as a Signaling Device for Pretrial Release Risk*, Monograph No. 5. Assessment of Pretrial Urine Testing in the District of Columbia. Washington, DC: Toborg Associates.

Index

ISBN 0-306-44879-3

90000

9 780306 448799